FRANCIS *and* ISLAM

FRANCIS *and* ISLAM

J. Hoeberichts

Franciscan Press

Francis and Islam
J. Hoeberichts

Franciscan Press
Quincy University
1800 College Avenue
Quincy, IL 62301
PH 217.228.5670
FAX 217.228.5672
WEBSITE http://www.quincy.edu/fpress

Maps designed by Keith Warner, OFM.
Cartography by John Isom.
Maps © 1997 St. Barbara Province of the Franciscan Friars

Book design and typesetting by Laurel Fitch, Chicago, IL.
Cover design and illustration by Terrence Riddell

Printed in the United States of America
First Printing: September 1997
1 2 3 4 5 6 7 8 9 0

Library of Congress Cataloging-in-Publication Data
    Hoeberichts, J., 1929-
        [Franciscus en de Islam. English]
        Francis and Islam / M.J.J. Hoeberichts.
            p.   cm.
        Includes bibliographical references (p. 269).
        ISBN 0-8199-0980-7
        1. Francis, of Assisi, Saint, 1182-1226--Views on Islam. 2. Christianity
and other religions--Islam. 3. Islam--Relations--Christianity. I. Title
BX4700.F6H49
261.2'2' 092--dc21   97-2595
                                                      CIP

To Fidelis,
my dearly beloved wife
whose love and support were invaluable
in writing this book
and
to all who, in the spirit of Francis,
are dedicated to the dialogue with people of other faiths.

Contents

Foreword

When first published in Dutch, *Francis and Islam* was described as 'an inspiring and thought-provoking' or even 'fascinating book,' which should be 'compulsory reading' for those who are involved in interreligious dialogue. In this study, J. Hoeberichts argues convincingly that the attitude of Francis of Assisi toward the "Saracens" provides a model for Christian-Muslim relations and for interreligious dialogue in general that is highly relevant today.

In the first part of his study, Hoeberichts establishes the late twelfth- and early thirteenth century European context for discussion of Islam and the crusade movement, quoting from documents and encyclicals by Innocent III, Honorius III, and Gregory IX, and writings by crusade preachers like James of Vitry. He then goes on to analyze in detail the 16th or 'mission' chapter of Francis' earlier rule, the *Regula non bullata* of 1221. It is here that Hoeberichts provides his original and radical reinterpretation of Francis' idea that the brothers who go among the "Saracens" must live among and "be subject" to them. Hoeberichts' notion of "being subject"—derived from an exhaustive analysis of *Regula non bullata*, 16 and a thorough grounding in Franciscan scholarship— precludes aggressive efforts at conversion, evangelizing and proselytizing, and makes matters of dogma secondary to sharing the lives of these "other believers."

In the second part of his study, Hoeberichts examines the state of Christian-Muslim dialogue today in light of Francis' example:

> When, during his [Francis'] stay among the Muslims, he experienced how God had graciously accepted them in the otherness of their religion and culture and blessed them with good gifts, he knew that he too had to accept the Muslims in their otherness and approach them with respect for God's sake. It is this respect for the other believers in their otherness which Francis asks from his brothers today. To this end, the brothers must develop in them-

selves a great sensitivity for the good that God works in the people of other faiths (196).

The idea that God works among persons of other faiths in ways that demand respect from Christians is a common theme in contemporary writing on interreligious dialogue. Ewert Cousins, for example, has written:

> [The] experience of God's transcendence is central to Islam. It is what we, in passing over, must contact as the primary element of the Islamic religious consciousness. Our method must be that of passing over rather than mere analogy to the Christian experience of God's transcendence. We must be cautious not to see Islam as a truncated Christianity or assume that God's transcendence is identical in both Islam and Christianity.[1]

What Hoeberichts is able to accomplish in this study is to link the respectful approach for other believers which characterizes contemporary interreligious dialogue directly to the life and writings of Francis of Assisi. As Hoeberichts urges at the end of his analysis of *Regula non bullata*, 16, our task is to:

> build an *oikoumene* of peace where the greeting of peace which Jesus gave to his followers is answered by the Muslim wish of peace, *salaam*, and Christians and Muslims together witness in word and deed to the greatness and goodness of God 'so that everyone may know that there is no one who is all-powerful except God' (LetOrder 9). In this way Francis' wish will be fulfilled that 'at every hour and whenever the bells are rung, praise and thanks always be given to the all-powerful God by all the people throughout the whole world' (1 LetCust 8).

In publishing this book, which was originally sponsored by the Franciscan Study Center at the Catholic Theological University of Utrecht and published by Van Gorcum at Assen, Holland, it is our hope that Francis' message of peace and respect will play an ever-greater role in the shaping of interreligious and intercultural dialogue as we enter the new millennium.

Terrence J. Riddell,
Director, Franciscan Press
July 7, 1997

Preface

In 1958 I went as a Franciscan to work in Pakistan where 95% of the population is Muslim. Yet it was only towards the end of the 70s that I discovered the meaning of chapter 16 of the Rule of 1221, the *Regula non bullata*, which Francis had written especially for those brothers who wanted to go among the Saracens. For many years I devoted myself, together with my colleagues—professors on the staff of Christ the King Seminary, Karachi—to spreading the new theological insights of the Second Vatican Council. We enjoyed our work until, in 1973, we became involved in a crisis of confidence with the ecclesiastical authorities. This led us to examine the place and significance of a Franciscan brotherhood within the church and society of Pakistan. During this process we went first of all back to the Franciscan sources, among which the writings of Francis obtained an ever greater importance. In our reflection on these writings, we found much help and inspiration in the insights of Asian theologians of liberation. They opened our eyes to the reality of Asia, a continent of great poverty, but also the cradle of all great religions. Although we had been living in the midst of this reality, it had until then exercised little influence on either our theological teaching or on our views concerning a Franciscan spirituality for Asia. In other words, we had remained foreigners, strangers who lived in our own little world, with our strongly Western-influenced theology and spirituality, who were not really touched by the problems of Asia. Awakened by the Asian theologians of liberation, we became more and more conscious of our First World ideology, and how this ideology had very profoundly influenced, and continued to influence, our thinking and our acting.

This insight was of great importance for us as a Franciscan brotherhood which only recently had started searching, albeit very tentatively, to find its own identity as a religious group in Pakistan. For now we were challenged to take Asian reality, with its own specific problems, as the starting point for our reflections on the Franciscan tradition; to read, or rather to re-read, the writings of Francis from within the Asian context which is determined by the poverty of the masses and the living presence of the great religions. This context invited us to become involved in a dialogue with the other religions, a dialogue which is of vital importance for Asia, for only if the different religions succeed in truly cooperating can the poor hope to be liberated from the degrading situation into which they have been forced. Unfortunately, the practice of this dialogue did not proceed very smoothly. Various reasons can be put forward to explain this situation. On the part of Christianity, one of the most important reasons for the slow advancement of the dialogue was that Christianity considered itself on theological grounds, but also very much because of the economic and technical progress of the West, to be superior to other religions. As long as this feeling of superiority continued, interreligious dialogue, so necessary for Asia, would not be able to make further headway.

Over the years I became ever more convinced of these ideas, especially because of the worsening economic situation and the increasing communalism of which the poor are always the victims. And the unexpected happened. I found an ally in Francis. Re-reading his writings, I discovered that he had developed an entirely different, even opposite approach to other religions than the one which had been common in the church for centuries: Francis asks his brothers that they live among the Muslims and be subject to them for God's sake. Of course, I had heard this text often before, but it had not made an impression on me. Only after I had become more conscious of the vital necessity of dialogue with Asian religions and of our lack of success in advancing this dialogue because of our feeling of superiority, could this text speak to me again and challenge me. Here unthought-of possibilities were given to the Franciscan brotherhood to provide new impulses to the dialogue in Asia on the basis of its own Franciscan tradition which had received little appreciation so far. Francis' advice to his brothers could mean a breakthrough and help to overcome the impasse in which the dialogue found itself.

From that moment on, my interest in chapter 16 of the *Regula non bullata* was roused. Although very little material was available, I started to study more in depth Francis' attitude towards Islam as it is formulated in the advice for his brothers. A really thorough study, however, was not possible until after I had returned to Holland and had been invited by the Franciscan Study Center in Utrecht to undertake, with its financial assistance, further research on this subject and, if possible and feasible, to prepare it for eventual publication. I accepted the invitation with both hands. For during my first explorations I had discovered that, notwithstanding the long presence of so many brothers in the Muslim world, a more historical study of this chapter had not been published so far. There existed thus a lacuna in Franciscan studies which affected first and foremost the Franciscan brothers and sisters living among Muslims and among followers of other religions. In trying to fill this lacuna, I hoped to be of service to them and to assist them in starting a dialogue from a Franciscan perspective, explicitly based on the insights which Francis and his brothers formulated in chapter 16. For such a perspective could inspire them to new initiatives. Moreover it would be more in accord with the views on interreligious dialogue which, after the Second Vatican Council, had been developed in the local churches of Asia on the basis of a greater openness to their own Asian context.

The pluriformity of religions, so characteristic of Asia, manifests itself more and more in Europe and North America. Hence this study may be important too for Franciscan groups in the Western world. It may show them a way to participate in the dialogue with other religions, especially Islam, in a Franciscan way, not from a position of power, but in an attitude of service. The importance of such a dialogue is day by day becoming more manifest. For without such a dialogue, the Western world will not be able to build a multicultural society in which there is a place for everyone, where no one particular group dominates and determines the norms and values by which the others are measured, but where all without exception are respected because of their own values and cultures and can make their own contribution towards establishing a society of justice and peace: a society where there are no lords and subjects, but where all are sisters and brothers mutually serving each other.

Now that my study has been completed, it is with great pleasure that I wish to thank most gratefully the members of the board of the Franciscan Study Center for my appointment as a part-time research-fellow at the center and for their consent to publish the results of my study as the first volume of their new series, *Scripta Franciscana*. Very specially I want to thank Gerard Ris, OFM, and Th. Steenkamer, OFM, director and secretary of FSC. Not only have they been instrumental in initiating this project, but they have also shown a real personal interest in my study and were always ready to support me with their advice and their assistance. My sincere thanks also to W. Geurts, OFM (✠), G. Schnijder, OFM, A. Camps, OFM and S. Verheij, OFM for their valuable observations and corrections, and to Henk Mager for the great readiness with which he, with all his technical skills, prepared the text for the printer. I owe a very special word of thanks to Anselm Wim Moons, OFM. Even during the years that we lectured together at Christ the King Seminary in Karachi, he encouraged me to publish, and continues to support me as a good friend. I owe very much, more than I can express in words, to his friendship, his creativity, his ever new ideas and initiatives. He was the person who, as custos, stimulated the brothers in Pakistan to start searching for their own identity as a Franciscan brotherhood within the Pakistani context, in which the Christian community constitutes a very small minority among a large Muslim majority, and thus put me on the track of *Regula non bullata*, chapter 16. Last but not least, my very special thanks to Fidelis, my dearly beloved wife. Notwithstanding the fact that she had often to miss me, she was always there to support me with her great love and particularly to protect me against myself, when my activities threatened to become too many and my work and health began to suffer. Hers was not an easy task, but she persevered and has thus made an essential contribution to the publication of this book which I dedicate to her in everlasting gratitude.

Abbreviations

1. WRITINGS OF FRANCIS

Adm	Admonitions
LetCler	Letter to the Clergy
1 LetCust	First Letter to the Custodians
2 LetCust	Second Letter to the Custodians
1 LetFaith	First Version of the Letter to the Faithful
2 LetFaith	Second Version of the Letter to the Faithful
LetLeo	Letter to Brother Leo
LetMin	Letter to a Minister
LetOrder	Letter to the Entire Order
LetRulers	Letter to the Rulers of the Peoples
OffPass	Office of the Passion
PrGod	Praises of God
RegB	Later Rule (1223)
RegNB	Earlier Rule (1221)
SalVirt	Salutation of the Virtues
Test	Testament
TrueJoy	True Joy

2. SOURCES FOR THE LIFE OF FRANCIS

AnPer	Anonymus Peruginus, in: *L'Anonyme de Pérouse, Traduction et Introduction par Pierre-B. Beguin*, Paris, 1979.
Bonaventura	Bonaventura, *Major Life of St. Francis*, in: *St. Francis of Assisi: Writings and Early Biographies: English Omnibus of the Sources for the Life of St. Francis*, Chicago, 1973, 627–787.
1 Cel	Thomas of Celano, *First Life of St. Francis*, ibid., 225–355.
2 Cel	Thomas of Celano, *Second Life of St. Francis*, ibid., 357–543.

3 Comp	*Legend of the Three Companions*, ibid., 885–956.
Jordan	*Chronicle of Jordan of Giano*, in: *Early Franciscan Classics*, Patterson, NJ, 1962, 235–272.
LegPer	*Legend of Perugia, English Omnibus*, 975–1091.

3. JOURNALS, WORKS IN SERIES AND OTHER COLLECTIONS

AFH	*Archivum Franciscanum Historicum*, Quaracchi-Grottaferrata, 1908ff.
BBT	G. Golubovich, *Bibliotheca bio-bibliografica della Terra Santa e dell'Oriente francescano*, Vol. I, Quaracchi, 1906.
BIMA	Bishops' Institutes for Missionary Apostolate.
BIRA	Bishops' Institutes for Interreligious Affairs.
BISA	Bishops' Institutes for Social Action.
BullFranc	*Bullarium Franciscanum*, Vol. I, ed. J. H. Sbaraglia, Rome, 1759.
COD	*Conciliorum oecumenicorum decreta*, ed. J. Alberigo et al., Bologna, 1973.
Espansione	*Espansione del Francescanesimo tra Occidente e Oriente nel Secolo XIII, Società Internazionale di Studi Francescani 6*, Assisi, 1979.
FABC	Federation of Asian Bishops' Conferences.
FAPA	*For All the Peoples of Asia: Federation of Asian Bishops' Conferences Documents from 1970 to 1991*, ed. G. B. Rosales and C. G. Arévalo, Manila, 1992.
FL	*Franciscaans Leven*, DenBosch-Utrecht, 1917ff.
FrancDig	*Franciscan Digest: A Service for Franciscan Spirituality*, Manila, 1991ff.
Francescanesimo	*Francescanesimo e vita religiosa dei laici nel '200, Società Internazionale di Studi Francescani 8*, Assisi, 1981.
Francesco	*Francesco d'Assisi e Francescanesimo dal 1216–1226, Società Internazionale di Studi Francescani 4*, Assisi, 1977.
FranzSt	*Franziskanische Studien*, Münster-Werl, 1914–1993.
Laur	*Laurentianum*, Roma, 1960ff.
Omnibus	*St. Francis of Assisi: Writings and Early Biographies: English Omnibus of the Sources for the Life of St. Francis*, Chicago, 1973.
PL	*Patrologiae cursus completus*, Series latina, accurante J. P. Migne, Parisiis, 1844–1905.

StFranc	*Studi Francescani*, Arezzo-Firenze, 1903ff.
VJTR	*Vidyajyoti Journal of Theological Reflection*, Delhi.
WissWeis	*Wissenschaft und Weisheit*, Münchengladbach-Düsseldorf, 1934ff.
ZMR	*Zeitschrift für Missionswissenschaft und Religionswissenschaftp*

Maps

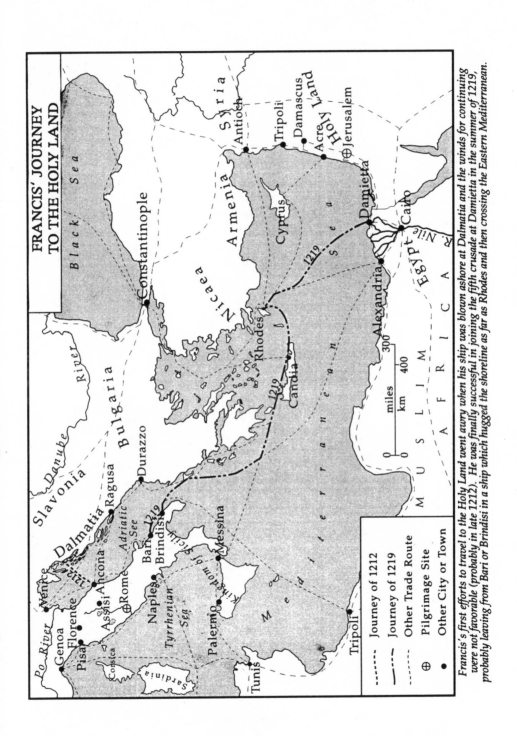

FRANCIS' JOURNEY TO THE HOLY LAND

Journey of 1212 ――――――
Journey of 1219 ――·――·――
Other Trade Route ――――――
Pilgrimage Site ⊕
Other City or Town ●

miles 0 ___ 300
km 0 ___ 400

Francis's first efforts to travel to the Holy Land went awry when his ship was blown ashore at Dalmatia and the winds for continuing were not favorable (probably in late 1212). He was finally successful in joining the fifth crusade at Damietta in the summer of 1219, probably leaving from Bari or Brindisi in a ship which hugged the shoreline as far as Rhodes and then crossing the Eastern Mediterranean.

FRANCIS & THE FIFTH CRUSADE AT DAMIETTA

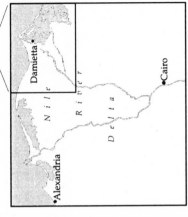

Area of Detail
Shown at Right

1Cel 57 narrates Francis' journey to the Fifth Crusade and his dramatic crossing of the battle lines in order to visit to the Sultan.

Mediterranean Sea

Contemporary Shoreline

Shoreline, ca. 1200

Shoreline, ca. 1200

Christian Camp

Damietta

Muslim Camp

Būrah

Fāriskūr

Delta

Nile River

River

Sharamsāh

Baramūn

Mansūrāh

Nile

part 1

FRANCIS *and* ISLAM

Introduction

In April 1213, pope Innocent III sent a whole stream of letters to the Christian world from Calabria to Scandinavia, from Hungary to Ireland.[1] First, his letter *Vineam Domini*, directed to all archbishops, bishops and abbots, and to all kings and princes, in which he announced his desire to hold the Fourth Lateran Council in order that his two greatest wishes might be fulfilled: the recapture of the Holy Land and the reform of the universal church.[2] Second, his encyclical *Quia maior*, sent to all Christians, which called upon them to prepare for a new crusade.[3] Finally, his letter *Pium et sanctum propositum*, which was meant for all those to whom he entrusted the special task of taking care that the crusade be preached in all parts of the Christian world—the crusade upon which he had decided by divine inspiration in order to vindicate the injury done to the Crucified.[4]

In his crusade encyclical, Innocent promulgated all sorts of concrete measures. They were meant to keep the idea of the crusade—this pious and holy undertaking—alive among the faithful and to motivate them to give not only their material, but especially their spiritual support to this cause which was most important for the whole of Christianity. Thus he wrote that once a month a procession had to be held for the men and, where possible, for the women, to pray for the liberation of the Holy Land. During this procession 'the preaching of the cross which brings salvation, should always be offered to the people in a way that is assiduous and encouraging.' Prayer had to be accompanied by fasting and almsgiving. Every day, during the celebration of mass, all men and women had to humbly prostrate themselves on the ground after the kiss

3

of peace when the saving sacrifice for the sins of the world was about to be consumed. In the meantime the psalm, 'God, the pagans have invaded your inheritance' (Ps 79), was required to be sung loudly by the clergy. When this ended with the antiphon, 'Let God arise, let his enemies be scattered, let those who hate him flee before his face' (Ps 68:1), the priest had to pray, 'God, who disposes all things with marvellous providence, we humbly beseech you to liberate from the hands of the enemies of the cross the land which your only-begotten Son consecrated with his blood and to restore it to Christian worship.' Also, chests had to be placed in each church in which clergy and laity, men and women, could put their alms. If they did so, they would share in the remission of sins, according to the amount of their aid and the strength of their devotion. The pope promised them this, trusting in the mercy of God and the authority of the blessed apostles Peter and Paul.[5] Two years later, the Fourth Lateran Council would officially confirm this extension of the crusade indulgence to almost all Christians, men and women, who in whatever way supported the crusade.[6]

While pope Innocent tried in this way to mobilize the whole of Christianity in the name of Christ for a new crusade, the fifth one, against the perfidious Saracens[7] who kept the Holy Land and the city of Jerusalem occupied, no trace of his call can be found in the writings of Francis and his first brothers. Similarly, they were not influenced by the decrees of the Fourth Lateran Council regarding the crusade nor by the letters of pope Honorius III, which repeated the call of Innocent III after his death. This forms a striking contrast with the decrees of the same Council and of Honorius III with regard to the eucharist and other matters. For even though we cannot find any literal quotation of a conciliar text in the *Regula non bullata*, the influence of the Council on the text of the Rule can be established in various places, especially in the first verse of chapter 17 on the permission to preach, and in chapters 18-20, on such diverse topics as the yearly chapter, orthodoxy, penance and the reception of the eucharist.[8] Also, in various letters, particularly those in which Francis spoke about reverence for the eucharist, like the Letter to the Clergy and the Letters to the Custodians, a clear influence of the Council and of the encyclical *Sane cum olim* of Honorius III (November 22, 1219) can be observed.[9]

Evidently, Francis was selective with regard to papal documents. He heard Honorius' call to promote reverence for the eucharist, but he appears not to have listened when the highest ecclesiastical authorities called for a crusade, not even when they went so far as to accuse those who did not give their names to take part in the crusade of 'the vice of ingratitude and the crime of infidelity,' for which the king of kings, the Lord Jesus Christ, would condemn them.[10] It looks indeed as if Francis did not give in to the moral pressure on the part of the authorities and did not want to use this 'opportunity to win salvation or rather this means of salvation,' as the crusade was called by Innocent III,[11] or to make propaganda for it. Thus Francis occupied an exceptional position among his contemporaries with regard to the crusades and the attitude they expressed towards the Saracens and Islam. This is all the more striking since virtually the entire church from high to low was committed to the crusade. The social pressure to which Francis and his brothers were subject must therefore have been very strong. We can hear an echo of this in the short dialogue which Francis had with one of his companions in the camp at Damietta when the crusaders were making the last preparations for the day of the decisive battle: 'The Lord has showed me ~~2Cel 30~~ that if the battle takes place on such a day, it will not go well with the Christians. But if I tell them this, I will be considered a fool; if I remain silent, I will not escape my conscience. What therefore seems best to you?' His companion answered: 'Father, consider it as nothing to be judged by men, for it is not only now that you will begin to be thought a fool. Keep your conscience free from blame and fear God rather than men.'[12] Francis then made up his mind to speak out, but his choice was not appreciated.

The choice which Francis made and which brought him into conflict with official ecclesiastical thinking and policy with regard to the crusades and Islam forms the subject of this study. I have briefly described the atmosphere that prevailed in the church of those days. In rough lines I have thus sketched the background against which Francis' choice must be understood: massive and ambitious planning on the part of the pope in order to insure that the fifth crusade would prove to be a success after the failure of the fourth one.[13] To this end all forces within the Christian world were to be mobilized. Yet, there was a small, insignificant man from Assisi who dared to oppose this church policy.[14] *Omnibus 1601*

This introductory sketch must be developed further. To do this, I want to make a more extensive study of some of Francis' contemporaries, like Innocent III, cardinal Hugolino and bishop James de Vitry, all of whom Francis knew personally and with whose ideas he was well acquainted. It is surprising that such a study has not yet been made, as far as I know. In the years after the Second Vatican Council, when greater emphasis was placed on the writings of Francis and on the evangelizing task in the world within the Franciscan movement, a few studies were published on chapter 16, the missionary chapter of the *Regula non bullata*, but none of them was explicitly concerned with an analysis of the ideas of Francis' contemporaries about the crusades as the historical context for Francis' ideas on mission and Islam.[15] Generally speaking, Franciscans consider this chapter of the Rule as more a spiritual than a historical document.

It is equally striking that authors who study the crusades in general or deal with those who were critical of them, like Peter the Venerable, Peter of Blois, Joachim of Fiore, and the participants in the so-called Children's Crusade, refer at times to Francis but do not consider chapter 16 of the *Regula non bullata* in their elaboration of Francis' position or when they try to establish a relationship between their subjects and Francis.[16] Thus there exists a clear gap not only in the work of those who explicitly study Francis' view on mission and Islam and refer briefly or not at all to the ideas then prevailing about the crusades, but also in the work of those who make a special study of the crusades and contemporary criticisms of them, and do not or do not adequately take into account the relevant ideas which Francis developed in his *Regula non bullata*. There is a need, therefore, to make a more direct and explicit link between ideas about the crusades at the time of Francis and his view on mission and Islam. Only then will Francis' choice and its originality stand out more clearly.

CHAPTER ONE

The Historical Context:

The Ideas of Some of Francis' Contemporaries on Crusades and Islam

Although, or, should we say, because Francis and his brothers had left the world (Test 3), they were forced again and again to clarify and define their position vis-à-vis this world.[1] The crusades belonged to this world; in fact, they reached a climax during the life of Francis. On October 2, 1187, Jerusalem fell into the hands of Saladin. In the same month, on October 29, only eight days after he had been elected pope, Gregory VIII called for a crusade, the third one, to recapture Jerusalem. During this crusade (1189–1192), in which Richard the Lion-Hearted played an important role, the crusaders succeeded in recovering the coastline of Palestine, but Jerusalem remained in the hands of Saladin.

In August 1198, Innocent III, who had been elected pope on January 8 of the same year, issued a call for the fourth crusade (1202–1204). It resulted in a complete failure and ended with the capture and looting of Constantinople by the crusaders who were particularly interested in the great treasure of relics. But Innocent did not give up. In April 1213 he wrote his most important encyclical, *Quia maior*, to unfold his plans for the fifth crusade which was to take place in 1217–1221. This means that three crusades for the liberation of the Holy Land were held during Francis' lifetime, apart from crusades against the Albigenses, the Moors, the Baltic countries, and against political opponents like Markwald of Anweiler who defended the interests of the German emperor in his fight with the pope over the kingdom of Sicily. It was the fifth crusade, however, which Francis and his brothers had to deal with at close range, not only because of Francis' visit with the sultan during that crusade, in 1219: it had already started with the encyclical in which Innocent announced the crusade. Francis and his first brothers were constantly confronted with this papal document. They simply could not avoid it. Wherever they were, the brothers came across it. When they were present at a eucharistic celebration in a church, prayers were said for the liberation of the Holy Land while people prostrated themselves on the ground; sermons were given about taking up the cross and joining the army of the crusaders. Thus they were forced to speak with each other about the encyclical and to determine their position in relation to it. It is therefore of great importance for our study to further analyze this encyclical.

1. Innocent III and his Crusade Encyclical *Quia Maior* (1213)

The fact that the crusades belonged to the most important activities of the pontificate of Innocent III (1198–1216), cannot be explained on the ground of the ecclesiastical tradition before him. For the earlier tradition considered the crusades above all as an activity of the emperor, which the pope might have eventually supported by issuing a call to the faithful, urging them to take part.[2] Innocent broke with this tradition when, completely on his own, he decided to organize the crusades. He came to this decision because, at the beginning of his pontificate, he had to conclude that the Holy Land urgently needed the help of the Christian world after the unsuccessful German crusade of Henry VI (1197–1198). There was, however, no emperor who could provide this help by taking the initiative for a crusade and leading it to a successful end. In these circumstances, Innocent, as head of the Christian world, felt himself forced, by the needs of the Holy Land, to take upon himself the responsibility for the organization of a crusade for its liberation. When he did not succeed in getting a firm grip on the fourth crusade and it failed, mainly due to lack of finances, Innocent learned from this and other experiences by the time he announced a new crusade in 1213.[3] This is why the encyclical *Quia maior*, in which Innocent called for the fifth crusade, consisted for the largest part of all kinds of concrete measures, regarding the most diverse matters, which were all meant to contribute to the success of the crusade. They ranged from indulgences to an order commanding the secular authorities to restrain the Jews from exacting usuries, to a prohibition on helping corsairs and pirates—those who helped them would be excommunicated.[4] Notwithstanding this practical, goal-oriented approach, the encyclical had at the same time an eminent theological significance. In fact it constituted the climax of thinking about the crusades as it had developed, especially under the influence of Bernard of Clairvaux (about 1090–1153).[5] Moreover, as was the pope's intention,[6] the encyclical greatly influenced the preaching of the fifth crusade. For this reason, a rather extensive summary of the encyclical seems appropriate here. It will enable us to obtain a better insight into the theology of the crusades at that time, which formed the background against which Francis' going among the Muslims must be interpreted.

A. The Main Lines of the Encyclical *Quia maior*

Innocent opened his encyclical[7] by pointing out that never before had there existed a greater need to come to the assistance of the Holy Land than at that moment. He did not, however, immediately clarify wherein this need consisted. In what followed, Innocent referred to the fact that 'the perfidious Saracens have recently built a fortified stronghold to put the Christian name to shame on Mount Thabor, where Christ revealed to his disciples a vision of his future glory.' By means of this fortress 'they think they will easily occupy the city of Acre and then invade the rest of the land without any resistance, since it is almost entirely devoid of forces or supplies.' Because of this need, Innocent resumed 'the old cry for help.' He did not do this on his own authority. He cried for help in the name and on behalf of Jesus Christ 'who when dying cried with a loud voice on the cross.' And as if this were not enough, Innocent continued that even at that very moment Christ cried out with his own voice, repeating the call of the Gospel: 'If anyone wants to come after me, let him deny himself and take up his cross and follow me,'—and so Innocent added—'as if to say, to put it more plainly: If anyone wants to follow me to the crown, let him also follow me to the battle, which is now proposed as a test of faith for all people.' Of course, God could have easily liberated the Holy Land by divine power, but God wanted to give the world, in which the love of many had grown cold, 'an opportunity to win salvation, so that those who fight faithfully for him will be crowned in happiness by him.'[8] Innocent was so touched by this divine initiative that he exclaimed: 'How much good has already come from this cause! How many men, converted to penance, have delivered themselves up to the service of the Crucified One for the liberation of the Holy Land and have won a crown of glory as if they had suffered the agony of martyrdom, men who perhaps might have perished in their wickedness. This is the ancient work of art which Jesus Christ has deigned to renew in these days for the salvation of the faithful.'

The urgent invitation of Christ to take up the cross, to follow him to battle and so to gain eternal salvation, is further strengthened by an argument which had its origin in the feudal world of the lord and his vassals. Preachers had used this argument before because it must have had a great appeal for the people of that time, but the popes did not make use of it, probably because it was not considered to be theologically flawless. It was Innocent who put these objections aside and became the first pope to use this argument in his letters.[9] 'If a temporal king is thrown out of his kingdom by his enemies, when he regains his lost kingdom surely he will condemn his vassals as faithless men...unless they risk for him not only their possessions but also their persons? In just such a way will the king of kings, the Lord Jesus Christ, who bestowed on you body and soul and all the other good things you have, condemn you for the vice of ingratitude and the crime of infidelity if you fail to come to his aid when he has been, as it were, thrown out of his kingdom, which he purchased with the price of his blood. So all should know that anyone who fails to serve his Redeemer in this hour of need is blameworthily severe and severely blameworthy (*culpabiliter durum et dure culpabilem*).'

Innocent then employed an old argument which had already been used by his predecessors Eugene III (1145) and Alexander III (1165) but had since disappeared into the background, i.e., the divine command to love one's neighbor which obliged Christians to liberate, in an effective way, their many thousands of brothers and sisters who 'are being held in the hands of the perfidious Saracens in dire imprisonment and are weighed down by the yoke of most severe slavery.'[10]

Next he pointed out that the Christians had formerly held almost all of the territories which were now occupied by the Saracens until after the time of pope Gregory the Great (about 540–604). Since then, however, 'a son of perdition has arisen, Mohammed, a pseudo-prophet, who has seduced many people from the truth by worldly enticements and carnal pleasures. Although his treachery has prevailed up to the present day, we nevertheless put our trust in the Lord who has already given us a sign that good is to come, that the end of this beast is approaching. For according to the Revelation of St. John, his number will come to an end within 666 years, of which already nearly 600 have passed."[11]

'In addition to the former great and grave injuries which the perfidious Saracens have inflicted on our Redeemer, on account of our offenses, the same perfidious Saracens have recently built a fortress on Mount Thabor to put the Christians to shame.' It was this new military initiative which, as we have already mentioned, had created a new and even more compelling urgency to send more men and material than ever, to prevent the little territory that was still held by the crusaders from being overrun by the Saracens. For thus the Saracens, who had already retaken Jerusalem, would also reconquer the rest of the Holy Land that the Christians, in previous crusades, had liberated. Innocent could not let this happen without taking action as leader of the Christian world.

'Therefore, most beloved sons,'—and here the real call for the fifth crusade started—'transform your quarrels and rivalries, brother against brother, into bonds of peace and affection, and gird yourselves for the service of the Crucified One. Do not hesitate to risk your possessions and your persons for him who laid down his life and shed his blood for you. Be certain and secure that if you are truly penitent you will achieve eternal rest as a reward from this temporal labor. For we, trusting in the mercy of almighty God and the authority of the blessed apostles Peter and Paul, by that power of binding and loosing that God has conferred on us, although unworthy, grant to all those who undertake this labor personally and at their own expense, full forgiveness of their sins which they confess orally and with contrite hearts, and as the reward of the just we promise them a greater share of eternal salvation.'

Full forgiveness was also granted to those 'who do not personally take part in the crusade but at least, at their own expense according to their means and station in life, send suitable men, and similarly to those who go personally although at another's expense.' Innocent continued, 'we wish and concede that all those Christians who donate a fitting proportion of their goods to the aid of the Holy Land, should share in this remission of sins, according to the amount of their aid and the depth of their devotion.' Innocent then promised the crusaders, 'we also take under the protection of blessed Peter and ourselves the persons and goods of those same people from the time they take the cross...and we decree that these goods are to remain untouched and rest unmolested until it is known for certain whether they have died or have returned home.' He also forbade potential creditors from exacting usuries from those who participated in these activities.

Innocent, however, was well aware that the easiest way to organize the necessary help for the Holy Land was to have as many people as possible take part in the crusade. Therefore, he continued, 'we implore each and every one through the Father and the Son and the Holy Spirit, the one only true and eternal God,—and we ask this as the vicar of Christ and on his behalf from archbishops and bishops, abbots and priors and chapters, whether of cathedrals or conventual churches, and all clergy, and also cities, villages and castles—, to provide, according to their own means, an adequate number of fighting men with the necessary expenses for three years. And if persons or groups are not capable of managing this on their own, they must join together. For we certainly hope that, if the expenses are provided, the men will not stay behind. We ask the same thing from those kings and princes, counts, barons and other magnates, who themselves perhaps are not personally taking part in the service of the Crucified One. We also demand naval help from maritime cities. And so that we should not seem to be laying on others heavy and insupportable burdens which we are not willing to move with a finger of our own, we declare truthfully before God that we ourselves will do with a willing heart what we have demanded others to do.'

As it was necessary to recruit as soon as possible as many people as possible, Innocent no longer insisted on an examination of the personal fitness of the candidates, because this meant that 'aid to the Holy Land would be much impeded or delayed.' In radical contrast with the past,[12] Innocent allowed 'anyone who wishes, except persons bound by religious profession, to take up the cross on condition that this vow may be commuted, redeemed or deferred by apostolic mandate when urgent need or evident expediency demands it.' For the same reason—the quick recruitment of as great a number of crusaders as possible—Innocent revoked 'the remissions and indulgences formerly granted to those setting out for Spain against the Moors or against the heretics in Provence.' For in both places affairs 'have gone so well, by the grace of God, that the immediate use of force is not needed.'

After having threatened all helpers of the Saracens with excommunication, Innocent gave a long list of his detailed decrees which were meant to keep the plans for the crusade alive among the faithful and lead it to a successful end. He entrusted the execution of these decrees in various countries to his special legates. Together with other 'men of foresight and integrity, [they] must on our authority lay down and determine whatever arrangements they consider useful to promote this matter. And they must see to it that their decisions are faithfully and carefully carried out in each diocese by suitable men especially appointed for this task.'

B. SOME OBSERVATIONS ON THE ENCYCLICAL *QUIA MAIOR*[13]

a. Innocent's Justification of the Crusade

In the opening lines of the encyclical, Innocent used the verb 'cry' or a derivative at least six times. With his cry he placed himself in the line of the tradition, because he resumed the old cry for help which was still necessary because of the great need of the Holy Land. This cry for help found its climax in the cry of Jesus himself which Innocent explicitly formulated in the present tense. It is Jesus who suffers now; it is Jesus, the king, who at this moment has been expelled from his land. Therefore, take up the cross and follow him in the battle to regain his kingdom.

It was not for the first time that the gospel text, 'If anyone wants to come after me, let him deny himself and take up his cross and follow me,' was used in connection with the crusades. Here too Innocent resumed the tradition which probably started with the call to the first crusade, which Urban II made in Clermont on November 27, 1095.[14] Further, the text was regularly quoted by crusade preachers throughout the history of the crusade movement. Although used in this way for centuries and sanctioned as such by ecclesiastical authorities, this interpretation of the text, i.e., that the armed crusade is an imitation of Christ, was certainly not the most obvious. But it worked. Thousands, tens of thousands, took up the cross and went to the Holy Land in order, as Innocent put it in his sermon at the opening of the Fourth Lateran Council, 'to fight the fight of the Lord and to vindicate the injury done to the Crucified One' by liberating the inheritance which he had bought with his blood.[15] The more they were committed to this fight and prepared to expose themselves to dangers and even to die in battle, the closer they would follow Christ.[16]

Other motives, mainly of a demographic and economic nature,

played a role too. Urban II, according to the account Robert of Reims made of his sermon at Clermont, called the knights to leave their land which produced hardly enough food for its own farmers, and to take the road to the Holy Sepulchre in order to liberate the Holy Land which, according to scripture, overflowed with milk and honey. He justified this call with the text of the Gospel, that everyone who left his house, his family or land in Jesus' name, would receive a hundredfold.[17] Also well known was the description which Fulcher of Chartres (1059–1127), the chronicler of the first crusade and of the beginning of the kingdom of Jerusalem, gave of the results of the colonization by the crusaders, 'Consider and reflect the way in which God in our time has transformed the West into the East. We, who were once Westerners have become Easterners. Those who were Roman or Frank, have here become Galilean.... Those who were once strangers, are now residents; the pilgrims have become inhabitants. Daily our relatives and neighbors come to join us, leaving behind the goods they possessed in the West. Those who were poor in their own land, are here made rich by God; those who had only a few pennies, have acquired here an unprecedented amount of bezants (gold or silver coins of Byzantium). Those who were only tenants, have been given here an entire estate by God.... God does not want that those who have taken up the cross, find themselves here in needy circumstances. You realize that we have here an awesome wonder, which must be admired by the whole world.'[18] The same motives still functioned in a sermon which Abbot Martin of the Alsatian monastery of Pairis preached in Basel cathedral in 1201 during the preparations for the fourth crusade. Towards the end, he mentioned both the eternal reward for the crusaders who died in battle, and the temporal reward for those who survived: 'I will pass over the fact that the land for which you are making is richer by far than this one and more fertile; and it could easily come to pass that many of you will find a more prosperous way of life there, even in temporal matters, than the one you have known here.'[19] The desire for war booty played a role, too. Hence it was not without reason that before the capture of Damietta the rule was set down that those who appropriated money or property, would lose a hand as well as their share in the war booty![20]

Yet, it remains very doubtful whether so many men and women would have taken upon themselves all the trials and tribulations of a crusade if it were only a matter of temporal gain. Moreover, as we have seen, Innocent complained about a shortage of manpower to defend Acre and its surroundings, a shortage which presumably was due to the fact that most of the crusaders who survived the fighting returned home rather than staying on in the Holy Land. Participation in a crusade, therefore, was also and even primarily an expression of deep religious feelings.[21] The crusade movement was a religious movement: the crusaders were the army of Christ; they were the new knights of Christ,[22] who, in his name, fought a holy and just war for the liberation of the Holy Land, Christ's inheritance which by right belonged to the Christians, and for the liberation of Jerusalem, the forerunner of the heavenly Jerusalem, in order to gain thereby their eternal salvation.[23] This ideal was very attractive because it opened for knights and other lay people a way to salvation which placed them on the same level as the religious, while the activities which were asked of them fit well with what they were accustomed to doing in their normal, ordinary lives.[24] The fighting in which they were continually involved in a feudal, martial society, was sacralized as it were in a holy war, fought in Christ's name. Strange as it may sound, the crusade was seen as an adapted form of lay spirituality in which continuous warfare between Christians was channeled into a war against the Saracens, which brought destruction and death to the Saracens and salvation to the Christians.[25]

The crusade as an opportunity for salvation was an idea which had been developed especially by Bernard of Clairvaux in his call for the second crusade (1146–1148). This call centered around the theme of the crusade as the beginning of the time of salvation: *Ecce nunc tempus acceptabile, ecce nunc dies salutis* (2 Cor 6:2). Bernard agreed that God could have liberated the Holy Land by sending legions of angels or by just saying the word. God had, however, granted Christians the possibility of proving themselves to be true faithful of Christ by taking part in the crusade. Christians should not let this opportunity pass by. Anyone who took up the cross was like the clever merchant who sold everything he owned to buy the one pearl; for him death during the crusade was profit, because full forgiveness awaited him.[26] Innocent adopted these ideas for the most part without any further comment. Looking back, he did not see, even for a moment, that the crusades had produced very few concrete results and that the need of the Holy Land had never before been so urgent, but he expressed his great admiration for the many good things which God had realized by making this opportunity of salvation available to the Christians. It was a real piece of art![27] However, Innocent did not say how much this piece of art had cost. He saw only the salvation of the Christian faithful and not the countless Saracen victims, at the cost of whose lives the Christians won their salvation.

This is not so surprising when we read that, according to Bernard, 'to inflict death or to die for Christ is no sin, but rather an abundant claim to glory. In the first case one gains for Christ, and in the second one gains Christ himself. The Lord accepts with pleasure the death of the enemy as revenge, and gives himself with greater pleasure to the [fallen] knight as consolation. The knight of Christ, I say, may kill with confidence and die with greater confidence, for he serves himself when he dies, and serves Christ when he kills the enemy. The knight of Christ does not bear the sword without reason, for he is the minister of God for the punishment of evildoers and for the praise of the good. If he kills an evildoer, he is not the killer of a human being, but, if I may so put it, a killer of evil. He is simply the avenger of Christ towards evildoers and the defender of the Christians. Should he be killed himself, we know that he has not perished, but reached his goal. When he inflicts death, it is to Christ's profit, and when he suffers death, it is for his own gain. The Christian glories in the death of the pagan, because by his death Christ is glorified; in the death of a Christian the liberality of the king is revealed when the knight is called forward to be rewarded. In the one case the just shall rejoice when they see that revenge has been taken; and in the other they shall say: truly there is a reward for the just; truly it is God who judges them on earth. I do not mean to say that the pagans are to be slaughtered when there is another way to prevent them from harassing and persecuting the faithful, but only that now it is better to kill them than that the rod of the sinners be lifted over the lot of the just.'[28]

It is difficult, if not impossible, for us to acknowledge a work of art in these ideas. How can we acknowledge that killing a pagan for the sake of Christ merits the highest praise? Or how can we glory in the death of a pagan, because therein Christ is glorified? Yet the church presented such killings to the Christians of Francis' days as something to be admired, as a work of art, because it offered the Christians an opportunity for and a cause of salvation, so that they who had faithfully fought for Christ would also be crowned by him with eternal happiness.

Earlier, we mentioned that Innocent was the first pope to use an argument which he borrowed from the the feudal system: just as the vassal committed himself with his whole person and all his possessions to his lord, so should Christians surrender themselves totally in the service of Jesus Christ, the King of kings, for it was from him that they had received body and soul and all other goods. Gratitude and faithfulness obliged them to come to the aid of their king, especially at this moment, because he had been thrown out, as it were, from his kingdom which he had redeemed by his blood. If Christians failed to do this, they were guilty of the vice of ingratitude and the crime of infidelity. Innocent explicitly returned to this obligation of gratitude once more in the decree *Ad liberandum* which he promulgated after the Fourth Lateran Council on November 30, 1215. Addressing those who refused to build or provide ships for the crusaders, he wrote: 'If indeed there be perchance any men so ungrateful to the Lord our God, we firmly state on behalf of the apostle Peter that they should know that they will have to answer to us on this matter in the presence of the Dreadful Judge on the last day of severe judgment. They should first consider whether they can make their confessions with clear consciences or with any assurance of salvation in the presence of Jesus Christ...if they have refused to serve him who was crucified for their sins, in this enterprise which is, as it were, particularly his own: for it is by his gift that they live, by his generosity that they are sustained and by his blood that they have been redeemed.'[29]

Here, Innocent used very beautiful, but also very forceful language. He wanted to exercise a strong moral pressure on the Christians in order to force them, as it were, to take part in the crusade in whatever way possible: by personally taking up the cross, by bearing the expenses for one or more crusaders, by building or providing ships, etc. Indeed, he wished to mobilize the entire Christian world to fulfill its obligation of gratitude towards its king by collecting men, material and money on a large scale in order to make the crusade against the Saracens a success and to liberate the Holy Land. In his opening address to the Fourth Lateran Council, he said: 'Beloved brothers, see, I commit myself completely to you; I place myself fully at your disposal and am prepared according to your advice, if you approve of it, to personally take upon me the heavy task and to travel to kings, peoples and nations, and even more than that, if by my cry for help I will be able to excite the people so that they will rise up to fight the fight of the Lord and to vindicate the injury of the Crucified One.'[30] In fact, when Innocent died in Perugia on July 16, 1216, he was on a tour to preach the crusade and to establish peace between all kinds of warring factions which because of their quarreling were not ready to go on a crusade. The crusade was seen as an act of gratitude for all the good Christians had received from Christ: but what about the Christians' respect for the good that could be found among other peoples which also found its origin in God? His negative attitude towards the Saracens blinded Innocent to the good among them. From his ideological point of view, he could only see evil among them.

The vision that Innocent had in mind when announcing the crusade was the restoration of the Christian world as it was when it had reached its climax in the days of the late Roman empire. The crusade was for him the means to realize this vision of the Christian golden age which lasted from the time of Constantine (✠337) until after the time of Gregory the Great (✠604). During this period the Holy Land and its surrounding territories were in the hands of the Christians. Hence, the perfidious Saracens occupied them unjustly and the Christians were fully justified in claiming their possession and even waging a war for their recovery. This vision fit Innocent very well, for he started his pontificate in the full awareness of his power as *vicarius Christi*. Until the middle of the 12th century, the popes used the title 'successor of Peter,' while the title *vicarius Christi* was mainly applied to bishops, even to clerics, and to lay princes. It was especially Bernard who gave this title a greater significance, while Innocent subsequently claimed it programmatically and exclusively for himself. For Innocent this title expressed the proper essence and the deepest meaning of the papal office. The pope was the vicar of Christ who was king and priest according to the order of Melchizedek. As such he stood between God and humankind, or rather under God and above all human beings; he was not only head of the church, but also the leader of the Christian world, the *mundus christianus*, the community of Christian peoples and kingdoms.[31] This formed a closed religious, political and cultural block against the outside world, with the result that all outsiders could easily be seen as potential, if not actual, enemies.[32] In his role as leader of the Christian world the pope had to go into action against these outsiders as soon as they started to become a threat to the Christian peoples and their interests. In Innocent's view, the appropriate means to counter their threat was the organization of a crusade. Thus, during his pontificate, crusades were being held against the Moors, the Albigenses, the Baltic states, and even against his political opponents. Riley-Smith considers Innocent a man 'obsessed by the crusades.'[33] The fifth crusade was supposed to be the climax of this series, and this all the more because the fourth one completely failed to reach its goals. Thus Innocent declared in the decree *Ad liberandum*: 'We desire with an ardent longing to liberate the Holy Land from the hands of the impious.... We declare that the crusaders should make preparations so that on the first day of June in the year after next [1217] all men who decide to travel across by sea should gather...at Brindisi or at Messina. We intend to be there in person on that date, God willing, so that the Christian army which is about to set out with divine and apostolic blessing may be organized to its advantage by our counsel and aid.'[34] Convinced of his own responsibility and completely focused on the success of his enterprise, Innocent could not harbor any doubts about the moral character of his crusade, even though these were sometimes expressed.[35] As vicar of Christ the King, he was called by God to restore the golden age of Christianity; hence he was personally responsible for the organization of the Christian army which he, with the blessing of God and of himself, sent to free the Holy Land, Christ's inheritance, out of the hands of the Saracens and so to realize once again the old ideal of the Christian world.

b. Innocent's Attitude towards Mohammed and Islam

Innocent used very negative language with regard to Mohammed and the Saracens. It fit very well with his intention to mobilize the Christians in order to liberate the Holy Land from the enemies of Christ and to rescue the captives who were suffering under the yoke of most severe slavery. It was here, however, that a gap gradually began to open between the stereotyped negative propaganda of papal crusade encyclicals and the changing views on the Saracens in the poetry and historiography of the crusades, as a result of the lively exchange with the world of the Middle East, especially through the contacts of the crusaders.[36] This is very well illustrated by a story which Usama ibn Munqidh recorded between the second and third crusade (1146–48 and 1189–90) as 'an example of Frankish rudeness.' He wrote: 'When visiting Jerusalem, I used to go to the al-Aqsa mosque. At its side there is a small oratory which the Franks had converted into a church. When I entered the al-Aqsa mosque where my friends, the Templars, were sitting, they put the small oratory at my disposal for reciting my prayers. One day I entered, recited the opening formula *Allah akbar* and stood up to start my prayers, when a Frank threw himself upon me from behind, caught me and turned my face to the East, saying: This is the way you must pray. Immediately some Templars came in between. They grabbed and removed him, while I turned to finish my prayers. But, when the Templars did not pay attention for a moment, he threw himself again upon me from behind, turned my face to the East and repeated: This is the way you must pray. Again the Templars intervened, removed him and excused themselves with me: It is a stranger who recently has arrived from the land of the Franks.'[37]

This story clearly shows the great and fundamental difference that existed between the attitude of the Templars who had stayed in Jerusalem for a longer time and had regular contacts with the Saracens living there, and that of the Frankish crusader who had just arrived and knew Islam only from crusade propaganda. Because of their contacts, the Templars had developed a different way of looking at the Saracens and, as a result, adopted a completely different attitude towards them.[38] No trace of these developments, however, could be found in the writings of Innocent III. Hence Roscher observes that Innocent's description of the Saracens as cruel, bloodthirsty barbarians must be seen as an anachronism. The difference in approach is also evident in the contempt which Innocent showed towards treaties with the Saracens. While, in 1188, according to the custom among knights, Frederick I Barbarossa first annulled the peace treaty with Saladin and then declared war upon him—thus treating him the same way he did a Christian prince— Innocent stated in 1199 that the truce which he concluded in 1198 for five years would not prevent him from preparing for a new crusade and would not influence his plans to liberate the Holy Land from the Saracens. To him, a treaty with a Saracen was nothing but a piece of paper.[39]

For this reason, it would seem that we must not attach too much weight[40] to the letter which Innocent, on the advice of prudent men,[41] wrote to the sultan of Egypt, al-Malek al-Adil, to propose to him a peace plan. And this all the more because he sent his letter to the Sultan on April 26, 1213, only a few days after he had sent out copies of his crusade encyclical and the other two letters, between April 19–23. This means that the pope had already started his campaign to mobilize the whole Christian world for the crusade, this pious and holy enterprise, upon which he had decided by divine inspiration and which he was determined to bring to a favorable conclusion.[42] In this situation, it is most unlikely that, only a few days later, the pope wanted to delay mobilization for some months in order to wait for an answer from the Sultan, which might never come. For time was pressing.[43] Moreover, as Innocent wrote in his crusade encyclical, God had already given him a sign that good was to come and that the end of the beast was near. Further, we may add that, notwithstanding its references to Jesus' humility and meekness, the letter had a rather threatening tone. Among other things, it stated that the sultan should not think that it was the army of his brother which conquered Jerusalem. On the contrary, God allowed the loss of Jerusalem because of the offenses of the Christians. Now that they had returned to the Lord, they might hope that God was once more on their side. Hence Innocent humbly asked his highness the Sultan to prevent further bloodshed and to return the land. If he was not prepared to do so, it could well bring him more difficulties than advantages.[44] What was the real reason that Innocent wrote this letter from which he did not expect much result? Was it perhaps only to convince himself, but particularly the prudent, God-fearing men around him, that he had tried everything to reach a peaceful solution? For only in the absence of such a solution—and he was almost certain that he would not receive an answer, or at least not a satisfying answer, to his peace plan— was Innocent, according to the canonists, justified in starting a crusade against the Saracens who kept the Holy Land occupied and were not prepared to give it back to the Christians.[45]

The gap mentioned above between papal-ecclesiastical language and the growing common one with regard to the Saracens, did not exist regarding the person of Mohammed and the teaching of the Koran. Thus William of Tyre (1130–1186), archbishop of Tyre and chancellor of the kingdom of Jerusalem, had a great appreciation for his Muslim contemporaries, but continued to consider Mohammed as a seducer, as the first-born of Satan, and his teaching as a teaching which corrupts.[46] A similar negative attitude was also present in someone like Peter the Venerable (✠1156). Although he wanted to develop a more objective approach to Mohammed and Islam, and to meet the Saracens 'not with weapons but with words, not with force but with reason, not with hatred but with love,'[47] he did not come to a revision of language with regard to Mohammed and the Koran either. Notwithstanding his greater openness towards and deeper insight into Islam, Peter the Venerable, in his *Contra Saracenos*, continued to see Mohammed as the mouthpiece of Satan and his teaching as 'a pile of lies' and 'a stupid, deadly error, devoid of all reason and deprived of all truth.'[48]

Innocent conformed to this negative theological language when, in his crusade encyclical, he called Mohammed 'a son of perdition who by worldly enticements and carnal pleasures has seduced many,' and applied to him the apocalyptic title of 'the beast.'[49] And, in his sermon at the opening of the Fourth Lateran Council, Innocent stated: 'All holy places are profaned, and the tomb of the Lord which was full of glory, has been deprived of it. Where Jesus Christ, the only-begotten Son of God was honored, there now Mohammed, the son of perdition, is honored.'[50] Given the accepted theological language of his time, it is not surprising that Innocent spoke in this way. Moreover, the fact that he wanted to organize a crusade against the Saracens, whom he saw as the great enemies of Christianity, made it virtually impossible for him to develop another outlook on Mohammed and Islam.

By identifying Mohammed and Islam with the beast of the Apocalypse, Innocent placed the crusade against the beast within the framework of God's final plan for human history: the beast will be overcome by Christ.[51] He was careful not to mention a precise date for the victory. However, there were some rather hopeful signs. With the help of God's grace, things had changed for the better in the fight against the Moors in Spain and against the heretics in Provence.[52] Moreover, since the arrival of Mohammed, almost 600 of the 666 years of the beast had passed. These facts were clear enough indications for Innocent that soon the power of the beast would come to an end and that he could look forward with confidence to a successful termination of the crusade which he had decided to start. Evidently, Innocent did not rush into a new adventure after all the previous failures. He looked for a sign, or, as we would say, he tried to read the signs of the times, for he wanted to be on the safe side, especially since there were people who might object to his decision. It is even likely that Innocent was thinking here of a real objection made against the crusade. For in his sermons to promote the second crusade, Bernard of Clairvaux had used as one of his main themes the text taken from Paul's second letter to the Corinthians, that it was now

God's acceptable time. But the second crusade had in fact turned into a complete failure. Because of this, several people started asking whether it was not presumptuous for the Christians and their leaders to determine by themselves that God's favorable time for a victory had come. Should they not leave this to divine providence?[53]

Such an opinion was followed by abbot Joachim of Fiore (ca. 1135–1202) among others. He held out the prospect of victory in the third crusade to Richard the Lion-Hearted during their meeting at Messina in December 1190. A few years later, however, he considered the crusade a useless enterprise. The victory over 'the beast' would not come as a result of military power. Rather, it would be won by a faithful remnant, the so-called spiritual men. Purified in their faith and their understanding of God's plan of salvation through persecution by pseudo-prophets and Saracens, they would, in God's time, convert the pagans not by the sword but by the word.[54] It is not known how widely this view had spread in those days. Its dissemination must have been considerable if Innocent, in his crusade encyclical, wished to defend himself against it. He did so by referring to the good signs which God had given him in Spain and in Provence, as well as by drawing attention to the end of 'the beast' that was approaching—a reference to the Apocalypse of John which played a central role in the thinking of Joachim. In this way, Innocent thought he had made it sufficiently clear that it was not he who determined the favorable moment for the crusade. On the contrary, it was God who clearly indicated that now was the correct moment to start a crusade against 'the beast.' The crusade fit very well in God's plan; it was God's will. It was not only the pope, it was Christ himself who called Christians to take up the cross.

c. Innocent's Strategy

The real call to the crusade started with the appeal to the Christians to put an end to their own dissensions and to make peace. This was a prerequisite for becoming reconciled with God and thus, by a moral transformation of life, for preparing oneself for the crusade and its success. For if previous crusades failed to achieve their goal, this was mainly due to the sins of the Christians. However, the appeal for peace had also (and mainly?) a very practical origin. As long as the Christians were fighting with each other, they would not be able to free men, material and money for the crusade. This is what in fact had happened at the time of the fourth crusade which was doomed to failure from its very start for lack of funds. Innocent wanted to do everything possible to prevent this from happening again to the new crusade he was planning. That was why in the encyclical he implored solemnly, in the name of the Father and the Son and the Holy Spirit, all archbishops and bishops, all abbots, priors and chapters, all cities and villages, all kings and princes, counts and barons, and requested them in the name of Christ and on his behalf to provide an adequate number of fighting men with the necessary finances for three years. He repeated this request in the decree *Ad liberandum,* in which he mentioned that he did not personally want to remain behind. In order to prevent the impression that he wanted to impose heavy and unbearable burdens on the shoulders of the people without himself lifting even a finger, he informed them that he himself would give 30,000 pounds for the crusade, besides a ship for the crusaders from Rome and its vicinity for which he earmarked a further 3,000 silver marks.[55] After the Fourth Lateran Council he also traveled to many cities in Italy to establish peace and thus to obtain men and money for the crusade. During this personal crusading mission, he died in Perugia on July 16, 1216. After his death, this mission fell first and foremost to cardinal Hugolino, whom the new pope, Honorius III, appointed as his special legate in central and northern Italy to establish peace among the Christians so as to be able to mobilize all forces for the war against the Saracens.[56]

Innocent's crusading plan differed from that of his predecessors mainly by trying to extend the participation of the people in the crusade. He ordered his legates to admit everybody who wished to take the crusader's vow without first examining whether they could serve in the army or in some other way contribute to the crusade. If later it appeared that they could not fulfill their vow, it could be redeemed by paying a sum of money that corresponded to their state in life. In this way Innocent tapped a new source of fund-raising for the crusade. He found another source in his extension of the crusade indulgence. For according to his new regulations, not only those who fulfilled the crusader's vow in person, but also those who paid the expenses for a substitute, would receive the promised total forgiveness of sins. Further, all those who contributed in some other way to the crusade would participate in the indulgence according to the quantity and the quality of their gift. Through these different measures, Innocent intended to obtain the greatest possible support for the crusade. The so-called children's crusade of 1212 had shown Innocent how strong the idea of the liberation of Jerusalem lived among the *pueri*—a term which did not so much refer to a certain age group as to a social group, the group of the new poor.[57] Whereas they were practically excluded from previous crusades, Innocent wanted to include them in his crusade. For he wanted to make the crusade a mass movement rather than the elite movement it had previously been. The entire Christian world must be drawn into taking part in the crusade in every possible way.[58]

The appointment of crusade preachers, too, had its own well-considered place within Innocent's planning. Innocent selected them very carefully, for he was convinced of their great importance in making the call for the crusade heard everywhere in the Christian world. He admonished them that they would only succeed in their mission if they showed by their behavior that they carried the wounds of Jesus Christ in their hearts. To this end he ordered that they deny themselves all financial rewards and not accept anything from anyone except food and other necessities, and even these with moderation; further, they must have no more than four mounts and six attendants; they must also be careful to watch their behavior in these and other matters, so that people would find no fault in them which could hinder the preaching of the gospel entrusted to them.[59] But in his attempts to reach the whole Christian world, Innocent expected the most success from the various regulations regarding daily prayers during Holy Mass and monthly processions with sermons and collections. These were especially apt to keep the plans of the crusade alive among the faithful and to remind them at regular times of their duty to contribute, as best and as much as they could, to the success of the crusade. If they did so in a befitting manner according to their state in life, God would certainly reward them!

With all these measures, Innocent clearly had only one thing in mind: the recapture of the Holy Land. From this perspective, it was rather obvious that the crusade encyclical did not speak at all about mission among the Saracens. Thus Innocent followed a tradition which went back to the beginning of the crusades. In none of the reports of Urban II's call for the first crusade was the conversion of the Saracens mentioned as an explicit aim. Also, in the writings of Bernard of Clairvaux, the motive of conversion was almost completely absent.

There were a few exceptions, however. In 1147, Bernard wrote a letter in support of the German expedition against the Wends in which he appealed to the Christians to take up the cross against them in order either 'to utterly annihilate or surely convert' them. Further, in his *De consideratione*, written in 1152 towards the end of his life, Bernard made a generally worded appeal for the conversion of the pagans and expressly requested that Eugene III send missionaries to them. But these appeals did not exercise any influence on the later crusade encyclicals of the popes. The recapture of the Holy Land was and remained the principal aim of the crusades. Even in papal letters to the prelates of the Latin kingdom of Jerusalem, the conversion of the Saracens did not occur as one of their important responsibilities.[60]

Not only in relation to the crusades, but also elsewhere, the idea of mission was absent from the writings of Innocent III.[61] Only once, and then indirectly, was the mission among the Saracens mentioned as a possibility in a bull which, as it appears now, was a copy of a bull written by Alexander III in 1175.[62] Moreover, the mention of mission did not occur in connection with the crusade to the Holy Land, but with regard to Spain. Innocent wrote in this bull that he wished the fighting in Spain to be conducted in such a way that the Christians would be protected against attacks by the Saracens and that the latter would be brought to the confession of the Christian faith. But when he heard, in 1211, that the sultan of Aleppo, although not baptized, was a Christian at heart, Innocent wrote him a letter in which he recommended him to God and asked him to show his Christian attitude by protecting the patriarch of Antioch. Apparently, it did not occur to him that this might be an opportunity to send missionaries to the sultan to instruct him in the Christian faith and eventually baptize him.

Alongside this negative tradition among church leaders, in which the idea of mission and conversion was almost entirely lacking, there existed yet another tradition, especially among the crusaders themselves, in which the motive of conversion came clearly to the fore. The development of this tradition among the crusaders was probably strongly influenced by the *Chanson de Roland*, which narrated how Charlemagne, in the middle of the fight, offered to convert the leader of the Saracens and how, after the victory, he drove the Saracens to the baptismal font and forced them to become Christians. This song, which dates from the time of preparation for the first crusade, 'has probably shaped the ethic

of the crusading stratum *par excellence*—the knighthood—more deci-
sively than many an encyclical or learned treatise.'[63] This perhaps
explains the fact that Albert of Aachen, in his chronicle of the first crusade, written around 1130, mentioned so many attempts on the part of
the crusaders to convert the Saracens, even though in the papal call to
this crusade the motive of conversion was completely absent.[64] A passage
from a report of Eudes of Deuil, the chaplain of king Louis VII of
France, seems to contradict this. For he informs us that the leaders of
the second crusade declared in October 1147 in Constantinople that their
aim was 'to visit the Holy Sepulcher and, by the command of the
Supreme Pontiff, wipe out our sins with the blood or conversion of the
pagans.' Their appeal to a command of the pope can, however, not be
substantiated. It only shows how, for many crusaders, the conversion of
the Saracens had become an obvious goal of the crusades, so much so
that they attributed it to a command of the pope, whether he had in fact
given such a command or not.[65]

During the fifth crusade, too, the conversion of the Saracens played
a role, as is evident from certain conversion activities of James of Vitry.
After the fall of Damietta, James not only expressed his hope that the
time had now come for the Egyptians to learn about the Lord and to be
converted, he also baptized many hundreds of orphaned children whom
he found in Damietta.[66] The *Gesta Obsidionis Damiate*, a report of an
anonymous eyewitness, is equally clear. According to it, on October 26,
1218, cardinal Pelagius, the papal legate, lead the crusading army to the
battlefield, while he prayed God in Christ to help the Christians so that
they would be able to convert the Saracens.[67] Yet, as stated above, the
motive of mission and conversion cannot be found in the writings of
Innocent III. His full attention was focused on the liberation of the
Holy Land which he wanted to bring to a successful close with all the
means at his disposal. In comparison to this, all other matters were of little or no importance.

C. Conclusion

In Innocent's crusade theology, based on the vision of Christ as
king of kings with Jerusalem as his city and the Holy Land as his inheritance, the crusade had various, interrelated facets: it was an imitation of
Christ, an adapted form of lay spirituality, an occasion for salvation, a

work of art of Christ which the crusaders created when, in Christ's name, they killed or were killed, an act of gratitude, a holy and just war of the entire Christian world against the Saracens, the enemies of the cross, through which the golden age of Christianity was to be restored. All these facets occurred in crusade preaching. Francis and his brothers were certainly acquainted with and reacted to them. In their reaction, profound differences with the papal crusade policy manifested themselves. In the final analysis, as we will see, they went back to a different vision of God, a radically different theology, which made Innocent opt for a crusade against the Saracens, while Francis, because of God, opted for staying among the Saracens and being subject to them.

2. Cardinal Hugolino and his Peace Mission

On July 18, 1216, two days after the death of Innocent III, who was perhaps the greatest apostle of the crusade movement,[68] Honorius III was elected as his successor. A week later he wrote a series of letters to the king and the patriarch of Jerusalem, to all the bishops and the entire clergy, in which he informed them of his election. He also emphasized that he accepted the crusade as an inheritance from his predecessor. Indeed, the crusade became the most important aim of his entire pontificate.[69] Since, according to the decision of the Fourth Lateran Council, the fifth crusade was to commence on June 1, 1217, he continued as forcefully as possible with its preparations. He did this all the more because, after Innocent's death, some hesitation about the crusade appeared to arise in places and interest in its preparations seemed on the decline.[70] For this reason Honorius devoted much of his attention to the further expansion of systematic crusade propaganda which Innocent had started with the appointment of crusade preachers throughout the entire Christian world. His greatest concern, however, was to restore peace between the Christian kings and nations, for without such peace the crusade would never succeed. Honorius felt that he was supported by the decree of Innocent, promulgated on the advice of the council, which stated that peace had to be preserved in the entire Christian world for at least four years. Moreover, those who did not wish to observe this decree had to be forced with a firm hand by their personal excommunication and by the imposition of an interdict on their land.[71]

For the execution of this peace mission, Honorius relied on the then

47 year old cardinal Hugolino, whom he appointed as his legate for northern and central Italy on January 23, 1217. In his letter of appointment Honorius commended Hugolino to both the ecclesiastical and the civil authorities as 'a man according to our heart, accepted by God and by the people, powerful in word and deed, a prominent member of God's church, whom we love with a special love among all our other brothers.'[72] It would be his task to motivate the authorities and the people to get ready for the passage to the Holy Land. To this end, he first had to establish peace between the various groups within Italian society in order to make men and money free for the successful outcome of the crusade.

In those days Italy was in a real state of ferment. This is evident from the history of Assisi where feudal power had to give way to the forces of the commune.[73] The same development was happening elsewhere too. However, as soon as the commune had established itself, there arose conflicts in many cities between the commune and the ecclesiastical authorities who felt that their old rights and privileges were being endangered by the new social and political order. Confronted with this danger, the ecclesiastical authorities made every possible effort to safeguard the church's possessions and even to increase them. Quite often they were supported in their struggle against the commune by members of the old feudal families who, by taking up the cross, placed themselves under the jurisdiction of the ecclesiastical court and its judges, and so were entitled to submit to them their legal claims against the commune.[74] There also existed many rivalries between the cities themselves. Thus we see why cardinal Hugolino traveled from one place to another in an attempt to establish peace among the warring parties. Regarding his second legation in 1221 this is well documented. Appointed on March 14, he traveled to Siena on March 26. Thereafter he visited Florence, Pisa, Emilia, Piacenza, Milan, Brescia, Desenzano, Verona, Venice, Murano, Potenciano, Venice, Padua, Treviso, Mantua, Reggio, Rubbiera, Bologna, Santa Maria del Reno, San Cesario, Columberio, Modena, Bergamo, Novara, Bergamo, Vercelli, Lodi, Reggio, Modena, Nonantola, and Bologna, from which he returned to Florence and Rome after seven months, on October 29. A very impressive list, indeed![75]

Hugolino's first legation lasted considerably longer: from 1217 until 1219. Unfortunately, we possess only three documents from this period, all dating from 1219.[76] Through other documents, we know that Hugolino had been active in Volterra in 1217, but without success. As a result, the people of Volterra refused to take part in the crusade. Hugolino was more successful in Lucca. Thanks to the fact that bishop Robert had a good relationship with the commune, Hugolino was able to reach an agreement with it. They committed themselves to equipping a contingent of crusaders and financing them by levying a tax of a fortieth, to be collected by the commune. Hugolino also had success in Pisa. In fact, he lived on in the memory of its citizens as the man who, by his preaching of the crusade, provided a solution for their many conflicts and, most importantly, brought about a peace treaty with Genoa. Thus the main aim of Innocent's last journey, which remained unfulfilled on account of his unexpected death in Perugia, was realized: the peace between the two rival ports of Genoa and Pisa. Finally, cardinal Hugolino succeeded in concluding a five-year truce between Venice and Padua, thereby making it possible for Venice to supply ships to transport a large number of crusaders and their material to the Holy Land. He even took great pains to obtain from the doge of Venice a discount on the price of the ships![77]

While Hugolino was making strenuous efforts to fulfill his peace mission (or, should we say, his war mission?), he met Francis in Florence. When Francis told him that he was on his way to France, Hugolino forbade him to continue his journey and ordered him to return to Rome. The reason given was that a number of prelates and others in the Roman curia wanted to interfere in the development of the fraternity, probably because of an alleged lack of discipline in the rapidly expanding brotherhood.[78] Francis responded by saying that he would feel greatly ashamed if he stayed in Italy, while sending his brothers to distant lands. Hugolino replied, in a tone of reproach, that Francis should never have sent his brothers so far away to undergo so many trials and die of hunger. Francis answered him 'with great fervor of Spirit and full of the spirit of prophecy: Lord, do you think and believe that the Lord has sent the brothers for these provinces only? Verily I say to you: God has chosen and sent the brothers for the good and salvation of all people in the entire world; they will be received not only among the believers but also among the unbelievers. Let them observe what they have promised the Lord and the Lord will give them among the unbelievers as well as among the believers all that they will need.'[79]

If we recall that cardinal Hugolino was, at that time, deeply involved in trying to collect men and money for the holy war against the unbelieving Saracens, then Francis' reply obtains a prophetic significance indeed. Francis assured Hugolino that his brothers would receive what they needed even from the unbelievers, provided they kept their promise to the Lord, namely that they would go through the world without any possessions, and certainly without arms, and that in whatever house they entered, they would first say: Peace to this house (cf. RegNB 14). A greater contrast than that between Hugolino's official papal peace mission (in reality, a war mission), and the peace mission of Francis is hardly imaginable.[80] Unfortunately, this contrast, and hence the prophetic significance of Francis' reply, has been lost because the story, as told in the Legend of Perugia, is completely silent about the real intention of Hugolino's legation in Florence.[81]

After the failure of the fifth crusade in 1221—the crusaders were defeated on August 26, and the sultan reentered Damietta with his troops on September 7—cardinal Hugolino committed himself fully to the new crusade which Honorius III and emperor Frederick II had decided upon as the quickest possible means of erasing the memory of this shameful defeat. By April 1222, they had their first meetings to prepare the new crusade. Due to all sorts of circumstances, Frederick was forced to postpone his departure for the Holy Land on several occasions. In 1225, Frederick promised solemnly, under pain of excommunication, to leave on August 15, 1227. However, Honorius died before then, on March 18, 1227. The next day cardinal Hugolino was elected pope, and took the name of Gregory IX. It was now his task to hold Frederick to his promise. When the latter, after his initial departure, returned to Italy because of sickness on board his ship, Gregory excommunicated him on September 29. Notwithstanding his excommunication, Frederick left again on June 28, 1228 and concluded a peace treaty with sultan al-Malek al-Kamil at Jaffa on February 18, 1229. In exchange for a truce, Jerusalem, Bethlehem and a few other places between Acre and Jerusalem were handed over to Frederick. On the other hand, the Saracens were allowed to visit the Dome of the Rock and the al-Aqsa mosque. Gregory IX raised some very serious objections against this treaty because, as a result of it, Jerusalem was liberated by negotiations with the pagans and not by a crusade. Because of this liberation by diplomatic means, it was no longer possible for crusaders to gain merit by sacrificing their lives in a crusade.[82] Here, the theology of the crusade as an occasion for salvation assumed a very questionable character: a crusade was preferred to a peace treaty in order that crusaders might gain merit by fighting against and killing Saracens! Francis could not have recognized himself and his ideal of peace, which the Lord had revealed to him, in these ideas and activities of Gregory IX, his erstwhile friend cardinal Hugolino.

3. James of Vitry and his Crusade Preaching

James of Vitry was born in the vicinity of Rheims.[83] After his studies in Paris, he devoted himself, at the request of the beguine Mary of Oignies (1177–1213), to preaching to the illiterate laity and motivating them to follow an evangelical life.[84] Thus James answered the great need for sermons for the people which had arisen because of the threatening activities of heretic preachers.[85] Since he had a lively style and used numerous popular anecdotes, he drew large crowds. He started his activity as a crusade preacher in 1213 around Oignies, preaching the crusade against the Albigenses. After the death of Mary of Oignies in June of that year, he preached with great success in the diocese of Rheims. And later in the same year, cardinal Robert Courçon, the papal legate for France, appointed James as official preacher for the fifth crusade which Innocent III had announced a few months earlier. James accepted this task as an exalted calling in obedience to God, as he later explained in one of his crusade sermons. For it was the Lord who enjoined the preachers 'to raise the sign of the cross like a standard of the supreme king on Zion, that is to say, in the church of God, by preaching the virtue of the cross, by vaunting its praises with the voice of a herald, and by inviting people to it.'[86] James fulfilled his task so well that he is considered one of the most important preachers of the fifth crusade, and even the most remarkable among them.[87] As a result of his preaching, a considerable number of crusaders from Lower Lorraine and the province of Rheims took the cross and travelled to Syria and Egypt.[88]

In 1214, the canons of Acre elected James bishop. After the pope confirmed his election in the course of the next year, James left in 1216 to be consecrated in Rome. On his exciting and dangerous journey he almost lost all his books and luggage while crossing a river whose waters had swollen enormously because of melting snow. As if by a miracle, he was saved thanks to a finger of Mary of Oignies which he carried with him in one of his chests. On his arrival in Perugia on July 17, 1216, he heard that Innocent III, who was on his way to Pisa and Genoa to establish peace, had just died the day before. While he was lying in state in a church, he was robbed of his precious vestments during the night and left naked and smelling badly. The next day Honorius was elected pope; he was consecrated the following Sunday. A week later, James received episcopal consecration.[89] During his stay at the papal court in Perugia, he came in contact with the Lesser Brothers and the Lesser Sisters. They were his only consolation in the midst of many things at the papal curia with which he could not agree because they hurt his feelings. For the members of the curia were so busy with worldly and temporal matters, with kings and kingdoms, with quarrels and legal cases, that they hardly allowed anyone to speak about spiritual matters.[90]

A. JAMES' PREACHING AND CONVERSION ACTIVITIES

After some time, James continued his journey to Genoa. When he arrived there in the beginning of September, the people of the city were about to attack a stronghold in the neighborhood. As was customary, they confiscated all horses, to whomever they belonged, including those of James and his entourage, for the time of the battle. He took this opportunity to preach the crusade to the women and the few men who were not taking part in the battle. A large group of rich and noble women accepted the cross. This made James observe: 'The men have taken away my horses, while I have signed their wives with the cross.' When the men returned and saw what had happened to their wives, they too accepted the cross with great fervor. James continued his preaching on Sundays and feastdays throughout the month of September. And although he did not speak their language, thousands of men took up the cross and were converted to the Lord. James was very happy with this result, for he mentioned expressly that these men were 'rich and powerful; they are strenuous and keen fighters. Moreover they have an abundance of the best ships and galleons. They also have expert sailors who know the way at sea and have often travelled to the land of the Saracens for purposes of trade.' In fact, James did not believe 'that there is one city which can contribute so much to the support of the Holy Land.'

Beside his preaching activities, James found time to rent 'a new ship which has never before been put to sea. It has just been built at a cost of four thousand pound; a bad ship, as I have heard, was bought for five hundred pound. I have reserved five rooms for myself and my people, that is, one quarter of the upper castle. In one room I shall eat, study my books and remain during the day, unless it storms at sea. I have reserved a second room where I shall sleep at night with my companions; a third one where I shall store my clothes and the food needed for a week; a fourth one where my servants will sleep and prepare my food, and a fifth one where the horses are kept that I am taking along on my journey. Further, in the hold of the ship, I have put wine, biscuits, meat and other necessities of life, enough for almost three months.'[91]

After a stormy journey, James arrived at the port of Acre on Friday, November 4, 1216. He was received with great joy by the whole city. He himself, however, was not very enthusiastic about the situation in the city. 'I found the city of Acre like a monster and a freak with nine heads that were fighting with each other': Jacobites, Syrians, Nestorians, Georgians, Armenians, three groups of Italians from Genoa, Pisa and Venice—they refused to come to his sermons so that James was obliged to go to them and preach in their neighborhood, and not without success— Pullans,[92] strangers and, finally, scribes and pharisees, 'a kind of people, worse than all others and more hardened and blinded.... While the others showed compunction and converted to the Lord, they alone resisted the word of God and all good, so that would be fulfilled what is written: publicans and prostitutes are entering the kingdom of heaven before you.'[93] In this monstrous city, murders were committed almost every day and night: men who strangled their women, women who poisoned their men with a slow or fast-acting poison. The city was full of brothels. 'Who can enumerate all the shameful deeds of this second Babylon, where Christians deny baptism to their Saracen servants, even if they themselves ask for it with great insistence and tears.' James did not allow himself to become discouraged and, with the help of God's mercy, he succeeded, in a short time, in converting the people to the Lord and 'to sign almost all of them with the cross, enjoining the men to prepare their arms and all other necessities for aiding the Holy Land, and the women to contribute financially to the army in accordance with their means, yet also imposing on them a moderate penance for their sins.'[94] When some of the Saracens heard how the Lord worked among the Christians, they wanted to be baptized. 'Many are admonished in their sleep, at least so they say, by the Lord Jesus Christ or by the Blessed Virgin or some other saint to abandon the error of Mohammed and to turn to God's grace. For the Blessed Virgin told them, they allege, that unless they become Christians, they will die a miserable death once the Christian armies will arrive in the near future and claim victory.' Further, James expected that those Saracens who, at that moment, were afraid of the revenge of their own people, would convert to the Lord after the landing of the crusaders' army.[95]

During the spring of 1217, accompanied by a military escort, James made a preaching tour of the coastal cities of Syria, which were under the crusaders' rule.[96] After the example of Acre, the people of those cities also wanted to hear the word of God. And after confessing their sins and receiving the sign of the cross for the defense of the Holy Land, they offered themselves and all their possessions to the Lord. In his sermons, James showed the Christians who lived in Saracen surroundings and often led corrupt lives, how 'they in a commendable way ought to live among the Saracens, so that the name of the Lord would not be blasphemed among the pagans because of them.' Further, he tried to explain, as best as he could, 'the fraud of Mohammed and his abominable doctrine, for there are some who waver between the law of the Christians and that of the Saracens.'[97] During his tour, James also baptized two Saracens from Antaradus in a small chapel which St. Peter had built there on his way to Antioch in honor of the Blessed Virgin. It was here that the Lord performed so many miracles that Christians and Saracens alike made pilgrimages to it.[98] However, he also wanted to extend his preaching activities to which Mary of Oignies had urged him (he always carried her finger, encased in a silver casket, around his neck) to the territory of the Saracens.[99] When this proved impossible, he preached in the border regions whenever he was able. Further, he sent letters to the Saracens in their own language in which he showed them both their errors and the truth of Christianity.[100] For, as James wrote at the end of his second letter: 'Many Saracens, I believe, would easily be converted to the Lord, if they would hear the sane doctrine.'[101]

James' interest in preaching disappeared into the background of his letters when the crusading army, mightier than ever before in arms, horses and soldiers, arrived in Acre in the autumn of 1217.[102] Yet his concern for the conversion of the Saracens continued, albeit in a different form. First, he mentioned that, during the siege of Damietta, many Saracens had gone over to the Christians and asked to be baptized. They would have been even more numerous if the crossing of the river that separated them from the Christians had been easier. In fact, some Saracens drowned during the crossing, while others were killed by their own people.[103] Next, James informed his readers at home that, after the fall of Damietta on November 5, 1219, the more wealthy prisoners were kept in order to be exchanged; all the others were sold as slaves to the Christians, except for the children, whom James personally was able to keep out of slavery with great difficulty and expense. After he had baptized them, five hundred died because they had been weakened so much by the long siege. Of the remainder, James kept some and gave the others to his friends to be educated and to learn the Scriptures to the honor of God.[104] Finally, James wrote that several Saracens who had become Christians of their own free will, afterwards 'returned secretly to the filth of the pagans to which they had been accustomed.' The explanation James gave for this behavior was that in Islam they could do whatever they liked, hence they found Christian life too hard and strict—an explanation which does not show much knowledge of the teachings and practices of Islam.[105]

B. JAMES' ATTITUDE TOWARDS CRUSADES AND ISLAM

James' letters contain several passages in which his views of the crusades and of Islam come clearly to the fore. In a first passage, James determined his position in a question which had frequently been raised, especially after Peter of Blois had written his *De Hierosolymitana Peregrinatione Acceleranda* (1188–1189). In this work, Peter explicitly asked whether it was the kings and their armies on whom the success of the crusade depended or whether the victory belonged to the 'poor'? The background of the question is to be found in the fact that, after the fall of Jerusalem (1187), the princes and the other powerful of the earth, even though they had accepted the cross recently, continued to fight with each other rather than to become involved in the preparations for a new crusade. Thus they showed themselves unworthy of God's kingdom because they were more concerned about their own perishable reigns and their own temporal gains.[106] In light of God's history with humankind, Peter thought it very likely that, in these circumstances, 'after the rejection of the powerful of the earth to whom the Lord had offered the rights to this pilgrimage, God will choose people of lesser fame for whom he has reserved the glory in this whole affair to the disgrace of the powerful. Yet it remains true that the Roman emperor and the king of France would have taken away the yoke of the tyrant and established eternal peace in the land, if they would not have set out with a great and undisciplined multitude, but with a small select group and in devout humility.' Hence Peter continued to hope that 'He who is the way, the truth and the life, will bring back those who have been signed with the cross, from their error unto the way of truth and life and that He will thus liberate the land which he has chosen as his dwelling place and, by living there, has made as it were into another heaven.'[107] Peter of Blois, therefore, was not against a crusade of the kings and the powerful of this earth, as some have concluded. However, he was deeply convinced that their crusade would only be successful if they put their trust not in money, weapons or their own strength, but in God, in a spirit of poverty and humility.[108]

The same idea is evident in a remark which James of Vitry made when, during the siege of Damietta, the crusaders were faced with the difficult task of conquering a tower built on the shore of the Nile at the other side of the city. From this tower a heavy chain, further protected by a boat bridge, led through the river to a tower in the city wall and prevented any ship from reaching the city by way of the Nile. To capture the city, the crusaders therefore had to take the tower first. John of Brienne, king of Jerusalem, made a first attempt, together with the Duke of Austria and other leaders, but without success. 'When the great and powerful of the army were about to despair, there appeared some poor people, devoted to God, and humble; they were Frisians. On the advice of Oliver, the chancellor of Cologne,[109] they had built with great difficulty and at a cost of 2,000 mark a wonderful and totally unheard-of war machine.... And since these Frisians do not trust in their own strength, but place all their hope in God, they held processions and fasted with tears and prayers. Thereafter they attacked the tower with their war machine. In the tower there were 250 of the Saracen elite troops beside other soldiers.... And while the pilgrims, both nobles and others, threw themselves in the sand and sprinkled ashes on their head, they cried out to the Lord with tears and sighs that He might show mercy to his people so that the pagans might not say: where is their

God? Thus fed by the tears and prayers of the pilgrims and strengthened in the Lord, our men were able to jump through the fire and the swords and arrows onto the tower and capture it.'[110]

It is clear where James' sympathy lay. He too was not against crusades. On the contrary! And as is evident from his sermons, he fully subscribed to the crusade ideology as it had been developed by Innocent III in his encyclical *Quia maior*. But also for him, what mattered most in the crusades was trust in God. Hence, when James used the word 'poor' here, it was not primarily meant in a socio-economic sense. Certainly, James did not speak about the rich, the kings and the powerful of the earth. But he also did not speak about people who possessed nothing, because, as we have read, those poor people were able to furnish the money necessary for building the war machine. As James himself indicated, we must think here of people who are humble and devoted to God's cause. Of course, kings and nobles were not excluded from this group, even though it may have been more difficult for them than for others to be 'poor.' If they had actually acquired this poverty of spirit, the crusades would have had much greater success in liberating the Holy Land.

Very interesting, too, is the opening passage of the sixth letter which James wrote in the spring of 1220, after the crusaders had captured Damietta on November 5, 1219. 'Let them praise the Lord for his mercy and for his wonders done for the sons of men; for He broke open the bronze gates and smashed the iron bars; He subjected the peoples under our dominion and put the nations under our feet. The city that was the glory of the pagans, the city in which the unbelievers had put their trust, the most fortified and unassailable city, repeatedly besieged by many kings and peoples and never conquered, this city the Lord has subjected in these days to the holy church and to the army of the Christians; He has broken the horns of the sinners. Thus he has opened wide the doors for us to subject the unbelievers and to expand the empire of Christ so that, after the wolves have been captured and thrown out, the vineyard of the Lord of hosts be cultivated as a new plantation.... And where so often the cursed name of the perfidious Mohammed has been invoked—an abominable name, which the mouth of the devil has named—, there people now invoke the blessed name of Jesus Christ—the glorious name which the mouth of the Lord has named—, so that the Egyptians may know the Lord and be converted to him, and the light of truth may return from the West to the East.'[111] Just as James was misinformed when he wrote in a previous passage that the Saracens could do what they liked, so he gave his readers here an erroneous picture of Islam when he said that the Saracens invoked the name of Mohammed. Further, it would be difficult to match the negative language which James used here with regard to Mohammed. The use of such language could in no way contribute to a good relationship with, or a greater openness toward the Saracens; it could only confirm and strengthen the existing, deep-seated enmity between Christians and Saracens. Beside the negative approach toward Mohammed, it is the triumphalistic tone of the passage which especially strikes the reader: God is on the side of the crusaders in their war against the unbelievers; God gives the crusaders their victory and subjects the pagans to them.[112] In James' mind, it was not possible to entertain any doubt whatsoever regarding the goodness and lawfulness of the crusades.

Yet, such doubts did exist in the Christian world at that time, as is evident from a sermon which James, probably as bishop of Acre, held for the members of a military order.[113] After a short introduction about the five basic rules for knights during battle, James replied to various objections which were being made by people to the use of violence by the military orders in their fight against the enemies of the church. In his reply James immediately attacked them: 'When people falsely assert that you are not allowed for any reason whatever to take up the physical sword or fight bodily against the church's enemies, it is the devil trying to attack the fabric of your order and by means of these people to utterly destroy it. They misuse the authorities of scripture and bring in worthless interpretations. For instance they quote the passages in which St Paul says: Revenge not yourselves, my dearly beloved; but give place unto wrath (Rom 12:19); and in the gospel of Matthew: Whoever takes the sword shall perish with the sword (26:52); and Luke: To him who strikes you on one cheek, offer also the other (6:29);[114] and when the Lord said to the servants who wanted to gather the cockle: Suffer both to grow until the harvest, and then I will say to the reapers: gather up the cockle, and bind it into bundles to burn (Mt 13:30). And they put forward many arguments like these to seduce the simple-minded and unwary.' After he had thus qualified the arguments of his opponents as worthless and false, James continued: 'The precepts of forbearance should be observed not so much in a false show of action as in circumspectness of heart: you should keep forbearance together with benevolence in the secret places of your soul. That is why the Lord, when struck on the cheek, was not seen to offer the other, but patiently bore it and exposed his whole body to death. When St. Paul was struck on the cheek in the same way he said to the high priest: God shall strike you, you whited wall. And so according to Augustine those precepts of forbearance should always be kept by a wary heart; this same benevolence ought always to fill the will, so that one does not repay evil with evil.'

After this rather twisted and distorted exegesis—who accuses whom here of misusing texts?—James gave a further justification of the crusade by pointing out that if the Christians 'were not resisting the church's enemies, the Saracens and heretics would have destroyed the whole church.' It was evident, therefore, that the military orders 'do not carry the sword without cause. Soldiering seems to have been instituted to repel violence, repulse injury and proceed with justice against wrongdoers.' Hence, James continued to the knights, 'it is clear that your order was founded with good reason and it is obvious how necessary it is to the church of God, especially in these days when man's life on earth is taken up not only with knighthood but also with knavery. And when you want to be useful to others, begin with yourselves so that you will not be...like the ass which carries the wine but does not taste it.... So always be prepared to shed your blood for Christ, that is to say to lay down your lives for God with the sword and do so eagerly, following the example of a certain soldier of Christ who on seeing a host of Saracens began to say to his horse with great confidence and rejoicing in his heart: Oh Morel, my good companion, I have done many a good day's work mounted and riding on you, but this day's work will be better than all the others, because today you will take me to eternal life. And then, after killing many Saracens, he himself died, crowned in war by blessed martyrdom.'[115]

These extensive quotations from sermon 38 give a good insight into James' attitude towards the crusades. He not only approved of them, he also defended them against critical voices which were being heard in certain places. I do not refer here to chronicles, poems, theological writings and even laws of the twelfth and thirteenth centuries which made unfavorable comments on crusades and crusaders, but rarely if ever touched the very principle of the crusade. They were primarily concerned with exposing certain abuses connected with the crusades, like the heavy taxes imposed on the people by popes and kings, the redemption or commutation of the crusader's vow by paying money, or the wrong mentality with which kings and princes took part in the crusades. In this way they hoped to improve both the organization and the efficiency of the crusades. Their criticisms, therefore, were more anticurial than pacifist.[116]

At times, however, more radical, pacifist voices emerged, like the one of the patriarch of Jerusalem. Basing himself on the gospel, he put, as a matter of conscience, the question to Peter Manducator, whether Christians were allowed to fight against the pagans and kill them.[117] And there were the nameless person or persons who questioned the existence and activities of military orders, and for this reason were attacked by James of Vitry, or still others who found it very hard to see the crusade as a time of salvation, that was acceptable to God.[118] To the latter belonged, perhaps, various clerics like Caesar of Spires, Rainerio, the prior of St. Michael, the Englishman Colin and others who, while in the Holy Land, joined the brothers, maybe because they found among them an alternative to the crusade with which they could no longer identify.[119] Unfortunately, these voices from the 'underside' of history are only indirectly known to us through the writings of their opponents who represented the dominant class and culture of those days and did not inform us of the strength and number of these critics. Certainly they were unable to influence the course of history. The crusade went on with its thousands of victims, with its violence and destruction. In the eyes of James, it was a time of salvation for all those who took up the cross in order to join the Christian army in the holy war against the Saracens, a war willed by God for the liberation of God's inheritance. If, as a result of this display of power, some Saracens converted to Christianity and were baptized, this was to be considered as a fortunate circumstance, as a happy coincidence which James accepted gladly.

C. CONCLUSION

These numerous and rather extensive quotations from James' letters and sermons portray to us a man who devoted himself zealously to the execution of the tasks which had been entrusted to him by the ecclesiastical authorities. He preached the crusade with great enthusiasm and did his utmost to raise the life of the Christians in his diocese to a higher spiritual and moral level and to motivate them to take part in the liberation of Jerusalem. He was also constantly intent on proclaiming the Christian message to the Saracens. Notwithstanding his ties with the movement of the beguines and his criticism of the Roman curia,[120] James was and remained a feudal bishop not only in his way of travelling but also in his unceasing efforts and his unwavering commitment to realize the church's policy of power which was directed to the recapture of the Holy Land and the subjection of the Saracens, a policy which he emphatically defended against the objections of opponents. His negative, strongly apologetic attitude towards Mohammed and Islam was in perfect agreement with all this. In all he said and did, James was the true opposite of Francis who, without arms and possessions, in a nonviolent way, went to meet the sultan and in whose writings not a single negative word about Mohammed and Islam can be found.[121] This fundamental difference is very well illustrated by the manner in which James, in his defense of the crusades, enervated the gospel text about turning the other cheek, while Francis acknowledged this same text as essential for the way in which he and his brothers wanted to go through the world in a spirit of nonviolence, as peacemakers.[122]

CHAPTER TWO

The Literary Context

Against the background of my investigations into the ideas of some of Francis' contemporaries—men he personally knew and met—I want to study Francis' ideas about crusades and Islam. Nowhere in his writings did Francis explicitly deal with this subject. In chapter 16 of the *Regula non bullata*, however, he left his brothers who wanted to go among the Saracens or other unbelievers, some advice on how they could live among them in the Spirit of the Lord. This advice did not fall from heaven. In the course of many years, Francis and his brothers gradually developed an essentially theological vision of church and world in continuous interaction with their surroundings in light of the gospel. On the basis of this vision they made their choices and determined their position with regard to what was happening in the church and the world in their day. They formulated these decisions in the so-called *Regula non bullata*. The genesis of their rule, therefore, runs parallel to the development of the early brotherhood and it is through the study of this rule that we can come to know the history of the first brothers.[1]

In this light, chapter 16 can be considered as the result of the position which Francis and his brothers, on the basis of their theology of church and world, adopted towards the Saracens and Islam after they had come into personal contact with them during their visit to the sultan. To understand chapter 16 properly, it is therefore necessary to study first the theological vision that inspired Francis and his brothers to go among the Saracens and relate to them in such a radically different way than the dominant church circles of those days. In other words, we must determine more precisely where and how chapter 16 and its unique way

43

of approaching the Saracens fit in with the theological vision developed and formulated in the *Regula non bullata*, especially in the chapters which immediately precede and follow chapter 16. In more technical terms, we must examine the literary context into which chapter 16 was inserted by Francis and his brothers. For it is this context which can throw light on the way in which we ought to interpret chapter 16, if we want to remain faithful to the theological vision of church and world developed within the early brotherhood. Before studying the literary context, however, we first want to address briefly the question of the date of chapter 16.

1. The Date of Regula non bullata, *Chapter 16*

In his pioneering study of the *Regula non bullata*, David Flood writes that chapter 16 was developed as a concretization of the way in which the brothers ought to go through the world (RegNB 14). It was made by Francis and his brothers in reply to the call of Innocent III on April 19, 1213, to hold a council with the twofold purpose of reconquering the Holy Land and reforming the universal church.[2] It is rather improbable, however, that in such a far-reaching matter the brothers would go only by a papal encyclical to which, for lack of experience on their part, they would reply in a rather *a priori* fashion, by working out a set of concrete recommendations on how to live among the Saracens whom they did not know. Such a procedure was alien to Francis and his brothers. In their elaboration of the rule, they let themselves be guided by questions which arose from their contact with reality. In other words, Francis and his brothers approached their problems *a posteriori*, on the basis of their own experience. On the other hand, it is possible, of course, that, confronted with all that was happening in church and society in preparation for the crusade—sermons, processions, prayers, collections—the brothers started asking what all of this meant for them and how they were to deal with it. On the basis of their earlier choices with regard to their place in society and their way of approaching people, they decided then that their peace mission must be extended to the Saracens as well. Hence, the brothers who were to go to the Saracens, must stay among them as brothers and servants. In that case chapter 16 must be seen as a contrast program. While Innocent III called for the recapture of Jerusalem and the Holy Land by fire and sword, if necessary, Francis and his brothers were convinced that the use of arms and violence could not be reconciled with their way of life as lesser brothers and as Christians. For the Lord had revealed to them that they should greet the people by saying: 'may the Lord give you peace' (Test 23).[3] But even with this presupposition, the concrete character of the advice and the way it fit the specific situation of the Saracens, cannot be adequately explained.

For this reason Walbert Bühlmann concludes that chapter 16 cannot be properly understood apart from Francis' personal mission among the Saracens; in fact, chapter 16 is a reflection on and a written fixation of a previous evangelical praxis. In Bühlmann's opinion, we can therefore accept as probable the view that the mission chapter of the *Regula non bullata* was written down after Francis' stay in Egypt (July 1219 through spring 1220).[4] Moreover, he thinks that we exaggerate the missionary impact of the Fourth Lateran Council if we accept that chapter 16 had been drafted under the influence of the council. For there is a world of difference between the call for a crusade and the concern for evangelization. Together with other authors, Bühlmann is therefore inclined to see chapter 16 as an echo and an elaboration of the experiences Francis had on his journey to Damietta and his stay among the Muslims. Without this personal missionary experience it would hardly have been possible for Francis to describe the two ways of being spiritually present among the Saracens in the manner he actually did in chapter 16.[5] Anton Rotzetter, however, is not convinced by Bühlmann's argument. According to Rotzetter, the Franciscan way of staying among the Saracens, described in chapter 16, is essentially determined by the Franciscan way of life elaborated in the earlier chapters of the *Regula non bullata*. Hence, chapter 16 may very well have been written before Francis' missionary journey to Egypt as an alternative to the crusade organized by the ecclesiastical authorities. This last point is, in Rotzetter's view, more important than determining the exact date of chapter 16.[6]

In the final analysis, the question is: which concrete experiences of Francis and his brothers formed the basis of the text of chapter 16 and inspired the extant formulation? The precision with which Francis and the brothers formulated the two ways of presence among the Saracens favors Bühlmann's thesis. In other words, Francis' concrete experiences during his stay among the Saracens, offer the best explanation for chapter 16, certainly for that part (1–9) which is explicitly concerned with the brothers who go among the Saracens. This holds true especially for the second way of presence in which Francis clearly indicated that the brothers could preach when they saw that it would please God (7). This can be interpreted as a general observation which is valid for everyone, at all times and places: everyone must always and everywhere act in accordance with God's pleasure. The fact, however, that Francis used this expression precisely in this context, and thus seemed to relativize the necessity of preaching and baptizing for salvation, can only be explained, in my opinion, on the basis of a profound personal experience on Francis' part of the presence of God among the Saracens, a presence which Francis expressly wished to respect.[7]

Also, the expression 'not to engage in arguments or disputes' (6), which Francis used in his description of the first way of presence, obtains a very special color when it is read against the background of Francis' experiences in the Middle East. In this case, too, it is possible to read the expression as a general characteristic of the peaceful way in which the brothers are supposed to move about in the world, as indicated in chapter 11:3 and also in *Regula bullata* 10:3. This does not adequately explain, however, why Francis and his brothers explicitly brought this characteristic forward precisely here, in the context of the brothers' stay among the Saracens. The explicit mention that the brothers should not engage in arguments or disputes, refers most likely to the fact that some brothers actually followed an apologetic method in their approach to the Saracens.[8] It speaks for itself that here we think first of the brothers who, at the chapter of 1217, had been sent to Syria under the leadership of brother Elias.[9] Under the influence of James of Vitry who devoted himself to explaining to the Saracens, orally and in writing, the lies of the pseudoprophet Mohammed and the truth of Christianity,[10] Elias and the other brothers may well have started using the same apologetic method. James of Vitry may then have had them in mind when he wrote: 'The Saracens gladly listened to the preaching of the lesser brothers as long as they explained the Christian faith and the doctrine of the gospel; but as soon as they in their preaching attacked Mohammed and openly condemned him as liar and traitor, then these ungodly men heaped blows upon them and chased them from their cities; they would have killed them if God had not miraculously protected his sons.'[11] Although the use of such an apologetic method by the brothers seemed rather obvious in the given circumstances, Francis evidently did not agree with it. For this reason he explicitly forbade his brothers to use this method any further. It seems very improbable that he would have issued such a prohibition even before he had gone to the East and observed the way Christian preachers approached the Saracens, purely and simply on the basis of a further elaboration of the fundamental characteristics of the Franciscan way of life. On the contrary, everything points in the direction of Francis having taken this measure because, during his stay among the Saracens, he had personally experienced the fact that good and fruitful contacts could be established with them if the brothers approached them as lesser brothers, without violence and arms, not subjecting them, but being subject to them.

For these reasons, chapter 16, 1–9 of the *Regula non bullata* probably has to be dated after Francis' visit to Egypt. This does not exclude the possibility that the preparations for the crusade may well have awakened him and his brothers to the existence of a non-Christian world[12] and made them decide to extend their peace mission to the Saracens as well, in opposition to the general ecclesiastical policy. Moreover, they certainly had many ideas about how they as lesser brothers were going to realize such a mission. After all, they had quite some experiences with peace missions over the years.[13] However, a more precise formulation of the way in which the lesser brothers must go among the Saracens—a formulation especially meant for the future brothers—had to wait until they had experienced themselves what such a mission really implied.[14]

However, there is more. All the authors who have written about chapter 16 presuppose its original unity. Yet, in my opinion, there exists a clear unevenness in the text which points to an insertion. It concerns the verses 3b through 5a, the passage which deals with the permission of the minister. The chapter opens with the gospel text about how the Lord sends out disciples as sheep, serpents and doves, and how the Lord, on this basis, prescribes a certain way of behavior: the disciples ought to be subject to those among whom they go, prudent and simple. One expects then the next sentence, which is introduced by 'therefore,' to draw from the quoted gospel text a number of more concrete practical conclusions for the way of behavior of those brothers who, by divine inspiration, as sheep, serpents and doves, wish to go among the Saracens and other unbelievers. However, the practical conclusions follow only in verse 5b where it is said that these brothers can live spiritually among the Saracens in two ways. These two ways correspond to the quoted gospel text: the first way consists in not engaging in arguments and in being subject like the sheep among the wolves, while the second way consists in prudently weighing the situation in order to discern whether it pleases the Lord that the brothers start preaching the word of God and, if so, in fulfilling this preaching ministry simply as it befits a lesser brother to do. The passage about the permission of the minister interrupts this train of thought by dealing first with a problem within the brotherhood. It must therefore have been inserted in the text at a later date.

This insertion fits in well with the other events that took place in the brotherhood at the time Francis returned from Egypt.[15] Francis found a brotherhood deeply affected by tensions, especially as a result of the activities of the ministers and the learned brothers. They wanted to move the brotherhood in another, more pastoral direction, and were supported therein by the papal curia. They wanted to transform the brotherhood of lesser brothers who, by their simplicity, confound and destroy the wisdom of the world (SalVirt 10), into a respected and powerful order of learned clerics who placed themselves at the service of the pastoral policies of the church.[16] In order to fulfill this ecclesiastical task well, they needed houses where the young brothers could make their studies, and papal letters which confirmed them in their pastoral role as preachers and protected them against eventual persecution (cf. Test 24–25). It is not surprising that these ministers and learned brothers showed little understanding of the way in which Francis wanted his brothers to go among the Saracens. Because of this, they made numerous objections to the departure of new brothers, whom they preferred to become involved as preachers or in some other way in the execution of the church's policies.

Even though Francis disagreed with the ministers regarding the future of the brotherhood, he could not do without them since the number of brothers had grown so enormously in such a short time. Hence he did the only thing possible given the circumstances. The brothers must ask permission from their ministers—this was simply necessary to have some idea of what was happening within the brotherhood and to prevent chaos—but the ministers on their part were not to refuse permission to go among the Saracens to any one of the brothers whom they saw fit to be sent. The ministers were thus told to respect the divine inspiration, the working of the Spirit, in the individual brother. When the Lord speaks (1), the ministers should not dare to contradict (4). If, all the same, they do so and proceed without due discretion, they must know that they are bound to give an account to the Lord. Francis used very forceful language in this insertion in order to protect the divine inspiration, which was holy to him, against the ministers.[17]

This presupposition of a later insertion does not interfere with the previous conclusion that chapter 16 must be dated after Francis' journey to Egypt. One can very well imagine that, during their months-long visit to Egypt and on their long sea voyage back to Italy, Francis and his brothers not only reflected on the purpose and manner of their stay among the Saracens, but also tried to find a formulation that could serve as a guideline for future brothers who, by divine inspiration, might want to go among the Saracens. Once back in Italy, circumstances forced them to make a final adaptation of the text because of the changed climate within the brotherhood.

2. The Literary Context of Regula non bullata, Chapter 16

Chapter 16 was inserted after chapter 14 as a further specification concerning the going about of the brothers in the world: 'to go' is therefore the key word that thematically unites chapters 14, 15 and 16.[18] Before this and other insertions were made, the text of the present chapter 14 originally continued in chapter 17:5.[19] With this verse there started a last admonition in which Francis reminded his brothers once more that humility, not taking pride in themselves nor appropriating anything (5–7), ought to be the fundamental attitude in their lives. They had to continue trying to maintain and to further deepen this attitude in their brotherhood and in the world in the unremitting struggle between the spirit of the flesh and the Spirit of the Lord (9–15).[20] By inserting chapter 16 precisely before this admonition concerning the fundamental attitude, Francis made it clear to the brothers that the essential characteristic of their going among the Saracens must be that they live spiritually among them in humility and patience in the Spirit of the Lord and so realize the pure and simple and true peace of the Spirit (16:5; 17:15):[21] the peace which the Lord had given to them as greeting (14:3) and as task, for all brothers must preach by their deeds (17:3).[22]

What did this mean concretely in the historical context of Assisi, of Italy, and, even beyond, of the Saracens? Assisi, too, offered its citizens peace. The warring factions of the city concluded with much pomp a peace treaty 'in the name of God and to the glory of our Lord Jesus Christ' at a meeting of the people on November 9, 1210.[23] The outward appearance of piety and holiness was fully on their side: with the bless-ing of God they possessed a wonderful document, which regulated everything in great detail. But for whom? From the point of view of the people who, individually or as a group, benefitted by it, this document fit exactly the situation of the rising classes in urban society, the classes of traders, bankers, lawyers, and notaries, all of whom, in their negotia-tions and discussions, relied mainly on words.[24] But, and this was Francis' concern, these practitioners of the 'culture of the word' were wanting in deeds (17:11–12): the *operatio*, that is, the liberating, transforming activity of men and women in the power of the Spirit through which they gave birth to Jesus again in this world, gave him again a concrete historical existence in their own surroundings (2 LetFaith 48–53). Because of the absence of those deeds, the peace treaty did not bring peace at all for many in and around Assisi: 'the people who are considered to be of little worth and who are looked down upon, the poor and powerless, the sick and the lepers, and the beggars by the wayside' (RegNB 9:2). On the con-trary, they were excluded; they did not count. Peace was only for those who had possessions and who were able to cooperate towards the increase of Assisi's goods. They alone had a right to speak; they alone had a decisive voice in the conclusion of a peace treaty. If the poor, the sick and the lepers were the losers, so be it. They, the rich, were even prepared, out of charity, to give them occasional alms. They knew very well their duties as religious people!

Francis and his brothers rejected this state of affairs. They did not want an illusory peace, a peace of words without deeds. They wanted true peace. That is the reason why they broke with the world of Assisi, a world which, in their eyes, was full of sin (Test 1–3). They did so first of all by selling their possessions and distributing the proceeds to the poor in accordance with the gospel (AnPer 10). After they had done this and had placed themselves thereby outside the accepted order of Assisi, the question arose: where do we go from here and how? In other words, they had promised to follow the footprints of Jesus (RegNB 1:1), but where could they find them?[25] Neither the bishop, nor the podestà could help the brothers because both were completely caught up in the system, in the sin of Assisi and the world (AnPer 17d; LetRulers 3–5). The brothers would have to search their way through this world all by themselves, guided by the light of the revelation of the Most High (Test 14). Individually and as a group, they would have to reflect on how, in the Spirit of the Lord, they would give shape to their ideals in their historical situation. Always intent on the struggle between the Spirit of the Lord and the spirit of the flesh, they themselves had to place the footprints of Jesus on the earth during their journey through history and thus once again make Jesus a historical reality in their situation.

The situation of the brothers at that moment was neither great nor spectacular. They would have to test their great ideals in the context of the ordinary reality of everyday life with which they were constantly being confronted. In this connection, a first rather obvious question put to them was: how are you going to keep yourselves alive? Their answer was: by working (RegNB 7). The growing economy of Assisi could certainly make good use of honest laborers. There was work enough in the fields and in the workshops. The preference of the brothers, however, went to the houses of the poor and the lepers. But wherever they worked, their work had for them a completely different meaning than it had within the system of Assisi. While Assisi considered work mainly within the context of its usefulness for the city's economic growth and hence wanted to involve the brothers in a way that was most profitable to Assisi, the brothers looked at their work mainly as a means to make the life of the brotherhood possible. The brothers, therefore, did not work to become rich, to gather possessions, or to enhance their social standing. On the contrary, in return for their work they accepted only what was necessary for their livelihood, with the exception of money (7:7). This economy of necessity, which the brothers wanted to practice, was radically opposed to Assisi's economy of growth, which favored the rich and victimized the poor, and so could not lead to true peace.

Assisi was not prepared to accept the opposition of the brothers. Notwithstanding the brothers' refusal to cooperate with the system, the citizens of Assisi tried to win them over to the world of money, status and power. And the spirit of the flesh is very inventive. They offered the brothers posts as financial administrators in charge of accounts or as officials of the commune supervising its service institutions (7:1).[26] For the brothers were hard working and honest. But they did not want these important posts. By accepting them they would have become part of the system that recommended an economy of growth and thus divided people, the rich—the winners—against the poor—the losers. The brothers would not bring peace, but division. Hence, they made a clear decision: they would be 'the lesser ones and subject to all who are in the same house' (7:2).[27] Making this choice in the Spirit of the Lord, they broke with the system of Assisi, based on money and might, and were able to build up an alternative structure, based on humble service and on sharing whatever they needed with each other and with everyone who knocked on their door, 'friend or foe, thief or robber' (7:14). In this way they hoped to create the conditions for a true peace, the fruit of the Spirit of the Lord (17:15).

This liberating insight, which enabled the brothers to bridge the divisions and experience true peace in brotherhood, was good news in a world that knew so much oppression and exploitation, and witnessed numerous wars between cities, between pope and emperor, between Christians and Muslims. The brothers could not keep this good news to themselves. They had to share with others their vision of a new world which confounds and destroys the old one (SalVirt).[28] Together with them, the brothers wanted to unmask the sinful world of Assisi and to build a new world where all people without distinction could find a place at the table of the Lord (Test 22) and receive their rightful share in the goods of the earth which Jesus had acquired for them (RegNB 9:8). Thus, when they wrote in the rule that the brothers must be *fratres minores*, lesser brothers who are subject to all, this did not signify that the brothers must submit to the system of Assisi where the leaders ruled over the people and kept them subject to their power.[29] On the contrary, they stated very explicitly on the basis of the gospel: 'It shall not be like this among the brothers' (5:10). The system of Assisi, of lords and subjects, of people who have rights and people who do not, was in no way to be continued. No one was to hold power or dominion over the other (5:9), for all are brothers who have but one father, the Father in heaven (22:33–34).

Francis and his brothers understood *minoritas* and 'being subject' in a completely different way than the rich and powerful. For the latter, these words implied a one-way traffic. The 'being subject' was forced upon someone, the servant, who must be subject to the master. For Francis and his brothers, however, it was a matter of a two-way traffic, or at least an attempt at it. Their 'being subject' was not exacted from them; rather, it was freely chosen, as a protest, but especially as an invitation to the rich and the powerful. They should break out of their thinking and acting in terms of power, which only created inequality and oppression, and instead, through mutual submission and service, lay the foundations for a society of equality, of respect for each other and of true peace.[30] Francis and his brothers were thus very explicitly concerned about a way of behavior that was mutual: the brothers must wash each other's feet (6:4). Obviously, they could not expect the whole world to be prepared to change all of a sudden and to convert to the ideal of the gospel. Someone must take the initiative. Francis and his brothers were ready for it. They decided 'to go about through the world' while proclaiming this good news of *minoritas* and *fraternitas*. In doing so, they made themselves extremely vulnerable.[31] The others might reject the invitation and in all sorts of ways try to put the brothers to shame. But then they were to encourage one another by referring to the example of Jesus (9:1) and confirm one another in their 'knowledge'—a knowledge that conflicted fundamentally with the knowledge of Assisi—'that such shame is credited not to those who suffer it but to those who caused it' (9:7).[32]

Against this background, it is not surprising that the gospel texts which Francis and his brothers selected[33] for the present chapter 14 in order to clarify for themselves their intentions with regard to their going about through the world, were clearly opposed to the way in which the citizens of Assisi moved about in the world and dealt with people.[34] In fact, with the help of these gospel texts, the brothers developed a new model of social action which struck at the heart of the social system of Assisi. Francis and his brothers went about the world, not as the rich and powerful, but without carrying anything for the journey, neither knapsack, nor purse, nor bread, nor money, nor staff (1). When they arrived at a place, they entered a house and first wished all who live there peace (2), that is, the true peace in the full meaning of the word as they themselves had experienced it after they had liberated themselves from the system of Assisi and its social rules and regulations, and had developed their own way to provide for their needs, not by appropriating goods, but by working and, in exchange for their work, receiving whatever they needed for their livelihood. When people offered them hospitality, they might stay with them and eat and drink whatever they had to share (3). This was their way of making Jesus' peace a concrete reality. But when people did not accept their peace greeting and turned against them, they must not be put off from their ideals.[35] Therefore they were not to resist, but to offer those who strike them the other cheek (4). And when something would be taken away from them, they were not to claim it (6). All they wanted was peace with the people in a mutual sharing of life, work and food.

In this summary of chapter 14 and its background, we place a different emphasis than does Dino Dozzi in his study on the Gospel in the *Regula non bullata*. He concludes his long analysis by stating that in verses 4–6, Francis and his brothers, taking their point of departure from texts of the Sermon on the Mount, no longer emphasized the material side of 'taking nothing for their journey,' but rather focused on a certain attitude of non-possessiveness. For while going about through the world, the brothers had not only to leave all material goods behind (1), they had also to give up their right of self-defense and of possessing goods (4–6). The advice not to take anything along for the road was thus extended from a material-spatial category to an anthropological-spiritual one which also included the attitudes, formulated in verses 4–6, which touch not only the going about through the world, but the whole life of the brothers. 'Not to take along anything' became a religious category. This extension, which at the same time implied an interiorization, enables us, according to Dozzi, to reread the next chapters in this perspective.[36] It is very surprising, however, that Dozzi in his conclusion does not mention verses 2–3 of chapter 14. These verses form, in my view, the very heart of this chapter: to bring peace to the people by sharing their lives. Not to take anything for the road is therefore not the leading idea of chapter 14, as Dozzi thinks, but rather a means or a condition for establishing peace. It is this peace which constituted the aim the brothers strove for while going about through the world.

In this light, the advice not to offer resistance and not to reclaim what had been taken from them, must be seen as a very concrete attempt by the brothers to realize, through their nonviolent behavior, the greeting of peace which they wanted to bring to all people, not only in words, but especially in deeds. To speak here of an interiorization of the rule's advice not to take along anything and of an anthropological-spiritual category instead of a material-spatial one, implies an ahistorical interpretation of Francis and his brothers and of the peace mission to which the Lord had called them. Such an interpretation does not reflect the intentions of Francis and his brothers, formulated in chapter 14. In contrast to a man like James of Vitry, the brothers indeed wanted to travel through the world without possessions and thus place themselves totally at the service of true peace which was threatened mainly by care and concern for possessions. In fact, for the sake of peace, they did not want to resist those who attacked or persecuted them. Nor did they want to demand that the things taken away from them be returned. For true peace could not be established by violence, nor was its realization served when the brothers would allow the fight for possessions to continue to divide people.

Francis and his brothers took a heavy task upon themselves with their peace mission. Once the brotherhood increased, some of the brothers thought that the ideal of peace was too difficult. They wanted to move in another direction which offered them a more accepted and less risky place within the pastoral policies of the church. A reflection of this conflict appeared in the Testament where Francis firmly commanded all his brothers through obedience not to ask any privileges from the Roman curia 'neither under the guise of preaching or even for the persecution of their bodies' (25). They must remain faithful to the original ideal which he reminded them of in verses 19–23. There he mentioned briefly the essential elements of the way in which the brothers must be present among the people. Thanks to this description we get a very good picture of the social identity and the relational patterns of the group of the first brothers. It confirms the conclusions that emerged from the analysis of chapters 7 and 14 of the *Regula non bullata*, given above. This picture shows an unsettled, wandering group, for the brothers were wearing breeches as a kind of travelling clothes (16);[37] they did not want anything more than the clothes and the food they needed; they did not look for positions of power, but wished to be subject to all, especially through the work they did; this work served to acquire whatever was necessary for their livelihood; at the same time it took them among the people. In fact, the most important form of presence of the brothers among the people was to be together with them in their working environment. In this connection Le Goff points out that the 'apostolate' of the first brothers was exercised preferably among the people in their houses. The house, not the church, was the cultural model of the first brothers.[38] It was there, in the house, that the brothers wished the people peace, in word and in deed, being subject to them.

By going about through the world in this way, the brothers, both clerics and lay brothers, followed a way of life which clearly did not fit the clerics and in fact had more of a lay character. This is first of all evident from the manual work which the brothers performed in the leper houses or in the fields. Further, their wandering existence points in the same direction. For clerics were bound by canon law to reside at the place where they received their benefice; moreover, they were forbidden to beg. The brothers, on the other hand, did not stay at a fixed place, but wandered around and were not ashamed to beg whenever they were refused the reward for their work. Finally, the lay character of their way of life is evident also from the clothes they wore, at least if Desbonnets is correct with his interpretation that the wearing of breeches could also mean that the brothers wished to distinguish themselves from the farm laborers of those days who did not wear them. In that case, the brothers adopted the clothing of farm laborers, that is, lay clothing, with the understanding, however, that they were also wearing breeches because of their travelling.[39] Their main and final concern in all this was, through their way of life and especially their manual work where service was central, to create the necessary conditions for true peace. They considered this peace to be better safeguarded by their lay way of life in solidarity with the poor than by joining and adapting themselves to the privileged group of clerics.[40]

It is quite surprising that not a single reference to preaching can be found either in Francis' memory of the first beginning or in the gospel texts of chapter 14 which the brothers selected to define their identity as a group going about through the world. This is all the more surprising because several of these gospel texts are taken from the missionary discourses of Luke 9 and 10 and Matthew 10, where preaching is considered fundamental to the mission of the disciples whom Jesus sent out. When Francis and his brothers, therefore, do not quote the texts about preaching, they appear not to consider preaching as a principal aim of the brotherhood on its journey through the world.[41] Hence, the emphasis which the first biographers place on preaching must be seen as a projection back to the first beginnings of the brotherhood of the later clerical development in the order.[42] Thus in his first biography, Celano makes Francis preach as soon as he has returned to Assisi, after he has heard the gospel of the sending of the apostles at the Portiuncula. Further, Celano informs us that we have here a miraculous coincidence, for

Francis 'first began to preach where as a child he had first learned to read and where for a time he was buried amid great honor' (1 *Cel* 22–23). However, in the Anonymous of Perugia we read that, even after Bernard, Peter and Giles had joined him, Francis still did not preach to the people (15d). It seems as if the anonymous author wishes to excuse himself before his readers who, because of other stories, may have a different picture of Francis and hence expect a different continuation of the story. Whatever the case may have been, it is certain beyond any doubt that Francis and his first brothers did not place much emphasis on preaching. Rather, they insisted on practicing a way of life[43] which, as their experience had taught them, was the only way to true peace. They knew, of course, that by following this way they ran the risk of persecution. But they encouraged one another to take this risk and, without offering resistance, to be ready to suffer persecution, and even to turn the other cheek to their persecutors. Peace was worth all these troubles and hardships!

In this connection, it remains strange that many authors opt for the model of wandering preachers (*Wanderprediger*) to characterize the first group of brothers around Francis.[44] An example of such a group, contemporary to Francis, was the group of the Waldensian Bernard Prim and his companions who were reconciled with the church by Innocent III in 1210 at Rome. They stated explicitly in their revised *Propositum* of 1212 that their main task was to study Scripture and, if they were fit, to preach and hold discussions against the heretic sects. Besides, they also worked with their hands, if time permitted. Manual work was for them a kind of ascetic practice to which they devoted themselves when there was some time left, and for which they did not accept any reward.[45] For Francis and his brothers exactly the opposite was the case: preaching was not their most important task, while manual work was for them the first means to provide for their livelihood.

By applying the model of the wandering preachers to Francis and his brothers, one is likely to give a distorted picture of their group and hence also of their ideals and of the purpose of their going about through the world. In fact, by putting such great emphasis on preaching, the proper character of the movement of Francis and his brothers threatens to disappear into the background. They wanted, as brothers, not in a position of power, but of submission, to stand next to the people in their simple everyday work, to share their lives with them in their houses and so bring them true peace indeed. In doing so, Francis and his brothers developed completely different forms of social relations, in sharp contrast to the dominant social structures of their time: no lords and masters on the one side and servants and subjects on the other, but only brothers who do not exercise any power over each other, and serve each other in submission.[46] Francis and his brothers were so convinced of the value and the significance of their way of life and action that, when they were confronted with the crusades and became aware of the existence of the Saracens, they decided to move beyond the borders of the Christian world and to extend their peace mission to the world of the Saracens and Islam:[47] a decision which was all the more remarkable because it was without parallel at the time.[48]

Unfortunately, not much of Francis' peace vision emerges in the stories about his visit to the sultan.[49] As the analysis of the stories by De Beer clearly shows, their authors had different intentions in mind and hence attributed different motives to Francis for his visit.[50] Confreres of Francis, like Celano and Bonaventure, interpreted Francis' visit as an expression of his desire for martyrdom.[51] Outsiders, like James of Vitry and Ernoul, on the other hand, interpreted his meeting with the sultan in the context of the crusade, as an attempt on Francis' part to convince the sultan of the truth of Christianity, not with arms, but with words, with 'good arguments.'[52]

Yet, in some places, we do find traces of Francis' rejection of the crusade and of his decision to go to the sultan to bring peace. In the *Historia Occidentalis* of James of Vitry, Francis called himself a Christian when the Saracens asked him for his identity.[53] In the given circumstances he indicated by this answer that he was not a crusader. Something similar can be found in the chronicles of Ernoul and Bernard the Treasurer.[54] First they tell us that Francis and his companion went to the sultan without the approval of cardinal Pelagius, the papal legate. Next they report that Francis stated before the sultan that he and his companion had not come with a message from cardinal Pelagius in reply to the peace offer of the sultan.[55] Rather, they had come 'with a message of the Lord God' (Ernoul), 'as ambassadors of our Lord Jesus Christ' (Bernard), who, in the words of Francis in his Testament, sent him and his brothers into the world with the greeting of peace: 'May the Lord give you peace' (Test 23). A clear opposition against the crusade is also evident from a short notice in the *History of Heraclius*: 'Brother Francis...

came into the crusaders' camp of Damietta, performed many good works and remained till the city was captured. He saw how evil and sin started to increase among the people at the camp and detested it. Hence he left the camp.'[56]

Finally, the story of 2 *Cel* 30 must be mentioned here. It deals explicitly with Francis' activities in the camp of the crusaders. In Celano's biography, this story serves as an *exemplum* to motivate the readers to listen to the voice of prophets. In its present form, the story ends with an implicit approval of the crusade. For Celano assures his readers that the crusaders would have won the battle if they had entrusted the battle to the Spirit of God. Yet, James Powell thinks that characteristics of a sermon against the crusade can still be discovered in the story, especially where it states that, although the crusaders would consider him a fool, Francis 'arose and approached the Christians with salutary warnings, forbidding the war, announcing its failure.'[57]

The harvest of texts about Francis' God-given peace mission is quite disappointing. Moreover, considerable searching is required. In some places, even opposite voices can clearly be heard. Thus brother Illuminatus informs us that, in a discussion, the sultan submitted the following problem to Francis: 'Your Lord taught in his gospels that evil must not be repaid with evil, that you should not refuse your cloak to anyone who wants to take your tunic, etc. (Mt 5:39–40): in that case, Christians should not invade our land?' Francis replied: 'It seems that you have not read the gospel of our Lord Jesus Christ completely. For in another place we read: if your eye causes you to sin, tear it out and throw it away (Mt 5:29). Here Jesus wanted to teach us that every man, however dear and close he is to us, and even if he is as precious to us as the eye in our head, must be repulsed, pulled out, expelled if he seeks to turn us away from the faith and love of our God. That is why it is just that Christians invade the land you inhabit, for you blaspheme the name of Christ and alienate everyone you can from his worship. But if you were to recognize, confess, and adore the Creator and Redeemer, Christians would love you as themselves.'[58] Whatever the case may be, the peace mission of Francis and his brothers to the sultan as an alternative to the violence of the crusades has left some traces in the sources, notwithstanding the fact the writers had quite different intentions than to remember Francis and his brothers as peacemakers to future generations.[59]

CHAPTER THREE

A Contextual Exegesis of *Regula non bullata*, Chapter 16

On the basis of the experiences during their peace mission among the Saracens, Francis and his brothers formulated chapter 16 of the *Regula non bullata* which is entitled: 'Those who are going among the Saracens and other unbelievers.'[1] In a more detailed commentary on each verse, I wish to draw on these experiences in order to deepen our understanding of the peace mission as Francis and his brothers developed it in a continuous interaction with the concrete situation prevailing within the church and world of their time with regard to the Saracens.

A. 'AS SHEEP IN THE MIDST OF WOLVES'

> 1. The Lord says:
>   'Behold, I am sending you as sheep in the midst of wolves.
> 2. Be therefore prudent as serpents
>   and simple as doves.' (Mt 10:16).

On various occasions Francis and his brothers inserted chapters in their rule when they were faced with new problems within the brotherhood. Chapters 3 and 8 are such insertions in which Francis and the brothers tried to formulate an answer to problems which had arisen about the divine office and fasting (ch. 3) and about the acceptance of money (ch. 8). Their answer was the fruit of much reflection and discussion among themselves. In both chapters, the final answer was preceded by a gospel text which they selected very carefully and which served as a kind of wedge in order to have the chapter inserted at its proper place within the rule.

In chapter 16, Francis and his brothers followed the same procedure when dealing with the extension of their peace mission to the Saracens. First, they reflected on and discussed their experiences in the light of their program of life; next, on the basis of their discussions, they decided on the way of action which the future brothers must follow when they go among the Saracens. Finally, they looked for a gospel text to support and confirm their decision with a word of Jesus. For in his name they had decided to leave everything. In his name therefore they also wanted to determine how they would more concretely fill in their program of life.[2] Thus the gospel text was rightfully placed at the beginning of the chapter, but had in fact been added last. In other words, the gospel text was, for Francis and his brothers, not so much a starting point which offered them the evangelical principles from which they could draw concrete guidelines for their going among the Saracens,[3] but rather a point of recognition or identification where they, reflecting on their own experiences, recognized themselves and their ideals.

In the final analysis, we are concerned here with the question of how the followers of Jesus make truly evangelical choices. This does not happen by reading and meditating on gospel texts. It is much more a matter of analyzing and interpreting the reality which they experience and of which they are a part, on the basis of a fundamental option for the good or, in Francis' words, on the basis of a profound uneasiness with 'the spirit of the flesh' and 'the sin of the world' and a growing sensitivity to 'the Spirit of the Lord.' In light of this interpretation they are able to make a clear choice of what they see as good within the situation in which they find themselves. In this way they create, as it were, the proper atmosphere in which a gospel text can resonate as such, as an evangelical appeal, an evangelical challenge, and thus offer the followers of Jesus a possibility to recognize their options and ideals. If people do not follow this path, it is very likely that a gospel text will not really resonate in a situation. As a result, the word of the gospel remains powerless and inoperative, because it is read and meditated upon apart from reality. Or it may happen that a gospel text resonates wrongly, because people are so preoccupied by power, possessions, self-interest, honor, etc., that they can only interpret the text to suit their own selfish ends.[4]

When Francis and his brothers made their choice after having thought about and evaluated their experiences, they placed great emphasis on the peaceful presence of the brothers as servants among the

Saracens: they were not allowed even 'to engage in arguments' and had to be 'subject to every human creature for God's sake' (6). Hence, preaching receded into the background and only 'when they see that it pleases the Lord, they may proclaim the word of God' (7). Because of this, a gospel text like the one in which Jesus sent his disciples on their mission into the world, 'Go, therefore, teach all nations and baptize them in the name of the Father and of the Son and of the Holy Spirit' (Mt 28:19) did not qualify as a confirmation of their choice. Although this text explicitly mentions that the disciples have to go, it places such great emphasis on the teaching, preaching and proclaiming, that it just did not harmonize with the proper character of the vision that Francis and his brothers had of their stay among the Saracens in the Spirit of the Lord.[5] The same must be said of the texts from the missionary discourses that stress preaching and the exercise of power over demons.[6] These too were not adequate as opening texts, because the brothers could not recognize themselves and their intentions in them.

This recognition did take place, however, when they heard the gospel text about the Lord sending his disciples as sheep among wolves. This text speaks very clearly about the way of being present and thus fit better the real aim of Francis and his brothers as bringers of peace. Moreover, this text probably expressed very well the feelings of Francis and the brothers before they went to the Saracens.[7] Under the influence of intense crusading propaganda, they had formed an image of the Saracens as 'wolves,'[8] an image that appeared to be fundamentally wrong, as Francis and his brothers would discover during their meeting with sultan al-Malek al-Kamil. For by going as sheep in a spirit of submission and service among the Saracens, the brothers personally experienced that the 'wolves' were not cruel animals which devoured everything that came their way. Rather, sheep and wolves could truly live together in peace:[9] the lost paradise was restored, the eschatological vision of the kingdom of God, as described by Isaiah, was brought near: 'The wolf lives with the lamb' (11,6). The text from the missionary discourse thus obtained a radically different meaning. In the gospel the text was really meant to encourage Jesus' disciples to face the threats to their lives that were connected with their mission. Originally it probably had the same meaning for Francis and his brothers. Now, however, after the visit to the sultan, it was no longer interpreted primarily as an encouragement to suffer possible martyrdom, but rather as an invitation to end

the existing enmity with the Saracens by living among them and being
subject to them. In doing so, they would restore the original order of
creation, the order of peace and harmony not only between human
beings, but even between human beings and animals (cf. SalVirt 15-18).[10]

Yet Francis remained enough of a believer and a realist not to forget
what happened to Jesus. Obviously, the same fate might also await him
and his brothers when going into the world in the name of Jesus to
establish peace. In fact, from the very beginning of their conversion, he
and his first brothers had personally experienced physical hardship and
persecution because of their choice to follow the gospel. It strikes the
attentive reader how often the word 'persecution' and its synonyms
occur in the writings of Francis.[11] Because of this experience, at the end
of chapter 16, in verses 10-21, Francis not only addressed the brothers
who wanted to go among the Saracens but all the brothers who, 'wherever they may be,' suffered persecution because of Jesus' name. Thus
Francis kept the possibility of persecution and martyrdom fully open for
his brothers. Above all, however, he was determined to build up a peaceful society with the Saracens, and with all the other people he met,
through his nonviolent approach: living as a sheep among wolves.

Next, the brothers, and especially the brothers-preachers, must not
think that they should immediately start preaching against the
Saracens, as James of Vitry and, under his influence, the first brothers
in Syria had done, convinced that in doing so they acted in accordance
with God's will and served the truth. In this matter, the brothers must
operate much more prudently, because they found themselves in a new
situation with people of a different culture. Hence they were to preach
only when they saw that it pleased God. In other words, only when God
gave them a sign, were they to proclaim the word of God. And they
must do so in a very simple manner, with the simplicity of a dove, so
that the Saracens might experience the Christian faith as a message of
'the simple and true peace of the Spirit' (RegNB 17,15). Thus they were
to show prudence in looking for signs of God in their new situation, and
simplicity in the proclamation of the gospel,[12] the simplicity which is
averse to 'all wisdom of this world' (SalVirt 10) and approaches the other
in a truly inviting way.

It is not easy to prove the correctness of this interpretation of the
opening verse of chapter 16. It surely has something artificial about it.
Presuming, however, that Francis and his brothers selected this gospel

text not in an arbitrary fashion, but with great care, we have to accept that it was precisely this text in which they recognized themselves and their ideas about going among the Saracens. This text therefore offers a short summary of what in the next verses will be said about the two ways of living spiritually in the midst of the Saracens.[13] It is remarkable, however, that Francis and his brothers attributed here a positive meaning to the word *prudentia* and mentioned it together with simplicity. For the most part, even in the next chapter, *prudentia* has a negative meaning in the writings of Francis: the *prudentia* of the flesh which is exactly the opposite of the simplicity which is the fruit of the Spirit of the Lord (RegNB 17,10.15). This opposition is most evident in the Letter to the Faithful: 'We must not be wise and prudent according to the flesh; rather we must be simple, humble and pure' (2 LetFaith 45).[14] All this did not disturb Francis and his brothers, when they read Jesus' missionary discourse in the gospel of Matthew. Evidently they found in the text about the presence of the sheep among the wolves, the prudence of the serpent and the simplicity of the dove, a very good summary of the way in which they wanted to live in the midst of the Saracens, and of the problems the brothers might have to face in this new situation.

When they placed their chosen gospel text at the beginning of the mission chapter, they did not use the perfect tense, *dixit*, as the gospel does, but the present tense, *dicit*.[15] Francis and his brothers thus indicated here, as in other places,[16] that they knew themselves to be called directly by the word of the Lord. There did not exist even the slightest doubt about that in their minds. Hence, as far as Francis and his brothers were concerned, the word that the Lord once, long ago, spoke to his apostles, did not belong to the distant past. Rather, in this text, the Lord spoke his word there and then to the brothers. At the same time they heard around them many other words of church officials and of preachers who in the name of God called them to a crusade against the Saracens. Francis and his brothers, however, decided not to heed these church appeals, but rather to follow the word which the Lord addressed to them in this gospel text: to live as lesser brothers, as peacemakers among the Saracens. In the words of the Testament (14), in which Francis recalled the beginnings of the brotherhood but which are also applicable here, it was the Most High, and no one else, who in fact revealed to Francis and the brothers how they must live among the Saracens according to the form of the gospel.

It is even the case that no one else but the Most High could possibly do this. For the pope, bishops, abbots and priors who gathered at the Lateran Council[17] had committed themselves to a violent crusade against the Saracens. And even though individual monks were excluded from active participation in the crusade, abbeys were closely involved in financing it. Not only did they lend money to members of the aristocracy to enable them to take part in the crusade, they also took it upon themselves to finance a ship for rich and poor crusaders for a period of three years, as, for example, the monastery of Santa Croce in Sassovivo near Foligno did. It even happened that a monastery, for lack of ready cash, had to dispose of gold and silver ornaments and sacred vessels to secure the necessary financial means.[18] In such a situation Francis and his brothers could not expect much support from the ecclesiastical authorities for their idea of going as peacemakers in a nonviolent way among the Saracens. Only the Most High could possibly guide them in this matter. Guided by God, they would always be in safe hands wherever they went. And so, full of confidence, in obedience to the Spirit of the Lord, the brothers set out to make themselves subject and submissive to all people, 'even to all beasts and wild animals, so that they may do whatever they want with them inasmuch as it has been given to them from above by the Lord' (cf. SalVirt 15–18). They hoped, of course, that their subjection and their nonviolence would be an invitation to the others, human and animal, to establish true peace. But whatever happened to the brothers, whether they would be accepted by the Saracens or persecuted, it would be God's good gift!

B. 'THE MINISTER SHALL NOT CONTRADICT THE LORD'

3. Therefore, any brother,
  who, by divine inspiration,[19]
  wishes to go among the Saracens and other unbelievers, may go
  with the permission of his minister and servant.
4. And the minister should give them permission
  and not contradict [the Lord],[20]
  if he sees that they are fit to be sent;
  for he will be bound to give an account to the Lord
  if he has proceeded without discretion in this or in other matters.

When determining the date of chapter 16, I have already indicated that, in my opinion, verses 3b–5a form an insertion in which Francis and his brothers first regulated an internal problem within the brotherhood, before they applied the gospel text they had selected to their way of life among the Saracens. In this short passage, Francis started by acknowledging the place and the authority of the ministers who had become indispensable within the brotherhood because of its spectacular growth in such a short time. According to the *Chronicle of Jordan*, three thousand brothers, professed and novices, were present at the chapter of 1221.[21] Such rapid growth did not allow the brotherhood to maintain the old structure under which Francis, at the chapter of Pentecost, personally appointed the brothers to be sent out. In this sense the arrival of the ministers was a definite improvement. Brothers who wished to go among the Saracens no longer needed to wait until the next chapter, or travel personally to Francis, to obtain permission to go. From now on they could also approach their respective ministers.[22] On the other hand, in this passage, Francis spoke up in defense of the individual brothers against certain ministers, who proceeded 'without discretion' and dared 'to contradict the Lord' and the word which the Lord spoke and through which the Lord inspired the brothers who wished to go among the Saracens. As is also evident from other passages of the rule, Francis refused to surrender his brothers unconditionally into the hands of their ministers because the ministers were not always able to discern adequately the true Spirit of the brotherhood, and hence made decisions which deviated from 'the right direction of our life' (RegNB 5:4).[23]

Evidently, Francis had some rather unfortunate experiences with the ministers after they had been introduced into the brotherhood at the chapter of 1217. Not only were there ministers who wanted to 'appropriate to themselves the ministry of the brothers' (RegNB 17:4) and were 'more upset about their office being taken from them than they would be over the loss of the office of [washing] feet' (Adm 4:3), there were also those who wanted to move the brotherhood in another direction. Francis wanted therefore to limit their authority: the brothers were not obliged to obey their ministers if they commanded the brothers to do something contrary to their life or against their consciences (cf. RegNB 5:2). He also ordered his brothers that they 'should reasonably and diligently consider the actions of the ministers' and admonish them or even report them to the chapter when they saw that 'any of them is living according to the flesh and not according to the Spirit in keeping with the right direction of our life' (RegNB 5:3–4).

In these circumstances, it was Francis' main concern to safeguard the Spirit of the brotherhood and, more concretely, the *divina inspiratio* of the individual brother. He did so very explicitly in his Letter to Brother Leo, and also in the case of the brother who, by divine inspiration, wished to go among the Saracens. If he was fit to be sent, the minister could not refuse him permission to go. Apparently, here or there, ministers had done just that or, at least, had wanted to do it because they had very little appreciation for Francis' ideas about going among the Saracens and wanted the brotherhood to turn in a different direction. It was not therefore a matter of the jurisdiction of the ministers who had the authority to determine the fitness or unfitness of a particular brother, as was the case later on in *Regula bullata* 12:2. Something much more fundamental was at stake: the rejection of a brother who was in fact fit to go, or, looked at from a different angle, the attitude of certain ministers who, without discretion, opposed the clear indications of the Lord, and thus dared to contradict when the Lord spoke. In fact, it was a conflict of principle between Francis and some ministers. Francis wanted nothing else than to live according to what the Most High revealed to him and to the brothers who, by divine inspiration, wanted to go among the Saracens. Some ministers, on the other hand, not only wished to take into account all sorts of matters of church policy, they also wanted to attach to these matters even more weight than they did to the word that the Lord spoke to the individual brother. That the text involves a very fundamental issue indeed, is also evident from the serious tone of Francis' admonition to these ministers: such a minister 'will be bound to give an account to the Lord if he has proceeded without discretion in this or in other matters.'[24]

One thing stands out very clearly: Francis' unconditional obedience to divine inspiration, his listening with his whole person when the Lord spoke the living word to him in a particular situation. But it is also clear that his obedience to divine inspiration brought him again and again into an inevitable conflict with the dominant culture. For who could have inspired him or one of his brothers at that time to go on a peace mission among the Saracens? No one: because church and society were dominated by the idea that the crusade against the Saracens was Christ's cause and a God-given occasion for salvation. Only the Most High could break through this cultural dominance.[25] The expression *divina inspiratio*, as it was used by Francis, invites us therefore to understand the going of the brothers among the Saracens dialectically within the historical and political context of the conflict between the ideas of church and society about the crusade and the insights that Francis and his brothers discovered when they saw and reflected on the world in light of the gospel.[26] Over against the ecclesiastical and social thesis of war and violence, Francis placed his antithesis of peace and nonviolence to which the Lord had inspired him when revealing to him the greeting: 'May the Lord give you peace' (Test 23), a greeting whose meaning and implications he gradually discovered ever more.

While church and society prepared for the crusade, a short passage from the First Letter of Peter was being read during the office on one of the Sundays after Easter: 'Dear friends, I urge you as strangers and pilgrims to abstain from carnal lusts that fight against the soul and to lead a good life among the pagans' (2:11–12).[27] Most likely, many brothers did not hear anything special in this text, but for Francis there was a flash of recognition, just as had happened earlier in the church of St. Nicholas, when he listened to the gospel with his first brothers.[28] Indeed, this was what he and his brothers desired. They did not want to fight against (*contra*) the Saracens, but to go among (*inter*) them, sharing life and work with them in order to establish peace.[29] For they did reject war and violence, and instead were intent on pursuing brotherly presence and solidarity as conditions for true peace.[30]

When, in 1219, the moment came that Francis and some brothers actually went among the Saracens, the things that had happened at the time of his conversion started repeating themselves. At that time the Lord led him among (*inter*) the lepers (Test 2). There, in their midst, Francis learned to understand the sin of the world. It was no longer the leper who stank, but money and vainglory.[31] There Francis also discovered a God who was different from the God Assisi worshiped with much external show as the legitimation of its socio-economic system and in whose name it was prepared to sacrifice the lives of many. This discovery led him to leave the world of Assisi in order to build up, gropingly, a new world with the brothers the Lord gave him; a world where everyone would find a place at the table of the Lord (Test 22; cf. 2 Cel 16). The same Lord now led him among the Saracens, while the camp of the crusaders lay at some distance behind him as a clear sign of the intentions of the Christian world with regard to the Saracens. Once again Francis went through a learning process. He discovered God's presence there where, according to the preaching of the church, only lies could be found; he saw the faith of the Saracens and was profoundly impressed by their prayer while everyone else called them unbelievers—a term that had become so much a part of the normal Christian vocabulary that even Francis and his brothers kept using it;[32] he listened with great attention to all that God was telling him through the Saracens' lives and history, and while others looked down on them, Francis was full of admiration: God had gone among the Saracens before him and had been the source of much that was good and beautiful. And where people had warned him of a 'wolf,' 'a cruel beast,' Francis met a friend.[33] A new world opened up before his eyes, a world which unfortunately remained closed for the crusaders because of their negative and hostile attitude.

C. 'TO LIVE SPIRITUALLY AMONG THEM'

> 5. The brothers who go,
>   can live spiritually among them in two ways.

After the insertion of the passage about asking permission from the minister, Francis and his brothers returned to the two[34] ways in which they could live among the Saracens and which had already been summarized as it were in the gospel text quoted in the opening verses of the chapter. However, before describing in more detail the two ways to 'lead a good life among the pagans' (1 Pe 2:12),[35] Francis and his brothers placed them, through a short, but well-chosen expression, within the broader context of the way they saw their presence in the world. Just as was the case with the world in general, so must the brothers see their presence in the world of the Saracens as a spiritual presence, as a presence therefore 'in the Spirit of the Lord.' Hence it is clear that for the brothers the life among the Saracens was nothing exceptional that stood apart from other important matters about which the brothers were concerned. On the contrary, it formed a part of the total vision which the brothers had of their mission as a brotherhood in the world. For they constituted a brotherhood which, as chapter 17 states once more by way of summary, was deeply involved in the never-ceasing struggle between the spirit of the flesh and the Spirit of the Lord in the world of their days.[36] As a brotherhood they were called to confound and destroy the spirit of the flesh and the wisdom of the world (SalVirt) in their own historical situation. In this way they were to make the way free for 'the Spirit of the Lord who strives for humility and patience, and the pure and simple and true peace of the Spirit' (RegNB 17:14–15).

When the brothers went about in the world, their lifestyle did not therefore fundamentally differ from when they went among the Saracens: in both cases the brothers did not go in the spirit of the world with arms and violence in order to defend or to recapture possessions, not even if it concerned the Holy Land or, as the crusading propaganda always called it, Christ's inheritance. On the contrary, they went without possessions and arms in order to bring peace to everyone whom they met on their way. Also, their 'strategy' was everywhere the same: to share the life and work of the people, to eat and drink with them whatever the table offered, and so in mutual solidarity to give concrete shape to God's original plan of creation, restored in Jesus Christ. In this paradise restored, all people, and especially the poor, could again occupy their rightful place at the table of the Lord (Test 22) and so take possession of the inheritance that was due to them because Jesus had acquired it for them (RegNB 9:8).[37] In this very concrete manner, Francis and his brothers wanted to give expression to the peace greeting the Lord had given them: 'Peace to this house' (cf. RegNB 14:1–3). Their going among the Saracens, however, because of the crusades and the attitude of the great majority of Christians toward the Saracens, presented some special problems. It was mainly to these problems that Francis and his brothers directed their attention in the next verses of chapter 16 where they further elaborated the two ways of going among the Saracens.

D. THE FIRST WAY OF BEING PRESENT

> 6. One way is not to engage in arguments or disputes,
>   but to be subject to every human creature
>   for God's sake (1 Pet 2:13)
>   and to confess that they are Christians.

a. 'Not to engage in arguments or disputes'

When the brothers want to live as peacemakers among the Saracens, they should not become involved in arguments and disputes, as they appear to have done on several prior occasions according to James of Vitry.[38] The use of such an apologetic method on the part of the brothers accorded very well with the overall manner in which church authorities depicted Mohammed as a liar and traitor. For confronted with his lies, the brothers could not remain silent. Just as the crusaders fought for the cause of Christ with arms, so the brothers were to take up the fight with words in order to refute the false claims of Mohammed and Islam before they could do even more harm than they had done already.[39] The truth urged them on: they could not act in a different way. It was not a matter of their being right, but of the truth of God, and of Jesus Christ who had given his life for the salvation of the whole world. It was out of love for, and in the service of this truth that the brothers were engaged in apologetic arguments in the hope of convincing the Saracens that Christianity was the only true religion[40]—a hope, which for them, just as for James of Vitry, was probably not so farfetched at all. For in one of his letters James writes: 'many Saracens, I believe, would easily be converted to the Lord if they would hear the sound doctrine.'[41]

Francis was not convinced by the arguments for an apologetic approach, however obvious such an approach must have looked in light of the theological thinking of that time. As already indicated, it is very probable that Francis, on the basis of his own experience or of that of his brothers, as described by James of Vitry, had come to the insight that disputes were not the most appropriate way to come into contact with the Saracens and to make known to them the truth about Jesus. In other words, it was a very practical matter of strategy, not to start by offending others, but by trying to gain their confidence.[42] But Francis' prohibition was not just a matter of strategy, of how his brothers could obtain the most success. For in his elaboration of the guidelines for his brothers, Francis was not so much influenced by a desire for practical success. Rather, he was profoundly concerned with translating all that he had come to know as the truth about God and about Jesus Christ during his stay among the Saracens into concrete advice for his brothers. In other words, Francis' approach was in the first place a principled, theological one. The motivation which is explicitly mentioned in the continuation of verse 6, namely that the brothers must be subject to every human creature 'for God's sake,' is thus presupposed here too. It was 'for God's sake' that the brothers must not engage in arguments and disputes with the Saracens. For God is, according to a very personal expression of

Francis, 'humility' (PrGod 4; LetOrder 28) and God wants the brothers to imitate this humility in their lives.[43] That is the reason why the brothers must not exercise power over others, nor pride themselves above others, nor feel themselves superior to others. On the contrary, they were to be 'lesser brothers' who, in humble service, wash one another's feet (RegNB 5:9–12; 6:3–4). Arguments and disputes did not fit such a way of life, however well they might have been intended by some brothers as a service in the defense of the truth. For arguments and disputes mostly start from a certain feeling of superiority, when a person thinks him- or herself to be above the other and looks down on the other as being inferior. As such they cannot be reconciled with Francis' understanding of the humility of God which the brothers are to imitate in their lives.

Francis experienced something still more important during his stay among the Saracens, namely that the truth about God and about Jesus cannot flourish at all in an atmosphere of arguments and disputes. In fact, arguments and disputes are counterproductive in the handing on of the truth. For, if truth is clothed with power, with a feeling of superiority, it is no longer itself and becomes unrecognizable for the other. It is no longer the gift freely offered to unite people with each other. It degenerates into a possession and hence into a means of power which leads to the condemnation and the exclusion of the other as a heretic. Having fallen prey to the human appropriation reflex, to the 'original sin' (Adm 2:3–4), the truth is violated and becomes a lie.[44] Thus Christianity wages war in the name of God who truly is love, and Christians feel themselves superior to others in the name of God who, in the explicit words of Francis, truly is humility. Indeed, the appropriation of the truth in arguments and disputes leads to an eclipse of the truth, an eclipse of God. It was this profound opposition which Francis had felt and had made him decide that his brothers must avoid arguments and disputes 'for God's sake.' In other words, it was his faith in God that made him set a different course for his brothers. Because of their faith in a God who is humility, the brothers must create, through a humble way of life, as subjects, without possessions and power, the atmosphere in which the truth about God and about Jesus can radiate unto salvation and peace for the Saracens. This confirms once again what we have observed before, that Francis' rejection of arguments and disputes must be seen not so much as a strategy to avoid antagonizing the Saracens in order to have a better chance of success with them. Rather, Francis' new way of approaching the Saracens was first and foremost a matter of principle: he wanted his brothers to act in this way because of God.

Undoubtedly, Francis' approach represented a radically new and liberating vision at a time of great enmity between Christianity and Islam: a new vision which unfortunately was not always understood even by his own brothers. This is clearly evident in the history of brother Berard and his companions who were the first brothers to suffer martyrdom in Morocco in 1220. They did exactly the opposite of what Francis prescribed for his brothers. On several occasions they were advised not to preach against Mohammed and Islam. Yet they took every opportunity to attack 'the most despicable superstition' of Mohammed, until finally they were captured and killed. When Francis was informed about their martyrdom, the legend makes him exclaim: 'Now I can say that I have five true lesser brothers.'[45] However, this exclamation does not agree at all with the instructions of Francis in chapter 16. The *Chronicle of Jordan* appears therefore to be more trustworthy when it says: 'When the life and the legend of the above-mentioned brothers martyrs were brought to blessed Francis...he rejected the legend and forbade it to be read: "Each one should glory in his own suffering and not in someone else's!" And so it happened that this whole first mission was brought to naught.'[46]

Further, the various stories about Francis' visit to sultan al-Malek al-Kamil do not show much understanding for his prohibition of arguments and disputes. Celano writes: 'But who can narrate with what great steadfastness of mind Francis stood before the sultan, with what strength of spirit he spoke to him, with what eloquence and confidence he replied to those who insulted the Christian law' (1 *Cel* 57). Ernoul, a French chronicler of the crusades, tells us about Francis' proposal that the sultan call the most learned men of his country together. In their presence Francis would demonstrate 'on the basis of good arguments that their doctrine means nothing.'[47] Bonaventure makes Francis challenge the sultan to an ordeal by fire,[48] while brother Illuminatus tells the highly improbable story about the sultan who wanted to test Francis by making him walk on a multicolored carpet, almost entirely decorated with motifs in the form of crosses. When Francis did indeed walk across this carpet from one end to the other, the sultan expressed his surprise about Francis' action. Francis replied: 'You must know that thieves were also crucified along with our Lord. We have the true cross of our Lord and Savior Jesus Christ; we adore it and show it great devotion. If the holy cross of the Lord has been given to us, the crosses of the thieves have been left to you as your share. That is why I had no scruple in walking over the crosses of thieves.'[49] It is evident that in the biographies little or nothing can be found of Francis' new approach, for the simple reason that it did not fit the ideas of the biographers, or rather their prejudices about Mohammed and Islam.[50] This suggests that the stories about the disputes between Francis and the Saracens must be banished to the land of fables.[51]

b. 'Subject to every human creature'

After stating their position with regard to the apologetic method of arguments and disputes, Francis and his brothers turned to the proper, positive description of the way in which the brothers must live their mission of peace among the Saracens in the Spirit of the Lord. In the process, they fell back on a word they had used earlier in order to determine the place of the brothers in the world, a word they evidently wished to repeat here because it fit so well the situation of the brothers who would go among the Saracens. It is the word *subditus* (subject, submissive), which occurs in *Regula non bullata* 7:2 and also in the Second Letter to the Faithful 47, the Salutation of the Virtues 16 and the Testament 19. It certainly can be called a key word of the spirituality of Francis and his brothers. This is particularly evident from the fact that Francis used it in his Testament to characterize his way of life 'according to the form of the holy gospel': 'We were illiterate and subject to all' (19). And he assured all those who were subject to every human creature for God's sake, that the Spirit of the Lord would rest upon them and be at home among them (2 LetFaith 47–48); they would again give birth to Jesus, i.e., they would give him a new historical existence in this world, by the works they would do in the strength of the Spirit (ibid., 53), especially by establishing true peace (RegNB 17:15).

It is difficult to explain why most authors, in their commentaries on chapter 16, do not bother to examine the deeper meaning of this 'being-subject.' They are satisfied with paraphrasing the text of the rule. Cajetan Esser writes that Francis repeated here his earlier admonition to all the brothers to live and work in the service of others, and applied it to the brothers who went to the missions. Francis expected of them that they would not only be present among the non-Christians, but would live among them as servants.[52] Leonhard Lehmann first makes a few general remarks about the foolishness of such an attitude of submission in the eyes of the people. He concludes that Francis' idea of 'being-subject' is 'diametrically opposed to the project of the crusades and the behavior of the crusaders. While the church officially wages war in the name of Christ and the gospel, Francis proclaims that 'being-subject' is the first and most important kind of missionary activity.'[53] Walbert Bühlmann gives a short paraphrase of the text of the rule. The first way of living spiritually among the Saracens is simple presence, the Christian witness of life. This means that the brothers do not engage in disputes, do not enter into polemics nor try to refute dialectically the people of another religious conviction. On the contrary, because of God's will, they must insert themselves into the society of others and be subject to their authority. This does not imply, however, that they must remain silent in every situation and simply allow injustices to continue. This would not be in accordance with the will of God and the example of Christ.[54] Optatus van Asseldonk makes a study of the place of the letters of St. Peter in the writings of Francis in which he mentions all places where our text is quoted. He sees in the submission to all, in love and affection, an example of a peaceful and loving obedience which pleases God and which will certainly produce fruits, even for nonbelievers.[55]

One of the very few authors who discovers a deeper meaning in Francis' idea of 'being-subject,' is Anton Rotzetter. Given the fact that this idea is mentioned in several other places, he too is of the opinion that 'being-subject' refers to a way of behavior that is of fundamental significance to Francis and his brothers. For them, this way of behavior is, in first instance, a matter of obedience to every human being and even to all wild beasts, as is evident from the Salutation of the Virtues 14–18. Thus, by introducing the idea of 'being-subject' in RegNB 16, the brothers emphasized that the missionary situation is also a situation of obedience, i.e., a situation in which the brothers must accept whatever dangers are implied, and to which they must submit themselves in both their analysis and their way of life. Now, their analysis of the missionary situation, both among the Saracens and others, showed Francis and his brothers that, if they wished to live in obedience to the Spirit and fulfill their mission among the Saracens and others, they must at the same time radically reject violence and power, choose those places in society where they were not in a position to command, and so undermine the hierarchical structures in society through their obedience and their submission. For the aim of their obedience, their submission, is brotherliness: a new way of dealing with people and with creation, not on the basis of violence and power, but in a spirit of love and tenderness.[56]

In this way, Rotzetter not only brings one of the other texts of Francis' writings into his interpretation of 'being-subject,' he also indicates very clearly that Francis and his brothers had a deeper intention in their particular way of behavior. They did not want so much to be subject to all people out of personal, ascetical motives, in order to practice the virtue of humility; rather, by their behavior, they wished in Jesus' name to introduce a new approach to people and even to the whole of creation which was opposed to the way in which people and other creatures were used within the hierarchical structures of medieval society. 'Being-subject' had thus a clear socio-critical significance for Francis and his brothers. It was an invitation to the brothers and to all people to build a new society, not on the foundations of violence and power which were inherent in the hierarchical structures of that time, but on the foundation of being subject to one another in love and tenderness, which are signs of true brotherhood. In this context, the brothers found themselves in continuous conflict with the surrounding world on account of their mission. Or, as Rotzetter says, 'Franciscan mission understood in light of the missionary discourses of Jesus, is to be defined as a situation of social conflict.'[57]

In my commentary on *Regula non bullata* 7, where the word *subditus* occurs for the first time in the writings of Francis, I reached a similar conclusion which was largely based on the studies of David Flood. In chapter 7, the choice of Francis and his brothers to be subject to all is intimately linked with their decision to separate themselves from the economy of Assisi which they had experienced as sinful because the poor and the lepers were excluded from participating in the goods of creation. The people of Assisi did their level best to coopt the brothers into their system by offering them work which entailed social prestige and a good salary and placed them on the side of the rich and the possessors over against the poor and those without possessions, but the brothers refused to comply. They did not want work that gave them status and power and thus integrated them into the system, but alienated them from the poor. They did not want work that confirmed and strengthened the division in society. Through their work—work that was necessary to provide for their needs—they wanted to place themselves at the service of others and to be subject to them, especially to the people who had no prospect in life and were excluded from society. Through their work they wanted to be close to the people, one with them, and to assist them as brothers in acquiring all that they needed. After mature reflection, they wrote this down in the rule so as to leave no doubt in their own minds and in the minds of others of their decision to keep themselves free from Assisi's intentions. They did not want to be *maiores* and *domini*, but *minores* and *subditi*.

In the view of Francis and his brothers, work and service, work and 'being-subject,' went together. This is another clear indication that for the brothers work was not directed toward the appropriation of goods and the maintenance of the economic system of Assisi, but toward sharing the goods of this earth and so toward laying the foundation for true peace. In other words, by dissociating themselves from Assisi and its purposes, Francis and his brothers increased their nearness to, and their solidarity with the people, especially the poor. In this context it is very remarkable that the emphasis which Francis placed on the link between 'being-subject,' work and peace, cannot be found in the *Regula bullata* where even the word *subditus* in the sense of 'being-subject-to-every-human-creature' is no longer present.[58] In all probability it had become the victim of the new tendencies within the brotherhood, according to which the learned brothers-priests could not be subject to ordinary illiterate churchgoers.

However others, even among his brothers, may think about it, Francis considered it of fundamental importance for his brotherhood to continue emphasizing the link between work and 'being-subject.' Hence he returned explicitly to it in his Testament, where he reminded his brothers for the last time about the original ideal and admonished them once more to realize this ideal in their lives: 'And we were illiterate and subject to all. And I used to work with my hands, and I still desire to work; and I firmly wish that all my brothers give themselves to work that is suitable to our life. Let those who do not know how to work learn, not out of a desire to receive wages for their work, but to give an example and to avoid idleness. And when we are not paid for our work, let us have recourse to the table of the Lord, begging alms from door to door. As our greeting, the Lord revealed to me that we should say: "The Lord give you peace"' (19–23). To be subject, therefore, was not only a virtuous attitude which the brothers ought to cultivate in their personal spiritual lives. Rather, it was an attitude that needed to be translated in a material-historical way in the work which the brothers did in the service of others and through which they, in contrast to the division and dissension that resulted from the economic system of Assisi, gave concrete expression to the greeting of peace which the Lord had given them.[59] Their 'being-subject,' therefore, was not the passive acceptance and endurance of a situation of oppression imposed on them by the rich and the powerful. It was a free choice of certain forms of work which were not much appreciated in their society, as a protest against the system of Assisi and as a realization of an alternative society which is not built on obtaining ever more possessions and power, but on service which leads to true sister- and brotherhood and to true peace. The fact that the word *subditus* occurs in the writings of Francis for the first and last time in the context of work, is thus of the greatest importance in determining its meaning and concrete content.[60]

To return to chapter 16: here, Francis and his brothers mentioned explicitly that the brothers who, by divine inspiration, wanted to go among the Saracens, must be subject, not just 'to all who are in the same house' (RegNB 7:2), but 'to every human creature' (16:6). This was not only meant to impress upon them a general characteristic of the brotherhood essential for all brothers wherever they were and thus for brothers on mission among the Saracens, too.[61] But, just as in the case of the injunction not to become involved in arguments and disputes, the attention of Francis and his brothers here was directed especially to the particular situation of the brothers who wanted to live in the midst of the Saracens. And, as in so many other places in the rule, the answer of Francis and his brothers was radically opposed to the patterns of behavior which were current in church and society and which, with regard to the Saracens, were even officially propagated and sanctioned by the church leaders on the authority of God and of the gospel. Because of this official justification by divine authority, one would expect Francis and his brothers to have made every effort to obey the papal call and to join the politics of the crusaders. And this all the more because the text of the first letter of Peter continues with the explicit exhortation to

Christians 'to be subject...to the king as the supreme authority, to the governors as commissioned by the Lord... for so is the will of God' (2:13–15).[62] The brothers, however, refused to do this. Here too they made a very selective use of the Scriptures!

While the crusaders were setting out, in the name of God and of Jesus Christ and in obedience to pope and king, to subject the perfidious Saracens, Francis asked his brothers to do exactly the opposite: he wanted the brothers for God's sake to be subject to the Saracens and to serve them while sharing their life, work and table unto peace.[63] The story of James of Vitry about the first meeting of Francis with the Saracens fits very well within this context. When the Saracens arrested him on his way, Francis replied to their question about his identity: 'I am a Christian.' In other words, he was not a crusader, or someone sent by them, as the Saracens might have expected since he came from the camp of the crusaders.[64] By his answer, Francis may at that moment unwittingly have touched a sensitive chord in the hearts of the Saracens, who subsequently heeded his request and took him to the sultan. For the Koran says: 'And you shall certainly experience that those who say: "We are Christians," are nearest to us in love' (5:85).[65]

Taking into consideration the intense crusade propaganda, especially by the crusade preachers, it is understandable that Francis and his brothers were faced with a very difficult task once they decided to go on a peace mission among the Saracens. Everywhere around them they heard people talk about war and conquest, about the subjection of the Saracens and the liberation of the Holy Land, about God who will humble the enemies and defeat them. This belligerent language became even louder when Francis and the brothers stayed in the crusaders' camp at Damietta. James of Vitry wrote in September 1219 from this camp: 'Once Damietta which is the key to the whole of Egypt, has been captured by our troops, it will be easy, with the help of the Lord, to subject the rest of the country to the authority of Christ. So we will finally return to the land of promise with joy and exultation, with triumph and thanksgiving, under the guidance of the Lord and with your prayers directing our course.'[66] And in the opening verses of his sixth letter, written after the capture of Damietta on November 5, 1219, James exclaimed: 'The Lord has subjected the peoples under our dominion and put the nations under our feet. The city, that was the glory of the pagans,... the Lord has subjected in these days to the holy church and to the army of the Christians; He has broken the horns of the sinners. Thus He has opened wide the doors for us to subject the unbelievers and to expand the empire of Christ.'[67] And further on in the letter: 'We trust in Him who in a wondrous way has opened the doors of Egypt for us, that He will also subject the rest of Egypt to the authority of the Christians by illuminating the darkness and by extending his church till the ends of the earth. And you must pray without intermission for the army of Jesus Christ so that the vineyard of the Lord may be planted in the land of promise, churches may be repaired, unbelievers thrown out, the faith restored.'[68]

It is evident that everything turned around the liberation of the Holy Land, which could only be accomplished if the Saracens were subjected by the Christian army. The ecclesiastical authorities justified the policy of liberation and subjection with scriptural and theological arguments about the inheritance which Christ had won by his blood. Further, they exercised a strong moral pressure by accusing people who did not want to take part in the war for the liberation of the Holy Land of ingratitude and criminal infidelity. At the same time they promised to all who contributed to the crusade, in the name and on the authority of God, total or partial forgiveness of their sins depending on the quantity and the quality of their contribution. Yet, Francis and his brothers stuck to their decision: the brothers who in the Spirit of the Lord wished to live among the Saracens, would be subject to them for God's sake. One can hardly imagine a greater theological contrast!

It is quite possible that Francis and his brothers had been confirmed in this decision by all the things they had seen before and during the capture of Damietta. The number of dead and wounded on both sides ran in the thousands. In *2 Cel* 30 we read that at the defeat of the crusaders on August 29, 1219, 'the losses were very great; six thousand men were killed or captured. The holy Father was deeply moved by compassion over them. He mourned especially over the Spaniards, when he saw that their greater impetuosity in the battle had left but a few of them remaining.' And this was only one battle! How many casualties there were on the side of the Saracens during the siege is not clear.[69] James of Vitry speaks about 60,000 soldiers who died 'without sword and without fight,' while master Oliver, the chancellor of Cologne, keeps the number to 30,000 whom 'the Lord struck down without sword and fire, scorning henceforth to endure the uncleanness committed in you [Damietta].'[70]

Whatever the case may have been, when the crusaders finally entered Damietta without meeting much resistance, they found a dying city. The dead were lying everywhere in the streets; they were so many that the few survivors were not able to bury them.[71] Just like Oliver, James attributes this victory to the Lord: 'The Lord has drawn his sword and killed the enemies from the greatest till the smallest.'[72] Francis, who was in the camp at that time, certainly did not remain untouched by all these events. He had come on a peace mission. All the violence and killing which he saw around him, cannot but have given rise to some intense questioning about the sense and the moral rightness of the war and of the plans of the church leaders to conquer the Holy Land and subject the Saracens.[73] The result was that Francis became even more firmly convinced than he already was, that through war and violence it simply was not possible to bring peace closer to its realization. On the contrary, in order to establish true and lasting peace, in order to remove the enmity between peoples, Francis and his brothers had to follow the opposite way: not to subject the others, but rather to be subject to them.

The capture of Damietta did not end the violence and destruction. The crusaders found in the city a great war booty of gold, silver, jewels, textiles, clothing and food. Despite the rules about the division of the booty, which were announced earlier, certain crusaders could not control themselves and started plundering when they saw such riches. James of Vitry clearly expressed his aversion for this way of behavior at the beginning of his seventh letter, sent on April 18, 1221. He also strongly condemned the fights between the Italians and French over their share of the booty, and objected especially to the fact that several crusaders spent the money that they had sacrilegiously kept for themselves, in a most scandalous way, on leading a life of luxury filled with gambling and prostitution.[74] Francis and his brothers too reacted with aversion, as the anonymous *History of Heraclius*, written in the second half of the thirteenth century, reports: 'Brother Francis...came in the camp of Damietta, did many good things and remained till the city was captured. He saw the evil and sin that kept increasing among the people in the camp and detested them. That is why he left from there and stayed for some time in Syria. Afterwards he returned to his homeland.'[75] It was like a repetition of his leaving the world of Assisi, after he had acknowledged its sin, not as an escape from reality, but in order to bring to all people Jesus' greeting of peace by sharing their life and work in humble service together with the brothers the Lord had given him (Test 1–3; 19–23).

With their decision to be subject to all people, Francis and the brothers also went against the canon law of their days. It is not clear to what extent the first brothers were familiar with the rules and regulations of canon law and so eventually wanted to take a stand against them. We may however presume that at a later stage the learned brothers would have had a better knowledge of the provisions of canon law. It is also possible that these learned brothers, with an appeal to canon law, may have been instrumental in the disappearance of the word *subditus* from the missionary statute which was reduced to just two verses in *Regula bullata* 12,1–2.[76] For several decrees concerning the relations between Christians and Saracens, collected in the first four of the *Quinque compilationes antiquae*, composed between 1188 and 1217,[77] and later taken up in the *Decretales* of Gregory IX in 1234,[78] presupposed or even stated explicitly that Christians may not be subject to Saracens.[79] These decrees were a practical expression of the manner in which Christians, and especially their church authorities, thought at that time about the increasing relations between Christians and Saracens. This implies that, even if the first brothers were ignorant of or inadequately informed about the decrees of canon law, it remains important to study the various decrees in order to gain a better insight into the ideas which lived in the Christian world in Francis' time and, explicitly or implicitly, influenced the way of thinking of Francis' contemporaries.

The *Decretum Gratiani*, composed around 1140, paid little attention to the Saracens. As a result, the material which concerns them is scattered all over the *Decretum* and hence difficult to trace. The *Compilationes*, on the other hand, contain a separate title or chapter about the Jews and the Saracens. This development indicates that, in the course of 50 years, the problem of the relationship with non-Christians, and especially with the Saracens, had acquired a certain urgency within the Christian community, largely because of the growing trade and of the crusades.[80] In order to face this new situation, earlier decrees with regard to the Jews were taken up again and extended to the Saracens. Thus the *Compilatio prima* (1188–1192) opened by reiterating a decree of the council of Mâcon (581) which, on divine authority, forbade Jews to keep Christian slaves. The reason which the council gave for this prohibition is that it was an abomination when someone who blasphemed

Christ detained in the chains of slavery those whom Christ the Lord had redeemed.[81] The second decree, a passage from the biography of pope Zachary from the *Liber Pontificalis*, gave the same reason in somewhat different words. When pope Zachary decided to redeem Christians who had been bought by Venetian merchants in Rome in order to be sold as slaves to the Saracens, he did so because it was not just that those who had been washed clean in the baptism of Christ would have to serve pagans.[82]

These arguments possessed a strong ideological color. For scriptural and theological arguments were applied in a very selective manner to safeguard or even to strengthen the Christian position of power. On the basis of scripture, however, Pope and council could also have reached exactly the opposite conclusion, that the followers of Jesus could very well be slaves of pagan masters. According to the Vulgate translation of the first letter of Peter, they must, as slaves, be subject to their masters in all fear, not only when they are good and kind, but also when they are brutish. For it is a grace if for the sake of God one endures afflictions, while suffering unjustly.... For it is to this that Christian slaves are called, because Christ suffered for them and left them an example so that they should follow his footsteps. He did not commit any sin, nor was there any deceit found in his mouth. When he was insulted, he did not repay with insults; when he was tortured, he made no threats but surrendered himself to the one who judged him unjustly (2:18, 21–23).[83] It is precisely this text of the letter of Peter about 'following the footsteps of Jesus' (RegNB 1,1), which made a deep impression on Francis and his brothers and which they wanted to realize in their own way by their freely chosen submission, their being subject to every human creature, as an alternative to and a protest against the use of power and violence by church and state in the world of their days.

Very instructive is a decree of the Third Lateran Council (1179) which was taken over by the *Compilatio prima*. It states that an anathema is to be pronounced on all those who prefer Jewish to Christian witnesses before the court, because Jews must be subject to Christians.[84] Another reason which the *Compilatio prima* gives is that the faith of Christians may be endangered when they work in the service of Saracens and stay with them. Thus a text was quoted from a letter of Alexander III (1159–1181) to the bishop of Marseille, in which the pope wrote that Christian slaves were not allowed to live with Jews (and

Saracens) so that they would not be converted to the perfidy of Judaism (or Islam) on account of their stay among them.[85] Similar argumentation, also taken from Alexander III, can be found in the *Compilatio secunda*, made by John of Wales after 1210.[86] This second reason, i.e., of a possible apostasy on the part of the Christians, disappeared in the later *compilationes* in order to again make a place for the first reason, that Christians cannot be subject to Jews or Saracens. Thus the *Compilatio tertia*, which Peter of Benevento composed in 1210 by order of Innocent III, contains a passage from a letter of the same Innocent written to the archbishop of Sens and the bishop of Paris in 1205. In this passage, the pope strictly forbade Jews to have Christian wet nurses or other servants in order that the children of the free (Christian) woman would not be the servants of the children of the slave (Jewish) woman; on the contrary, as slaves rejected by the Lord in whose death they maliciously conspired, the Jews must acknowledge that they are the slaves of those who have been freed by the death of Christ.[87] This is underlined once more in the *Compilatio quarta*, composed in 1217 by Johannes Teutonicus, where a text from the Fourth Lateran Council is quoted; 'Since it is all too absurd that a blasphemer of Christ exercises power over Christians, we renew in this general council because of the audacity of the transgressors what has been decided with foresight at the council of Toledo (589), and forbid Jews to hold any public office. We extend this same ruling also to pagans.'[88]

This survey of legal rules which canon lawyers at the time of Francis collected with regard to the relations between Christians and Saracens is perfectly clear. The rules themselves, but especially their theological justification by popes and councils, reflect very accurately the commonly accepted views of the church leaders of that time. In their opinion, the Christians, redeemed by Christ's death, occupied by divine providence a special, if not a higher place within the history of humankind: they were the children of the free woman. As such they could claim by divine right that the Saracens, the children of the slave woman, be subject to them, while the Saracens on the other hand were not entitled to any power over them. Within this theological view which emphasized the God-given superiority of the Christians and translated this into concrete rules, there is no room for the attitude of being subject to the Saracens for God's sake, which Francis and his brothers advocated on the basis of their experiences in dealing with the Saracens and their theological reflection upon them. In short, there existed such a fundamental difference in their theological starting points and the approaches that follow from them, that the position of Francis and his brothers on the one hand and of the official church on the other appear irreconcilable. As became evident earlier, everything ultimately centered around the way in which God is seen and experienced, for the ecclesiastical authorities also explicitly appealed to a divine inspiration to justify their position.[89]

Whichever way one turns, the conclusion is inevitable: the God of the crusaders was fundamentally different from, and even opposed to, the God of Francis and his brothers. The God whom the brothers had come to know and experience, was not the God of power and possessions who, according to the view of the pope and the council, justified the crusade, but the God who was revealed in Jesus as humility (Adm 1:16; LetOrder 26–27). This God invited the brothers to imitate the humility of Jesus in their lives and thus to make it the foundation of a new world of peace by being subject to the Saracens, staying among them without any feeling of superiority and sharing work and food with them. By living in this way in the midst of the Saracens in the Spirit of the humble Lord (LetOrder 28), the brothers confessed that they were Christians (RegNB 16:6),[90] and not crusaders.[91] In other words, their life of being subject to the Saracens was their declaration of identity,[92] that they were followers of Jesus who did not come to lord it over others and make his authority felt, but to be their servant and slave (Mt 20:25–27; RegNB 5:9–12). He did not want to be served but to serve and to give his life (Mt 20:28; RegNB 4:6).

This theological intuition of Francis and his first brothers, and the way of life based on it, gradually lost their attraction for the brothers. The ever more numerous clerics and priests were no longer able to have a proper understanding of and appreciation for the original lay character of the way of life of Francis and his brothers, and became alienated from the ideals which inspired the brotherhood at the beginning. They strove not so much to be subject to every human creature, but to become preachers since preaching was an activity that was more adapted to their education and status.[93] And so it could happen that, only two years after the final redaction of the *Regula non bullata* had been formulated at the Pentecost chapter of 1221, the mission chapter (16), with its totally new theological and practical approach toward the Saracens, disappeared almost completely from the *Regula bullata*. As far as the first seventeen chapters of the *Regula non bullata* are concerned, chapter 16 is indeed the worst off. From 21 verses it is reduced to 2 with a predominantly juridical character. Further, the two verses that were left were moved to the end of the rule and degraded to a kind of appendix that no longer had any connection with the preceding chapters.[94] Indeed, it looks as if they did not dare to leave the mission chapter completely out of the rule, but at the same time they could not really manage to show a proper appreciation for this text which seemed rather strange in their eyes, so that they did not know what to do with it.[95] However, what is most regrettable in this matter is that the disappearance of the call to the brothers to be subject to every human creature for the sake of God meant the removal of that element from the rule which was most characteristic of the Franciscan missionary vision and constituted its very heart.

The same objection also holds true with regard to the biographies which, in their various stories about Francis' visit to sultan al-Malek al-Kamil, do not deal with his original approach to the Saracens and other unbelievers. On the other hand, it is possible that a story with an entirely opposite tendency emerges in the *Legend of Perugia*. The author made Francis answer to a question of a novice who wanted to have a psalter: 'The emperor Charles, Roland, and Oliver, all paladins and valiant knights who were mighty in battle, pursued the infidels even to death, sparing neither toil nor fatigue, and gained a glorious and memorable victory over them; and in the end, these holy martyrs died fighting for the faith of Christ. There are many however who want to be honored and praised by the people only because they tell what these heroes have done.'[96] This answer sounds very strange, if not entirely impossible, in the mouth of Francis, who did not even want to engage in arguments and disputes with the Saracens, but wished to approach them without arms in a spirit of peace and to be subject to them. The fact that the author of the legend placed such an answer in Francis' mouth demonstrates clearly how little understanding many brothers had with regard to Francis' original way of approaching the Saracens. This lack of understanding explains in turn why, in the course of history, Francis' approach did not lead to a specific Franciscan mission method of living among the Saracens and being subject to them, a method which finds its deepest foundation in Francis' experience of God.[97]

c. 'For God's sake'

In this light it is difficult to understand why the words 'for God's sake' which, in my opinion, are the heart of Francis' approach as well as its justification, hardly received any attention in the commentaries. Lehmann reaches no further than the observation that Francis refers explicitly to God and to the gift of eternal life, because from a purely human point of view it is complete foolishness to be subject to every human creature, as the brothers are supposed to be. In this situation, the brothers needed, for their motivation, to be able to fall back on God and on the promise of eternal life.[98] According to De Beer in his book *We Saw Brother Francis*, originally published in French in 1977, the words 'for God's sake' point to the unselfish character of the brothers' service to the Saracens. They did not search their own gain. They were prepared to forgo even this 'for God's sake.'[99] In a later article (1981), De Beer gives some more thought to these words and acknowledges that they are of essential importance for the understanding of Francis' intentions. According to him, 'for Francis the *propter Deum* is always the principal motive: the adoration of God for no other reason than because God is God. To serve the Muslim brother in a spirit of adoration is from now on the fundamental basis of the Franciscan attitude.'[100] With this interpretation, De Beer places his accent elsewhere than I have. Whereas he emphasizes the adoration of God, I stress the imitation of God whose humility has been revealed in Jesus. Undoubtedly, the adoration of God is a theological category that is of great importance to Francis. I do not think, however, that it plays such a prominent role in this context where Francis speaks rather about the service of his brothers to their fellow humans for the sake of God who in Jesus became our servant. Except for De Beer and, to a lesser degree, Lehmann, all the other authors remain practically silent on this important theological element of the Franciscan missionary vision. The final result therefore is a rather poor harvest which in no way does justice to the theological intuition of Francis and his brothers. It is this intuition which formed the basis for their entirely different approach to the Saracens and Islam. For this reason, I have taken it as the starting point for my exegesis: the brothers did not become involved in arguments and disputes and were subject to every human creature for the sake of God whom they in Jesus had come to know and experience as humility.

Because of this approach, the brothers were able to open themselves to everything they saw and heard among the Saracens, and thus create the space for new discoveries in a learning process that was full of surprises.[101] When we take the later writings of Francis as a criterion, it is evident that Francis indeed started looking at Islam with different eyes and learned some new and unexpected things. In fact, he experienced how the Spirit of God was also at work among the Saracens. It is this experience which offers an explanation for the fact that we do not find any evidence of the negative outlook on the Saracens and Islam, which was so prevalent in church circles at that time, in the writings of Francis. Moreover, and this is perhaps even more important, this experience was the real source of Francis' positive approach to the Saracens and Islam. Thanks to his openness, Francis was able to see with his own eyes the deep religiosity of the Saracens and to admire it. He was struck by the great reverence they had for their holy book, the Koran, which they always kept beautifully covered in a special place, and for the holy names of God, which they continually recited with great devotion and reverence.[102] He was also struck by the daily public calls to prayer to the praise of the all-powerful God.[103] The Saracens were believing, praying people, whatever others may have said about them!

Back in Italy, deeply impressed by these experiences, Francis wrote in his Letter to the Clergy, that the clergy must not only show more respect for the Eucharist, as the Lateran council and pope Honorius required, but also for the written names and words of the Lord which together form the Scriptures (12). In those Scriptures, the Lord still speaks the words to us through which the Lord creates and redeems us (3) and thus makes God's name, or rather many names, come true for us at this moment in our world. These names continued to captivate Francis' mind and, in an outburst of joy and thanksgiving, he eventually listed them in his Praises of God, composed after his stigmatization on Mount La Verna and written down in his own hand, on a little parchment for brother Leo. Next he called on the custodians of the brotherhood to cooperate in making the appeal to the clergy more successful (1 LetCust 2). Even in his Testament he returned to this subject when he asked his brothers that, wherever they found 'the most holy written names and words of the Lord in unbecoming places,' they must see to it that 'they be collected and placed in a suitable place' (12). The respect and reverence for the most holy names and words of the Lord was clearly one of the major concerns of Francis, ever since he returned from his visit to the Saracens.

In his Letter to the Rulers of the Peoples, it was the Muslim public call to prayer which Francis had in mind when addressing the rulers. He admonished them: 'You should manifest such honor to the Lord among the people entrusted to you that every evening a call be made by a messenger or some other signal that praise and thanks may be given by all people to the all-powerful Lord God.' And the rulers should not take this lightly for they must know that, if they do not do this, they 'must render an account before the Lord [their] God, Jesus Christ, on the day of judgment' (7–8). In this way Francis hoped to realize the vision which he had during his stay among the Saracens, of a Christian-Muslim ecumenism in praising God so that 'at every hour and whenever the bells are rung, praise and thanks are given to the all-powerful God by all the people throughout the whole earth' (1 LetCust 8).[104] Given this positive appreciation of Francis for Islam and especially for the way in which the sultan and his people lived and expressed their faith, it is difficult to understand how Bonaventure could conclude his story about Francis' visit to the sultan with the observation: 'Besides he [Francis] could not see the smallest sign of a genuinely religious spirit in the soul of the sultan.'[105]

The discovery of God's presence among the Saracens added a new and important perspective to Francis' approach 'for God's sake.' For this discovery invited Francis to acknowledge in gratitude God's presence among the Saracens and to admire all the good God had worked in their midst. Reverence for this God, who was so graciously manifest among the Saracens, encouraged him still more to be subject to them and to the plans which God in the divine pleasure had for them. It is a further expression of Francis' deep respect for and obedience to all that the Spirit of the Lord, by divine inspiration, works out in people in the intimacy of their consciences (cf. LetLeo 3; Adm 3:7; RegNB 5:2).

Reverence for this God, source of all that is good (cf. RegNB 17:17)[106] and thus also of the good that is present among the Saracens, invited Francis to have great respect for the writings of the pagans. This comes very much to the fore in the interesting story which we find in 1 Cel 82. 'Whenever Francis would find anything written, whether about God or about man, along the way, or in a house, or on the floor, he would pick it up with the greatest reverence and put it in a sacred or decent place, so that the name of the Lord would not remain there or anything else pertaining to it. One day when he was asked by a certain brother why he so diligently picked up writings even of pagans in which the name of the Lord is not mentioned, he replied: "Son, because the letters are there out of which the most glorious name of the Lord God could be put together. Moreover, whatever is good there does not pertain to the pagans, nor to any other people, but to God alone, to whom belongs every good."[107]

It is known that during the eleventh century there arose in the West a greater openness with regard to Greek and Latin literature and philosophy. Little or no attention was paid to the differences which existed between this literature and Christianity. The great representatives of antique culture were even made into Christians before Christ. A profound change took place with regard to the image of the 'pagan,' so much so that in the royal portal of the cathedral of Chartres, Cicero and Aristotle, Pythagoras and Euclid gathered around Mary as patrons of the liberal arts. This new appreciation led to a feeling that they belonged to 'us.' Hence people started talking about *Plato noster, Aristoteles noster, Cicero noster.* They too, the 'pagans,' had thus a place in God's salvific plan. Christians must therefore approach them and their writings with respect.[108]

The story about Francis could very well fit in with the climate of this medieval humanism. Yet it does not appear very plausible to look there for the context of the story, especially since in speaking about the writings of the pagans Francis most likely did not refer to the works of Plato and Aristotle which he never knew, but rather to the Koran which he had seen during his visit to the Saracens, who were commonly called 'pagans.'[109] It is this Koran which was the source of all the good things which Francis discovered in the behavior of the Saracens and which made such a deep impression on him: their prayer, their faith, their respectful use of the word of God. And since all these good things in the Koran did not come from the Saracens, but from God from whom all good comes (RegNB 17:17), Francis wished to also respect the Koran. It is precisely this respect for the Koran in which Francis differs from medieval humanism, as represented by William of Tyre (1130–1186), archbishop of Tyre and chancellor of the kingdom of Jerusalem.

Born in Jerusalem, William studied arts and theology at Paris with Peter Lombard, and civil and canon law at Bologna. The growing appreciation for antique culture was very welcome to him, because from his youth he had been accustomed to an open, pluralistic religious society. His *Historia rerum in partibus transmarinis gestarum* shows this very clearly. But while the book is full with kings and emperors from antiquity, with mythological figures and gods, who without any problems find themselves in the company of persons from the Old and New Testament, Mohammed and Islam appear in a completely different light. They are clearly rejected from a theological point of view. As already mentioned, William saw Mohammed as a seducer who was so foolish as to deceptively call himself a prophet, and so arrogant as to declare himself to be sent by God. He was the first-born of Satan. Hence his doctrine was nothing but a bundle of lies which could only lead to perdition. And although William had high esteem, even from a religious point of view, for a man like Nur ad-Din whom he called not only just, but also religious and God-fearing, yet he continued to consider Islam a superstitious tradition, an antithesis to Christianity.[110] In this he was not alone. Everywhere around him in church and society the negative language with regard to Mohammed and Islam prevailed, even in the writings of a person like Peter the Venerable who commissioned a translation of the Koran. He did so, however, not out of respect for the Koran, but in order to be able to combat this 'collection of lies.'[111]

A similar attitude can be found in Oliver, the chancellor of Cologne, who together with Francis was present in Damietta, but probably did not meet him, for he never mentions him in his *Historia Damiatina*.[112] After Damietta had been recaptured by sultan al-Malek al-Kamil in 1221 and the crusade with arms had turned into a failure, Oliver wrote a letter to the sultan in which he tried to convert him to Christianity by words.[113] In this letter he profusely praised the sultan whose name he interpreted as meaning 'the perfect one.' He was especially grateful to him for the humane treatment of the crusaders who had been taken captive by him and his troops. 'Since time immemorial an example of such great generosity towards prisoners has not been heard of.' The sultan did not behave as a tyrant or lord, but as a father, a helper and companion. He had taken care that, at his expense, the weak and wounded were transported to the harbor of Damietta. Struck by so much goodness, Oliver expressed his wish: 'Kemel, may the Lord increase the good that is in you and may he take away the veil of darkness from your eyes so that you may see the fullness of the truth.'[114] Oliver thus acknowledged the goodness of the sultan. It came from God, but had nothing whatsoever to do with the Koran. For it was the Koran which held the sultan in darkness, as it was the work of Satan. Oliver therefore could not show any respect for the Koran, the holy book of Islam, and would never have kept it in a sacred or decent place. On the contrary, he was a fervent crusader who dreamed of the destruction of Islam, when he heard the stories about huge groups of Christians which were coming from the East on their way to Jerusalem.[115] And when these dreams did not become reality and his attempt to convert the sultan failed, he returned home to Germany to again devote himself to the preaching of the crusade.[116] This Oliver would definitely have done everything in his power to banish the perfidious Mohammed and all that reminded people of him from Damietta forever.[117]

On the basis of his personal experience, Francis placed over against this negative attitude his much more positive theological vision of Islam. All the good that he had discovered in Islam, had its origin in God, the source of all good (cf. RegNB 17:17). It was because of the presence of all these good features which came from God and which he gratefully wanted to return to God, that Francis wished to keep the writings of the pagans 'in a sacred or decent place.' In his reverence for the Koran, Francis stood practically alone in his time. Further, his brothers have not followed him in this respect for many centuries. Like the brother in the story of Celano, they joined the common opinion according to which, in those writings, 'the name of God is not mentioned.' Until the Second Vatican Council, the Koran was therefore kept in a special section of Catholic theological libraries which was called 'the hell.' That this situation has changed, is due, among other things, to the presence at the council of many bishops from Africa and Asia who knew Islam from personal experience and were in part responsible for the declaration *Nostra Aetate*, which was promulgated by the council on October 28, 1965. This declaration is in fact the first document in the history of the Roman Catholic church that deals explicitly with the attitude of the church towards non-Christian religions. Taking a much more positive view of those religions, the declaration invites Catholics to initiate a dialogue with people of other faiths. With his experiences and insights, briefly formulated in his advice to the brothers who want to go among the Saracens, Francis gives, in my view, the only true basis for a sincere dialogue between Christianity and Islam and, in particular, for an intensive dialogue on the existential level of everyday life where, out of reverence for God, Christians and Muslims are mutually subject to each other and thus create the possibility for a true ecumenism of peace.[118]

E. THE SECOND WAY OF BEING PRESENT

    7. Another way is
        to proclaim the word of God
        when they see that it pleases the Lord,
        so that they believe in the all-powerful God,
        the Father and the Son and the Holy Spirit,
        in the creator of all,
        in the Son, the redeemer and savior,
        and that they be baptized and become Christians,
        for whoever is not born again
        of water and the Holy Spirit
        cannot enter into the kingdom of God (cf. Jn 3:5).

a. 'When they see that it pleases the Lord'

In Francis' approach, as I have described it so far, the emphasis is placed on being subject for God's sake, i.e., on a way of living and doing which is inspired by a very definite theology and directed towards the establishment of true peace. Preaching and baptizing do not have first priority.[119] In itself this fits very well in Francis' vision, for according to him the witness of life always holds priority over the witness of the word. In the given circumstances, however, when the brothers stayed among the Saracens, it was not so obvious that for them preaching and baptizing came in second place and might even be absent. Yet, this was the case in Francis' view, for, as he said, the brothers-preachers may only proclaim the word when they see that it pleases the Lord. In other words, they may not proclaim the word of God unless the Lord gives them a sign.[120]

By making preaching dependent on the fulfillment of certain conditions, while, on the other hand, no one of the brothers could be dispensed from being subject, Francis underlined first the essential lay character of the presence of the brothers among the Saracens. Also, for the brothers who were priests and hence could officially proclaim the word of God, 'being-subject' was therefore their first and most essential task as lesser brothers,[121] a task which at the same time offered them the opportunity to enter into a learning process among the Saracens which might be of great value to them precisely as preachers. For if in this learning process they became aware of the presence of God among the Saracens, they would proclaim the word of God in an entirely different way once they actually became involved in preaching because they saw that it pleased God.

Next, by taking this position with regard to preaching and binding it to the fulfillment of certain conditions, Francis differed from the common way of thought and practice in the church. Starting from the church's possession of the truth which leads to eternal life, a man like James of Vitry felt the urge to preach this truth and to expose the lies which held the Saracens captives, as soon as he was confronted with them. Undoubtedly, this preaching was for him not only a matter which pleased God, but simply a duty, because it concerned the eternal life of the Saracens. And when he was not able to preach to them, he sent them letters in which he refuted their errors and showed them the truth of Christianity in the hope that they would be converted.[122] In his letter to al-Malek al-Kamil, written in 1221, Oliver of Cologne even went so far as to threaten the sultan with a new crusade if he did not allow Christian missionaries to publicly proclaim the Christian faith.[123] And Francis, being a man of the church: shouldn't he also think in like manner about the necessity of preaching? Did he not see that the Saracens did not know the truth about Christ and thus were deprived of the truth that leads to life? In such a situation, how could it possibly please God to delay preaching the word of life? Yet, Francis did not think that preaching took first priority and could not be delayed. Apparently, he had seen and experienced something different during his stay in the midst of the Saracens than James or Oliver. Here, then, lies the reason why he acted differently from them. To summarize briefly, Francis followed a different practice because he started from a different theory, in this case a different theology.

The basis of this theology is to be found in the words: 'when they see that it pleases the Lord' (RegNB 16:7). These words refer first to the fact that in the process of meeting the Saracens the brother-preacher is not the lord, not the possessor of the word.[124] Here, too, he is the hearer, the listener who must try to become immersed in the situation in order to learn there what God's will, God's pleasure, really is. As already indicated in the opening verse of chapter 16, the brother must act with great prudence, the prudence of the serpent.[125] This way of acting was in itself nothing special. In fact, the brothers had to act in this way always and everywhere. For it was around God's pleasure that the whole life of Francis and his brothers was concentrated. Thus Francis prayed at the end of his Letter to the Entire Order: 'Almighty, eternal, just, and merciful God, grant us in our misery to do for you alone what we know you want us to do, and always to want what pleases you' (50). And in chapter 22 of the *Regula non bullata* Francis admonished his brothers: 'Now that we have left the world, we have nothing else to do except to take care to follow the will of the Lord and to please him' (9). The question, however, is why here, in the particular case of preaching to the Saracens, Francis explicitly advised his brothers that they must first search for what pleases God. Are there, within the historical context, indications to be found which may help to clarify Francis' advice?

Not only Francis and his brothers, but the ecclesiastical authorities also wished to act according to God's pleasure. Hence Innocent III looked for signs in order to be able to determine whether the crusade he wanted to undertake was pleasing to God or not. As I have indicated already, Innocent operated very prudently in this case, probably as a result of the controversy which had arisen after the second crusade. With reference to 2 Cor 6:2, Bernard preached this crusade as being a time acceptable to God. Yet it failed miserably. Since this defeat, many people started asking whether they should not be somewhat more modest with regard to such affirmations. They felt they should leave it to God to set the day and the hour to conquer the Saracens and liberate the Holy Land in accordance with God's pleasure. Innocent did not agree with this opinion and decided all the same to organize a crusade, because he thought he saw clear signs coming from God which convinced him that it pleased God to hold a crusade then.[126] Honorius III was of the same opinion, as is evident from the fact that the letter which he wrote to the bishops of Lombardy and Tuscany on January 23, 1217, opened with a quotation from 2 Cor 6:2.[127] James of Vitry too followed this view when, at the end of his second sermon to the crusaders, he appealed to all Christians to take up the cross as vassals of Christ, because now was the acceptable time, now was the day of salvation.[128]

Against this background it is not improbable that a similar type of discussion about the crusades took place during Francis' stay in the crusaders' camp at Damietta.[129] Celano reports Francis' stay in the camp and his activities there, together with a number of 'seer stories,' in the second, thematically organized part of his second biography of Francis, completed in 1247.[130] His story was first of all meant as a kind of *exemplum* in order to motivate the readers, and especially the princes of the world, to follow the salutary advice of seers and prophets and not to harden their hearts against the will of the Lord. For if they would go against the Lord's will, they would lose the battle. Celano therefore did not enter into the discussion, probably held in the crusaders' camp at the time of Francis' stay, about whether or not the crusades were pleasing to God. In fact, Celano had no difficulty whatsoever with the crusades as such and did not condemn them at all. Implicitly he even gave his approval to them. For his only concern was to show the princes, with the help of a concrete example from Francis' life, how they should behave if they wanted to win a crusade or any other battle for that matter. Hence he concluded his story about the defeat of the crusaders prophesied by Francis with the following advice to the princes: 'Rashness generally ends in disaster, for since it relies on its own powers, it does not deserve help from heaven. But if victory is to be hoped for from on high, battles must be fought in the Spirit of God.' That this advice breathes a totally different spirit than the Spirit of the Lord who called Francis to a mission of peace, goes without saying.

According to Powell, however, this *exemplum* shows, on closer examination, characteristics of a sermon, an admonition against the crusade which Francis gave in the crusaders' camp. Celano's story gives the impression that Francis spoke about one particular battle which he would have liked delayed because, according to him, the right moment had not yet come to start the battle. In fact, however, Francis' sermon was not directed against one particular battle (*pugnam*) which the crusaders wanted to start at an inopportune moment, but was meant to forbid the crusade as such (*bellum*) and to announce its failure.[131] In the words, 'forbidding the war, announcing its failure,' we still hear an echo of Francis' original intention, which, sadly enough, can no longer clearly be heard in the present story because Celano does not mention the original context of the discussion going on in the camp. For this context was not necessary for, and might even interfere with, the meaning which the story of Celano had as an *exemplum* for the princes of this world. Within the original context, however, Francis' words manifested a clear opposition against one of the fundamental themes of crusade preaching, namely that the crusade was an acceptable occasion of salvation.[132]

If Powell's interpretation is correct, it appears that Francis explicitly used the criterion of being acceptable to God, of being pleasing to God, in his evaluation of the crusade. This, then, could explain why Francis, with regard to other problems occurring within the context of the crusade as well, appealed to the same criterion and mentioned it explicitly when he had to determine his position in a controversial matter like that of preaching to the Saracens. For while the majority within the church was convinced that it simply pleased God when the word of truth and life, necessary for salvation, was proclaimed to the Saracens without delay, and that therefore no further examination of the situation was required—the preaching activity of James of Vitry illustrates this very well—Francis differed from this generally accepted opinion. He did not want the brothers to start preaching immediately, and surely not by using the apologetic method. On the contrary, he declared explicitly that his brothers were allowed to preach only after they had lived among the Saracens and discerned in their midst that it pleased the Lord, i.e., they had to look prudently for a sign from the Lord in the given situation which would indicate to them there and then that the proclamation of the word was indeed pleasing and acceptable to God.

Beside this possible dependence on the more general climate of discussion about the crusades, it is probable that there is still a more direct influence on Francis' choice of words to be found in the events that took place during Francis' visit to sultan al-Malek al-Kamil.[133] Because of the fact that every historiographer gives his or her own personally colored view of persons and events, it is only natural that we proceed carefully here and do not draw any hasty conclusions. Yet there seems to be a clear point of contact which we cannot overlook. It is found in a letter which James of Vitry wrote in the spring of 1220, a few months after Francis' meeting with the sultan. Briefly reporting this meeting, James mentions how the sultan used the idea of 'pleasing God' in his conversation with Francis. How are these words to be understood? Is it possible that there is a connection with Francis' use of the same idea in the mission chapter of his rule?

Before answering these questions, it is first necessary to take a closer look at the report of James of Vitry. He writes in his letter that, although Francis preached to the Saracens for several days, he had 'little success' except that 'the sultan, the king of Egypt, asked him secretly to pray to the Lord for him, so that by divine inspiration he might join the religion which was most pleasing to God.'[134] Francis' preaching had thus caused doubts in the mind of the sultan. And although he could not admit this before his own people, he had become a man in search of the religion which would be most pleasing to God. Once he had found this, he intended to convert to it, as in his successful search he could only have been guided by divine inspiration. Francis may have had little success, but he had at least achieved this much in James' eyes: the highest representative of Islam was no longer certain of his own religion after he had been confronted with Christianity in the person and the preaching of Francis. To James, this was yet another proof that Christianity pleased God more than Islam. And, according to him, even the sultan could not deny this, if he really dared to face the fact of his own uncertainty, as he secretly did in his meeting with Francis. The report of James of Vitry has thus a clear apologetic undercurrent: if the sultan examined his situation fairly and squarely, he could not but acknowledge that Christianity was the reason why he had started doubting his own religious conviction and that Christianity therefore must be the religion which pleased God most.

James of Vitry returns once more to the meeting between Francis and the sultan in chapter 32 of his *Historia Occidentalis*, probably written before September 8, 1221.[135] In this report, Francis does appear to be more successful with his preaching, so much so that, according to James, 'the sultan was afraid that some of his soldiers might be converted to the Lord by the force of Francis' words and go over to the army of the Christians. He therefore had him led back to our camp with many signs of honor and with security precautions, but not without saying to him: "Pray for me that God may reveal to me the law and the faith that is the more pleasing to him."'[136] Despite differences in the reporting, the overall impression is the same: the sultan had to acknowledge the force of Christianity, whether he liked it or not. In this acknowledgement also lay the answer to his prayer for a revelation from God. For the success of Francis' preaching among his soldiers manifested clearly which law and which faith were pleasing to God. Thus, in this story too, there exists a predominant apologetic interest in showing the superiority of Christianity over Islam. This interest is very understandable on the part of James of Vitry, the crusade preacher and bishop of Acre, as we have come to know him through his letters. But does it also do justice to the actual meeting between Francis and the sultan? And more particularly: what do the words 'to please God' mean to sultan al-Malek al-Kamil?

Despite the apologetically colored interpretation of James of Vitry, his reports appear to contain traces of an actual conversation between Francis and the sultan. Specifically, the words 'to please God,' which occur in both reports, seem to point in this direction. The main reason for this is the fact that these words fit very well in the mouth of a Muslim. For one of the most important words which occurs over and over again in a conversation with a Muslim, is *in'shallah*, if it pleases Allah, if Allah wills it. Through the frequent use of this word, that very often serves as an interjection or exclamation, believing Muslims express their most profound conviction of faith, namely that their lives are completely in God's hands. This conviction, of course, also lives among believing Christians. 'God willing' is an expression which older believers very readily use. Yet, one cannot avoid the impression that God's will plays a bigger role in the ordinary lives of Muslims. For everything in their lives centers around *islam*, around submission, surrender to the will of Allah. Hence, it is only natural that the sultan spoke about this in his conversation with Francis. This impression is further confirmed by what James of Vitry reports about this conversation. The sultan wished nothing but to surrender himself totally to the will of Allah and to do only what pleased Him. He would therefore do everything in his power to discern what pleased Allah and to act accordingly. If it pleased Allah to do something, it was good, whatever might happen to the sultan; if it pleased Allah to ask something from him, he would commit himself to it with his whole person. This need not mean at all, as James of Vitry supposes because of his apologetic interest, that the sultan would have started having doubts about Islam. On the contrary, it was exactly Islam which, in and through the Koran, revealed to him the will of God and led him to that attitude of faith and life which Francis had come to admire so much. For just as Francis had been deeply touched by the prayer practice of the Muslims as an expression of their faith in Allah, the All-powerful, so he was now, in his conversation with the sultan, touched by the predominant place which the will of Allah, that which pleases God, occupied in the life of the sultan and of every Muslim believer.

This experience was still vivid in the mind of Francis and his brothers when they reflected on preaching to the Saracens. Arguments and disputes had already been rejected by them as not being in accordance with their vision of God who had invited them to a mission of peace in humble submission. But what about preaching? Does it please God? During his stay among the Saracens, Francis had come to greatly admire how it had pleased God to be actively present among them and to be the source of much good in their lives. He knew therefore that God had not rejected them, and had not left them to their own devices. On the contrary, even though they were different, God accepted them and was continually interested in them. And thus Francis too was ready to accept and to respect them for God's sake. Because of this positive approach, Francis was able to correct many wrong ideas about Islam and discover its many good qualities.

It is even more important that this approach enabled Francis to penetrate ever deeper into the 'incomprehensible and unfathomable' mystery of God, 'creator of all and savior of all' (RegNB 23:11; cf. 16:7), who, in gracious goodness, goes beyond the bounds of Christianity and is greater than all our theological ideas which are conditioned by place, time and culture. Out of reverence for this God, Francis wanted to be subject to the Saracens and to the plans which God in divine pleasure had for them and which God, being patience (SalVirt 4), would realize in good time. That is also why Francis was prepared to delay the proclamation of the gospel until he received a sign that it pleased the Lord. The starting point for Francis with regard to the question of whether to preach to the Saracens or not, was therefore not an abstract theological doctrine about what is necessary for people's salvation, but his own personal mystical experience[137] that God, in ineffable goodness and unfathomable pleasure, did not exclude, but rather included the Saracens. Because of this experience he felt confident that he could let go of the question of the Saracens' salvation and leave it to God,[138] in the meantime waiting patiently[139] until he discerned that it pleased the Lord that he proceed to the actual proclamation of the gospel. Things are done well when they are done in accordance with God's pleasure. Who was he, Francis, that in his impatience he would dare to let his ideas and wishes prevail over the plans which God in divine pleasure took the time to realize with regard to the Saracens?

This theological vision, based on reverence for and subjection to the mystery of God, who, in divine pleasure, also included Islam, was at odds with the common theological opinion about salvation as expressed in the adage, *extra ecclesiam nulla salus*.[140] In interpreting this adage, theologians and canonists hardly left open the possibility of an inculpable ignorance. With an appeal to Paul, they took as their starting point that the gospel had been proclaimed till the ends of the earth and that therefore everyone had been able to hear it. Hence an inculpable ignorance with regard to Christ and his gospel was practically excluded.[141] And if it existed, it could not be applied to the Saracens for, besides other matters, they denied explicitly the divine sonship of Christ. Interpreting this denial from his perspective on the history of salvation, Peter the Venerable placed Mohammed, that Satan, as the promoter of this heresy, between the devil who conceived it and Arius who sowed it, on the one hand, and the Antichrist who will complete it, on the other. Thus he situated Mohammed among the explicit antagonists of Christ on the stage of world history. As followers of this Mohammed, the Saracens found themselves therefore outside God's order of salvation. In fact, the Saracens were the people who prepared the coming of the Antichrist and hence had to be opposed relentlessly.[142]

Francis' experience with the Saracens as people of faith among whom God is present through grace, was not at all compatible with these very negative conclusions. There was, then, no trace whatsoever of this negative view to be found in the writings of Francis, notwithstanding the fact that it belonged to the dominant culture of his day. Francis, however, did not possess the mental categories of a theologically trained person to further elaborate his positive, experience-based intuition and so to develop a new theological vision. At times, therefore, we see him fall back on traditional theological language.[143] This leads to a certain contradiction, especially when in the next verse Francis seems to affirm the necessity of baptism for salvation, while earlier he attached a conditional character to baptism by making the actual preaching and the eventual baptism resulting from it, dependent on a sign of God's pleasure. The fact that a person was an unbeliever was not in itself an adequate reason for Francis to start preaching the Christian faith.

This contradiction between the experience of, and the theological reflection on, Islam and its followers is not something typical of Francis alone. In fact, it exists even today. An analysis of the way pope John Paul II approaches Islam shows a similar contradiction between the words and images of the language which he uses in his more personal and direct approach to Muslims and Islam during his visits and audiences, and the traditional theological language he uses in his mission encyclical and other official ecclesiastical documents to determine the place of Islam in God's plan of salvation.[144] But while it looks as if the pope does not really acknowledge the questions which arise as a result of meeting with Muslims and other believers, Francis let himself be guided by his personal experience of God's presence among the Saracens in the advice he gave to his brothers who wanted to go among them. Francis had seen something that remained hidden from others. He caught a glimpse of the mystery of God that could not be contained within the bounds of Christianity. This experience, and not traditional theology, determined for Francis the way in which his brothers must live among the Muslims in the Spirit of the Lord, namely by being subject to them for God's sake and waiting patiently for a sign from God, meanwhile delaying their preaching and baptizing activity until they saw that it pleased the Lord.

This passage about the moment when the brothers may start preaching to the Saracens was not taken up in the *Regula bullata* of 1223. The consequence of this omission is that the original lay character of the Franciscan mission method, which emphasized a way of life of being subject to all, while preaching and baptizing came second, soon disappeared. From 1225 onward, a new type of Franciscan missionary appeared on the scene. They were clerics and priests who were sent to the 'kingdom of Miramolim,' the present Morocco, by pope Honorius III by virtue of his bull *Vineae Domini custodes* of October 7, 1225. They did not go primarily to live in the Spirit of the Lord among the Saracens to whom they wanted to be subject. The bull does not say a word about that! On the contrary, insofar as the Lord gave them time and opportunity, the brothers still had to try to convert the Saracens just as they also had to lift up the fallen and support the weak, but their first and foremost mission in name of the pope was to preach for the Christians who lived in the midst of the Saracens, and to administer the sacraments to them.[145] In this way they had to try to build up their church so that one among them might then be appointed bishop. The priestly pastoral care for the Christians had clear preference. Consequently, the Saracens practically disappeared from the brothers' sight.[146] This quick turnabout is clear evidence of the fact that chapter 16 must not so much be considered the beginning of a new Franciscan mission era, but rather as the close of the first Franciscan missionary period. The reason for this turnabout must not be sought in the faulty character of the method proposed by Francis, but in the rapid increase in the number of clerics and priests within the brotherhood and in the consequent alienation from the original ideal.[147] Francis continued to oppose this development within the brotherhood until the bitter end, as is evident from the Testament and the way in which Francis there reminded his brothers of the original ideal: 'We were illiterate and subject to all. And I used to work with my hands. The Lord revealed to me a greeting: "May the Lord give you peace."' (Test 19–24).

It is rather unfortunate that Francis and his first brothers did not elaborate any further on what these signs of the Lord consisted of which were to indicate that the brothers might start preaching. From the observations made above with regard to their not becoming involved in arguments and disputes, it is evident that, according to Francis, it did not please God when the brothers would preach in an atmosphere of controversy, even when others might challenge them to defend their Christian faith. Therefore, they must not see their sermons as a kind of extension of or substitute for the crusade, waged not with weapons but with words, at the end of which martyrdom might perhaps be waiting for them.[148] Any feeling of superiority from the side of the brothers was not in accordance with God's pleasure, for as lesser brothers they were supposed to be subject to the Saracens for God's sake. In more positive terms, this means that the brothers' preaching would please God only when an atmosphere of reverence and respect for each other had already developed. Obviously, one thinks here of a situation in which the Saracens had been impressed by the way of life of the brothers and were ready to listen to them or even to invite them to speak about their faith.[149]

If we can believe James of Vitry, it is exactly such a situation in which Francis found himself on his visit to the sultan. For James reports, albeit in his usual negative style with regard to the Saracens, 'On seeing the man of God, the sultan, that cruel beast, became sweetness itself, kept him with him for a few days and with a great deal of attention listened to him preach the faith of Christ to him and to his followers.'[150] Francis' personality, his simplicity, his nonviolence and his love of peace, captivated the sultan to such an extent that he was ready to listen to his message. Maybe he saw Francis as a *Sufi*, as a wandering ascetic whose words were worth listening to.[151] Yet the question still remains whether Francis actually did preach before sultan al-Malek al-Kamil. Or is it rather the case that Francis' preaching is entirely the view of James of Vitry who from his background could hardly imagine Francis behaving in any other way, and certainly not in the way he describes in his rule as the first manner of being present among the Saracens. Whatever the case may be, it was Francis' wish that the brothers live among the Saracens without violence, and also without the verbal violence of arguments and disputes, and be subject to them. When this way of life led in fact to the creation of an atmosphere in which the proclamation of God's word was welcome to the Saracens, the brothers could see this as a sign that it pleased God that they start preaching.

b. 'To proclaim the word of God'

Francis speaks only in rather general terms about the content of the brothers' proclamation. He wanted them to proclaim their faith to the Saracens in all simplicity 'so that they believe in the all-powerful God, the Father and the Son and the Holy Spirit, in the creator of all, in the Son, the redeemer and savior.' Striking in this short summary of the Christian faith is that it pays attention both to what the Christian faith has in common with Islam and to what is specifically Christian,[152] while every negative criticism of Islam and the prophet Mohammed is absent.

The summary opens with the profession of faith in the all-powerful God. As such we have here a traditional Christian formula. But when Francis started precisely with this formula in the concrete context of preaching to the Saracens, it is possible that his choice was also determined by the fact that the Saracens consider omnipotence one of the first and most important attributes of God. Francis could then have chosen this formula precisely because he wanted to draw attention to faith in the all-powerful God, the creator of all that exists, a faith which Saracens and Christians share.[153] This common faith in the one, all-powerful God is followed by the proclamation of the triune God, the Father, the Son and the Holy Spirit. Here too Francis placed his own emphasis by extending the trinitarian formula: the Father is called 'the creator of all' and the Son 'the redeemer and savior,' while the Holy Spirit is connected with baptism, in which people are born to new life through the working of the Spirit.

This addition, 'creator, redeemer and savior,' returns at two other places in the writings of Francis. But whereas here the titles 'redeemer and savior' are given to Christ, at the other two places they are, together with the title 'creator,' given to 'the one true God' (RegNB 23:9) and to the Father (ExpOurFather 1). This promiscuous use—at other places Francis attributes the title creator to Christ—indicates that Francis saw the work of creation, redemption and salvation essentially as the work of the triune God, which he in one place attributed to the Father and in another to the Son.[154] By the use of these three titles, as is evident from RegNB 23:3–4, 8–9, Francis clearly referred to three distinct moments of the action of God which together comprehend the whole history of salvation: creation at the beginning of time, redemption by Christ's death on the cross, and salvation by Christ's glorious coming at the end of time.[155]

It was Francis' amazement at this history of salvation which in his prayer of thanksgiving in chapter 23 of the *Regula non bullata* made him burst out in exuberant praise of God who as creator, redeemer and savior is so deeply involved in human history and wants it indeed to be a history of salvation for all people. 'Therefore let us desire nothing else, let us wish for nothing else, let nothing else please and delight us, except our Creator, Redeemer and Savior, the one true God, who is the fullness of good, all good, every good, the true and supreme good; who alone is good, merciful, kind, gentle and sweet; who alone is holy, just, true and right; who alone is benevolent, innocent and pure; from whom and through whom and in whom is all pardon, all grace, all glory of all the penitent and the just, of all the blessed who rejoice together in heaven... Let all of us wherever we are, in every place, at every hour, at all times, everyday and continually, believe truly and humbly, and hold in our hearts, and love, honor, adore, serve, praise and bless, glorify and exalt, magnify and give thanks to the most high and supreme eternal God, Trinity and Unity, the Father and the Son and the Holy Spirit, creator of all, savior of all who believe in him, hope in him and love him' (RegNB 23:9 and 11). This prayer of thanksgiving clearly describes the associations that the titles, creator, redeemer and savior, called up in the mind of Francis. Hence it manifests the God that Francis held in his heart and loved and adored. It is this God whom the brothers must preach to the Saracens: a God who cares for creation and wants nothing but good for all people. And if they have separated themselves from this God, God will receive them back again for God is merciful, kind and benevolent and the source of all pardon. God is not one who condemns and punishes, but rather a God who forgives and welcomes even the Saracens, among whom God has already worked so much good. However briefly Francis indicated the themes of preaching, they are evidence enough that there existed a very profound, even essential difference with the negative and condemnatory apologetic proclamation of a person like James of Vitry who was very much concerned about refuting the lies of the pseudo-prophet.[156]

It is also remarkable how, except for the addition 'and in the Son, the redeemer and savior,' this brief proclamation of faith hardly differs from the beginning of the 'exhortation and praise' which 'whenever it may please them, all the brothers can proclaim...among all the people with the blessing of God' (RegNB 21:1). Lehmann,[157] basing himself on Rotzetter,[158] concludes from this that with regard to preaching to the Saracens, Francis did not primarily have in mind the official more dogmatic preaching which is reserved to priests. In fact, as Jeusset observes, the words 'to preach' or 'preacher,' and also the word 'priest,' do not at all occur in chapter 16.[159] On the contrary, Francis referred here to the exhortation and praise[160] which all brothers 'with the blessing of God' may proclaim and for which he provided a kind of model in chapter 21. The only difference between chapter 21 and the model here is that the latter is adapted to a non-Christian audience in that it starts with a call to faith and next focuses on redemption and salvation through Jesus and on baptism, whereas in the exhortation to Christians, the emphasis is placed on penance. Since this type of proclamation, like the first way of being present among the Saracens, is not reserved to clerics or priests, the lay character of the Franciscan mission is once more clearly affirmed. Or as Rotzetter writes, 'The Franciscan mission method is not to be described in hierarchical-priestly terms, but consistently to be defined from the perspective of the lay-brother... as a simple, attracting presence... through a life of peace, responsibility, nonviolence, brotherhood and tenderness.'[161]

The similarities between RegNB 16:7 and RegNB 21:2 are striking indeed. But there are also differences! Are these differences the result of an adaptation to the new situation of a non-Christian audience, which does not affect the basic character of the proclamation itself? Or are they the result of an adaptation which is of such a nature that the proclamation receives a different character? There are good reasons to assume the latter. In the new situation of a non-Christian audience, it is no longer a matter of an exhortation to fear and honor, praise and bless, give thanks and adore the Lord God almighty, an exhortation which ends in a call to penance, to a change of life. On the contrary, as the text of RegNB 16:7 expressly indicates, it concerns an instruction in the faith, 'so that they believe,' an exhortation which is crowned by the reception of the sacrament of baptism and conversion to the Christian faith, 'that they be baptized and become Christians.' According to canon 10 of the Fourth Lateran Council[162] this kind of proclamation belongs to a priest, who has been delegated by his bishop. As such the bishop is responsible for the preaching in his diocese but, when he cannot fulfill this task, he has to ordain suitable men to help him in the exercise of the office of preaching and in the administration of the sacraments.[163] Within the context of the brotherhood this means that this proclamation of the faith, which is geared towards the administration of baptism, cannot be the task of all the brothers but is reserved to the brothers who are priests. Moreover, if the text were to speak about an exhortation that is allowed to all the brothers, we would obtain the somewhat strange situation that lay brothers by their proclamation would lead the Saracens to the faith, after which the brothers-priests would then have to administer them the sacrament of baptism.

That in our text the official proclamation of the faith by the brothers-preachers is intended, also appears more acceptable when we read the text in its more immediate context of the opening verses of chapter 17. Francis and his brothers deal here with the new situation that had arisen within the brotherhood because of the growing number of priests who joined and wanted to continue exercising the office of preaching. This situation required clarification both in relation to the church, where at that time many problems existed because individuals and groups appropriated to themselves the office of preaching,[164] and in relation to the brotherhood where the exercise of the office of preaching by the brothers-preachers threatened to cause a division. Regarding the church, Francis and his brothers prescribed that 'no brother may preach contrary to the forms and institutions of the holy church' (17:1), as they had been determined in canons 3 and 10 of the Fourth Lateran Council. This implies that no brother was allowed to exercise the office of preaching 'without authorization from the Apostolic See or the local catholic bishop.'[165] Regarding the brotherhood, Francis and his brothers decreed that a brother was not allowed to preach 'unless he has been permitted by his minister' (17:1) and that 'at whatever hour he is enjoined to do so he should give up his office without any protest.' Under no condition was he 'to appropriate to himself the office of preaching' (17:4).

Thus, according to Francis, the office of preaching was not a task which a brother-priest could, at any time or for any reason, not even for reason of priestly ordination, consider his rightful possession and hence legitimately claim for himself. It was rather a temporary function which was given to a brother-priest, but which should never threaten the proper mission of the brothers, 'all brothers should preach by their deeds' (17:3). Over against the tendency which appeared to exist among the brothers-preachers to hold on to the clerical office of preaching, Francis and his brothers insisted on the original lay calling which had brought them together as brothers and must keep them together, united in one brotherhood, to witness by their life and their deeds, in accordance with the gospel, that they are followers of Jesus and bringers of peace (cf. Test 14, 23). It was this, then, that Francis in the end desired for all his brothers, for 'those who preach, those who pray and those who work, whether cleric or lay,' that they, together as brothers, 'strive to humble themselves in all things' (17:5). By thus emphasizing the lay vocation which united the brothers, both cleric and lay, into one brotherhood, Francis and his brothers tried to meet the danger of the division between preachers (clerics) and non-preachers (lay brothers) as best as they could.[166]

It is only natural that this problem, so characteristic of the situation of the brotherhood around 1219–1220, also had its repercussions in the description in chapter 16 of the two ways in which the brothers can go among the Saracens and live in their midst in the Spirit of the Lord.[167] The first way of being present concerns the fundamental mission of all brothers, whether cleric or lay, to be subject, precisely as lesser brothers, to the Saracens for God's sake and so by their lives and their deeds to confess that they are Christians. The second way concerns the proclamation of faith directed towards an eventual reception of baptism. And although for all kinds of theological and other reasons, great pressure could be exercised on the brothers-preachers to take up preaching, yet Francis attached certain conditions to their preaching. The brother-preacher must understand that he is not the lord, the possessor of the word, that he cannot appropriate the word to himself, but that he must always submit himself to whatever pleases the Lord. This may imply that in a given situation he must decide not to engage in preaching for the time being. So be it! But the brother-preacher is never dispensed from the Christian lay witness of a life in humility, of being subject. He, too, must not, in the first place, preach with words, but with deeds!

This description shows that the passage about the two ways of being present among the Saracens fits very well with what the opening verses of chapter 17 say about the problems which had arisen around the place of the preachers within the brotherhood. Since chapter 17 clearly places the witness of life next to, and even to some extent over against, the official proclamation of the word, it seems evident that both these forms of proclamation are also intended in chapter 16. This means that, in all probability, the proclamation of the word of God in 16:7 must be understood as the official proclamation of the word by the brothers-preachers.[168] More important, however, is that in this interpretation, the emphasis lies on the irreplaceable lay vocation of every lesser brother to witness to the gospel by his life, lived without arguments and disputes, and in being subject to the Saracens—a vocation which the brother-preacher has to fulfill before he devotes himself to the official office of preaching.

The official proclamation of the word is directed towards an eventual baptism. Since, as we have seen, the brothers are only to become involved in this proclamation when they see that it pleases the Lord, it is *a fortiori* to be concluded that they also have to wait to administer baptism until God's will is made known to them. Hence, the brothers are not supposed to baptize as quickly as possible as many people as possible in the presupposition that this would please God. On the contrary, just as in the case of preaching, they must surrender themselves confidently to the plans which God in unfathomable goodness has for the Saracens and wait patiently until God gives them a sign. Thus the administration of baptism is dependent on the fulfillment of certain conditions and hence not as absolute and urgent as the quotation from the gospel might have us think. For this gospel text links the entrance into the kingdom of God unconditionally with the reception of baptism: 'Whoever is not born again of water and the Holy Spirit cannot enter into the kingdom of God' (cf. Jn 3:5).[169] On the basis of this text, one would presume a clear insistence on Francis' part that his brothers who are going among the Saracens do everything in their power not to delay the administration of baptism, since the Saracens' salvation is at stake. Yet this is not the case, as we have seen in the previous verses, where Francis and his brothers emphasized the priority and the irreplaceable character of their vocation of 'being-subject' to the Saracens, and thus moved baptism into third place, after the preaching of the word of God.[170] This 'contradiction,' as we have observed earlier, is probably the result of the fact that in this case Francis and his brothers did not have the necessary mental categories of theologically trained persons to think through the experiences they had during their stay among the Saracens and to discern all their theological implications. The consequence is that they quoted a traditional gospel text with regard to baptism which can hardly be reconciled with the missionary praxis they formulated for the brothers, and with the theology that is implicit therein. This unevenness, however, does not diminish the originality and the value of Francis' missionary praxis and the theology behind it, a theology based on God's pleasure, which includes the Saracens, and to which Francis and his brothers submit themselves in faith, especially with regard to the urgency of preaching and administering the sacrament of baptism.[171]

F. TO CONFESS JESUS BEFORE THE PEOPLE

    8. These and other things which please the Lord
       they can say to them and to others,
       for the Lord says in the gospel:
       'Everyone who confesses me before the people,
       I will also confess before my Father
       who is in heaven.' (Mt 10:32)
    9. And: 'Whoever is ashamed of me and my words,
       the Son of Man will also be ashamed of him
       when he comes in his majesty
       and that of the Father and the angels.' (Cf. Lk 9:26)

Francis did not want to be exhaustive in mentioning the most important themes for proclamation by the brothers.[172] On the contrary, the brothers could also say other things. They thus possessed a great freedom and it was left to them to determine whether in a particular concrete situation something could be said or not. The only criterion which they had to observe as decisive for their judgment, was whether the things they wanted to say were pleasing to the Lord or not. How are we to understand this? On the negative side, we can certainly say that all those things which could lead to arguments and disputes or which were not in accordance with being subject to the Saracens for God's sake would not please the Lord: all things, therefore, by which the brothers-preachers wanted to show the superiority of Christianity, for this happened mostly at the expense of the others, the Saracens, who were discredited or even falsely accused.[173] Looking at it from the positive side, the things which pleased the Lord and about which the brothers might preach, were first and foremost those things which aroused respect, admiration and gratitude for all the good which the Lord, the creator of all and the savior of all those who believe in the Lord (RegNB 23:11), had worked, through the divine pleasure, everywhere in the world, even among the Saracens. However, such a manner of preaching presupposed that the brothers-preachers took very seriously the first way of living among the Saracens and being subject to them, and so opened for themselves the possibility of discovering God's creative and saving presence among them. Only then would they be able to let reverence and respect for the Saracens sound through their preaching: something which definitely would please the Lord very much!

This way of preaching would lead the brothers almost naturally to the proclamation of Father, Son and Holy Spirit and their respective roles in the economy of salvation, as already indicated by Francis in his short summary of sermon themes. It was here however that difficulties might arise, because the Saracens denied this specifically Christian vision of faith. Hence the brothers might run the risk of getting involved in useless arguments and disputes which, as already observed, would certainly not make their proclamation pleasing to the Lord. For arguments and disputes did not accord with the humility which they, as lesser brothers, had to practice in their words and deeds. Moreover, disputes of this kind violated the truth.[174] It might also happen that the proclamation of the triune God would expose the brothers to persecution and endanger their lives, notwithstanding the fact that they had been as prudent as possible in their examination of the situation and their discernment of the signs which the Lord gave them. However, this risk of persecution or even of their lives should not frighten them. They must continue to look for signs from the Lord. They must continue very prudently to examine the new situations which they met, in order thereby to learn what pleased the Lord. Was it the will of the Lord that they patiently suffered persecution and so confessed their faith in Jesus, even unto death? Or did the Lord give them a clear sign that it was better for them to move to another place, to bear witness there, in word and deed, to the kingdom of God (cf. RegNB 16:14)? But regardless of what happened, under no circumstances might the brothers give up the work which they had started in the Spirit of the Lord. They must go on confessing Jesus before the people. This was never allowed to suffer.

Francis and his brothers underlined this vision with an explicit reference to two words of Jesus that are complementary. The first, Mt 10:32, probably known to Francis as it is the first antiphon of the lauds, the vespers and the prime of the common of a martyr,[175] twice repeats the verb 'to confess' of verse 6. Precisely as a word of Jesus, 'the Lord says,' it emphasizes once more the first and most important task mentioned in verse 6, namely that the brothers, by living among the Saracens and being subject to them, must confess to being followers of Jesus. This first word of Jesus is reinforced by a second that expresses even more forcefully the intention of the first through its negative turn. To the twofold 'confession,' there corresponds a twofold 'being ashamed.'[176] Further, it is remarkable that this second word is not taken from the continuing text of Matthew 10:33 or its parallel in Luke 12:9, as one would expect, but rather from the longer and more solemn text of Luke 9:26.[177] By means of this choice, probably made by Caesar of Spires, Francis and his brothers stressed once again the seriousness of the situation in which the brothers might find themselves when they went among the Saracens and might actually be threatened by great dangers. When even then they would not be ashamed of Jesus, but rather continued to confess him before the people, Jesus would certainly not be ashamed of them and would confess them before his Father. With these encouraging words and the hopeful perspective they opened, Francis and his brothers concluded their particular advice for the brothers who, in the Spirit of the Lord, wanted to go among the Saracens on their mission of peace, and who might be confronted with serious dangers, even to their lives.

G. 'THEY HAVE GIVEN THEMSELVES TO THE LORD'

> 10. And all the brothers, wherever they are,
>   should remember
>   that they have given themselves
>   and have abandoned their bodies to the Lord Jesus Christ.

11. And for his love
  they must expose themselves to enemies,
  both visible and invisible,
  for the Lord says:
  'Whoever loses his life for my sake,
  will save it (cf. Lk 9:24)
  for eternal life.' (Jn 12:25)

a. 'All the brothers wherever they are'

The address indicates that this verse starts a new passage which concerns not only the brothers who want to go among the Saracens, but all the brothers wherever they are. However, the commentators do not interpret this clear caesura in the same way. Lehmann sees verses 10–21 as a clear continuation of the preceding verses with which they form a unity. From this he concludes first that the mission statute possesses a universal validity, because from verse 10 onward it addresses all the brothers wherever they are.[178] With this conclusion, Lehmann says precisely the opposite of what the text intends to say. The first part (verses 1–9) is explicitly addressed to, and meant for, the brothers who want to go among the Saracens. The text centers around certain words and ideas, like 'being-subject,' which have been used before to characterize the brotherhood and its place in the world. These same words and ideas are now repeated in chapter 16 because they indicate very accurately what the brothers, in opposition to the ecclesiastical views and practices of that time, are really concerned about when they go among the Saracens. This part, therefore, and especially the description of the two ways of being present among the Saracens, is to be seen instead as an application of the universal to the particular. In this application, all the attention is naturally directed to the special character of the brothers' going among the Saracens within the context of the church and the society of that time. To conclude the universal validity of the particular from the broadening of the circle of addressees in verse 10 not only makes little sense—the universal validity of 'being-subject,' for example, has already been accepted by all—but it may also draw our attention away from the real intention of the text. By focusing on what is universally valid, the danger arises that the particular character of verses 1–9 is not sufficiently acknowledged and that these verses therefore are not read in, and interpreted on the basis of, their specific context, as in fact has happened all too often in the past.

Because of the presumed unity of the text, Lehmann also concludes, as does Esser, that the two ways of presence among the Saracens which Francis and the brothers deal with in verses 5–9, are followed by a third one which is described in verses 10–21,[179] and which he characterizes as 'a situation of being handed over, being abandoned.'[180] It is difficult to see why these authors feel so strongly the need to correct Francis and his brothers who explicitly speak of only two ways of presence. Moreover, it is not very obvious why the undergoing of suffering and persecution is a way of being present. The brothers may in fact live among the Saracens without having to suffer or be persecuted. Suffering and persecution, therefore, are not to be considered as a way of presence, but rather as a possible consequence of the brothers' choice of living among the people as peacemakers.

Finally, continuing with his proposed correction, Lehmann compares the length of the passages dealing with the different forms of presence and reaches certain conclusions the reasons for which are not very obvious. Thus he writes that 'the two ways of missionary activity which are repeatedly praised as an original Franciscan contribution and achievement, and which actually in a somewhat fortunate manner correspond with the present understanding of mission, are only treated in three short sentences (verses 5–7),' whereas 12 verses are devoted to 'the third way.' This indicates very clearly, according to him, that 'Francis attaches much more importance to explaining to his brothers that their way of life will lead to the diverging of opinions, challenge the surroundings and cause conflicts. It is not only a matter of confessing one's faith in words (verses 7–9), but in deeds, by one's way of life, by one's suffering. This constitutes the theme of the entire third and last part of chapter 16.' After an analysis of this part, Lehmann concludes that his study 'has shown that, for Francis, there exists an order of precedence in the attitudes and activities of the missionaries. Most important is not the *actio*, but the *passio*.'[181] This conclusion fits very well with a certain form of religious spirituality, but implies at the same time a real distortion of the advice that Francis and his brothers give in verses 5–9. The brothers who go among the Saracens, do not go, in the first place, in order to suffer and to be persecuted, but in order to bring the Saracens true peace through deeds of humble service, in contrast to the deeds of war and violence of the crusaders, and so to show them the true face of Christianity.

In my opinion, verse 9 constitutes thus the end of the mission statute proper in which Francis and his brothers gave 'those who are going among the Saracens' clear advice that was specifically geared to their particular situation and the problems they might face. Thereafter Francis continued with certain, more general advice which concerned all the brothers wherever they were. He resumed chapter 14, as it were, and reminded all the brothers that on their peace mission through the world they might be confronted with persecution anywhere. Naturally, this reminder was also valid for the brothers who wanted to go among the Saracens. But, as already indicated, this does not mean that Francis proposed suffering and persecution as 'a third way of presence' which the brothers who were going among the Saracens would have to practice as a way of life, in the same way that they were not supposed to engage in arguments and disputes, but rather to be subject to the Saracens. On the contrary, the advice which Francis gave to the brothers about their way of life among the Saracens was precisely intended to create such conditions that the Saracens would welcome the brothers in their midst. This advice was thus meant to prevent persecution and suffering as much as possible in the given situation. Francis did not want to antagonize the Saracens, but to open ways of contact, of dialogue with them; he wanted to break through the predominant way of thinking about the Saracens as enemies, and to foster friendly, or rather brotherly and sisterly relations among all people: he wished to establish true peace.

Francis was firmly convinced that the brothers 'will be received not only among the believers but also among the unbelievers. Let them observe what they have promised the Lord and the Lord will give them, among the unbelievers as well as among the believers, all that they will need.'[182] That is, as long as the brothers go as sheep among the wolves and are subject to the Saracens, as long as they 'speak well and act well when [they] see or hear evil said or done' (RegNB 17:19), as long as they show the enemy 'love by their deeds' (Adm 9:4), Francis believed that, by their nonviolent, peaceful behavior, they would likely succeed in putting an end to the existing enmity between Christians and Saracens and thus create an atmosphere in which Christians could live together with Muslims in peace.[183] However, in case people did not welcome them in spite of all their efforts to make peace, Francis advised his brothers 'to flee into another country to do penance with the blessing of God' (Test 26; RegNB 16:14).

Against this background it is not possible to accept the desire for martyrdom as the most important motive for Francis' going to the Saracens, even though it is considered as such by the Franciscan authors, especially by Celano. Rather, their stories are to be understood as applications of a certain model of interpretation in which martyrdom is seen as the most perfect imitation of Christ.[184] According to Celano, this martyrdom came within reach of Francis and his brothers the moment they went to the Saracens. For, in conformity with the dominant way of thinking, the latter are depicted as cruel enemies, as 'wolves' that spare no one. For this reason, according to Ernoul, the cardinal-legate Pelagius refused Francis permission to visit the sultan, 'for he was convinced that, if they would go, they would never return.'[185] Yet, Francis did not give up, for to sacrifice one's life as martyr in imitation of the poor, naked and crucified Redeemer is the highest a disciple of Jesus can reach. It is the fulfillment of a truly apostolic life in the service of preaching the gospel.[186] However, Francis' ardent desire was not fulfilled, because, as Celano concludes his story, 'the Lord had reserved for him the prerogative of a singular grace,' namely the stigmatization. It is sad, though, that by placing so much emphasis on the motive of martyrdom, Francis' original intention of a peace mission was almost completely obscured. The typical character of Francis' approach, that is, to carry Jesus' greeting of peace to the Saracens by assuming a radically different attitude towards them and so to bring the eschatological vision of peace closer to its realization, thus disappeared, with all the harmful consequences this had for the way in which the brothers would later go among the Saracens.

Francis and his brothers knew all too well that something might go wrong with their peace mission, notwithstanding all their good intentions and their profound conviction of moving in the right direction. They, and especially Francis, had personally experienced persecution and rejection within the Christian world. Thus it is not at all impossible that the collection of gospel texts which Caesar of Spires brought together in verses 11–21, was strongly influenced by the profound impression which the reports about the maltreatment of the brothers in the countries beyond the Alps made at the chapter of 1221![187] In any event, with this long passage, Francis and his brothers wanted to encourage the brothers wherever they were, in case they were not accepted by either Christians or Saracens on their mission of peace. In such a situation, they should first carefully examine the circumstances and try to discern God's will. It might be that God would give them a sign indicating that they should flee from this particular city or country to another place (14; Test 26). It might also be, however, that this possibility would no longer be open to them. In that case they should not shun persecution and death, but face them courageously as a consequence of the choice they had made 'to give themselves to the Lord Jesus Christ and to abandon their bodies to him' (10).

b. 'They have abandoned their bodies'

It is this original choice which Francis and his brothers recalled at the beginning of this long passage of encouragement. And they wished that all the brothers would take this choice to heart again (*re-cor-dentur*) whenever they were being persecuted. According to Lehmann, their formulation may have been influenced by the system of vassalage of that time. Just as a vassal surrendered himself to his lord and by his oath of allegiance made himself socially and economically dependent on him, so did the brothers surrender themselves to the Lord. There exists however an important difference. Whereas the feudal lord often dealt in an arbitrary manner with his vassals and exploited them, Jesus invited the brothers to a voluntary following and to a common sharing of the same destiny.[188] It is remarkable indeed that here Francis and his brothers used the verb *'se exponere'* (11). This was also used by Innocent III in his crusade encyclical when, for the first time in a papal document, he used the image of vassal and lord to remind the people of their duty to expose their goods and their whole persons, just as vassals did, and to take up the cross out of gratitude towards the king of kings, Jesus Christ, the Lord.[189] However, this does not prove that Francis was influenced by the system of vassalage, especially since no such influence can be found elsewhere in his writings. Moreover, the expression can be adequately explained without referring to this system. Also remarkable in this context is that Francis never used another related image, even though it was predominant at that time, namely that of the Christian as *'miles Christi,'* as soldier of Christ, who fights under the banner of his Lord Jesus Christ and is ready to lay down his life for him.[190]

It seems more important, therefore, to read this particular formulation of the original choice of Francis and his brothers, namely that 'they have given themselves and abandoned their bodies to the Lord Jesus Christ,' against the background of Francis' own writings, especially the beginning of the fifth Admonition. There Francis briefly summarized his theology of the body: 'Consider, O man, in how excellent a position the Lord God has placed you, because he created and formed you to the image of his beloved Son according to the body and to his likeness according to the spirit.'[191] In this text, we can very clearly hear an echo of the creation story in Genesis. However, Francis was not satisfied with an allusion to the story in Genesis alone. He had to place it within the New Testament context of the person and the life of Jesus who is the center of the brothers' life and to whom they have given themselves completely. And so we also hear in the words of the Admonition an echo of texts from the New Testament like, 'God co-operates with all those who love him. They are the ones he intended to become true images of his Son, so that his Son might be the eldest of many brothers' (Rom 9:28–29), or the opening verse of the hymn to Christ in the Letter to the Colossians: 'He [the beloved Son] is the image of the unseen God and the first-born of all creation' (1:15). The references to these texts contain the danger of all kinds of abstract theological reflections. Thus Eric Doyle asks if, by stating explicitly that the human body was created and formed in the image of the Son, Francis meant 'to say that the incarnation of God's Son—Jesus of Nazareth—was first in the mind of God before Adam? His words are clearly a seminal formulation of that view of the reason of the incarnation which is theologically expressed as the unconditional primacy of Christ.'[192]

In saying this, however, we are far removed from Francis' interest in the concrete, historical person of Jesus who 'was poor and homeless and lived on alms, he and the blessed Virgin and his disciples' (RegNB 9:5). For it was by this earthly Jesus that Francis had been touched! It is the image of this Jesus that Francis had in mind when he spoke about God's creation of the human body in the image of the beloved Son. The dignity, the excellence of the human body must therefore be sought in all that happened to Jesus and his body during his life here on earth. Jesus gave his body in a life of service, especially to the poor (RegNB 4:6). By thus emptying himself, he wanted to undo the division among people, a consequence of the original sin of appropriation (Adm 2), and to restore the lost paradise of peace and solidarity, where even the poor have their rightful place at the table of the Lord (RegNB 9:8; Test 22).[193] In order to realize this ideal, he even lost his body, dying on the cross in obedience to the will of his Father (2 LetFaith 10–11). In the eucharist, Jesus repeats this historical act and so continues to give his body over and over again (Adm 1:10). For in the eucharist Francis heard Jesus saying: 'This is my body,' given in humble service (Adm 1:16–17; LetOrder 27–29) for the liberation of humankind, expelled from paradise and held captive by its possessions (RegNB 23:3). Thus Francis discovered the dignity of the human body in the way Jesus had lived it before in his own body. And he began to see and understand that he could realize the dignity of his body only by following in Jesus' footsteps, leaving the world of Assisi behind, that is, the world of power and possessions, of violence and exploitation, and committing himself with his whole person, with body and soul, to the building up of God's world. In this way, Francis, like Jesus, 'loses his body in obedience' (Adm 3:1–3) to God's plan of liberation for humankind.

The tragedy of humankind, which Francis and his brothers had experienced in their own lives, consists in the fact that people all too often refuse to obey God. While all other 'creatures, under heaven, each according to its nature, serve, know and obey their Creator,' people 'delight in vices and sins' (Adm 5:2–3). They let themselves be guided 'by the desires of the flesh, the cares and anxieties of this world, and the preoccupations of this life,' and in this way 'they serve the world with their body' (2 LetFaith 65), that is, the world of Assisi and its economic and political interests. Thus the body becomes an instrument of sin; it becomes an enemy (Adm 10:2). People have the power to hold this enemy captive and wisely guard themselves against it (ibid., 3), but in many situations they do not exercise this power and let the body follow its own way. This is bound to lead to sin, for 'it is sweet to the body to commit sin and bitter to serve God' (2 LetFaith 69). Acting in this way, people show clearly that they are truly 'blind, because they do not see the true light, our Lord Jesus Christ' (ibid., 66). For if they were to see Jesus, or, more particularly, if they were to see his most holy body in the eucharist and believe in it (Adm 1:21), they would know in what the dignity of the body, created in the image of Jesus, consists: not in the appropriation of power and possessions, but in the giving of their bodies in humble service. They would then 'hate their bodies with their vices and sins' (2

LetFaith 37; RegNB 22:5), and 'hold them captive' (Adm 10:3) 'under the yoke of service and holy obedience' (2 LetFaith 40).[194] They would 'keep their body mortified to obedience to the Spirit and to obedience to their brother, and be subject and submissive to all people' (SalVirt 15–16).[195] They would do all this following the example of Jesus, who came 'to serve in true and holy obedience' (RegNB 5:11 and 15), to realize the will of his Father, God's plan of love for the liberation of the people (RegNB 23:3), and to that end 'offer himself as a sacrifice and oblation on the altar of the cross...leaving us an example that we should follow in his footsteps' (2 LetFaith 11 and 13).

All these ideas must have been in the mind of Francis and his brothers when they reminded each other that they 'have abandoned their bodies to the Lord Jesus Christ': Jesus had personally done this first on the cross and continues to do it in the eucharist where 'he gives himself totally to you' (*se exhibet*, LetOrder 29). Thus Jesus had shown them the value and the dignity of the human body. At the same time, he invited them to follow him and, like him, to give their bodies in humble service, even to the very end, and so to confirm the excellence to which their bodies had been created in the image of Jesus. 'In answer to Jesus' love,' the extraordinary love because of which Jesus had sacrificed his body, the brothers, therefore, must not hesitate to expose themselves and their bodies 'to enemies, both visible and invisible,' and 'not fear those who kill the body and after that have nothing more they can do' (RegNB 16:11 and 18; Adm 10:4). For by undergoing martyrdom, the brothers will be truly 'formed to the image of [God's] beloved Son according to the body' (Adm 5:1), and they will save it for eternal life. Exactly the opposite happens to the rich man. When death approaches, 'deceived by our enemies, the flesh, the world, and the devil,' and deprived of 'the true wisdom,' he places his soul and body and all his possessions into the hands of family and friends. 'Certainly, that man is cursed, who entrusts and exposes (*exponit*) his soul and body and all that he has into such hands' (cf. 2 LetFaith 63–77). Or, as Francis writes elsewhere, in such a case the devil has succeeded in making a person 'live according to the flesh. Thus he has taken from [him or her] the love of Jesus Christ and eternal life and cast [him or her] into hell' (RegNB 22:5).

c. 'For his love'

The brothers, therefore, must never allow themselves to be alienated from the love of Jesus in which God's love for humankind has received its visible expression. On the contrary, they must always remember his liberating love unto the end, as it daily becomes visible among the brothers in the eucharist (Adm 1). And in answer to and in imitation of this love, they must commit themselves in love with their whole persons, with soul and body, to the liberation of captive humanity and the restoration of the lost paradise of peace and solidarity (cf. RegNB 23:3). In the fulfillment of this mission, the brothers must not try to keep out of the way of their enemies, knowing that they ultimately cannot be harmed. Rather, in imitation of Jesus, who 'called his betrayer "friend" and freely gave himself up to those who crucified him,' the brothers must consider friends 'all those who unjustly inflict upon [them] trials and anxieties, shame and injuries, suffering and torments, martyrdom and death' (RegNB 22:2–3), and they must submit themselves in obedience 'so that they may do with [them] whatever they want inasmuch as it has been given to them from above by the Lord (SalVirt 18). In summary, the brothers must imitate Jesus in his liberating love and obedience, and so 'carry him in [their] heart and body through love and a pure and sincere conscience, and give birth to him through holy works' (2 LetFaith 53), that is, give him in and through the body and its activities a new historical existence for the liberation of humankind. This is the chosen life, the calling which the brothers have to take to heart again and again and from which they cannot escape, whatever suffering and persecution this may entail for them in accordance with God's will.

From the aforesaid it is clear that the dominant motive for the brothers' perseverance in their chosen life lies in Jesus' love for us. Because of his love and in answer to it, the brothers must be ready to expose themselves to their enemies. These and similar expressions are typical for Francis.[196] In the great prayer of praise and thanksgiving in chapter 23 of the *Regula non bullata*, Francis rendered thanks to God because 'through [God's] holy love with which [God] loved us,' God caused Jesus to be born, and wished 'to redeem us from our captivity (due to the sin of appropriation) by his cross and blood and death' (3). And so, 'in the love which is God,' and which has become visible for us in Jesus, Francis admonished all his brothers, 'those who preach, those who pray and those who work, whether cleric or lay, to strive to humble themselves in all things, not to pride themselves nor to rejoice in themselves nor to exalt themselves interiorly about their good words and works, in fact, about any good which God sometimes does, says or works in them and through them' (RegNB 17:5–6). Thus, they must strive not to appropriate to themselves whatever is good, because every good belongs to God and has to be returned to God (ibid., 17).

For the same reason, Francis admonished his brothers who are priests, 'If there should be several priests in a place, for love of charity let one be content to assist at the celebration of the other priest' (LetOrder 31). For through this one celebration 'the Lord Jesus Christ fills both those present and those absent who are worthy of him' (32). When therefore a brother celebrates the eucharist privately, such celebration is not needed to render Christ present. Hence the brother concerned does not place himself at the service of Jesus Christ, but holds his priestly ministry (24) as it were for himself. In other words, he appropriates the priestly ministry to himself and uses it for his own glory. He is not humble, as would befit him because of his ministry, but he exalts himself and prides himself on account of the good which the Lord works through him (cf. RegNB 17:4–6). In this way he denies the deepest essence of the eucharist, for in the eucharist Jesus gives himself totally out of love, humbling himself and thus inviting the brothers-priests to humble themselves and to hold back nothing for themselves (LetOrder 27–29).[197]

In the great admonition in chapter 22 of the *Regula non bullata*, Francis broadened the application by begging all his brothers 'in the holy love which is God, to remove every obstacle and put behind them every care and anxiety, and in the best way they can to serve, love, honor and adore the Lord God with a clean heart and a pure mind' (26). In a similar way, he asked and implored his readers at the end of the second Letter to the Faithful 'in the love which is God, to receive these words and others of our Lord Jesus Christ with humility and love, and to put them into practice and observe them' (87). One of these words is Jesus' word about the love of enemies. Francis quoted this word several times (RegNB 22:1; RegB 10:10; 2 LetFaith 38; Adm 3:8; 14:4), a clear indication that he was very interested in breaking through that way of thinking which was so predominant in his days and which considered others, whoever they were, as potential or actual enemies.

In his ninth Admonition, Francis connected the love of one's enemies explicitly with the love of God. Someone who truly loves an enemy is not upset at any injury which the other inflicts, but is disturbed because of what really matters, namely the sin which the other committed against God. 'Out of love of God,' who has been offended by this sin of the other, one experiences the other's sin as if it were 'burning' (*uritur*) one's own heart (3). For by injuring a neighbor, a brother or sister, the other person has violated the love of God for humankind and frustrated God's plan for a world in which all people live together as brothers and sisters. In such a situation, the only way to realize God's plan is not for people who have been injured to try to be vindicated by all possible means, but for them to be good for their enemies because of the love which God has for humankind. Or, as Francis writes: 'And let him show love to the other by his deeds' (4), by not treating him or her as an enemy but as a brother or sister. Thus, 'no matter all that he has to suffer in this world [at the hand of his enemy], he will preserve peace [with him or her] for the love of our Lord Jesus Christ' and so realize God's plan, God's kingdom, and be blessed because of it (cf. Adm 15:2).

These texts from his various writings clearly show that Francis, on various occasions and for various groups of brothers and faithful, appealed to the love which is God and which had become visible in Jesus' love for us. Thus, these texts confirm once again that the love with which God has loved us in Jesus constituted, for Francis and his brothers, the most important motive for gratefully imitating Jesus in his love of enemies and in his loving commitment to liberate humanity from its captivity due to its sin of appropriation. And since the imitation of Jesus' love urges them, the brothers cannot refuse: just like Jesus, they must remain faithful to their mission of bringing liberation and peace and expose themselves with confidence to their enemies, both visible and invisible, never mind the consequences this may entail for them.

Who are these visible and invisible enemies? It seems obvious that the visible enemies are those people who opposed the brothers in their mission of peace, persecuted them, and eventually brought some of them to death. Because Francis addressed himself in this text to all brothers wherever they were in the world, it is evident that he did not specifically intend the Saracens, but all those people, be they Christians, Saracens or other 'nonbelievers,' who were hostile to the brothers. Notwithstanding the fact that the brothers tried not to make enemies by avoiding all arguments and disputes and being subject to people, there will always be enemies, people who allow themselves to be deceived by the invisible enemy, by the flesh, the world and the devil, and refuse to serve God (cf. 2 LetFaith 69). The visible and invisible enemies make common cause. It is through the visible enemies that the invisible ones, and especially the devil, try to ensnare the brothers and make them give up their original choice of life. But when, as we have seen, the brothers continue to remember the love of Jesus and, in answer to this love, keep giving their bodies in obedience to God's plan of liberation, the enemies, visible or invisible, will not be able to harm them (cf. Adm 10). For even if they kill the brothers, Jesus will keep his promise toward those who gave their lives because of his love, and save them for eternal life, 'For the Lord says: "Whoever loses his life for my sake, will save it for eternal life"' (RegNB 16:11).

This word of the Lord, which is composed out of Lk 9:24 and Jn 12:25,[198] opens a long series of gospel texts which are intended to encourage the brothers and offer them a hopeful perspective in the difficult circumstances they may have to face because they have abandoned their bodies to the Lord.

H. 'BLESSED ARE THOSE WHO SUFFER PERSECUTION'

12. 'Blessed are those who suffer persecution
    for the sake of justice,
    for theirs is the kingdom of heaven (Mt 5:10).
13. If they have persecuted me,
    they will also persecute you' (Jn 15:20).
14. And: 'If they persecute you in one city,
    flee to another (Mt 10:23).
15. Blessed are you when people will hate you,
    and malign and persecute you
    and drive you out and abuse you
    and cast out your name as evil
    and when they utter every kind of slander against you
    because of me.
16. Rejoice on that day and be glad,
    for your reward is great in heaven' (cf. Mt 5:11–12 and Lk 6:22–23).
17. And 'I say to you, my friends,
    do not be afraid of these things
18. and do not fear those who kill the body
    and thereafter can do no more (Mt 10:28; Lk 12:4).

19. See that you are not troubled (Mt 24:6).
20. For through your patience you will possess your souls (Lk 21:19)
21. and whoever perseveres to the end
   will be saved' (Mt 10:22; 24:13).

Obviously, these texts were not chosen at random. On the contrary, they were selected from the perspective of encouragement which was already indicated in verse 11, the opening verse of the series. Whatever enemies may try, whatever suffering they may inflict on a disciple of Jesus, the disciple's life is in safe hands. Even when one loses his or her life for Jesus' sake, it will be saved for eternity (11). The text places special emphasis on the words 'for my [i.e., Jesus'] sake' for they return at the end of verse 15 after a long summing up of all the things which a disciple of Jesus may have to undergo. Also important is the verb 'to save,' which functions as a kind of inclusion, because in the opening as well as in the closing verse (11 and 21), it is the word around which everything turns: to save life, to be saved for eternity. For this reason, all those who suffer persecution and even lose their lives for Jesus' sake are called 'blessed.' This is underscored twice by beginning the two subunits, verses 12–14 and verse 15, with the acclamation 'blessed.' Precisely as an opening acclamation, which resounds before the real summing up of the persecutions starts, the words 'blessed are you' receive an extra emphasis in the context of the difficult and painful situation of persecution. These beatitudes find their climax in verse 16, 'Rejoice on that day and be glad for your reward is great in heaven.'[199]

This climax could have been a fitting end to the text of encouragement. However, human reality is such that, in times of persecution, 'to rejoice and be glad' are not the most obvious reactions. In such situations, the brothers too had experienced how they could be seized by fear and anxiety, how they could be troubled and confused and perhaps even tempted to give up the fight. It was this experience which the brothers wanted to face. That is why, in the concluding verses (17–21), they explicitly encouraged each other once more with words of the Lord, 'I say to you my friends' (17). There was, then, no need for the brothers to be afraid of anything that might happen to them. Rather, in patience, they must persevere to the end. For 'whoever perseveres to the end, will be saved' (21).

As a text of encouragement, this collection stresses final happiness, eternal salvation. Yet it is remarkable how persecution and all that this may entail is also described rather extensively. Thus, the words 'to persecute' and 'persecution' are used five times in verses 12–15. Further, in verses 15–16, two beatitudes of Matthew and Luke are so skillfully intertwined that not a single word that can contribute to the description of the negative, hostile attitude with which the disciples of Jesus may be confronted has been left out. All these words find their place in a summary which, because of its completeness and its ingenuity, undoubtedly manifests the hand of a master in harmonizing gospel texts. Since this harmonization is fully independent of other known harmonizations, like the *Diatesseron* of Victor of Capua and that of Tuscany, B. Vollot, following the testimony of Jordan of Giano, attributes the composition of verses 15–16 to Caesar of Spires. In his analysis, Vollot speaks of 'a successful slalom,' in which the author, with great skill, 'slaloms' from one text to the other without omitting anything of importance. It is, therefore, impossible that we have a spontaneous mixture of two texts here, in which Francis freely formulated his thoughts on the basis of biblical texts he remembered. The harmonization is too complicated and too accomplished for such an assumption.[200]

Further, the completeness of the summary clearly indicates the deep impression which negative experiences on the journey through the world had made on the brotherhood and especially on the brother who composed the text. They did not want to omit anything the brothers had experienced before when warning them of the persecutions they might have to face in the future. But over against these persecutions, however severe, the text emphasizes, as already noted, the beatitudes of the Lord. The use of such beatitudes is typical of Francis, as Admonitions 13–26 and 28, which are all formulated as beatitudes, show. In these beatitudes, Francis first of all expressed, in the ever recurring 'blessed,' his faith in the love which is God and which only wants the happiness of humankind. Next, he indicated the way which people have to follow in answer to God's love to reach the happiness to which they have been called. Along this way, they will meet many obstacles within themselves as well as within the world, but it is worth the trouble to remove them, for at the end of the road happiness awaits all those who have persevered: 'All who love the Lord...and hate their bodies with their vices and sins, and receive the Body and Blood of our Lord Jesus Christ, and produce worthy fruits of penance: Oh, how happy and

blessed are these men and women when they do such things and persevere in them, because the Spirit of the Lord will rest upon them and he
will make his home and dwelling among them, and they are children of
the heavenly Father whose works they do' (1 LetFaith 1:1–7).

Notwithstanding this long and impressive text of encouragement, it
soon became evident that, even during Francis' lifetime, brothers sought
to escape future persecution with the help and support of the Roman
curia. Thus, in his bull *Ex parte vestra* of March 17, 1226, a few months
before Francis' death, Honorius III granted the brothers their request
and gave them permission to wear different clothes and to grow their
hair and beards in order to be able to exercise their pastoral ministry
untroubled by the Saracens. They also received permission to use
money although this went against the rule of the order.[201] Most probably,
Francis also had this bull in mind when, in his Testament, he 'commands
all the brothers through obedience that, wherever they are, they do not
dare to ask any letter of privilege at the Roman curia, either personally
or through an intermediary under the pretext of preaching or as protection against the persecution of their bodies' (25).

Francis could not have expressed himself more explicitly in his rejection of those papal bulls whereby the pope granted the brothers privileges which, according to Francis, were not in conformity with the original ideal. But what really happened? First of all, it is rather strange, to
say the least, that the brothers in Morocco approached the pope directly
in matters which concerned their way of life among the Saracens. Was
not the chapter the proper place to discuss questions pertaining to the
life of the brotherhood? And when this was not possible because of the
urgent character of the matter, why not consult Francis first? Or did
they already know how he would react to their request? He would
undoubtedly forbid them to take any precautionary measures to protect
themselves against possible dangers. For the brothers had abandoned
their bodies to the Lord and committed themselves, body and soul, to
realizing God's plan of liberation and peace by being subject to the people, whatever the consequences of this commitment might be for them
personally. Hence they must not try to escape persecution and imprisonment, not even in order to safeguard the exercise of certain pastoral
tasks. But this was exactly what the brothers in Morocco wanted to do,
to try to maintain pastoral care among the Christians. Because they
expected little support for their plans from Francis, the brothers pre-

ferred to turn to Honorius, for he had sent them to Morocco precisely for the purpose of pastoral work. That in the exercise of this work certain aspects of the Franciscan way of life might suffer did not pose a real difficulty for the pope. As is evident from the bull, 'inevitable necessity and the great and evident usefulness for others' were reason enough for the pope to justify a dispensation.

Francis' evangelical ideal, as he had gradually discerned it in the course of years, stands here in opposition to the pastoral policy of the popes. Several brothers who were priests chose to align themselves with this papal policy to which they gave preference over the ideal of the brotherhood. In this view they were supported by Honorius who in his bull *Vineae Domini* (October 7, 1225) wrote to the brothers in Morocco that 'no sacrifice is more pleasing to God than the endeavour to gain souls.'[202] It was to this care of souls, this sacrifice most pleasing to God, that they wanted to devote themselves. It was this care of souls that they wished to maintain, even though this implied certain adaptations in their Franciscan way of life. It seems to have escaped them, however, that by acting in this way they appropriated to themselves, as it were, the pastoral ministry, and defended it as some possession of theirs, while they no longer gave themselves in humility and obedience to God because of the love of Jesus (cf. RegNB 17:4–5), nor allowed the divine pleasure to do with their lives what God willed (cf. SalVirt 18).

Francis, on the other hand, was concerned precisely with these values which were at the very heart of his life according to the form of the gospel. It was not the church's pastoral policy, therefore, however useful and even necessary it may have seemed, but the love of God as it appeared among us in Jesus' humble service unto the end, which was for Francis the norm the brothers had to follow in their lives in the footsteps of Jesus. This implied that they must not try to protect themselves in advance with the help of papal bulls against possible inconveniences and dangers, not even when it concerned 'gaining souls.' In other words, they must not try to control the situation. Rather, they must be subject to all, without any privileges, as sheep among wolves, devoting themselves to their mission of peace, to the restoration of the original harmony of paradise, whatever might happen to them. For Francis was deeply convinced that by such an evangelical way of life in total obedience to God and God's plan of salvation, the brothers would ultimately achieve more than they would by their conformity with the policy of the church. In fact, the church let pastoral care prevail over what the Lord had revealed to Francis and his brothers, namely that the brothers who went among the Saracens must be subject to them for God's sake and always remember that they had given themselves to the Lord Jesus Christ to realize his mission of liberation and peace, even if this meant that they must abandon their bodies after the example of Jesus himself, who gave his body on the cross and continues to do so daily in the eucharist.[203]

I. CONCLUSIONS

1. It is evident that Francis and his brothers on the one hand, and their contemporaries, like Innocent III and cardinal Hugolino, on the other, lived in two different worlds, with different theologies and different language systems. For many of Francis' contemporaries in church and society, God was a God of power and possessions, who justified the crusades and their violence to reconquer the Holy Land. For Francis, however, God was a God of humble service who invited the brothers to go among the people in a spirit of nonviolence and peace, to share their work and lives and so to build a fellowship that comprehended all people throughout the whole world. This mission of peace was basically one and the same, whether lived among Christians or among Muslims.

2. On the basis of his view of God, Francis reached a radically different reading of the gospel than the church authorities. This appears very clearly in the way Francis interpreted certain gospel texts which in his conviction were foundational for the life of the brothers but which, in church documents and in the church's preaching, were understood in a totally different, even opposite way. It concerned texts like Mt 16:24 (in RegNB 1:3) about taking the cross and following Jesus; Mt 19:29 (in RegNB 1:5) about leaving everything and receiving a hundredfold in return; Mt 5:39 or Lk 6:29 (in RegNB 14:4) about turning the other cheek. Francis understood these gospel texts as an invitation to follow Jesus by possessing nothing and by acting in a nonviolent way, in order to establish the peace of the Lord even among the Saracens. Church authorities, like Urban II, Innocent III and James of Vitry, on the other hand, used the very same texts to call the faithful to a holy war to reconquer the Holy Land where the crusaders expected to receive a hundredfold of what they had left behind in an impoverished Europe. Some peo-

ple did object against all this violence with an appeal to the gospel, and especially to the text from the Sermon on the Mount where Jesus spoke of turning the other cheek. A churchman, like James of Vitry, accused them, however, of falsely interpreting and abusing the gospel under the influence of the devil. For, according to James, the crusade was a just war, and the soldier of Christ who gave his life in this war for the reconquest of the inheritance which Christ had won by his blood, would receive the crown of martyrdom and gain eternal happiness. But for Francis, the inheritance of Christ was something totally different. In light of his understanding of Christ's mission as a mission of restoring the original paradise of peace, the inheritance of Christ consisted for him in the right of the poor to alms (RegNB 9:8). Due to this right, which Jesus had acquired for them, the poor could occupy their rightful place at the table of the Lord and share in the goods of the earth which the Lord has meant for all people without exception.

3. There thus existed an undeniable conflict between Francis and his brothers and the dominant culture in church and society. It is within this context of conflict that the expression *divina inspiratio* in RegNB 16:3 must be understood. Only the most high God could inspire Francis and his brothers to go on a peace mission among the Saracens. The leaders of church and society could not possibly achieve this, given their view of God. Over the years, however, the influence of the dominant culture became stronger within the brotherhood thanks to the increasing presence of learned brothers. In those circumstances Francis and his brothers felt the need to protect the *divina inspiratio* of the brothers who wanted to go among the Saracens from the learned brothers who had little or no appreciation for Francis' views about living among the Saracens.

4. In Francis' view, the simple, ordinary life of people was of decisive importance: the fields, the workshop, the leprosarium, the house, were the places where Francis and his brothers met the people. By being subject to them and serving them, they brought them the Lord's greeting of peace, not only in words but in deeds. In this sense, Francis and his brothers invited people to a dialogue of life where truth was not someone's possession, but was discovered together with others in sharing the experiences of life.

5. Francis' approach, which made him and his brothers move among people of different cultures and beliefs in a spirit of humble service and

without any feeling of superiority, was therefore first a learning process, a journey of discovery. Gradually, Francis and his brothers learned to discern the presence and workings of God among the Saracens, and to appreciate the good that God had worked in and through their lives and history. Gratefully acknowledging this *divina operatio*, they found a further reason to subject themselves to the Saracens and to whatever plan God, in the divine pleasure, had for them in the economy of salvation.

6. Francis' rejection of all arguments and disputes was not so much a matter of tactics or strategy, but a matter of principle. It originated in the profound awareness that God is humility. Hence God wishes people to follow this humility by not acting as if they are the lords and possessors of the truth, but by opening themselves to the truth as it becomes manifest in the lives of people wherever they are. Here, Francis differed fundamentally from a man like Peter the Venerable who, precisely by engaging in arguments and disputes, wanted to convince the Saracens, in an aggressive way, of the truth of Christianity: *'Aggredior...non armis, sed verbis.'*

7. Francis' ideal of going among the people and sharing their lives suits a lay group better than a clerical one. Therefore, it comes as no surprise that this ideal disappeared rather quickly when the clericalization of the order started to make its way. We also have to look to the clericalization process for an explanation of the fact that the words 'subject to every human creature for God's sake' were no longer quoted in the Rule of 1223. For it was not only inappropriate for Christians to be subject to Saracens according to canon law, it was also contrary to the dignity and status of the learned brothers-priests, especially when, as Francis reminded his brothers in his Testament, being subject is intimately connected with working with their hands (19–20).

8. Francis' approach to reality presupposed a great sensitivity to the 'sin' of the world and to the ways in which it deeply affected church and society and all their structures. Francis acquired this sensitivity by going among the victims of sin: 'the people who are considered to be of little worth and who are looked down upon, the poor and powerless, the sick and the lepers, and the beggars by the wayside' (RegNB 9:2). If this sensitivity fails, it is easy for people to remain caught in the existing prejudices of the dominant culture which are intended to legitimate and even, if possible, to strengthen the position and power of the rich and mighty. Thus the church continued to be a captive of its own unevangel-

ical crusading policy. Francis, on the other hand, sensitive to the disastrous consequences of violence and war to which the original sin of appropriation could lead, wished to establish peace between Christians and Saracens without violence and weapons, even without the weapon of the word, by going among them and being subject to them.

9. In Francis' approach, preaching did not take priority. He differed here from the accepted way of thinking and acting in the church, according to which preaching the truth of Christianity was a matter of the highest priority, a matter of salvation. The reason for this difference in practice lay in the fact that Francis started from a different theory, in this case, a different theology. This theology was based on Francis' personal experience that God, in the unfathomable divine pleasure, was present and active among the Saracens and was the source of much good in their lives and history. Normative for Francis, therefore, was not an abstract theological doctrine about what is necessary for salvation, but God's pleasure, which in his experience included the Saracens. This positive appreciation enabled Francis to do away with many negative ideas about Islam and to penetrate ever deeper into the mystery of God who, desiring to save humankind, went beyond the frontiers of Christianity and thus was shown to be greater than all historically and culturally bound theological ideas. Out of reverence for this God, Francis was ready to consider what, according to the dominant theology, was necessary for salvation, to be of secondary importance.

10. Because of his experience of God, who did not exclude the Saracens, but included them in the plan of salvation, Francis could confidently entrust the matter of their salvation to God and wait patiently until he saw that it pleased God that he start preaching the word of God. Unfortunately, Francis did not have at his disposal the theological categories necessary to further elaborate his positive, experience-based theological intuition and to integrate it within the whole of theology.

11. Francis' theology of God's pleasure constitutes a very valuable contribution to the theology of religions and of interreligious dialogue. Starting from Francis' experience that God, in the divine pleasure, includes the Saracens, this theology offers the basis for a true dialogue between Christians and Muslims, and especially for a dialogue of life in which, out of reverence for the gracious way in which it pleases God to be actively present among all people, Christians and Muslims are mutually subject to each other for God's sake and so collaborate in peace towards the creation of a new world.

12. By emphasizing that the brothers must avoid arguments and disputes and be subject to the Saracens for God's sake, Francis clearly indicated that he and his brothers were not motivated by a desire for martyrdom when by divine inspiration they went among the Saracens. However, when the brothers were treated with hostility on their mission of peace and even threatened with persecution, they would not try to escape such a situation, but face it patiently and with great perseverance after the example of Jesus. Just as Jesus gave his body on the cross in obedience to the Father and continues to do so in the eucharist, in order to restore the paradise that was lost because of sin and to gather all people around the table of the Lord, so for love of Jesus the brothers must give their bodies in humble service to continue the Father's work of creation and redemption and to establish true peace among Christians and Saracens and all people. This task is still valid now: to build an *oikoumene* of peace where the greeting of peace which Jesus gave to his followers is answered by the Muslim wish of peace, *salaam*, and Christians and Muslims together witness in word and deed to the greatness and goodness of God 'so that everyone may know that there is no one who is all-powerful except God' (LetOrder 9). In this way Francis' wish will be fulfilled that 'at every hour and whenever the bells are rung, praise and thanks always be given to the all-powerful God by all the people throughout the whole world' (1 LetCust 8).

part 2

FRANCIS' ATTITUDE:

A Challenge Today

Introduction

The rich and original vision of going among the Saracens, which Francis and his brothers developed in chapter 16 of the *Regula non bullata*, has found little or no resonance within the brotherhood or the church. Even during Francis' lifetime, a number of his lesser brothers went to Morocco, not to live there among the Saracens in the Spirit of the Lord and to be subject to them, but in order to undertake the pastoral care of local Christians under the protection of papal bulls. After Francis' death, brothers like Gilbert of Tournai (✠1284) joined the crusade preachers,[1] while others, like John of Wales (✠1285) became involved in disputes with the Saracens.[2] Also, the use of negative language with regard to the Saracens, which Francis had always avoided, continued as if nothing had happened. Thus Bonaventure spoke about the heart of a Saracen as 'the savage heart of a barbarian.'[3] Nothing could be seen of the original approach of Francis. The lesser brothers were no different from other religious in their attitudes toward the Saracens and Islam. Like the latter, the lesser brothers also became instruments of the papal and curial ideology which, under the guidance of the pope, was focused on defending the unity of Christian Europe against any threat, both from within—Judaism—and from without—Islam.[4] In the fifteenth century especially, the lesser brothers were actively involved in preaching and organizing wars against the Turks who occupied an important part of southeast Europe and were advancing against Vienna. The best known among them was undoubtedly St. John of Capistrano (✠1456). By acting in this way, they were clearly in conflict with the original ideal of Francis, who wished his lesser brothers to live among the Saracens in the Spirit of the Lord, in humble service and in peace. The dominant ecclesiastical ideology, however, was so strong and all-pervasive that the brothers did not even question it. They were faithful servants of the church, which called upon them to fight the dangerous threat that Islam posed to the Christian unity with all available means.

In the nineteenth century a change took place. It was a time when Western power and influence grew, while the Muslim countries lost ground, both politically and economically. As a consequence of the extension of the Western sphere of power, the church also discovered new possibilities, especially in colonial territories. These possibilities were not found in the area of the direct proclamation of the gospel. For this, as experience had proven, did not lead to any result. Rather, the churches saw new opportunities in the area of the so-called indirect mission. Schools, hospitals, orphanages and other social institutions were established throughout the Islamic world in order to gain access to the Muslims and to find a way to convert them to Christianity. The lesser brothers took part fully in this missionary activity of the church. They did so not on the basis of Francis' specific approach to the Saracens, but adapted themselves readily to the current missionary policy of the church.[5] In most cases, they were not even aware of the existence of their own Franciscan mission method, for Francis was generally considered a simple, illiterate brother who had always been an obedient servant of popes and bishops. The idea that he could have developed a mission method which differed from the accepted theological opinions of his day was not at all current among his followers. In fact, it was not until after the Second Vatican Council that the originality and importance of Francis' approach to the Saracens was rediscovered.

During the Second Vatican Council a clear and profound change occurred in the theological approach to other religions. For the first time in the history of the church, a council declared that 'the Catholic church rejects nothing which is true and holy in these religions [which] often reflect a ray of that Truth which enlightens all people.' The members of the church were therefore admonished 'prudently and lovingly, through dialogue and collaboration with the followers of other religions...to acknowledge, preserve, and promote the spiritual and moral goods found among them, as well as the values in their society and culture.'[6] In this statement, new words emerged which signify precisely the opposite of the words which were characteristic of the church's approach to other religions until then. Christians should no longer engage in a monologue on the grounds of their exclusive possession of the truth, but rather recognize the riches of other religions and enter into a dialogue with them; they should not deny the values of other religions, but gratefully acknowledge them; they should not try to destroy other religions but preserve and even promote their spiritual and moral goods.

Many followers of Francis, and especially many of those working among Muslims, welcomed this new theology of religions. All the same, it would take more than 15 years before they became aware that the theology of the Second Vatican Council was commensurable with the theology of reverence and respect which Francis had developed on the basis of his personal experience during his stay among the Saracens. Further, they discovered that Francis' specific emphasis on being subject to the Saracens for God's sake might constitute a positive contribution to the further development of the council's theology. After the inter-Franciscan mission document compiled in Mattli, Switzerland, in September 1982, it was the letter of the first Franciscan conference on Islam, held in Assisi in October 1982, which elaborated this idea for the first time, albeit rather briefly, on the basis of a short analysis of chapter 16 of the *Regula non bullata*.[7] Its statement about the significance of *minoritas*, of being the lesser one, was especially important for dialogue with other religions, particularly Islam.

According to the letter of the Islam conference, '*minoritas* demands from us, lesser brothers, today that we abandon the spirit of superiority which so often leads us to place our Christian culture above theirs. This is not really Franciscan or Christian: Christ humbled himself and came to serve, not to be served (Mk 10:45). *Minoritas* will also favor our fraternity in being true brothers to the Muslims: fraternity demonstrated through our love for them, our participation in sorrow and joy with them in the events of life, and in being sensitive to, and avoiding, whatever hurts them and is offensive to them.' *Minoritas* will also influence our attitude toward Islam, for it will open our hearts and our minds to the recognition of the working of God's Spirit in Islam. It makes it possible 'to perceive different emphases in a commonly shared doctrine, e.g., God's transcendence in today's world, reverence for the Word, the holiness of God's name' and to appreciate them. Further, *minoritas* leads us to also 'reconsider the absoluteness of our own formulations of truth: God is greater than all formulations.' This brief description of the implications of *minoritas*, of being subject for God's sake, clearly shows the profound significance that this basic Franciscan attitude can have for the dialogue with other religions.

This first impulse, provided by the letter of the conference in Assisi, was not really followed up. I hope to compensate for this failure by studying in depth what could only be summarily indicated at the Assisi conference. Therefore, in the first part of my study, I gave an extensive, contextual commentary on RegNB 16, in order to obtain a proper understanding of the significance of Francis' advice for his brothers who wished to go among the Saracens. In the second, shorter part, I would like to determine clearly and precisely how Francis' advice to his brothers is relevant for dialogue with other religions, and particularly Islam. Thus, Francis' advice may not only become a special source of inspiration, but also offer a truly Franciscan challenge to all the lesser brothers who try to live in the Spirit of the Lord among Muslims at this moment, especially in Asia and Africa. To this end, I start with a description of the present position of the ecclesiastical magisterium with regard to interreligious dialogue. I study the speeches, encyclicals and other documents in which John Paul II directly addresses Muslims or speaks about Islam to Christians. After the papal magisterium, I turn to the magisterium of the bishops. In line with my interest in the Franciscan brotherhood in Asia and Africa, I study the developments which have taken place in the Federation of Asian Bishops' Conferences (FABC) in the field of mission and dialogue since its establishment in 1972. During this period, after the Second Vatican Council, Asian bishops tried to design an Asian theology of dialogue and mission on the basis of the experiences of the Asian churches. In my analysis, in which I frequently quote the FABC documents, it will become evident that the Asian churches, with their newly acquired theological insights, make an important contribution to the universal church. Finally, I will try to indicate precisely where and how the Franciscan approach, which I discovered in my exegesis of RegNB 16, fits in with developments in the theology and praxis of interreligious dialogue in the church after Vatican II. Further, I hope to indicate how the Franciscan approach can give new stimulus to interreligious dialogue, not only in Asia and Africa, but also in Europe and North America, and so promote solidarity among people of different religious convictions to build a new world of justice and peace where no one is excluded, but all without exception find their rightful place at the table of the Lord.

CHAPTER ONE

John Paul II
and the Dialogue with Islam

In his address to a large number of Muslim religious leaders in Senegal in February 1992, John Paul gave thanks to God for the numerous opportunities he had received during his pontificate to meet Muslim leaders as well as faithful, both in the Vatican and on his many travels, especially in Africa.[1] A year later, in February 1993, he visited Africa again and addressed Muslim leaders in Benin, Uganda and Sudan. These many meetings, from the beginning of his pontificate through the present, have undoubtedly made John Paul II the pope who, in the course of the church's history, has given the greatest attention to relations with Islam. As he has indicated in several of his speeches, he continues to proceed in the direction set out in the documents of Vatican II,[2] and especially in *Nostra Aetate*, promulgated on October 28, 1965, the first document in the history of the Roman Catholic church which explicitly deals with the relation of the church to non-Christian religions. These documents contain the most important themes which recur, with variations, in the addresses of John Paul. Hence, an exposition of John Paul's relation to Islam must start with the teachings of Vatican II. Next, there are some highlights of his pontificate to which John Paul continually refers, particularly his address to thousands of Muslim youths in Casablanca on August 19, 1985, and the world day of prayer for peace in Assisi on October 27, 1986. The addresses given on these occasions also deserve our attention.

Vatican II

The paragraph of *Nostra Aetate* on Islam describes a completely new Roman Catholic approach to Islam. Whereas a strongly negative atti-

143

tude prevailed within the church even in the recent past, the declaration
of the council starts with the recognition of a spiritual bond between
Christianity and Islam: 'The Church has also a high regard for
Muslims. They worship God who is one, living and subsistent, merciful
and almighty, the Creator of heaven and earth, who has also spoken to
humankind. They strive to submit themselves without reserve to the
hidden decrees of God, just as Abraham submitted himself to God's
plan, to whose faith Muslims eagerly link their own. Although not
acknowledging him as God, they worship Jesus as a prophet; his virgin
mother they also honor, and even at times devoutly invoke. Further, they
await the day of judgment and the reward of God following the resurrection of the dead. For this reason they highly esteem an upright life
and worship, especially by way of prayer, almsgiving and fasting.' This
common faith in one God, creator and judge of all humankind, and the
common concern for the moral values of individuals and society are an
invitation to Muslims and Christians to forget their many quarrels and
hostilities of the past, 'and to strive sincerely for mutual understanding.
On behalf of all humankind, let them make common cause of safeguard-
ing and fostering social justice, moral values, peace and freedom.'[3]

This short but impressive statement regarding Islam would never
have been made without the presence and influence of those bishops
who, as leaders of minority churches in predominantly Muslim countries in Africa and Asia, had acquired a new view of the significance of
Islam based on their personal contacts and experiences with Muslim
believers. They found further support in new developments which had
taken place in the theology of religions, mainly due to the influence of
Karl Rahner.[4] The statement of *Nostra Aetate* was thus the fruit of a profound change in thinking which had already occurred in the minds of
several participants in the council. At the same time, the statement was
also a stimulus to promote this new positive view and help it to gain
acceptance in those churches where the negative view of Islam still prevailed. This led to a new situation in the church. The idea and practice
of 'dialogue and cooperation' with the followers of Islam and other religions did not only find their way into the life of the churches, but form
an essential part of it. Among other indications, this is evident in papal
visits to countries in Africa and Asia, and even Europe, which almost
always include a meeting with representatives of other religions, especially Islam. It is obvious that the themes of the pope's addresses on such

occasions have been influenced by *Nostra Aetate,* namely that the common insights of faith together with the recognition of common moral values form a sure and solid foundation for a stable and strong cooperation in the building up of a just and peaceful world. The addresses, however, do not limit themselves to a mere repetition of the statements contained in the documents of Vatican II, but also add various new elements.[5]

Paul VI

While *Lumen Gentium* and *Nostra Aetate* only speak about 'Muslims' and do not mention Islam as a religion, Paul VI took the Council one step further in his encyclical *Ecclesiam suam* (August 6, 1964) when he wrote that 'the Muslim religion deserves our admiration for all that is true and good in [its followers'] worship of God.'[6] In his address to representatives of the Muslim communities at Kampala (Uganda), Paul VI expressed his 'profound respect for the faith which they profess,' and hoped that 'what we possess in common may serve to unite Christians and Muslims in an ever closer way, in an authentic brotherhood.' Further, he was certain that his Muslim listeners would 'unite themselves to the prayers which [he addressed] to the Almighty, that He may grant all African believers the desire for pardon and reconciliation which is so often encouraged in the gospel and in the Koran.' Finally, while remembering the Christian martyrs of Uganda, Paul VI wished 'gladly to celebrate those confessors of the Muslim faith who were the first to undergo death, in 1848, because they refused to transgress the precepts of their religion.' Such a public homage on the part of a pope to Muslims who had been put to death because of loyalty to their faith had never been heard before. It came as a welcome relief after all the negative and false statements about Islam that had been made until then.[7]

After this statement, there followed a period of more than ten years during which Paul VI remained publicly silent about Islam.[8] Did this silence have anything to do with disturbing tendencies which the authorities in Rome suspected in the churches in Africa and especially in Asia? It was rumored that those churches placed such a great emphasis on reverence and respect for other religions that the proclamation of the gospel was being neglected. Missionaries were said to hold the view that it was no longer the mission of the church to convert people to

Christianity, because they could find salvation within their own religions. The mission of the church should therefore consist in helping people to become better people, and Muslims better Muslims, by building up basic human communities in solidarity with them in a continuous dialogue of life, and so to establish the kingdom of God, a kingdom of justice and peace, here on earth. That the Vatican authorities were really disturbed is confirmed by the apostolic exhortation *Evangelii Nuntiandi* (December 8, 1975) in which Paul VI wrote in general terms about other religions, without explicitly mentioning Islam: 'We wish to point out, above all today, that neither respect and esteem for these religions nor the complexity of the questions raised is an invitation to the church to withhold from these non-Christians the proclamation of Jesus Christ. On the contrary, the church holds that these multitudes have the right to know the riches of the mystery of Christ.' And this all the more because 'the religion of Jesus, which the church proclaims through evangelization, objectively places the human person in relation with the plan of God, with his living presence and with his action.... In other words, our religion effectively establishes an authentic and living relationship with God which the other religions do not succeed in doing, even though they have, as it were, their arms stretched out towards heaven."[9]

If we compare this last statement with the address of Paul VI at Kampala, it is evident that there is a fundamental difference. The reader cannot escape the impression that two different language systems are functioning here. On the one hand, there are the positive, very appreciative words with which Paul VI addressed his Muslim guests at Kampala while respectfully recalling the memory of the Muslim martyrs who had given their lives out of loyalty to their faith. It is the language of *Nostra Aetate*, of the Secretariat for non-Christians, where, on the basis of numerous contacts with Muslims, the officials had developed a great respect for them and their religion. On the other hand, there are the rather harsh, disparaging words with which the encyclical tried to remove the unrest and fear which had arisen in certain circles, by emphasizing the traditionally accepted teaching on the inadequacy of other religions, including Islam, vis-à-vis Christianity: even though they stretch out their arms towards heaven, even though 'they carry within them the echo of thousands of years of searching for God,' they will never lead to a living relationship with God. The latter is explicitly reserved to Christianity alone. In these statements we meet the language of those who guard the orthodoxy of faith and test all new ideas against the well-defined teachings of the church. They are not concerned about moving into new directions and developing a new theology of religions on the basis of new experiences. On the contrary, starting from what in their view are fixed theological principles, they try to find out whether the new ideas fit within the old framework. If they do not, they are rejected without any further consideration, however harsh such a rejection may sound. For them, it is the truth which is ultimately at stake.

For many people, the statement of Paul VI's encyclical signified a revocation of the positive view of *Nostra Aetate*. Yet, this statement did not put an end to the dialogue with Islam. Although Paul VI, as already mentioned, issued no direct statement regarding Islam during the remainder of his life, the dialogue continued at a lower level. Mainly due to the initiative of cardinal Sergio Pignedoli, who in 1973 was appointed president of the Secretariat for non-Christians, dialogue meetings with Muslims were organized in various countries.[10] Moreover, in 1977, the Secretariat sent the first special message to the Muslims on the occasion of the festivities at the end of Ramadan—a custom which later was taken over by many bishops' conferences as well as by individual bishops.

John Paul II

THE ENCYCLICAL *REDEMPTOR HOMINIS*

After long years of silence under Paul VI, there followed a dramatic revival under John Paul II. Even in his first encyclical, *Redemptor Hominis*, of March 4, 1979, he clearly stated that the 'activities for coming closer together with the representatives of the non-Christian religions' must continue. 'These activities are realized through dialogue, contacts, prayer in common, investigation of the treasures of human spirituality, in which, as we know well, the members of these religions also are not lacking.' The pope was well aware of the fact that, in certain circles, objections were made to these activities which, according to them, 'are harmful to the cause of the gospel, are leading to a further rupture in the church, are causing confusion of ideas in questions of faith and morals and are ending up with a kind of religious indifferentism.'

However, the opposite seemed to be the case. For, as the pope asked, 'does it not sometimes happen that the firm belief of the followers of the non-Christian religions—a belief that is also an effect of the Spirit of truth operating outside the visible confines of the mystical body—can make Christians ashamed of being often themselves so disposed to doubt concerning the truths revealed by God and proclaimed by the church and so prone to relax moral principles and open the way to ethical permissiveness?'[11] Describing the non-Christian religions in this way, it seems obvious that the pope had Islam especially in mind.

Further in the encyclical, John Paul returned once more to the relationship with other religions. In this particular passage he gave a summary of *Nostra Aetate* in which he clearly placed his own emphases. According to him, the council document 'is filled with deep esteem for the great spiritual values, indeed for the primacy of the spiritual' in the other religions. These show 'that, though the routes taken may be different, there is but a single goal to which is directed the deepest aspiration of the human spirit as expressed in its quest for God and also in its quest, through its tending towards God, for the full meaning of human life.' The pope concluded this passage with the observation that the council 'also expressed its esteem for the believers of Islam, whose faith also looks to Abraham.'[12]

I want to pay extra attention to some of the ideas in these passages because they are important for what follows. First, John Paul wrote that 'the firm belief of the followers of the non-Christian religions is an effect of the Spirit of truth.' Commenting on this text, Thom Michel, a member of the Secretariat, writes that, according to the pope, it is not true that the Spirit of truth can only operate in the lives of followers of other religions in spite of their religious convictions, as is sometimes said. For their convictions, so it is said, concern a religion that is not true; hence, it cannot come from the Spirit of truth. On the contrary, Michel observes, John Paul 'considers the action of the Holy Spirit in the lives of the non-Christians to be operative not in spite of their religious adherence, but rather at its essence and foundation.'[13] With regard to the Muslims, this statement would imply that their religious conviction, which is inseparable from the Koran and the prophet Mohammed, is a grace of the Holy Spirit. As such the statement represents a revolutionary breakthrough which could create completely new perspectives. However, if we look at the further context of the encyclical and later documents which explain the relation between Christianity and Islam on the basis of fixed theological principles, we are forced to interpret the passage above in a restrictive way, notwithstanding the more positive interpretation of Thom Michel. For according to John Paul, the operation of the Spirit of truth is limited to whatever is good and true in the lives of Muslims and in their religion. In their lives it is indeed a great good when, freely following their consciences, they hold fast to their faith.[14] Hence their firm belief, their faithfulness to conscience, is indeed a grace, but within the context of the whole theology of John Paul, this does not say anything about the truth and, consequently, the salvific value of the religion itself. For someone who follows a false religion in ignorance, and confesses it as well as possible according to his or her conscience, is not excluded from salvation, for this person cooperates with the grace of the Spirit.[15] However, salvation comes to him or her not because of adherence to this religion, but rather in spite of it, because of faithfulness to conscience.

We also have to interpret the statement that the Muslim faith goes back to Abraham in the same vein. Here John Paul moved beyond the council documents. *Nostra Aetate* stated very carefully that Muslims 'like to refer to Abraham,'[16] while *Lumen Gentium* said that they 'profess to hold the faith of Abraham.'[17] The council documents did not therefore make a clear pronouncement as to whether the Muslims indeed possess the faith of Abraham. They simply said that the Muslims think they do. If, for this reason, there was still doubt about this matter in the minds of Christians, John Paul removed it with his affirmation, repeated before the Catholic community of Ankara on November 30, 1979: 'They [i.e. the Muslims] have, therefore, like you, the faith of Abraham in the one almighty and merciful God.'[18] Does this mean, in light of the theology of St. Paul, that John Paul holds the view that Muslims, like Abraham, are saved by their faith? Thom Michel thinks that the soteriological implications of this view should be thoroughly examined by theologians. They should ask whether the Muslims can come to salvation like the Jews, as sons and daughters in the faith of Abraham, who are heirs of the promises made to Abraham because of their faith.[19] Taking into consideration the pope's theology of religions, to which I have already alluded, such an interpretation is rather unlikely in the case of John Paul. *Redemptor Hominis* leaves no doubt of this: 'the only direction for our intellect, will and heart is towards Christ, our Redeemer, the Redeemer of humankind. We wish to look towards him, because there is salvation in no one else but him, the Son of God.'[20] Later documents explicitly confirm this.

As already mentioned, it is striking how John Paul summarized the main ideas of *Nostra Aetate* in his own way. He admired the 'deep esteem for the great spiritual values, indeed for the primacy of the spiritual' in the other religions. It is not surprising that the pope, coming from the once atheist-materialist Eastern bloc, stresses this characteristic in other religions. Moreover, he sees the emphasis on the spiritual dimension as a very important counterweight against the secularist tendencies which are felt everywhere. They lead to a weakening or even a disappearance of attention to the spiritual, the transcendent, in which the ultimate meaning of the human person rests. Because of his view on the necessity of the transcendent in the present world, the pope considers other religions, especially Islam, to be allies in the struggle for a world in which the dignity of the human person, rooted in God's transcendence, is acknowledged and safeguarded.

Finally, in the description of the activities which must lead to closer cooperation with the followers of other religions, the pope also mentioned common prayer. However, when he called representatives of the other religions together in Assisi for a world day of prayer for peace in 1986, common prayer seemed impossible. Pressure from within the church and accusations of syncretism forced the pope to forgo his plan. I will return to this below.

THE FIRST SPEECHES

John Paul made his first speech on Islam on November 29, 1979, at Ankara. Over the next fifteen months, he made seven more speeches in Africa (Kenya, Ghana), Asia (Pakistan, Philippines) and Europe (France, Germany). The Secretariat seemed so delighted with this favorable change after the long public silence under Paul VI that it published the eight speeches in a separate booklet.[21]

In almost all of these speeches, the pope followed the line of thought of *Nostra Aetate*: because of their common faith in God, creator and judge, Christians and Muslims can and should cooperate so that God's plans for humankind may be fulfilled in a world which threatens to sink into materialism. Thus he said in Ankara: 'Faith in God, professed by the spiritual descendants of Abraham—Christians, Muslims, and Jews—when it is lived sincerely, when it penetrates life, is a certain foundation of the dignity, brotherhood and freedom of man and a principle of uprightness for moral conduct and life in society. And there is more: as a result of this faith in the transcendent God, the creator, man finds himself at the summit of creation. He was created, the Bible teaches, "in the image and likeness of God" (Gen 1:27); for the Koran, the sacred book of the Muslims, although man is made of dust, "God breathed into him his spirit and endowed him with hearing, sight and heart", that is, intelligence (Sura 32:8).... [Let us] draw from this the principle of a collaboration with a view to the progress of man, emulation in good, the extension of peace and brotherhood in free profession of the faith peculiar to each one.'[22] In Nairobi on May 9, 1980, the pope made it known that on his part he wished 'to do everything possible to help develop the spiritual bonds between Christians and Muslims...in a world that runs the risk of being absorbed by materialism. Our relationship of reciprocal esteem and the mutual desire for authentic service to humanity urge us on to joint commitments in promoting peace, social justice, moral values and all the true freedoms of man.'[23]

On June 2, 1980, John Paul addressed the Muslims in France as 'our brothers in faith in the one God.' And he concluded his speech with the words: 'Our common ideal is a society in which men can recognize each other as brothers walking in God's light and striving for what is good.'[24] In Germany, he praised the Muslim migrant workers on November 17, 1980, on the square before the cathedral of Mainz: 'When you have taken along your faith in God with a sincere heart from your homeland into a foreign land and here pray to God, your Creator and Lord, you too belong to that great group of pilgrims who since Abraham have set out over and over again to search and find the true God. When you are not afraid to pray also in public, you give an example to us, Christians, which deserves our esteem. Live your faith also in a foreign land and let no human or political interest take advantage of you.'[25] Also in Karachi, on February 23, 1981, John Paul spoke about '..Abraham to whose faith Christians, Muslims and Jews alike, eagerly link their own.'[26] Finally, in Davao, in the Philippines, on March 2, 1981, the pope began his speech to the representatives of the Muslim community by 'deliberately' addressing them as 'brothers.' For 'that is certainly what we are, because we are members of the same human family, whose efforts, whether people realize it or not, tend towards God and the truth that comes from him. But we are especially brothers in God, who created us and whom we are trying to reach, in our own ways, through faith, prayer and worship, through the keeping of his law and through submission to his designs.' Referring to various efforts of dialogue, the pope stressed that 'dialogue is built upon trust, and trust presupposes not only justice but mercy.' And he continued: 'Dear Muslims, my brothers.... Just like you, we Christians seek the basis and the model of mercy in God himself, the God to whom your Book gives the very beautiful name of *al-Rahman*, while the Bible calls him *al-Rahim*, the Merciful One.'[27] These first speeches set the tone for the many others that followed in the course of John Paul's pontificate but that we cannot deal with in detail here.[28]

The short passages which I have quoted show a great appreciation for Islam. It is especially striking how the pope develops the theme of the faith of Abraham and calls the Muslims brothers and sisters in faith in the one God. However, the question about the eventual theological implications of this brother- and sisterhood in the faith of Abraham is not addressed here. Further, it is important that in the speeches at Ankara and Davao the pope not only mentions the Koran, but quotes from it and qualifies it as 'the holy Book of the Muslims' for the first time. After all that had been said about the Koran by church authorities in the past, this statement is very remarkable indeed. Moreover, the question can be asked: what theological significance can be attributed to the fact that the pope calls the Koran 'holy' and fully agrees with the content of the texts he quotes? Does this imply that, according to the pope, the Muslims will come to salvation by their observance of all that is written in their 'holy Book?' Is this also the meaning of the pope's appeal to the Muslim migrant workers at Mainz, 'Live your faith?' In light of what I said above with regard to similar issues—the firm belief of the Muslims which is a gift of the Spirit of truth, and the faith of Abraham which Muslims and Christians share—my answer will have to be negative. Here again we have an example of the language of the Secretariat which does not fit the theology of religions as proposed by the papal magisterium. It even seems that in 1985, because of possible misunderstandings, an end was put to direct quotations from the Koran, which earlier was called a 'holy Book.'

MEETING WITH YOUNG MUSLIMS IN CASABLANCA, MOROCCO

In spite of the fact that a papal visit to Morocco was not without political risks, John Paul decided to accept the invitation of king Hassan II to address the young Muslims of Morocco during the year of the youth. And so the impossible happened. On August 19, 1985, pope John Paul II met 80,000 young Moroccan Muslims from all parts of the country in the stadium at Casablanca. Quite understandably, the pope saw this meeting as a climax to his contacts with the Muslims to which he would refer on many occasions afterwards. The content of his speech, which naturally required careful preparation, did not differ from what he had said to other Muslim audiences. Thus he stated at the beginning: 'We, Christians and Muslims, have many things in common, as believers and as human beings. We live in the same world, marked by many signs of hope, but also by multiple signs of anguish. For us, Abraham is a very model of faith in God, of submission to his will and of confidence in his goodness. We believe in the same God, the one God, the living God, the God who created the world and brings his creatures to their perfection.... It is of God himself that, above all, I wish to speak with you.... I wish also to speak with you about human values, which have their basis in God.... The mystery of God, is it not the highest reality from which depends the very meaning which man gives to his life?' This common faith calls for a common 'witness to him by word and deed in a world ever more secularized and at times even atheistic.' The witness to God, 'the Father of all mankind' cannot be separated from our 'common witness to the dignity of the human person,' for 'he is a creature of God and, in a certain sense, his image and his representative.' This implies that 'we must respect, love and help every human being,' that we honor his or her rights because they 'are the expression of God's will and the demands of human nature such as it was created by God.' This love and respect 'require reciprocity in all spheres, especially in those which concern the basic freedoms, more particularly religious freedom.' Next, the pope spoke extensively about the responsibility to cooperate in building a more human, pluralistic world of greater solidarity in which all people may find 'the means to nourish themselves, to take care of themselves, and to live in peace.'

In the last part of his speech, after repeating our common religious values, John Paul referred to the differences that exist between Muslims and Christians. 'Loyalty demands also that we should recognize and respect our differences. Obviously, the most fundamental is the view that we hold on the person and work of Jesus of Nazareth. You know that, for the Christians, this Jesus causes them to enter into an intimate knowledge of the mystery of God and into a filial communion by his gifts, so that they recognize him and proclaim him Lord and Saviour. Those are important differences, which we can accept with humility and respect, in mutual tolerance; there is a mystery here on which, I am certain, God will one day enlighten us.... I believe that, today, God invites us to change our old practices. We must respect each other, and also we must stimulate each other in good works on the path of God.... Ideologies and slogans cannot satisfy you nor can they solve the problems of your life. Only the spiritual and moral values can do it, and they have God as their fundament.... I wish that you may be able to help in thus building a world where God may have first place,' and where we, believers, give expression in our our lives and in our cities to 'the most beautiful names which our religious traditions attribute to God.'[29]

It is remarkable that the pope did not quote a single verse from the Koran in his speech at Casablanca, while he did a few months earlier in a speech to the participants in the colloquium on Holiness in Christianity and Islam, held in Rome on May 9, 1985.[30] In this connection, M. Borrmans, who was probably closely involved in the preparation of the speech, remarked that one can safely assume that the Muslims would be grateful to the pope for making this change in policy. He clarified his remark by saying that one can properly quote the Koran only in Arabic, after which a translation may be added. This would have been difficult, and even more so because it might have been interpreted as an official recognition of the canonical value of the text in its totality. A Christian could not allow this without compromising the faith, especially because the Koran denies certain fundamental mysteries of Christianity. Various people were therefore surprised to hear the pope quoting verses from the Bible and the Koran during his speech at the colloquium in Rome.[31] It is quite evident that objections had been raised within church circles. Apart from the fact that such a practice might give the wrong signal to the Muslims, it could also lead to syncretism. Sensitive as the Vatican is to such an accusation, the quotations of texts from the Koran were henceforth omitted.

Against this background, it is striking to see how much the pope emphasized the common faith and the need for a common witness of

Muslims and Christians. This is evident in his frequent use of 'we' and 'our.' In most instances, the pope did not intend these words in the sense of 'we Christians,' as opposed to 'you Muslims,' but in the sense of Muslims and Christians together who, as he stated at the beginning of his speech, 'have many things in common, as believers and as human beings.' Thus the speech expressed a profound spiritual bond. At the end of the speech, the pope related this to the most beautiful names which we attribute to God in both our religious traditions. However, the pope did not address the question of the salvific meaning of this common faith in the one God.

The pope paid attention, though, to the important differences which exist between Muslims and Christians, especially in regard to the person and the work of Jesus of Nazareth. These should not lead to polemics and even to war, as they did in the past. We must accept them with humility, knowing that we find ourselves here in the presence of a mystery, which will be fully revealed to us at the end of time.[32] In this context, the Secretariat stated in the same year that 'we live in the age of the patience of God for the church and every Christian community, for no one can oblige God to act more quickly than he has chosen to do.'[33] And in *Dialogue and Proclamation*, published jointly by the Pontifical Council for Interreligious Dialogue and the Congregation for the Evangelization of Peoples on May 19, 1991, we read: 'All, both Christians and the followers of other religious traditions, are invited by God himself to enter into the mystery of his patience, as human beings seek his light and truth. Only God knows the times and stages of the fulfillment of this long human quest.'[34] Does this imply that, for the time being, we can suspend the question of truth and salvation and entrust it to God, who wants the salvation of all humankind?[35] And, in the meantime, can we acknowledge the religions through which most people know and serve God as ways of salvation? God's plans are unfathomable indeed and the Spirit works the salvation of humankind in a mysterious way which is known to God alone. However, according to the pope, this recognition of the mystery of God can never come into conflict with what the same God has revealed to us in Jesus, namely, that Jesus Christ is the only way to salvation for humankind. There does not exist any other way of salvation than his.[36]

THE WORLD DAY OF PRAYER FOR PEACE IN ASSISI, OCTOBER 27, 1986

During a eucharistic celebration in the presence of representatives of other Christian churches on January 25, 1986, the final day of the Week of Prayer for Christian Unity, John Paul II announced that, in the course of that year, the international year for peace, he 'wishes to contribute to the arousal of a world movement of prayer for peace which, surpassing the boundaries of individual nations and involving believers of all religions, will reach the point of embracing the entire world.' Part of this 'spiritual commitment of prayerful solidarity' was his plan to organize, together with the leaders of all churches and of all world religions, 'a special meeting of prayer for peace, in the city of Assisi, a place which the seraphic figure of St. Francis has transformed into a center of universal brotherhood.'[37] While the leaders of churches and world religions accepted the pope's invitation, conservative Catholics raised objections. The pope answered them in a speech during the general audience of October 22, 1986, five days before the day of prayer. He stated very explicitly that 'it is only in Christ that all humankind can be saved.... Christ is united in a certain way with everyone; he is the center of the created world and of history.' That is why in other religions 'seeds of the Word' can be found which the church respects. One of them is prayer. However, respect for the prayer of others does not mean, according to the pope, that 'we intend to make our own formulae that express other views of faith. What will take place at Assisi will certainly not be religious syncretism but a sincere attitude of prayer to God in an atmosphere of mutual respect. For this reason the formula chosen for the gathering at Assisi is: being together in order to pray. Certainly we cannot "pray together," namely, to make a common prayer, but we can be present while others pray.'[38] On the day itself, the pope turned once more to this problem when he stated that their coming to Assisi did not imply 'a concession to relativism in religious beliefs,'[39] and was not a matter of 'reducing the content of our prayers to a kind of common denominator.'[40]

It is not clear what content and form John Paul wanted to give the world day of prayer for peace when he announced his plans for its organization in January 1986. As he explained on the day itself, his main concern was 'to witness before the world to the transcendent quality of peace.' Together with other believing people, he wanted to express the conviction which binds them together, that 'peace goes much beyond human efforts, particularly in the present plight of the world, and that therefore its source and realization is to be sought in that Reality beyond all of us.' He wished to do this because the world is in urgent need of real peace. 'Either we learn to walk together in peace and harmony, or we drift apart and ruin ourselves and others.' He continued: 'We hope that this pilgrimage to Assisi has taught us anew to be aware of the common origin and the common destiny of humanity. Let us see in it an anticipation of what God would like the developing history of humanity to be: a fraternal journey in which we accompany one another towards the transcendent goal which he sets for us.'[41]

However, in the pope's view of a common pilgrimage of brothers and sisters, united in their conviction of the common origin and destiny of humanity, there was no place for praying together, but only for being present at the prayer of others; many see this as contradictory. What is the value of what believers hold in common on essential matters, if they cannot give it common expression? What is the basis for their common commitment to the recognition of God in a secularist, and even atheist world, if they cannot express their concern about this to God together? And in connection with Islam, what does it mean that Muslims and Christians are brothers and sisters in the faith of Abraham in one and the same God, creator and judge, when common prayer is not possible and they must turn separately to God, each with their own prayer? Is God after all not the same for them? There are still more questions. It is a fact, however, that the pope took the objections of syncretism very seriously, because they touched his own christological views. He did not want to do anything that could look like or be interpreted as a recognition of other religions as ways of salvation, and that could harm the unique place of Christ in God's plan of salvation.

In his Christmas address to the Roman curia, looking back on the meeting at Assisi, 'the religious event that attracted the greatest attention in the world in this year which is drawing to its close,' the pope returned to this question. In fact, he interpreted the meeting exclusively from the perspective of his own christology: 'On that day, and in the prayer which was its motivation and its entire content, there seemed for a moment to be even a visible expression of the hidden but radical unity which the divine Word, "in which everything was created, and in whom everything exists" (Col 1:16; Jn 1:3), has established among the men and women of this world.'[42] Whether the followers of the other religions had seen and interpreted the meeting in the same way, seems rather doubtful.

Conclusion

The tension which has existed since Vatican II between dialogue and proclamation, between respect for other religions and the uniqueness of Christ, continues in the pontificate of John Paul II. However, the mission encyclical *Redemptoris Missio* of December 8, 1990, gives the impression that the emphasis has definitely shifted again towards the renewed affirmation of the uniqueness of Christ and the necessity, based thereon, of the proclamation of the gospel, which becomes ever more urgent as the number of people who have not heard the gospel continues to increase.[43] This impression is further confirmed by *Dialogue and Proclamation*, the document that appeared five months after *Redemptoris Missio*, in which the Pontifical Council for Interreligious Dialogue and the Congregation for the Evangelization of Peoples jointly published their reflections and insights on interreligious dialogue and the proclamation of the gospel of Jesus Christ. Among other things, it states that dialogue 'remains oriented towards proclamation in so far as the dynamic process of the Church's evangelizing mission reaches in it its climax and its fullness.'[44]

This change of emphasis does not come as a surprise. For we have seen that various impulses towards a new theology of religions, which became manifest in the practice of dialogue, did not receive a proper follow-up. The most important reason for this failure lies, as already indicated, in the fact that the official theology of religions does not start its reflections with the experiences of Christians with people of other faiths, but with certain preconceived ideas about other religions. For its main concern is to determine the place of these religions in God's plan of salvation in light of traditional christological dogmas, rather than to inquire about the meaning of other religions in the lives of their followers and the questions that arise therefrom. Even when the pope could admire the firm belief of the Muslims, he could not make room in his own theological reflection for this phenomenon in its own right, namely, that it is precisely their Muslim belief, derived from the Koran and proclaimed by the prophet Mohammed, which gives direction to their lives in relation to God and brings them closer to God. And when he stated that 'every authentic prayer is called forth by the Holy Spirit, who is mysteriously present in the heart of every person,'[45] this did not allow him to pray together with people of other faiths at Assisi, although we may presume that the pope considered their prayer authentic and thus called forth by the Holy Spirit. In such a situation, his concern for orthodoxy gained the upper hand over anything that may create the slightest impression of relativism or indifferentism—two characteristics of the modern mind which, according to the pope, have brought about a situation in which the present world 'seems to have lost its sense of ultimate realities and of existence itself.'[46]

It is obvious that the pope puts interreligious dialogue under pressure because of these beliefs; this is especially clear in statements like the following: 'Christ is the one Savior of all, the only one able to reveal God and lead to God.... No one, therefore, can enter into communion with God except through Christ, by the working of the Holy Spirit.'[47] And: 'It is the Spirit who sows the "seeds of the Word" present in various customs and cultures, preparing them for full maturity in Christ.'[48] And: 'Dialogue should be conducted and implemented with the conviction that *the Church is the ordinary means of salvation* and that *she alone* possesses the fullness of the means of salvation.'[49] Without really listening to what they have to say, the pope classifies other religions *a priori* as theologically immature, incomplete, in need of help. They contain 'gaps, insufficiencies and errors.' Therefore, only one possibility exists for followers of other religions, namely to convert to Christianity and to become a member of the church which alone possesses the fullness of the means of salvation. This view, however, can hardly be reconciled with the openness, humility and mutual support on the road of religious search, which the encyclical itself mentions as conditions for a true dialogue. This anomaly, which is also found in the pope's book, *Beyond the Threshold of Hope*, will continue as long as the official theology of religions holds on to traditional high christology, and refuses to acknowledge questions which are raised by such realities as the plurality of christological statements in the Second Testament, the historical character of dogmas, and religious pluralism. It is necessary, therefore, that the papal magisterium not consider itself first and foremost the authority which examines the working of the Holy Spirit in other religions on its own terms, rather, it should open itself to the Spirit and her creative presence in the living faith of the Muslims.[50]

The Federation of Asian Bishops' Conferences and the Dialogue with People of Other Faiths, Especially with Muslims[1]

When the bishops of Asia met for the first time in November 1970 at Manila, they wanted an insight into the Asian situation.[2] In their evaluation, they were struck by the fact that Asia, with its more than two billion inhabitants, was marked by poverty and undernourishment, war and suffering. At the same time, however, with the ending of the era of colonialism, a new consciousness emerged in which Asian people sought to discover their own identity and to confirm it in continuity with the heritage of their past. The bishops were concerned that Catholic communities in Asia would become increasingly integrated into this process and become part of the new Asian culture that slowly but surely was coming to birth. The bishops asked themselves particularly how Catholic communities could be of greater service to the people of Asia and become more involved in the broader task of building a society which would respond to the deepest aspirations of the Asian people as well as to the demands of the gospel. In spite of all the good the church had done, and continued to do, especially in the fields of education and health care, the bishops regretfully admitted that they had only fostered their own narrow, 'domestic' church interests. They could have shown more compassion for the poor and spoken out more vigorously in favor of justice and in defense of human rights. Also, the church was not sufficiently integrated into Asian culture and thus remained an alien who did not look for a better understanding of and greater cooperation with the brothers and sisters of other faiths.[3]

On the basis of this evaluation of the situation, the bishops resolved that they primarily wanted to be more truly 'the Church of the poor.'[4]

Secondly, the bishops were more than ever convinced that dialogue with people of other faiths would become increasingly more important.[5] Hence, in the resolutions of the meeting, the bishops 'pledge [themselves] to an open, sincere and continuing dialogue' with the followers of the great religions of Asia so that they 'may learn from one another how to enrich [themselves] spiritually and how to work more effectively together in the common task of total human development.'[6] This last aspect in particular received much more attention in later years, when greater emphasis was placed on the dialogue of life. In line with this development, dialogue with other religions would be directed mainly to the discovery of those common ideas and values which could promote cooperation in establishing the kingdom of God. Finally, in order to prevent their resolutions from disappearing into a filing cabinet, the bishops urgently requested the Asian bishops' conferences represented at the meeting 'to authorize and support a permanent structure for the effective implementation of the decisions of the meeting.'[7] This resulted in the establishment of the Federation of the Asian Bishops' Conferences (FABC) in 1972.

Local Churches in Dialogue

The first plenary assembly of the FABC was held in Taipei, Taiwan, in April 1974. Its theme was *Evangelization in Modern Day Asia*. In contrast to the conclusions of the meeting in Manila, the bishops stated that 'the primary focus of [their] task of evangelization is the building up of a truly local church.'[8] It was thus not so much the poverty of Asia, according to the bishops, which first demanded their attention when it came to evangelization in Asia, but the fact that the church, properly speaking, was still alien. For if the message of the gospel was to be credible in this situation, the church in Asia had to shed its Western character and immerse itself in the various cultures of the Asian peoples. In this context, the bishops described the local church as a church which, after the example of Christ's incarnation, has become 'incarnate in a people, a church indigenous and inculturated. This means concretely a church in continuous, humble and loving dialogue with the living traditions, the cultures, the religions—in brief, with all the life-realities of the people in whose midst it has sunk its roots deeply and whose history and life it gladly makes its own. It seeks to share in whatever truly belongs to that people: its meanings and its values, its aspirations, its thoughts and its language, its songs and its artistry. Even its frailties and failings it assumes, so that they too may be healed."[9]

In this dialogue with the great religious traditions of Asia, the bishops declared, 'we accept them as significant and positive elements in the economy of God's design of salvation. In them we recognize and respect profound spiritual and ethical meanings and values. Over many centuries they have been the treasury of the religious experience of our ancestors, from which our contemporaries do not cease to draw light and strength. They have been (and continue to be) the authentic expression of the noblest longings of their hearts, and the home of their contemplation and prayer. They have helped to give shape to the histories and cultures of our nations. How then can we not give them reverence and honor? And how can we not acknowledge that God has drawn our peoples to himself through them?'[10] This recognition had definitely been lacking in the past. The church showed little respect for the great religious traditions and certainly did not acknowledge that, by means of these religions, the peoples of Asia were drawn to God. Therefore, when the bishops expressed themselves in such positive statements about other religions, it looked as if they were involved in a kind of maneuver to catch up. So much time had been lost for which they now had to try to make up. There had been a great lack of understanding, which they now had to try to amend. For the situation was urgent. If the church did not become seriously involved in a dialogue with other religions, it would remain alien and unable to realize its mission in Asia.

Dialogue with other religions was thus seen in the perspective of the local church and its mission, like the dialogue with the poor would be later.[11] This was only natural when we take into consideration the theme of the conference, the evangelization of modern day Asia. However, by putting so much emphasis on the building up of the local church, the positive declaration with regard to other religions and the questions which such a declaration raised, did not receive due attention. For example, what consequences for a theology of religions are implied by the statement of the bishops, that the peoples of Asia have been drawn to God through their own religious traditions? Instead of asking this question, the bishops moved in the direction of what the church could learn, and eventually assimilate, from other religions. Thus the bishops wrote, 'this dialogue will allow us to touch the expression and the reality of our peoples' deepest selves, and enable us to find authentic ways of living and expressing our own Christian faith. It will reveal to us also many riches of our own faith which we perhaps would not have perceived."[12] This church-centered approach was, in a certain sense, an expression of 'fostering narrow and "domestic" church interests,' about which the bishops at their earlier meeting in Manila had expressed their regret.[13] Moreover, because of this approach, the Asian bishops did not use their experience of living among people of other faiths to formulate a proper Asian theology of religions through which their local Asian churches could contribute to the catholicity of the church.

On the contrary, from the very start, they clearly presupposed the traditional theology of God's plan of salvation in Jesus Christ as the framework within which other religions, purified and healed, had to find their place.[14] But do they really fit within this framework? Or do they invite us to break out of it? For other religions are important and positive elements in God's plan of salvation. It is through them that the Asian peoples have been drawn to God.

The Voice of God's Spirit

The second plenary assembly was held in Calcutta in November 1978 and was devoted to *Prayer-The Life of the Church of Asia*.[15] In their introduction to this theme, the bishops did not overlook the fact that the conference was taking place in India, which, in the words of Paul VI, is 'a land of ancient culture, the cradle of great religions, the home of a nation that has sought God with relentless desire, in deep meditation and silence, and in hymns of fervent prayer.'[16] In this context, it was only natural that the conference expressed itself on the subject of the inculturation of Christian prayer and the dialogue with other religions. This was done, however, under the heading 'Some means for the renewal of the prayer-life of the church of Asia.'[17] Thus inculturation and dialogue were only considered insofar as they could help the church, especially since, as the bishops admitted, 'it is sometimes said that we ourselves and our Christian communities do not impress those of other Asian religious traditions as men of prayer, as contemplative communities. This prevents the church from being, for Asian peoples, the sign and sacrament of God's presence in our midst.'[18] In order to improve this situation, inculturation and dialogue were very necessary for the church in Asia. It was this limited view, together with the traditional theology of religions, which led them to the following statement under the heading of inculturation: 'In keeping with the economy of the Incarnation, which is the law of the church's life and mission, the prayer-life of our local churches should "take over the riches of our nations, which have been given to Christ as inheritance." '[19] Even though this statement quoted a passage from the mission decree *Ad Gentes* of the Second Vatican Council, it did not show the sensitivity and disinterestedness toward people of other faiths which the final document later mentioned as requirements for deepening and expanding the dialogue.[20]

The passage about interreligious dialogue showed a very positive spirit. Among other things, the final document spoke of the spirituality which is characteristic of Asian religions. This spirituality 'stresses a deeper awareness of God and the whole self in recollection, silence and prayer, flowering in openness to others, in compassion, in non-violence, generosity.... Sustained and reflective dialogue with them in prayer will reveal to us what the Holy Spirit has taught others to express in a marvelous variety of ways. These are different perhaps from our own, but through them we too may hear his voice, calling us to lift our hearts to the Father.'[21] This last sentence implies that Christian churches can not only discover the working of the Spirit in all that Christianity has in common with other religions, but also in those expressions of faith that are different from Christianity's. For those different expressions have also been taught to them by the Holy Spirit. This is a very important conclusion which breaks through the exclusive Christian framework where other religions are evaluated on the presence of the 'seeds of the Word' and not sufficiently acknowledged in their difference. Unfortunately, the final document did not further elaborate this statement. Once again, Asian experience, obtained while living among other believers, did not lead to an Asian theology of religions. This may be explained in part by the fact that this document limited itself to prayer, so that it would be asking too much of it that it also deal with other theological questions. Perhaps we ought to be happy that the bishops' statement on Christian prayer expressed itself in such a positive manner about the spirituality of the Asian religions in which, even where it is different, Christian believers can discover the presence of God's Spirit and hear the Spirit's voice, calling them to lift their hearts to God.

Further, this recognition asked for a serious dialogue with Asian religions, a dialogue which, according to the bishops, had to be 'fostered and safeguarded by those attitudes which lead to its deepening and its patient, loving growth. These are: openness and sensitivity, honesty and humility of spirit, a sincere disinterestedness and that fraternal love which holds in reverence the feelings of the other and seeks to enter into his heart.'[22] In the description of these attitudes, an echo can be heard of the positive experiences of the Asian bishops and others who, in their dialogue with other believers, have heard, and still hear, the voice of God's Spirit. Because of these experiences, they recommended a completely different attitude toward other religions than was customary in the context of the exclusive Christian thinking about truth and salvation. This was a great step forward. Yet, sometimes the bishops fell back into their old ways of thinking and, as I observed before, sinned against the sensitivity and disinterestedness which they themselves recommended. Maintaining a church-centered approach, it was rather difficult for them to leave the traditional, exclusive Christian way of thinking behind and to meet the other believers in a humble and disinterested manner on the basis of the experience that the voice of God's Spirit is heard in their religious traditions, too.

While FABC II dealt explicitly with inculturation and dialogue with other religions, it was only in its conclusion that it mentioned the dialogue with the poor as one of the tasks 'which the Gospel and the Spirit speaking in the "signs of the times" have given to us and our communities.'[23] Apparently, the bishops found it difficult to connect prayer, the theme of the plenary assembly, with dialogue with the poor. A year later, during the International Congress on Mission, held in Manila in December 1979, the dialogue with the poor returned as one of the forms of dialogue which constitutes the essence of evangelization. Referring to the final document of FABC I, the congress stated that 'the continued building up of the local church [is] the focus of evangelization today, with dialogue as its essential mode, through a more resolute, more creative and yet truly discerning and responsible inculturation; through interreligious dialogue undertaken in all seriousness; through solidarity and sharing with the poor and the advocacy of human rights.'[24] All the same, the repeated stress on the building up of the local church is somewhat surprising, because, at the time, a new view of evangelization was emerging, one which did not start with the church, but was directed more towards the kingdom of God, for the building up of which the church is only an instrument.

The Kingdom of God

This view occurred for the first time in the documents of the so-called Bishops' Institutes for Social Action (BISA).[25] This seems appropriate since, under the influence of liberation theology, the social action of the church was increasingly seen as a commitment to the liberation of the poor in the Spirit of Jesus in order to establish God's kingdom on earth.[26] In this connection BISA III (November 1975) stated that local churches must become more involved in the process of building God's kingdom on earth by promoting, together with the followers of other religious traditions in Asia and with all people of good will, the gospel values of justice, truth, love and peace.[27] From the BISAs, this idea spread to other institutes where, due to the new perspective of liberation theology, concern for problems of poverty and injustice was increasing. Thus the first Bishops' Institute for Interreligious Affairs (BIRA I, October 1979) mentioned 'the needs of our people, a desire for a more just and human society' as the first of 'many contemporary challenges for dialogue,' without, however, speaking explicitly about the kingdom of God.[28] This was done at BIRA II (November 1979), when dialogue with Islam was specifically discussed.

The starting point was that 'from all eternity God has spoken his message to humankind, to make the power of his word rule over the individual and social life of man.'[29] This eternal message of God 'became incarnate in Jesus who announced the Good News of God's reign in this world. The church continues Christ's work of dialogue. Her duty is always to proclaim the reign of God, to bring the proclamation of this message into every aspect of human life, and to seek the fulfillment of all things in Christ.' However, Christians also believe that 'God's saving will is at work, in many different ways, in all religions. It has been stated clearly again by the Second Vatican Council, that the Spirit of Christ is active outside the bounds of the visible church. God's saving grace is not limited to members of the church, but is offered to every person. His grace may lead some to accept baptism and enter the church, but it cannot be presumed that this must always be the case. His ways are mysterious and unfathomable, and no one can dictate the direction of his grace.' When the church proclaims the gospel in this situation, it is 'to call people to the values of the kingdom of God. We find such values also present in Islam. In dialogue, therefore, a Christian hopes that both he and his Muslim brother will turn anew to God's kingdom, their own

faiths richer by their mutual interchange, their mission to the world
more fruitful by their shared insights and commitments.'[30] For most
Christians, this dialogue consists of the so-called 'dialogue of life. This
is the most essential aspect of dialogue, and it is accomplished by
Christians and Muslims living together in peace.'[31]

Excursus: The Salvific Meaning of Islam

BIRA II strongly emphasized the cooperation of Christians and
Muslims in building the kingdom of God. Such cooperation seems fitting because the values of the kingdom of God are also present in Islam.
Remarkable in this connection, however, is the reference to the mysterious and unfathomable character of God's ways. How is this reference to
be explained? For centuries, Christianity tried to find an opening to
Islam, but without visible success. If it is true, however, that God also
gives grace to the Muslims, this centuries-long failure is rather surprising. For why did God's grace not lead the Muslims to faith in Jesus
Christ? Why did they instead refuse to be baptized and to join the
church, even though they were under the influence of God's grace?
Their refusal raises serious questions about the necessity of baptism and
church for salvation. The document answers these questions with some
hesitation: it cannot be presumed that the grace which God offers the
Muslims must always lead to baptism. For the facts seem to contradict
such a presumption in all those countries where Christian minorities
live among Muslim majorities, and have for centuries, without making
any progress. Out of reverence for the mysterious character of God's
gracious presence, in such situations proclamation must not be directed
towards baptism and church, but towards all that Christian and Muslims
have in common because of the working of God's Spirit: the values of
the kingdom of God. By sharing them, Christians and Muslims can
enrich each other's faith and become more committed to their mission
in the world.

While BIRA II was still hesitant in its reply, the special *Consultation
on Christian Presence among Muslims in Asia*, which was organized in
November 1983 by the FABC Office for Interreligious Dialogue and the
Office for Evangelization, spoke more clearly. In their theological reflections, the participants stated explicitly that 'in the mysterious and provi-
dential plan of God Islam possesses a salvific and liberating purpose....

Thus the genuine beliefs and practices of Muslims form the vehicles of God's favor to them and constitute the basis of their human communion and action. The dynamic impact of the character of Mohammed and of the Koran on Muslims throughout their history is something which a Christian cannot overlook. The church believes that salvation is a gift from God offered to all in Jesus Christ.'[32] Besides this statement on the salvific meaning of Islam, the participants also gave some practical advice. Thus they stated that 'dialogue is an encounter with others which demands an attitude of humility, acceptance, honesty and respect.'[33] Further, they pointed to the fact that 'the terms "mission" and "evangelization" ...unfortunately bear negative overtones. In Asia, both terms often connote a sense of cultural superiority, disrespect for the beliefs of others, and colonial chauvinism. We are still paying for the failures of the past, and we must not be surprised if our neighbors of other faiths react negatively to the concepts of "mission" and "evange- lization," although we ourselves may understand them according to a theology which acknowledges the universal activity of God's Spirit.'[34] The participants, however, did not ask how others would react to this theology of God's Spirit. Would this theology, as was suggested, really remove the objections of the people of other faiths? Or would these objections continue, especially when the other people hear that God's Spirit is the Spirit of Christ who operates in the history of humankind to establish Christ's reign on earth and bring all things to fulfillment in Christ? While the participants in the Consultation did take into consid- eration their experiences with Muslims and their religion and so reached a positive evaluation of Islam, they were not yet able to revise their own christology in light of these same experiences. In the end, they tried again to give Islam a place within the framework of christology as it was formulated many centuries ago in a Christian world which did not have the experience of living together with people of other faiths and work- ing together with them in a multireligious society.

The Church at the Service of God's Kingdom

At the Consultation which expressed itself more clearly than BIRA II with regard to the place of Islam in God's plan of salvation, the per- spective of the kingdom of God, so important at BIRA II, was complete- ly absent.[35] It returned, however, very forcefully at BIRA IV/2

(November 1985) which was entirely dedicated to the theme, *The Church at the Service of God's Reign*.[36] The final document opened with a sketch of the situation, in which it was stated once again that the church was still an alien in Asia, 'struggling to free herself from her historical burden, from the stigma of being foreign,' while living 'as a small flock in the midst of vast numbers of peoples who have different beliefs and persuasions.' Further, attention was drawn to the fact that 'the vast majority of the people of Asia are living in utter poverty due to injustice and several other factors.' In this Asia, characterized by religious pluralism and by poverty, the church has 'come to believe more firmly and realize more clearly that the reign of God is the very reason for the being of the church. The church exists in and for the kingdom.' The church is therefore 'an instrument for the actualization of the kingdom.' As such the church 'empties herself and dies like her master... so that she may rise to a new life which approaches the reality of the kingdom.'

This kingdom of God, the document stated, 'is far wider than the church's boundaries.' Even outside the church, 'the kingdom, God's gift and initiative, is made present through the Spirit. Where God is accepted, where the gospel values are lived, where man is respected ...there is the kingdom.' This being so, it is the task of the church in a situation of pluralism and poverty to make common cause with persons of all faiths 'in a dialogue of action to respond to the cry for human dignity, brotherhood and freedom.' This implies that the church must emerge from its 'selfcenteredness' and, together with people of other faiths, dedicate itself 'in a spirit of humble servanthood' to the building of God's kingdom which 'is oriented towards the final manifestation and full perfection of the reign of God.' To this end, 'the formation programs for priests, religious and laity, [must] be geared towards a spirituality which lays greater stress on the values which are expressed in the Word of God, especially in the Beatitudes.' Moreover, the church has to become more aware that it is 'a servant of all in God's reign.' This should lead to a situation where 'Basic Christian Communities' develop into 'Basic Human Communities [in which] men and women of faith and goodwill, strengthened by the experience of common humanity, will join in the building of God's kingdom. In this way, the church of Asia can truly become servant of all.'[37]

For the first time, the Asian bishops stated in an explicit manner that the reason for the existence of the church lies in its being an instrument for the building up of the kingdom of God, which is not to be identified with the church. For the kingdom, more comprehensive and extensive than the church, is also visibly present among people of other faiths. This emphasis on the kingdom of God and the servant role of the church creates a completely different image of the church than the traditional one. Since their first meeting in Manila in November 1970, the Asian bishops had pointed out that the church in Asia was too self-centered, too concerned about its own interests. Hence they called upon the church to truly become the church of the poor and to commit itself, together with people of other faiths, to the establishment of a just society and to the defense of human rights. It was in this connection that they spoke about servanthood and service. Mostly, however, this referred to the bishops themselves and to other church leaders who, after the example of Jesus, had to dedicate themselves to their tasks in a spirit of service.[38] In the final document of BIRA IV/2, on the other hand, servanthood is seen not so much as a virtuous attitude of bishops, but as a constitutive element of the church itself: the church does not exist for itself but for the kingdom of God.

This view of the church also implies that the church has a relative, and hence a temporary and provisional character. The church must empty itself, lose its life and die for the kingdom of God which is the only reason for its existence. The kingdom of God is the reality which ultimately matters. A further consequence of this approach is that several christological questions which occupied an important place in other documents are not considered in BIRA IV/2. This owes to the fact that the concrete problems which are connected with the establishment of the kingdom of God in Asia, marked by the poverty and the exploitation of millions of people, are so immense that the more abstract christological problems lose much of their urgency. The common commitment to the realization of the kingdom of God, in which God's salvation becomes visible and tangible here and now for all people, demands all attention and energy; questions arising from traditional christology around the final place of Christ in the divine economy of salvation are justifiably moved into the background. The important point is that, during his life on earth, Jesus committed himself totally to the establishment of God's kingdom, even unto his death on the cross. It is this point which is repeatedly emphasized in later documents.

Fellow Pilgrims with All People of Good Will

The ideas developed above returned in BIRA IV/3 (November 1986) which had as its theme, *Discerning the Spirit at Work in and Beyond the Church in Asia*. Here, too, we read that 'the Asian realities... compel the church to move out of herself and into fellowship with all people of goodwill as an effective way to work for the reign which Christ proclaimed.' This fellowship is made possible by the fact that 'the same Spirit, who has been active in the incarnation, life, death and resurrection of Jesus and in the church, was active amongst all peoples before the incarnation and is active amongst the nations, religions and peoples of Asia today.' This active presence of the Spirit 'may be discerned in situations where people come together to build human communities based on love and justice.' Further, the document pleads for a broader and deeper knowledge of Asian religions. More important than this knowledge, however, is 'the inculcation of the correct attitude to the working of the Spirit beyond the boundaries of the church.' This working 'may be perceived in a variety of ways. This is due, in part, to the fact that people encounter the Spirit within their context, which is pluralistic in terms of religions, culture and world views.' In this connection, the document recommends 'a stance of receptive pluralism,' thanks to which Christians and people of other faiths open themselves to 'the many ways in which people respond to the promptings of the Holy Spirit,' and receive them with their hearts and minds and see to it that they remain 'continually in conversation with one another.' Thus they may create 'a relationship of dynamic tension [which] may open the way for mutual information, inspiration, support and correction.' This will undoubtedly lead 'to a new era when [Christians], along with [their] Asian brothers and sisters, will jointly make the reign of God more visibly present, a reign of freedom, justice, love and peace.'[39]

The theme of the kingdom of God also played a prominent role in the other meetings of BIRA. It would take too long to study these in detail. Following Jacques Dupuis, I would like to quote some salient texts in which an important thought or special expression is connected with the idea of the kingdom of God. Thus BIRA IV/4 (August 1987), basing itself on FABC III (October 1982),[40] states that 'interreligious dialogue flows from the nature of the church, a community in pilgrimage journeying with peoples of other faiths towards the kingdom that is to come. Interreligious dialogue is an ongoing process of common search for mutual understanding and trust, leading us and our fellow pilgrims towards a deeper appreciation of truth—the truth about God and the human person.'[41] In BIRA IV/6, an ecumenical consultation of the FABC and the Christian Conference of Asia (CCA) on *Living and Working Together with Sisters and Brothers of Other Faiths* (July 1987), this idea is further developed: 'All life has a pilgrim character, and neighbors of other religious traditions are our fellow pilgrims on the way.' This image of being pilgrims together no longer emphasizes the special position of the church possessing the full truth. On the contrary, as pilgrims on the way, all people are equal. The church as pilgrim is, therefore, like all other religions, subject to the uncertainties of pilgrim existence. The church does not possess the truth, but together with other religions it is continually searching for God and God's kingdom which can break through in a surprising way anywhere in this world. For the Spirit of God is not only actively present in the church, it is also actively present in other religions. Hence, on their pilgrimage, all people have to be open to the working of the Spirit. Only then can their conversation, their dialogue on the way, become 'a process of mutual learning and growth,'[42] in which all become more aware of the kingdom of God that is present among them. On the basis of this awareness, they will be able to support and inspire each other in their common commitment to the realization of the kingdom which is the ultimate aim of God's activity in the world.

This last point is emphasized again in another text of the ecumenical consultation, which, in somewhat different language than is customary in FABC documents, states that 'God's recreating activity is prior to and more comprehensive than the church's mission. [Hence,] it directs our attention beyond the church to the kingdom.'[43] In God's plan of salvation, the church clearly has the task of pointing to and serving the kingdom of God. The church shares this task with other religions with which it travels on a pilgrimage toward the kingdom of God, toward ultimate salvation. The coming of the church, therefore, does not mean that other religions cease to be ways of salvation. On the contrary, they remain fellow travelers on the pilgrimage of humankind towards God's kingdom.[44] This will be revealed in its fullness at the end of time, but it is rendered visible among us today when people of all faiths confront the forces of injustice, violence and oppression, and struggle for a better world in the strength of the Spirit. Therefore, as BIRA IV/10 emphasizes, 'we Christians need to abandon our self-image as sole possessors of the kingdom.'[45]

An Indigenous Asian Theological Tradition

This survey of several FABC documents shows clearly that the church in Asia, on the basis of its experiences as a minority in a continent of immense poverty and in the midst of a pluralism of religions, has begun to change its emphasis in its understanding of mission and dialogue. Over the years, the church has developed its own theological tradition within the FABC and its various offices. This, in turn, has led to a clear missionary agenda which has received concrete expression in numerous pastoral directives. Most striking in all this is the emergence and development of the so-called regnocentric or kingdom-centered vision of the mission of the church instead of the more traditional ecclesiocentric vision. In the regnocentric vision, as seen above, the kingdom of God stands at the center while the church, freed from its self-centeredness, commits itself in a spirit of service to the realization of this kingdom through a dialogue of life with people of other faiths in whose struggle for a better world the Spirit of God is actively present. This indigenous Asian vision, however, was not approved by the highest authorities in the Roman Catholic church. This is evident from the opening speech which cardinal J. Tomko, prefect of the Congregation for the Evangelization of Peoples, gave at the fifth plenary assembly of the FABC. This was held in Bandung, Indonesia, in July 1990 and had as its theme, *The Emerging Challenges for the Church in Asia in the 1990s: A Call to Respond*. In his speech, the cardinal anticipated the teachings of the encyclical *Redemptoris Missio* of John Paul II, which appeared half a year later. It was the beginning of a well-orchestrated campaign to discredit the achievements of Asian theology as one of the most important causes of the alleged decrease in missionary activities in Asia.[46]

The Asian church developed its theological vision on mission and dialogue on the basis of its experience within the concrete historical context of Asia. Cardinal Tomko, on the other hand, stated that 'the question of evangelizing the immense continent of Asia..., the challenge of proclaiming Jesus Christ, the Savior of all' must be faced 'apart from the sociological, economic, cultural and religious challenges, and even in some way *above* them.... Conversion and baptism [are to be considered as] a human right of the person concerned, even before they constitute a divine right of the church.'[47] In spite of this pressure, the assembly tried to find its own way. On the whole, it succeeded in this, but here and there compromises were made in order to safeguard Asian theological achievements. Therefore, the final document, *Journeying Together toward the Third Millennium*, showed a certain lack of balance at times, because insights of a contextual experience-based Asian theology were placed next to statements of a more traditional, strongly Western, deductive theology. In this survey, I will limit myself to describing the most important Asian insights with regard to mission and dialogue.

In the Spirit and with the Power of Jesus

The mission of the church is 'a continuation in the Spirit of the mission of Christ. [It] involves a being with the people, as was Jesus: "The Word became flesh and dwelt among us" (Jn 1:14). Therefore, mission includes: being with the people, responding to their needs, with sensitiveness to the presence of God in cultures and other religious traditions, and witnessing to the values of God's kingdom through presence, solidarity, sharing and word. Mission will mean a dialogue with Asia's poor, with its local cultures, and with other religious traditions.... The acting subject of mission is the *local church* living and acting in communion with the universal church. It is the local churches and communities which can discern and work out (in dialogue with each other and with other persons of goodwill) the way the gospel is best proclaimed, the church set up, the values of God's kingdom realized in their own place and time. In fact, it is by responding to and serving the needs of the peoples of Asia that the different Christian communities become truly local churches.'[48] Thus, in contrast to the centralist tendencies of the Vatican, the document explicitly affirmed the competence of the Asian churches to develop their own vision on the mission of the church in light of their specific context.

In line with this affirmation, the document continued, 'Mission may find its greatest urgency in Asia; it also finds in our continent a distinctive mode.... The proclamation of Jesus Christ in Asia means, first of all, the witness of Christians and Christian communities to the values of the kingdom of God, *a proclamation through Christlike deeds*. For Christians in Asia, to proclaim Christ means above all to live like him,

in the midst of our neighbors of other faiths and persuasions, and to do
his deeds by the power of his grace. Proclamation through dialogue and
deeds—this is the first call to the churches in Asia.... But we shall not be
timid when God opens the door for us to *proclaim* explicitly the Lord
Jesus Christ as the Savior and the answer to the fundamental questions
of human existence. We shall proclaim the gospel in the manner of the
Lord Jesus, who expressed his mission in these terms: to preach good
news to the poor...to proclaim release to the captives and recovering of
sight to the blind, to set free those who are oppressed (Lk 4:18–19).[49]

It is evident that, in developing their own vision of mission and dialogue, the Asian churches did not stress the proclamation of the word,
but the witness of life through presence among, and solidarity with,
people. In other words, they did not give in to the strong pressure of the
Vatican which thought that the proclamation of the word had been
neglected and therefore emphasized its urgency, especially in Asia, apart
from the concrete situation in which the churches found themselves. On
the contrary, the Asian churches defended their own, clearly distinct
way of mission, which found its origin in the specifically Asian context
of religious pluralism and massive poverty. In this situation, God wants
them to be good neighbors to people in need. And they can only start
thinking of an explicit proclamation of the word when, through a fundamental change in the situation, God gives them, as it were, a clear sign
that it is pleasing that they start proclaiming, and thus opens the door
for such proclamation. As long as this sign has not been given and the
situation remains as it is, Christians are called 'as *servants of the Lord* and
of *humanity*...to serve the Asian peoples under the leading of the Spirit
of Christ and in the manner of Christ himself who did not come to be
served but to serve and to lay down his life as a ransom for all.' This service to humanity must be given 'in *compassion*, the compassion of Jesus
himself who, like the Good Samaritan, came to bind the wounds of
humanity. It will be a compassion that makes the church weak and powerless with those who are weak and powerless. But it will also be a compassion that will denounce, in deeds, if it is not possible to do so in
words, the injustices, oppressions, exploitations and inequalities resulting
in so much of the suffering that is evident in the Asian situation. Such
compassion will see as fellow members of the one human family under
the Fatherhood of God all exploited women and workers, unwelcome
refugees, victims of violations of human rights, and in fact every needy

human person. This compassion will see even deeper, and will welcome in each human being—but especially the poor, deprived and oppressed— the very person of Christ who has united himself to every human being though he/she may be unaware of it. Such a church will not boast of human power but will serve with the power of the Lord Jesus who emptied himself and took the form of a servant (Phil 2:7), but is, for all who believe, the wisdom and power of God (1 Cor 1:23–24). This church, witnessing by its very being and deeds to the values of the kingdom of God, will be credible when it proclaims with its lips that Jesus is the Savior of the world and the answer to all its longings.'[50]

An Asian Christology

The most striking element in the Asian churches' vision of mission was that it did not start with stating that Christ is the only way to salvation, as cardinal Tomko did in his opening talk and the encyclical *Redemptoris Missio* would do a few months later, in order to conclude with the urgency of the church's task to proclaim the word: 'Woe to me if I do not preach the gospel' (1 Cor 9:16).[51] Confronted with the great needs of the peoples of Asia, the Asian churches found their starting point in the Jesus of the gospels who, confronted with the needs of the people of his own day, committed himself totally, in the power of the Spirit, to proclamation, but above all to the establishment of the kingdom of God, a kingdom of justice and peace. And even though there were references to a more traditional christology, e.g., when 'seeds of the Word' or 'God's plan to bring all things together under Christ as head' are mentioned,[52] they were infrequent and did not change the overall vision of their own mission which the Asian churches had developed. What really mattered to them was 'to patiently work out in collaboration with Christians of other churches and peoples of other religions and persuasions the steps needed to liberate our people from the bondage of sin and its societal manifestations, and to inscribe the values of the kingdom in Asian society.'[53] For the kingdom of God was also Jesus' first and foremost concern. In fact, it was his whole life. Thus the whole life of the Asian churches too must be directed toward the kingdom of God and its establishment in this world.

Therefore, christological questions which emerged after Jesus' death, slowly at first but with ever greater force, did not occupy a primary place in the reflections of the Asian churches. The christocentric interpretation of mission yielded to a gospel-based regnocentric approach.[54] As mentioned already, this shift was influenced by the fact that the experience of God's presence in other religions raised questions within the Asian churches with regard to traditional christology. Does this christology still fit reality as they have come to experience it? Moreover, during the centuries, this christology had blinded many Christians to the treasures of wisdom and beauty in other cultures. Thus it led them to a negative and often rather insensitive attitude toward other religions and gave them a feeling of superiority which is completely alien to the Spirit of Jesus.[55] Against this background it is quite understandable that the Asian bishops found it difficult, if not impossible, to continue with this christology, and looked for the starting point of their reflections to another vision of Christ as it appeared in the gospels.[56] At the same time, one can understand why the Asian bishops placed so much stress on a spirituality of *kenosis*, of emptying oneself in humble service.

An Asian Spirituality of kenosis

Because of traditional christology with its negative attitude toward other religions, the church in Asia found itself in isolation for a long time, which was exacerbated by its links with Western colonial powers. In this situation it was only natural that the church became very self-oriented, continually concerned about maintaining and extending, where possible, the position of power which it had built up through schools and other institutions, with the help and support of colonial authorities. This ecclesiocentric attitude continued to exist even after the colonial powers withdrew from the Asian scene. Living in its own world, the church paid, in many instances, little or no attention to what was happening outside its walls. When, after Vatican II, the leaders of the church became aware of this situation, they wanted to do everything possible to put an end to their isolated position and to start building a truly local church. However, it was not immediately clear what this entailed. It was a long term project. When, in the course of years, they clearly discerned that it was the calling of the church in Asia, in the Spirit of Jesus, to answer the needs of the people by working together with people of other faiths for the realization of God's kingdom, it became evident to them that the church must give up its position of power. After the example of Jesus, the church would have to empty itself and assume the condition of a slave, thus identifying itself with the poor and the marginalized.

This insight, in which the earthly Jesus, and not Christ in glory, occupied a central place, emerged in various parts of the FABC documents, before it was dealt with explicitly in the central chapters of the final document of FABC V (see above). But, as if this were not enough, FABC V returned to it again in its last chapter, which was devoted entirely to developing a spirituality for our time. This spirituality was 'nothing more and nothing less than a following of Jesus-in-mission, an authentic discipleship in the context of Asia. [It] is the spirituality of those who place their complete trust in the Lord. It is the spirituality of the powerless, of the *anawim*. Renunciation and simplicity, compassion for and solidarity with all, and especially with the poor, meekness and humility—virtues promoted by active nonviolence—are some of the significant features of the spirituality we need, and these gospel values resonate deeply with the cultures of Asia. It is a spirituality of harmony. It expresses our intimate communion with God, our docility to his Spirit, our following of Jesus, as we challenge the disharmonies of our Asian world. It moves us away from images of exterior organization, power or mere secular effectiveness to images of simplicity, humble presence and service. By itself then, such spirituality is already a living proclamation of Jesus, the Lord and Savior, unequivocal in its meaning, powerful and far-reaching in its impact.'[57]

The Crucial Role of Other Religions in God's Plan of Salvation

Discussions with the Roman authorities did not cease after the encyclical *Redemptoris Missio* of John Paul II was published on December 8, 1990. On the contrary, they were deliberately continued when, in February 1991, BIRA IV/12 was held to conclude the series of seminars which had been held since 1984 on the theology of dialogue. Against the background of the controversy that had arisen with the Roman authorities, several statements of BIRA IV/12 expressed the position of a local church which had become conscious of its own responsibility and, on the basis of this awareness, wanted to make its own contribution to the universal church.

Summarizing the insights of the previous BIRAs, the final document stated that 'primary among these insights is the realization that the religions of Asia have a crucial role to play in God's great enterprise to bring peace, communion and a more humane way of life to all peoples in Asia, indeed to the whole human family. Following from this insight, is the inescapable truth that God's Spirit is at work in all religious traditions, moving the faithful believers of each tradition to a greater commitment to truth and more authentic communion within and beyond their own tradition.' And with regard to the role of Christians and their churches in Asia, the document declared: 'Finally, we have come to the compelling conviction that for us, Christians, our way to participation in God's enterprise is Jesus, who died in order to find and give life.'[58] Jesus' mission now consisted of sharing 'the Good News of God's dream for the world. He spoke of the dream through the image of God's reign and described it in parables often of life and growth or of reconciliation. We may describe the dream as one of people and communities fully alive.'[59] However, this life is being threatened from all sides by massive poverty, exploitation of resources and destruction of the habitat of many peoples, militarization, discrimination against women, exploitative sex-tourism, the great stream of migrant workers and refugees, and cultural imperialism. 'In the face of these threats to life, human persons and communities are called to stand together in solidarity. Our very survival demands a transcending of social, ethnic and indeed religious boundaries.'[60] This implies for Christians that they can no longer maintain their ghetto mentality. Rather, they have to cooperate with sisters and brothers of other faiths in a dialogue of life which 'must go beyond symptoms (of poverty, injustice, oppression) and attempt to eradicate the causes of dehumanization.' Thus they can create the conditions in which it will be possible to defend and promote true human values. Further, 'for Christians these values are also values of the reign of God.... As Christians we see such work [for the promotion of human values] as proclamation of and preparing the way for the coming of the reign of God.'[61]

It is evident then that Christians find in their own faith and spirituality the necessary support and encouragement to become involved in a dialogue of life. This is not surprising because 'Christian spirituality is at heart a *spirituality of dialogue*... a response in the Spirit to the call of God which comes to us through the Word.... Our response to the Word in the Spirit should be open to the presence of the Word in all creation and particularly in the different cultural and religious traditions.... Such openness demands a *kenosis* modeled after that of Jesus. Christian spirituality is a *spirituality of kenosis*—of powerlessness, of continual purification from self-centeredness, of growing more in openness to our partners in dialogue.'[62] Such openness to the other, especially in showing great sensitivity to the language of the other and to the limitations of our own (which is linked to a Jewish-Christian worldview)[63] makes it possible to feel 'at home with the inner world of the other, seeing and relishing as the other sees and relishes, resonating with the awe and profound reverence with which the other experiences the sense of the divine.'[64] Thus we can 'join other believers on the pilgrimage beyond, celebrating our interdependence and our oneness before the ever-greater Mystery.'[65]

In this light it is clear that 'the church is called to be a community of dialogue. This dialogical model is in fact a new way of being church. Such a church is never centered on itself but on the coming true of God's dream for the world. It seeks not to exclude others but to be truly catholic in its concerns, in its appreciation of the gifts of others, and in its readiness to work with others for a world at once more human and more divine. A church that thus stands with sisters and brothers of other faiths in confronting issues of life and death will necessarily be transformed in the process. In other words, it will become inculturated—at a level which includes but goes deeper than changes in ritual and symbol. Such a church may at last become a church of Asia, not simply a church in Asia. It may then be perceived as no longer an alien presence.'[66] 'In this model of church, dialogue, liberation, inculturation and proclamation are but different aspects of the one reality':[67] a church that is called 'to be more effectively a sign of reconciliation, a sign of the reign of God, a sign of the love of God in Asia,' and therefore works 'with other believers and believing communities for a world where people and communities are fully alive, for a communion of all life, for the final coming true of God's dream.'[68]

The Ever-greater Mystery of God

The final document of BIRA IV/12 thus continued the regnocentric stance of previous BIRA seminars and of FABC V. Both at the beginning and the end, the document explicitly mentioned the kingdom of God as the goal to which the church, together with all believers and all people of good will, must strive through the realization of human values. From the outset it is evident that its definition of mission finds its basis in the earthly Jesus. He is for Christians the way to participate in God's plan for the world. Given this starting point, it is not surprising that BIRA IV/12 placed such strong emphasis on the spirituality of *kenosis*, for it was this emptying out that was the most fundamental characteristic of Jesus' earthly life. This spirituality, however, obtains new content in accordance with the development of interreligious dialogue in the final document. It seems to me that the real contribution of BIRA IV/12 to the building up of an Asian theology of dialogue is to be found here.

At the first possible occasion, the final document stated very forcefully that the religions of Asia fulfill a crucial role in God's plan. In previous documents, the bishops spoke about cooperating with the people of other faiths toward the establishment of God's kingdom, and about contributing to the mutual growth of all believers by recognizing and realizing human values. Nowhere, however, did they refer in such explicit terms to 'the crucial role' of other religions in God's plan. Also, they described the active presence of the Spirit in somewhat different terms. The Spirit does not lead people of other faiths to be more committed to finding the truth outside their traditions in Christianity, but within their own traditions and beyond in the ever-greater mystery of God, before which Christians and other believers are one. Moreover, the Spirit moves people of other faiths to become more involved in building a true communion within their own Hindu, Buddhist or Muslim traditions and beyond these in the common realization of the kingdom of God. The communion of the church is not mentioned here as one of the realities to which the Spirit moves the other believers.

If the Spirit of God is actively present among the people of other faiths, it is a matter of great urgency for Christians to try to understand or, as the document says, 'to feel at home with the inner world of the other,' in order to hear the voice of God. This task can only be accomplished if they understand the languages of others, for language is the bridge to others, to their cultures. It is in this context that BIRA IV/12 speaks about the need for a kenotic spirituality which motivates Christians to empty themselves of that particular intellectual and emotional content that is, often unconsciously, present in Jewish-Christian religious language and that, on account of its close link with the Jewish-Christian tradition, may form an obstacle to real communication with people of other faith traditions. For only by practicing such a *kenosis*, will Christians be able to grow toward a greater openness to other believers, their myths, their rituals and symbols, and so feel at home with them and their experiences of the sacred, of God. This plea for a kenotic spirituality not only manifests a great respect for other believers and their deepest religious feelings, but, surprisingly for a church document, it also speaks a very refreshing and inviting language, in which Asian Christians express their sincere admiration and gratitude for the presence of God's Spirit, which they have been allowed to experience in all the good and beautiful things the Spirit works out among people of other faiths.[69]

It is remarkable that, while making these new emphases, BIRA IV/12 does not make any attempt to give its views a christological foundation. This is all the more remarkable because, as already mentioned, the mission encyclical *Redemptoris Missio*, with its strong christocentric approach, was known to the participants of BIRA IV/12. In fact, this encyclical did not play any significant role in the final document where it is only mentioned once, in a passage of little importance towards the end, as a document which encourages interreligious dialogue.[70] It is evident that, during BIRA IV/12, the Asian churches followed their own way in the development of a regnocentric view of mission and dialogue which was founded on a profound reverence and respect for the mystery of God and for God's presence in the Spirit who inspires Christians and people of other faiths to a greater commitment to the realization of God's dream—the dream for which Jesus gave his life.

The Church: Servant of the Asian Peoples

This development continued in the *Conclusions of the Theological Consultation, FABC Office for Evangelization* (November 1991). However, it clearly met greater opposition, which resulted in a final document that is very unbalanced because both views, the traditional and the Asian, are placed next to each other. After an analysis of the Asian situation, the document continued with a rather critical consideration of the local church as a social institution: 'The lingering colonial image survives in its traditional ecclesiastical structures and economic dependence on the west.... The church remains foreign in its lifestyle, in its institutional structure, in its worship, in its western-trained leadership and in its theology.... The church is often giving a counter-witness to its evangelizing mission. This is most notable in its lack of practical identification with the poor, its lack of concrete involvement in interfaith dialogue and its lack of real interest in interculturation. In many cases the church fails to raise a prophetic voice in matters of injustice because of her minority situation as a community.... We are still reluctant to study Asian languages, cultures and the arts. Often enough the church exculturates new converts from their own societies. In short, there is a gap between the vision statements of FABC on the triple dialogue with the poor, with cultures and with religions and the everyday life of the churches. The church is an institution planted in Asia rather than an evangelizing community of Asia.'[71] Against this background, the participants continued 'to dream of an Asian church which feels at home in her own culture: well-educated and ensouled in the cultural traditions of the Asian countries.... In this effort [of inculturation] we need courageous and creative initiators rather than detailed directives and norms. To this end, the churches must be free to exercise their legitimate autonomy in making important decisions, without undue interference from higher authority.'[72]

This Asian church, of which the participants dreamed, must be 'a servant church.' In a very beautiful and inspiring passage, the document states: 'We dream of a servant church: servant of God, servant of Christ, servant of his plan of salvation; servant also of the Asian peoples, of their deep hopes, longings and aspirations; servant of the followers of other religions, of all women and men, simply and totally for others. A servant church has no pretensions and no exigencies. A servant church does not insist upon its rights; she offers her services, without getting offended when they are not accepted. A servant church keeps silence when bypassed, forgotten or unfairly treated. In a servant church, the structures of the church herself are at the service of the gospel and of the people.... Thus structures are for the church, not the church for structures.... A servant church is not afraid of being a minority. She is a pilgrim church on the way to the kingdom. She is primarily a faith community, expressing and proclaiming kingdom values. She does not place herself at the center. Thus in theology, she is not centered on herself but on Christ. In her teaching she clearly distinguishes between the gospel and her own doctrinal understanding of it. In daily life, she puts doing the truth before formulations of doctrine.'[73] And the document ends: 'Since doing the truth comes before the formulation of doctrine, the churches in Asia should not await a satisfactory theological answer before going further in the praxis of dialogue and proclamation. It is in the systematic reflection on sustained praxis that we shall discover what God is saying to the churches. Therefore everybody has to be encouraged to become more and more involved in the threefold dialogue and proclamation at grassroots level. In the meantime theologians should be given the freedom to work creatively on these issues, reflecting upon the dialogical praxis of the local churches.'[74]

Undoubtedly, the participants in the theological consultation did not want to force their experiences with the practice of interreligious dialogue into the straitjacket of traditional doctrinal formulations. On the contrary, they wanted to make their experiences the starting point of a new theology. Notwithstanding their plea, which they justified with an appeal to the legitimate autonomy of local churches, they did not succeed in executing their plans at the consultation. They gave in to the pressure of 'higher authorities.' Thus, a series of theological reflections on 'the evangelizing mission of the local churches' was added onto their conclusions.[75] These reflections proceeded in a purely aprioristic manner and hence were full of quotations from various church documents, mainly the encyclical *Redemptoris Missio* and the document *Dialogue and Proclamation*, jointly issued by the Pontifical Council for Interreligious Dialogue and the Congregation for the Evangelization of Peoples on May 19, 1991. Here and there, the participants tried to rescue something, but on the whole the voice of Asian experience and of the theology based thereon was buried under the doctrinal pronouncements of the central authorities. These only repeated traditional christology and the urgency, deduced therefrom, to proclaim Jesus Christ to the masses that do not know him, especially in Asia. They did not show, however, any understanding of the new insights that were developing in the local churches of Asia on the basis of their experiences as communities of faith in a world of multiple religions.

The participants still succeeded, though, in inserting into the conclusion of the final document the statement that they 'have reflected upon and tried to clarify some theological issues raised by the Asian situation where the church is in a religious minority, in particular upon the question of the centrality of Jesus Christ in the context of evangeliza-

tion, dialogue and proclamation.' But they 'do not claim to have fully
succeeded.' Their response remains 'open and tentative.' Moreover, they
admitted in all honesty that 'it has become clear that there are more
questions than answers.' Certainly, there have been all kinds of documents produced from Vatican II to the present time. These 'have been a
first prophetic attempt at formulating the crucial problem of the relationship between dialogue and proclamation. Yet they are not the last
word. They are open to new horizons,' which will become clear in
'reflecting upon the dialogical praxis of the local churches.'[76] Will this
ever happen? For a person of faith, nothing is impossible. Many obstacles, however, will have to be overcome, as the results of the consultation
clearly show. The central authorities will use every opportunity to try
to impose their own views. And as is evident from the talk of cardinal
Tomko at the consistory, they will not hesitate to put theologians in Asia
in a bad light.[77]

CHAPTER THREE

Francis' Relevance Today

A comparison between Francis' approach to Islam and the ideas that are now alive at the center of the church and in the local Asian churches with regard to interreligious dialogue, shows many points of contact. It is not my intention to pursue these in detail. I limit myself to a general consideration of some fundamental points. In doing so, a certain repetition of words and ideas from the previous chapters is unavoidable.

'Among the Saracens'

Both the papal magisterium at the center of the church and the episcopal magisterium in the local Asian churches at the periphery have undergone a process of development since Vatican II. When we compare these developments, it appears that center and periphery are moving in opposite directions. Both start from the documents of Vatican II, but, under the influence of conservative forces, the papal magisterium returns increasingly to the traditional theology of salvation in which election and salvation in Christ are central. The Asian bishops, on the other hand, continue to move further in the direction indicated by the council which begins with the theology of creation.[1] For, following the lead of the council, the Asian bishops begin their reflections on the meaning of other religions with God's universal salvific will, which embraces the whole of humanity. All people have been created by God; they receive their life from God on their pilgrimage through history and are destined by God to find eternal happiness. God is origin, provider and final goal for all people. Through the creating and lifegiving Spirit, God is always graciously present and active in the life of every human person as source of all that is true and good.

The choice of this starting point and its continuous reaffirmation in the documents of their conferences is not accidental. On the contrary, the Asian bishops and their Christian communities had to proceed in this way when, after the Second Vatican Council, they were confronted with the task of becoming local churches in Asia. For it was then that they became aware, for the first time, of the place in which they lived, and of the cultures and traditions which they shared with millions of people of other religious convictions. It was then, too, that they were able to discern the creative activity of God's Spirit among people of other faiths who, inspired by their faiths, live the religious and moral values that are preserved in their age-old traditions. The kingdom of God, the kingdom of justice and peace, is not the monopoly of Christians. It is also manifest in the wonderful variety of good and beautiful things which the people of other faiths realize in their everyday lives. If they are prepared to listen, Christians can hear the voice of the Spirit everywhere around them, calling them to work together with people of other faiths in building the kingdom of God. This voice calls them ever more insistently, as is evident from the later documents of the FABC which show a great admiration for the cultures and religions of other believers and for the crucial role they play in God's plan of salvation. This profound change from the earlier negative attitude of the Asian churches is thus intimately connected with the fact that the churches abdicate their privileged position of power and give up their feeling of superiority in order to share in the ordinary everyday life of other believers. Or, as Felix Wilfred formulates it briefly, this change occurs when the churches shift from the macro to the micro level.[2]

Undoubtedly, it will be rather difficult and painful for the churches to find a place at the periphery and no longer put themselves in the center, to see themselves as servants of the kingdom of God, which they are called to establish with all people of good will, and not as the one, divinely elected community of salvation with all the privileges flowing from this election. The Asian churches are not alone in having to make this shift. In the course of history, people and movements have continually been obliged to change place in order to discern and realize their callings in the world. So it was for Francis and his first brothers. They explicitly refused to accept the church's macro-political thinking in terms of power, which manifested itself at that time in the crusades against the Muslims. Instead, by divine inspiration, they went, without arms and violence, to the Saracens in order to live among them in peace and to be subject to them. In other words, Francis and his brothers opted for a dialogue on the micro level where they could share and experience the life of the Saracens. In so doing, they began a learning process through which prejudices could be broken down and a new mutual understanding and trust be built up. From their new place among the Saracens, they were able to experience all the good in the lives and faith of the Saracens, and learn that God, who is the source of all good, was also present and active among them. They were, therefore, not allowed to damage or destroy the good that was present among the Saracens and had its origin in God. Rather, they had to give it back to God in gratitude. After his return to Italy, Francis did so, among other ways, by calling the Christians to a greater respect for the names and the written word of God, in accordance with what he had seen and admired among the Saracens. He also showed great respect for the books of the pagans, for all the good to be found therein did not belong to the pagans or any other person, but to God (1 *Cel* 82).

By bringing this approach to life again in today's world, especially in Asia, the followers of Francis can make an important contribution to interreligious dialogue. Inspired by Francis' attitude, they too will be able to show great respect for the holy books of other religions and to develop a greater sensitivity to the myths and symbols in which the people of other faiths try to give expression to their deepest experiences of God; but above all, out of reverence for the active presence of God's Spirit among other believers, they will be ready to cooperate with them in a dialogue of life for the establishment of the kingdom of God. Thus none of the good that God works among the people of other faiths will be lost. On the contrary, it will be returned thirty, sixty, even a hundredfold to God from whom it comes and to whom it belongs.

An indispensable condition for realizing this approach is that the brothers 'change place.' The brothers must find a place among people of other faiths and share their lives as fully as possible. Only then will they, like Francis, be able to discern and experience the presence of God among the other believers. Only then will they be able to allow this experience, together with all the questions it raises, to penetrate their minds and hearts and change and convert them. This also implies that those who find themselves at the center of the church and are very much concerned with preserving the Christian faith in all its purity, will find it difficult, if not impossible, to understand the developments that are occurring at the periphery. For this reason there will always be conflicts unless the leaders at the center become more aware of the limited, historically and culturally conditioned character of their expressions of faith. This awareness will create the necessary atmosphere in which they can acknowledge the legitimacy of the views developed at the periphery and accept them as a real and important contribution to a greater catholicity.

In the Spirit of Jesus

In his mission encyclical *Redemptoris Missio*, John Paul II starts his reflections with a christology in which Christ is the only mediator and there is no salvation except in him. This implies, among other things that, in the case of missionary activities, a strong emphasis is placed on the proclamation of Jesus Christ as the savior of the world and on the establishment and the extension of the church founded by Christ as the community of salvation in which he is visibly and audibly present among the faithful through word and sacrament. This leads to an ecclesiocentric view of mission. The Asian bishops, however, no longer consider such a view adequate for their situation. For in the recent past it produced a church which was alien to Asia and self-centeredly sought to maintain and even strengthen itself and its position of power. The Asian bishops after Vatican II wanted to change this situation. Through their efforts they wanted to achieve a church that is no longer a church in Asia, but a church of Asia which, in the Spirit of Jesus, together with the followers of other religions, commits itself to an intense dialogue of life which will lead to the establishment and the extension of the kingdom of God. Especially in the later documents of the FABC, which formulate a more developed Asian theology of mission and dialogue, the bishops speak frequently of the church as a servant of the kingdom of God. In doing so, they are not inspired by Christ in glory, but rather by the earthly, historical Jesus who did not come to be served, but to serve and to give his life in faithfulness to his ideal: the kingdom of God.

Against this background, the Asian bishops stated at FABC V (July 1990) that, for them, mission 'involves a being with the people, as was

Jesus...responding to their needs, with sensitiveness to the presence of God in cultures and other religious traditions, and witnessing to the values of God's kingdom through presence, solidarity, sharing.' And a little further on, the bishops repeated their view: mission, 'the proclamation of Jesus in Asia means, first of all, the witness of Christians and of Christian communities to the values of the kingdom of God, *a proclamation through Christlike deeds.* For Christians in Asia, to proclaim Christ means above all to live like him, in the midst of our neighbors of other faiths and persuasions, and to do his deeds by the power of his grace.'[3] If the Asian churches want to realize this missionary task, a one-time change of place is not sufficient. They will have to cultivate a completely new attitude, a new spirituality. In this context, the Asian bishops speak about a 'spirituality of the powerless, of the *anawim*,'[4] and 'a spirituality of *kenosis*.'[5] Both are characterized by not being self-centered, by renunciation and simplicity, and by openness to the other, by compassion and solidarity, by humble presence and service.

This description of the bishops' view on mission and the spirituality required for its realization, raises immediate associations with the way in which Francis and his brothers understood their mission, their going among the Saracens in the Spirit of the Lord. The brothers did not go as representatives of those in power; they did not go to subject others. They went in order 'to live among the Saracens' and 'to be subject to them for God's sake' (RegNB 16:5–6). Their model was the historical Jesus in whose life of service and solidarity God was revealed as humility.[6] Because of this God, they did not want to hold power or dominion over others, nor to be greater. Rather, after the example of Jesus, they wanted to be the lesser ones, ministers and servants (cf. RegNB 5:10–12), and as such stay among the Saracens in the Spirit of the Lord in humility, being subject to them. In this way, they hoped to put an end to the existing enmity and to build a new relationship of friendship and solidarity; they hoped to realize the vision of peace where sheep and wolves live together: a new world, not based on power, but on mutual service to each other in everyday life. When the brothers live in this manner, then, Francis said, 'they confess that they are Christians' (RegNB 16:6), not by words, but by the witness of their lives.

The similarities between the way in which Francis, at the beginning of the thirteenth century, saw the relation between Christians and Muslims, and the way in which the Asian bishops at the end of the twentieth century speak about mission and dialogue, are very striking indeed. Both Francis and the Asian bishops emphasize being among other people and living together with them, in humble service and solidarity. Both emphasize the proclamation of Jesus Christ not by words, but by deeds. This is not very surprising because both start with the historical Jesus and base their mission method on the way in which Jesus dealt with people in his attempt to bring them peace and to establish the kingdom of God. It is all the more remarkable, though—or maybe not, considering Jesus' own fate—that this evangelical approach in which the kingdom of God is central, meets with such strong opposition and all too often has to give way to the more ecclesiocentric approach. This danger also threatens the church of Asia at the present moment due to pressures from the center. In this situation, the followers of Francis in Asia can make an important contribution to the development of a truly Asian view and practice of mission and dialogue. Inspired by the example of Francis and his first brothers, they should go among the people of other faiths in humble service in the Spirit of Jesus. Thus they will be in a position, through a continuous dialogue of life, to discern the presence of God among the other believers and to appreciate all the good God has worked in their midst. Grateful for all this, they will want to bring the good God has begun to its fulfillment with others through their common commitment to establishing the kingdom of God. It is in this way, by their lives and their commitment to the values of God's kingdom, rather than by their direct proclamation, that the brothers will confess to be Christians. In turn, this Asian missionary practice could inspire the local churches, especially in Europe and America, in their mission to work together with people of other faiths in building up God's kingdom in an increasingly multicultural and multireligious European and American society.

'When it pleases the Lord'

As I observed earlier, the creative, lifegiving presence of the Spirit of God among people of other faiths is one of the most important insights of which the Asian bishops have become convinced over the years. It is this Spirit who has helped to give form and shape to the cultures and religious traditions of Asia. They are therefore not purely natural, humanly made religions, as was often said in the past. On the contrary, in the Asian religions, although differently from Christianity, the voice of God's Spirit can be heard calling both other believers and Christians to direct themselves in prayer to God. The other religions are vehicles of grace and ways to salvation and liberation for their followers. God's creating and redeeming activity thus passes beyond the boundaries of the church. Naturally, this insight has its impact on the place and role of the church within God's plan of salvation. It invites a greater modesty with regard to certain claims that were made in the past about the church as a necessary means of salvation—a claim that still resounds at this moment in the mission encyclical of John Paul II. This is especially evident in the way in which the encyclical, from the very beginning, speaks about the urgent necessity to give new impulse to missionary activity in Asia. For there the number of people is still growing 'who do not yet believe in Christ, who are far from Christ, in whom the church has not yet taken root and whose culture has not yet been influenced by the gospel.'[7]

The way in which John Paul formulates the reason why Christians must proclaim Christ with great urgency to the Asian people and plant the church among them, contrasts sharply with the way in which the Asian bishops speak about their experience of the working of the Spirit in the lives of their Asian neighbors. They have seen with their own eyes how the Spirit makes the values of the gospel, of the kingdom of God, grow among them. Out of reverence for this gracious presence of the Spirit, the Asian bishops do not consider it justifiable to follow John Paul's view on church and mission. Their main concern is to work as Jesus did, guided by the Spirit of God, to establish the kingdom of God and, together with the other believers, to help it sink deeper roots in the Asian world for the liberation of the poor and oppressed. The bishops cannot wait any longer for this mission, because time presses. However, regarding the proclamation of Jesus Christ and the establishment of the church, they take a rather expectant attitude. It depends on the circumstances or, as Vatican II says, on the signs of the times. In the present situation of Asia, with the poverty of its masses and the riches of its religious pluralism, the signs point clearly in the direction of a dialogue of life with the people of other faiths for the building up of God's kingdom of justice and peace. It cannot, however, be ruled out that, as the bishops formulated it at FABC V, at a certain moment 'God opens the door for us to proclaim explicitly the Lord Jesus Christ as the savior and the answer to the fundamental questions of human existence.' When this happens, they will 'not be timid,' notwithstanding what is sometimes suggested by their opponents. Rather, they will then 'proclaim the gospel in the manner of the Lord Jesus, who expressed his mission in these terms: The Spirit of the Lord is upon me, because he has anointed me to preach good news to the poor. He has sent me to proclaim release to the captives and recovering of sight to the blind, to set free those who are oppressed, to proclaim the acceptable year of the Lord (Lk 4:18–19).'[8]

Again, the similarity between the views of the Asian bishops and those of Francis and his brothers is striking, regarding both their starting points and their ultimate solutions. For Francis and his brothers, too, the starting point for their view was the experience they had during their stay among the Saracens. There and then, from their new place, they experienced for themselves how God is the source of much good in the life of the Saracens. This experience truly enriched them. It enabled them to acknowledge the limitations of accepted theological arguments and to penetrate more deeply into the mystery of God whose gracious presence even extends beyond the boundaries of Christianity. Out of reverence for and obedience to this God, who includes the Saracens in the divine pleasure, Francis and his brothers subject themselves to the plans which God has for the Saracens. Before they pass on to explicit proclamation, they will wait until the Lord gives them a sign so they can see clearly that it pleases the Lord that they announce the word of God (RegNB 16:7).

The true spirit of admiration and reverence for the mystery of God, which is evident in this approach, did not often prevail, even among Francis' followers, and had to make room for a dangerous shortsightedness which originates in the absolutizing of doctrinal formulations about Christ and his church as the necessary means of salvation. It is this shortsightedness which, in the course of history, produced an aggressive proclamation of the Christian faith which caused more harm than good for the realization of God's plan of salvation. For in the name of God and Christ, peoples and their cultures have been destroyed. Yet God, from whom all good comes, wants nothing more than that people live together in peace and mutual service to each other and cooperate so that the God-given good may grow and bear fruit in the realization of God's kingdom. The followers of Francis ought to recognize this shortsightedness wherever it occurs in an open or hidden form. Here, too, they can be of great help, on the basis of their Franciscan inspiration, in solving a very real problem which not only affects the local churches in Asia, but the entire church everywhere in the world.

The Ever-greater Mystery

In the beginning, following the documents of Vatican II, the Asian bishops showed a positive appreciation of other religions, because of the presence of the so-called 'seeds of the Word.' This appreciation was thus based on what these religions had in common with Christianity. Slowly, however, a change occurred. The religions became increasingly appreciated because of their differences from Christianity. This change, too, had everything to do with the 'change of place' which the Asian churches opted for when they discovered that they were aliens in their own countries. Initially, the bishops tried to fit the other religions into the framework of the traditional theology of salvation by considering them preparations for Christianity in which the 'seeds of the Word' present in them would find their fulfillment. But their new experiences among other believers started moving bishops in a different direction. The other religions were, precisely in their otherness, seen as expressions of the ever-greater mystery of God. For this mystery cannot be fully understood and expressed in any religion, Christianity included. Every religion, therefore, can be no more than a limited, historically and culturally conditioned expression of the one divine mystery. This implies that, in order to create the possibility of an ever richer and fuller knowledge of the divine mystery, it has to be expressed in as many different cultures and in as great a variety of narratives and symbols as possible. For this reason, the pluriformity of religions is not a sinful imperfection which has to be ended as soon as possible in the name of the one Truth and the one true religion. On the contrary, the one Truth asks that, out of reverence for each religion's otherness in giving expression to the Truth, all religions join in supporting and enriching each other on their common pilgrimage to God, to the Absolute. Moreover, as partners, they ought to cooperate, each in their own way, in transforming their insights into the mystery of God into a liberating truth through deeds of liberation and salvation for humanity.[9]

Reverence for each religion's otherness as a gift of God from whom all good things come, and the bringing together of all these gifts in harmony for the peace and salvation of humanity: these matters were also very dear to Francis. Francis did not want uniformity, precisely because he had such great reverence for all that the Spirit of God inspired individual persons to do (RegNB 2:1; 16:3; LetLeo 3). For this reason he also wished to respect the individual consciences of his brothers and their decisions (RegNB 5:2; Adm 3:7). When, during his stay among the Muslims, he experienced how God had graciously accepted them in the otherness of their religion and culture and blessed them with good gifts, he knew that he too had to accept the Muslims in their otherness and approach them with respect for God's sake. It is this respect for the other believers in their otherness which Francis asks from his brothers today. To this end, the brothers must develop in themselves a great sensitivity for the good that God works in the people of other faiths. They must never cease to look with admiration and gratitude to all the deeds of goodness and love, of justice and peace, to which the Spirit of God inspires them through their own religious traditions. If the brothers follow the example of Francis, they will learn to discern the true value of the pluriformity of religions and to look at it as an invitation to journey together with other believers on their common pilgrimage to the ever-greater mystery: the most high and supreme God to whom they return all good things, wherever they find them, because they come from God who alone is good (cf. RegNB 17:17–18; 23:9).

Endnotes

FOREWORD

1. Ewert H. Cousins, *Christ of the 21st Century* (Rockport, MA: Element, 1992), 112.

PART ONE: Introduction

1.   H. Roscher, *Papst Innocenz III und die Kreuzzüge*, Göttingen, 1969, 140–169; J. M. Powell, *Anatomy of a Crusade, 1213–1221*, Philadelphia, 1986, 15–32.
2.   PL 216, 824.
3.   PL 216, 817–822. An English translation can be found in L. and J. Riley-Smith, *The Crusades, Idea and Reality, 1095–1274*, London, 1981, 118–124.
4.   PL 216, 822.
5.   PL 216, 818–821 passim; Riley-Smith, o.c., 121–124.
6.   COD 271.
7.   PL 216, 818. The etymological origin of the word 'Saracens' is uncertain. As early as the sixth century, Greek authors used the term 'Saracens' as an ethnic classification for both the pagan and the Christian inhabitants of the Arab peninsula. Hence the term was also applied, without any prejudice, to the Arabs after they had become Muslims. Only afterwards did the term acquire negative religious connotations. A similar development took place in the Latin world. Until the end of the eighth century, the name Saracens was religiously indifferent. A change occurred in the course of the ninth century when Italy was continually attacked by the Saracens. This threat to the Christian world resulted in a different religious and theological appreciation of the Saracens who had become enemies of the Christians. This found expression in the use of adjectives like *nefandi, odibiles, impii, perfidi, nequissimi*, and *barbari*. Also, the heavily loaded idea of the Antichrist emerged at that time. See R. C. Schwinges, *Kreuzzugsideologie und Toleranz: Studien zu Wilhelm von Tyrus*, Stuttgart, 1977, 70; 98–104; C. A. Willemsen, 'Sarazenen,' in *Lexikon für Theologie und Kirche* 9 (1964) 326. Within this negative context, we must also place the opinion of several canonists who, under the influence of St. Jerome, hold that the Saracens should really be

called *Agareni*. For the name Saracens is according to them derived from
Sara, Abraham's wife. This derivation, however, is in their opinion historically incorrect since the Saracens do not descend from Sara, but from
Hagar, the slave woman. See H. Gilles, 'Législation et doctrine canoniques
sur les Sarracins,' in *Islam et chrétiens du Midi (XIIe–XIVe s.)*, Toulouse, 1983,
195–213, here 198; Schwinges, o.c., 70. Innocent III uses the name *Agareni* in
his sermon at the opening of the Fourth Lateran Council: 'What a shame,
what an embarrassment, what a disgrace that the sons of the servant, the
most despicable *Agareni*, detain our mother: the mother of all the believers
has been made a servant' (PL 217, 676).

8. D. Flood, *Die Regula non bullata der Minderbrüder*, Werl, 1967, 125–133. Cf.
also F. Vocking, 'Franciscus en het IVe Lateraans Concilie,' *FL* 45 (1962) 47–59,
78–94, 132–152; 46 (1963) 6–20, 40–50, 67–81, 109–123, 131–143.

9. *Francis and Clare: The Complete Works*, trans. Regis J. Armstrong, OFM Cap.
and Ignatius C. Brady, OFM, New York, 1982, 49–53.

10. *Quia maior*, PL 216, 817; Riley-Smith, 120.

11. Ibid.; Riley-Smith, 119.

12. *2 Cel* 30.

13. Roscher (o.c., 273) observes that it is remarkable how often Innocent III uses
words like *effectus*, *efficax*, etc. A very clear example of Innocent's desire for
an effective outcome of the crusade is, according to Roscher, the following
play on words: the *affectus*, the will to help the Holy Land, is in itself not
sufficient; the Christians have to persevere until the *effectus* follows. Cf. PL
216, 892.

14. Cf. the witness of Thomas of Split, *Omnibus*, 1601.

15. K. Esser, 'Das missionarische Anliegen des hl. Franziskus,' *WissWeis* 35 (1972)
12–18, also found in 'Missionszentrale der Franziskaner,' *Bruder aller
Menschen, Der missionarische Aufbruch in Franziskus von Assisi*, Werl, 1976,
11–19; W. Bühlmann, 'Das Missionsverständnis bei Franziskus nach der
Regula non bullata,' in A. Camps und G. Hunold, *Erschaffe mir ein neues
Volk*, Mettingen, 1982, 13–29. English translation: 'Francis and Mission
According to the Rule of 1221,' in 'Mission in the Franciscan Tradition,'
Spirit and Life: A Journal of Contemporary Franciscanism 6 (1994) 87–107; L.
Lehmann, 'Grundzüge franziskanischen Missionsverständnisses nach
Regula non Bullata 16,' *FranzStud* 66 (1984) 68–81. English translation: 'Main
Features of the Franciscan Understanding of Mission According to the Rule
of 1221,' *FrancDig* II, 1 (Jan. 1992) 1–20; abbreviated: Features; A. Rotzetter,
'Die missionarische Dimension des franziskanischen Charismas,' *FranzStud*
66 (1984) 82–90. English translation: 'The Missionary Dimension of the
Franciscan Charism,' *Spirit and Life: A Journal of Contemporary
Franciscanism* 6 (1994) 47–57; abbreviated: Missionary Dimension; D. Flood,
'Assisi's Rules and People's Needs: The Initial Determination of the
Franciscan Mission,' *FranzStud* 66 (1984) 91–104, reprinted in *FrancDig* II, 2

(June 1992) 69–89; abbreviated: Assisi's Rules; J. G. Jeusset, *Dieu est courtoisie: François d'Assise, son Ordre et l'Islam*, Nantes, 1985, 55–68; H. Sevenhoven, 'Leven te midden van de Saracenen: De universaliteit van Franciscus' zending,' *FL* 73 (1990) 201–211. Whenever an English translation is indicated, I will refer to it in the notes.

16. Beside the studies of Roscher and Powell mentioned above, cf. especially B. Z. Kedar, *Crusade and Mission*, Princeton, 1984; R. Pernoud, *The Crusaders*, Edinburgh; P. Raedts, 'The Children's Crusade of 1212,' *Journal of Medieval History* 3 (1977) 280–323. Further literature will be indicated when these persons and tendencies are dealt with more explicitly. Special reference must be made here to a recent study which appeared after the publication of the original Dutch version of this book in January, 1994: Christoph T. Maier, *Preaching the Crusades: Mendicant Friars and the Cross in the Thirteenth Century*, Cambridge, 1994. In the first chapter, Maier explicitly deals with Francis and his attitude toward the fifth crusade. To my great amazement, however, he never even mentions RegNB 16 or any other of Francis' writings. Instead, Maier bases his treatment of Francis only on the biographies, and especially on the stories of Brother Illuminatus. For these stories, see 59–60, 74–75.

PART ONE: Chapter 1

1. For this view, see especially D. Flood, *Francis of Assisi and the Franciscan Movement*, Quezon City, 1989; abbreviated *Francis of Assisi*.
2. Roscher, o.c., 49–50; Schwinges, o.c., 7–8.
3. Roscher, o.c., 57–58.
4. 'In Gregory VIII's call for the third crusade, the 'statuta' made up one seventh of the text. In Innocent III's call for the fourth crusade in August 1!98, they take half the space, while in the call of April 1213 they are extended to about two thirds of the encyclical' (Roscher, o.c., 271).
5. 'the apogee of papal crusading propaganda' (Riley-Smith o.c., 118); 'the synthesis of the ideology of the crusade movement' (Powell, o.c., 17).
6. Cf. the separate letter *Pium et sanctum propositum* which Innocent wrote to instruct the crusade preachers: 'In order to vindicate the injury of the Crucified One, you must animate his faithful with great care and accurate attention, as it is contained in the encyclical, executing carefully and effectively everything you will see has been included in the same letter for the aid of the Holy Land, which we wish you to note most carefully' (PL 216, 822). See Riley-Smith, o.c., 131.
7. I will closely follow the line of thought of the encyclical. In order not to overburden the reader, I will not give a reference for each passage. As far as the translation is concerned, I use that of Riley-Smith, mentioned in the Introduction, with some minor modifications.

8. The motive of the *occasio salutis* was developed especially by Bernard of Clairvaux. After a long introduction, he starts the real call for the second crusade with the text from Paul's second letter to the Corinthians: 'Now is the favourable time; now is the day of salvation' (6:2). See Roscher, o.c., 269–272. Later, I will return to this motive.

9. Roscher, o.c., 282–283. Riley-Smith makes the following observations regarding this feudal imagery: 'And his [Innocent's] fondness for using images drawn from the everyday world could be theologically dangerous. For instance, he liked to compare Christ to a secular king, to whom was owed the loyalty of a subject and the services of a vassal, and it is clear that these words of his made a great impression.' Yet, 'churchmen were not happy with the feudal analogy, because a feudal relationship was contractual and involved reciprocal obligations, which was most definitely not the case with man's relationship with God.' But they 'could hardly avoid using it when trying to put across an appeal to fight for God in terms the laity would understand' (o.c., 22, 133 and 8).

10. Roscher, o.c., 143.

11. Mohammed (✠ 632) started his preaching in Mecca after 611, and made his first converts around 613, according to Muslim tradition.

12. Roscher, o.c., 278–282. He mentions that Bernard of Clairvaux explicitly asked Pope Celestine II to forbid the abbot of Morimond to go to Jerusalem: 'Who does not see that fighting soldiers are more needed there than singing monks' (PL 182, 561). Around 1200, Innocent himself was still of the opinion that only healthy and combative men could take part in the crusade; women and men who could make the journey but could not fight should be excluded from the crusade because they were only a hindrance in the Holy Land (PL 216, 1261–1262).

13. For the exegesis of the encyclical we refer to Roscher, o.c., 141–147, Powell, o.c., 17–22, P. J. Cole, *The Preaching of the Crusades to the Holy Land, 1095–1270*, Cambridge, MA, 1991, 104–107.

14. The text of Urban's sermon has been lost, but two accounts of the sermon report that he preached on the text 'Anyone who does not carry his cross and come after me cannot be my disciple' (Lk 14:27) or its parallel, 'Anyone who does not take his cross and follow in my footsteps is not worthy of me' (Mt 10:38). Cf. Riley-Smith, o.c., 10, 45 and 53. Further, we find the text in a letter to the pope by the leaders of the first crusade and in the opening passage of an eyewitness account of the expedition. See Riley-Smith, o.c., 90–91.

15. PL 217, 676.

16. Cole, o.c., 124. In her analysis of the *Brevis ordinacio de predicacione crucis*, 'a preaching manual designed especially for crusade preachers,' Cole writes about the crusade as imitation of Christ: 'As a true imitator of Christ, the

crusader is fortified by his fear of God, by his resistance to temptation, and by his ability to bear tribulation with patience. This exalted, Christocentric conception of the crusader and of crusading is reinforced by examples of the heroic conduct of crusaders in battle. The first comes from the time of the First Crusade.... When Godfrey of Bouillon was wounded in the Holy Land, he asked his brother Eustace not to join battle until he had recovered. But Eustace, a "true soldier of Christ," desiring only "to die and be with Christ," refused to wait and entered the battle, where he was martyred. The second concerns James of Avesnes, who, when his companions urged him to retreat from the Saracens, responded, "I will go there voluntarily, and let no man restrain me."' Powell adds still another *exemplum* which 'recounts the tale of a knight who was wounded four times in battle. The physicians said that his wounds were mortal, but he insisted on returning to battle, saying, "My lord Jesus Christ suffered five wounds for me; I will return to battle and suffer a fifth for him"' (o.c., 60).

17. 'The Lord says in the Gospel: "Everyone who has left house or father or mother or wife or children or lands for my name's sake, shall receive a hundredfold and shall possess life everlasting." Let no possession keep you back, no care for domestic affairs, for this land you inhabit is everywhere shut in by the sea, is surrounded by ranges of mountains and is overcrowded by your numbers; it does not overflow with copious wealth and scarcely furnishes food for its farmers alone. This is why you devour and fight one another.... Stop these hatreds, still the wars.... Take the road to the Holy Sepulchre, rescue that land from a dreadful race and rule over it yourselves, for that land that, as scripture says, flows with milk and honey, was given by God as a possession to the children of Israel. Jerusalem is the navel of the world, a land fruitful above all others, like a second paradise of delights' (Riley-Smith, o.c., 43–44). Schwinges writes in this context: 'The pure, idealistic aim of the crusades was, since the days of Clermont, only to be found in the heads of the spiritual elite of the West, while the majority of the crusaders took the road to the Holy Land with material as well as emotional motives' (o.c., 3). More specifically with regard to the idea of reward, he writes: 'That this idea of a reward did not necessarily imply only religious merit in the mind of the majority of the crusaders, need not expressly to be emphasized. Solid social and economic considerations have thus made many crusaders dream of a land where milk and honey flow at least in the form of a rich war booty' (o.c., 6).

18. Quoted by J. Le Goff, *De cultuur van Middeleeuws Europa*, Amsterdam, 1987, 91–92.

19. Riley-Smith, o.c., 71. For a more complete analysis of Martin's sermon, see Cole, o.c., 92–97.

20. Powell, o.c., 162.

21. A. Bredero, *Christenheid en Christendom in de Middeleeuwen*, Kampen, 1986, 90–91. For a short summary of the various motives, see also Schwinges, o.c., 2–8.

22. For this idea, see especially Bernard of Clairvaux, *De laude novae militiae*, PL 182, 922–940. Written for Hugh, the first master of the Templars, between 1128–1137, its ideas can also be applied to the crusaders. See Riley-Smith, o.c., 101–102.

23. 'Basically, the following motives can be distinguished whose influence on the crusaders was definitely not always of the same importance: the strongly eschatologically oriented desire for Jerusalem, the idea of pilgrimage, the concept of the holy war and the fight against the pagans, the leading authority of the pope...and the idea of merit and reward in the crusade indulgence' (Schwinges, o.c., 5). The Jerusalem motive is hardly present in Innocent's encyclical *Quia maior*, yet more so in his sermon at the opening of the Fourth Lateran Council, where he speaks at length about the *Pascha corporale*, the *transitus corporalis*, for the liberation of Jerusalem that is in great misery (PL 217, 675–676).

24. Roscher, o.c., 269 Riley-Smith, o.c., 9–10: '[According to] Guibert of Nogent, one of the most intelligent commentators on the First Crusade, God had instituted a holy war precisely in order to give knights and laymen a path to salvation that did not entail entering a monastery and could be taken following their normal profession. There is strong evidence that this idea...struck a real chord, the sound of which was still reverberating half a century later.' See also J. Riley-Smith, *What were the Crusades*, London, 1977, 64–65, G. Basetti-Sani, *L'Islam e Francesco d'Assisi: La missione profetica per il dialogo*, Firenze, 1975. The latter writes that the church, mainly under the influence of Bernard of Clairvaux, 'has christianized knighthood.... The Christian knight becomes the "soldier of Christ," whom the church consecrates with a special liturgical rite' (3).

25. Schwinges, o.c., 11: 'They "sacralized" the vehement bellicosity of the feudal warrior societies and offered them the fight against the enemies of the faith as a safety valve.' Powell concludes, 'Troubled by violence at every level, its [i.e. the Christian world's] highest powers, both secular and spiritual, possessed but limited means to maintain order. From its inception, the ideology of the crusade movement had emphasized the substitution of a just war against the enemies of Christianity for the continued violence of Christian against Christian' (o.c., 201).

26. Bernard, Epist. 363, 565–567. Schwinges writes: 'Precisely the motive of the spiritual reward played a prominent role throughout the time of the crusade movement. It was mainly Bernard of Clairvaux, who from a diversity of motives and traditions...selected this particular motive and made it the predominant, though not the exclusive one. Bernard offered the faithful a favorable opportunity to close a spiritual deal, to become a clever merchant.

The time of the crusades was for him a *tempus acceptabile*, a favorable time, the time of penance in the form of taking the cross, in order to win salvation.... In Bernard's case, the motive of the fight against the pagans clearly receded into the background behind the subjective-religious aim, for whose achievement it was only (!) the acceptable means' (o.c., 6–7).

27. This idea of the *artificium*, the work of art that Jesus realized by making salvation possible through participation in the crusade, also comes from Bernard who used the expression for the first time in his crusade manifesto for England, *Ad gentem Anglorum*, where he writes: 'See, how great a work of art he uses to save you.' Later the expression can also be found in the bull *Inter omnia* of Alexander III (July 29, 1169) and in the bull *Audita tremendi* of Gregory VIII (October 11, 1187). V. Cramer, *Die Kreuzzugspredigt zur Befreiung des Heiligen Landes, 1095–1270*, Köln, 1939, 194, note 10.

28. PL 182, 924. For an English translation, see *Treatises III: The Works of Bernard of Clairvaux*, Volume 7, Kalamazoo, Michigan, 1977, 134–135. I used this translation, but made several adjustments.

29. COD 268: '... *cuius munere vivunt, cuius beneficio sustentantur, quin etiam cuius sanguine sunt redempti.*' Cf. Riley-Smith, o.c., 126.

30. PL 217, 676; see also H. Tillmann, *Pope Innocent III*, Amsterdam, 1980, 273–288, here 275.

31. Roscher, o.c., 20–27, especially 25–26; G. Schwaiger, 'Innocenz III,' in *Theologische Realenzyklopädie* XVI, Berlin 1987, 175–182.

32. E. R. Daniel, *The Franciscan Concept of Mission in the High Middle Ages*, Lexington, KY, 1975, 1–5.

33. 'With the election of Innocent III on 8 January 1198 there came to the papal throne the most important figure in the crusading movement after Urban II. It is no exaggeration to say that Innocent was obsessed by the crusades' (o.c., 22). Interesting too is the remark which Riley-Smith makes earlier: 'The crusading movement is often treated as an eleventh- and twelfth-century phenomenon that went into rapid decline in the thirteenth. But in fact no period can equal the activity of the 87 years from 1187 to 1274, in almost every one of which a crusade was being waged somewhere' (ibid., 19).

34. COD 267; Riley-Smith, o.c., 125; Tillmann, o.c., 282.

35. Roscher, o.c., 285. It is not possible to mention here all the doubts that were expressed in those days. Moreover, they can only be traced indirectly in answers of theologians and canonists to questions which they were asked and which therefore can be supposed to have been actual and important at that time. Thus around 1202–1210, an anonymous author replied to the question whether it is allowed to start a war to conquer cities which never belonged to the Christians. In his answer he mentioned that, according to Peter the Chanter, this is not allowed; others, however, think it to be permitted because all pagans were once true believers. For the preaching of the apostles reached till the ends of the earth. Thus every country has once

been the property of the Christians who, therefore, can now lawfully reconquer them (P. Herde, 'Christians and Saracens at the Time of the Crusades: Some Comments of Contemporary Medieval Canonists,' *Studia Gratiana* 12 (1967) 365–366). This last opinion, of which Herde says that 'this obviously far-fetched explanation...satisfied few canonists' became the more common opinion under Pope Innocent IV (1243–1254) (H. Gilles, 'Législation et doctrine canoniques sur les Sarracins,' in *Islam et chrétiens du Midi (XIIe–XIVe s,)*, Toulouse, 1983, 195–213, here 201).

About half a century earlier, a patriarch of Jerusalem put a question to Peter Manducator or Comestor, provost of Troyes from 1147–1167. The question showed clearly that highly placed ecclesiastical persons had their doubts about the morality of the crusades. His question was: 'Is it lawful for Christians to fight against the pagans and kill them, for the Lord says in the law: You shall not kill, and in the Gospel: Anyone who takes the sword, shall perish by the sword?' In his reply Peter quoted texts from the Scriptures and the Fathers according to the *Decretum Gratiani* and concluded, 'And therefore, when pagans try to fill the holy places with their filth and to extinguish the memory of Christ and the Christian name, he who repels them from the holy places, even by killing them, or retakes the holy places that have been taken away, if in doing so he does not seek his own, but Jesus Christ's, serves the Lord—the more dangerous the fight, the greater the reward—, especially when he acts on the orders of the lord pope, whom Jesus has left us as his vicar on earth. And when he dies in battle, he will have to be placed among the martyrs of our time.' But Peter reserved the most forceful language for the end when he directly addressed the patriarch: 'To you, however, I say finally this, while God and my conscience are my witness: Consider in what position you are placed. Your hesitation could never remain alone, but would draw many with it into error. Therefore, act manly, be firm, pour out the blood of Christ's enemies. Be to others an example of strength, not of fear, for woe to the man through whom the obstacle comes. You wear the sign of the cross on your chest unto damnation, if the zeal for the Crucified One recedes from your heart, if you are afraid, which I do not think, to defend the place of the crucifixion' (J. Leclercq, 'Gratien, Pierre de Troyes et la seconde croisade,' *Studia Gratiana*, 2 (1954) 585–593). See also E. Siberry, *Criticism of Crusading 1095–1274*, 210–211.

36.   'A clearly defined enemy image, the image of someone who deviates from the divine norm, underlies the holy war, which forms an essential aspect of the crusade idea. It is known that this enemy image was very negative and distorted at the beginning of the crusade movement. It changed into a more positive one in the course of the 12th and 13th century, mainly due to the experiences which the crusaders at that time gathered on the spot. This change in the image of the pagans could first be observed in the crusade

poetry of the West.... M. Plocher shows that, in the course of the 12th and 13th century, Western historiography, particularly that of the crusades, experiences the same change in ideas and attitude as the poetry' (Schwinges, o.c., 13–14). Later he adds: 'It must be emphasized that this change did not completely reform the way of thinking within the old cadres; it rather developed parallel to the continuation of the old image of the pagans, which, depending on the circumstances, could always flare up again' (ibid. 105).

37. F. Cardini, 'I musulmani nel giudizio dei crociati all'inizio del Duecento,' *Archivio Storico Italiano*, 146 (1988) 371.

38. See especially N. Daniel, *The Arabs and Mediaeval Europe*, London, 1975.

39. Roscher, o.c., 286.

40. Roscher draws a different conclusion when he writes: 'Yet this diplomatic attempt is revealing: Innocent was not concerned about the crusade as a holy war, but about the liberation of the Holy Land, for which he would have liked to avoid a war' (o.c., 148). Later he returns to the same letter: 'Among other things, this letter confirms our observation that Innocent was first and foremost interested in the external result of the liberation of the Holy Land. The liberation by diplomatic means, which avoids all fight-ing, and thus excludes every possibility to earn merit through the sacrifice of one's life on a crusade, appears even as the more desirable solution' (ibid., 287). Powell also pays attention to the letter: 'Innocent emerges from this letter not as an intransigent supporter of holy war, but as a leader attempt-ing to keep his options open for a favorable peace settlement' (o.c., 28). J. Donovan is of the same opinion: 'If this new crusade was to be a success, it would be in great part a tribute to the indefatigable zeal of Pope Innocent himself. Yet it could not be said that Innocent wanted a crusade for its own sake, that is, to the glory of the papacy; he was hopeful of attaining his objective—the Holy Land—preferably by peaceful means. To this end he tried to persuade the Sultan al'Adil' (*Pelagius and the Fifth Crusade*, Philadelphia, 1950, 27).

41. Innocent explicitly mentioned this in his letter to Albert, the patriarch of Jerusalem, whom he ordered to send messengers with his letter to the Sultan. He also informed Albert that he did not expect much from his peace proposal to the Sultan (PL 216, 830–831).

42. See Introduction.

43. *Vineam Domini*, PL 216, 824: 'The recovery of the Holy Land...cannot be further delayed without great and serious danger.'

44. PL 216, 831–832.

45. In his *Decretum* Gratian quoted a passage from a letter of Alexander II (1063) in which the pope wrote: 'There is a disparity between the cause of the Jews and that of the Saracens. For against the latter who persecute the Christians and expel them from their cities and their own settlements, a

just war is waged; on the other hand, the first are everywhere prepared to serve' (C.23 q.8 c.11). At the time of Innocent III, canonists like Alanus Anglicus and Laurentius Hispanus made a distinction with regard to this canon *Dispar*. According to them, the present, harsh approach towards the Saracens was due to the state of war. However, if the Saracens wanted to live in peace with the Christians, they were not to be attacked or killed, but had to be tolerated. In other words, the Christians were only allowed to wage war when it was a matter of self-defense or of the recuperation of land which originally belonged to them but had been occupied by the Saracens. Thus the canonists applied the doctrine of the just war as it had been developed by Gratian to the crusades. Were those prudent, God-fearing men on whose advice Innocent wrote his letter to the sultan, perhaps curial canonists who insisted that Innocent should first make certain that the Saracens were indeed not willing to live in peace and to return the Holy Land to the Christians? For this problem, see Herde, a.c., 364–367; Gilles, a.c., 200–201. The same opinion can also be found in Bernard when he says that the pagans may not be killed when they can be prevented in some other way from persecuting or oppressing the faithful. See above, 16.

46. Schwinges, o.c., 116–117. See also my commentary on RegNB 16:6, 91.

47. PL 189, 673. Peter's apologetic approach has been influenced by his contacts with Islam in Spain, and also by the growing significance of the scholastic method with its emphasis on reason. Thus an opportunity was given to enter into discussion with non-Christians on the basis of reason. An example of this approach is Anselm of Canterbury's *Cur Deus homo*, in which he wanted to convince an unbeliever with rational arguments of the rationality of the Christian doctrine of redemption (*ratio fidei*). According to Julia Gauss, Anselm's unbelieving partner in the discussion was a Muslim. Anselm wrote his treatise under the influence of the council of Clermont where Urban II made his call for the first crusade (1095). It was Anselm's intention to give the crusaders a guideline for their discussions with unbelievers. Thus Julia Gauss places Anselm, even before Peter the Venerable, as the first in the line of apologists within the Latin Church who have dealt with Islam (Schwinges, o.c., 51–64).

48. '...*per eum loquebatur Sathanas*' PL 189, 680; '...*agger mendaciorum*' PL 189, 717; '...*errore stulto, mortifero, carente omni ratione, destituto omni veritate*' (ibid). For this double language, the language of reason and the language of religious prejudice, see J. P. Torrell, 'La notion de prophétie et la méthode apologétique dans le *Contra Saracenos* de Pierre le Vénérable,' *Studia Monastica* 17 (1975) 257–280, especially 275–279. An explanation might be found in the fact that Peter thought his work to be of little or no use for the conversion of the Saracens whom he believed to be lost. Yet he considered a book like his valuable as a Christian weapon against the 'pest' of Islam. For even though the erring Muslims did not convert to Christ, such a book

could strengthen the weak Christians in their faith, whereas otherwise they might be seduced by this evil. Peter wrote his book therefore for Christians rather than for Muslims, and adapted his language accordingly. See Epist. 111 ad Bernardum, in *The Letters of Peter the Venerable*, ed. Constable, Cambridge, 1967, 298. See also J. Kritzeck, *Peter the Venerable and Islam*, Princeton, 1964, 44–45; Kedar, o.c., 102–103.

49. PL 216, 818; Riley-Smith, o.c., 120. See also the opening sentence of the letter *Vineam Domini*: 'Beasts of many kinds are destroying the vineyard of the Lord of hosts' (PL 216, 823).

50. PL 217, 675.

51. In this connection, Cardini rightly observes that, especially in clerical circles of the West, people were inclined to conclude that 'Islam belonged to the world of the eschatology, if not to that of metahistory, rather than to the world of history: Islam was the Metaphysical Enemy, the Evil, a terrible reign of idolators and of adorers of Satan' (a.c, 372). Within these circles, Islam was looked upon 'only in the deforming mirror of the crusade propaganda or of the epic literature of the knights.' About the latter, Cardini writes: 'In the *chansons de geste* and in the romances which contributed to the spreading of the crusade ideal and of the fashion of *aventure* in the East during the entire twelfth century and beyond, we find ourselves before an Islam that is described as a 'false' religion, whose basic characteristics are polytheism, idolatry, the cult of Mohammed as divine, and in ultimate analysis demonolatry. It may even be said that this type of Islam is considered as a diabolic 'antireligion,' an antichristianity...Mohammed is more than a false prophet: he is a false Christ; the Muslim ethic is the overthrow of the Christian ethic which becomes manifest mainly through the refusal of any order or check as regards carnal pleasures' (ibid. 375).

52. In the passage about 'the beast,' Innocent mentioned only that the Lord had already given him a sign that good was to come, without indicating of what this sign consisted. It was later on, when he explained why he felt justified in revoking the indulgences for those going on a crusade against the Moors in Spain or the heretics in Provence, that he informed us about the nature of God's sign: both in Spain and in Provence the situation had developed so well that, at least for the moment, further use of violence was not needed (PL 216, 820). For Innocent's reaction to the victory over the Moors at Las Navas de Tolosa in 1212, see his letter to King Alfonso VIII of Castile, where he attributed this victory to the invincible power of God (PL 216, 703–704; Riley-Smith, o.c., 59–61).

53. 'The failure of that [i.e., the second] crusade...may well have raised the question of whether it was not presumptuous of Christians to expect victory according to their own timetable, rather than at the time ordained by Divine Providence' (Powell, o.c., 18). 'There is no indication that they [i.e., the preachers] felt the need to defend the crusade against any major opposi-

tion, though the emphasis they placed on the theme "Now is the acceptable time" may well have been a response to an effort on the part of some to argue that God would take care of the Moslems and liberate his Holy Places in his own good time' (ibid., 63). From the same author see also 'Francesco d'Assisi e la Quinta Crociata: Una missione di pace,' *Schede Medievali* 4 (January–June 1983) 68–77, here 74–75.

54. E. R. Daniel, 'Apocalyptic Conversion: The Joachite Alternative to the Crusades,' *Traditio* 25 (1969) 127–146, here 134–139; see also *The Franciscan Concept of Mission in the High Middle Ages*, Lexington, 1975, 14–21. A somewhat different interpretation is given by Kedar who thinks that Joachim did not completely reject the idea of the crusade. Also in the future a crusade might obtain divine support if the participants would turn away from their sins. However, Joachim appeared to expect the final victory not from a crusade but from the preaching of the *viri spirituales* (o.c., 112–116).

55. COD 268; see also Tillmann, o.c., 282.

56. For the activities of cardinal Hugolino, see below.

57. 'We thus cannot conclude that the crusade of 1212 was really a "children's" crusade. The word *puer*, gratuitously translated 'child' by most scholars, seems to denote a social situation rather than an age. Moreover, the sources mention participants other than *pueri*, such as *mulieres, homines* and *pauperes*.... The works of Ariès and Duby, who ascertained that *puer* is more a social than a psychological concept, form my point of departure. Ariès finds that the term is used primarily for people in relationships of dependence, such as farm hands, while Duby has placed it in a more specific context. He sees the beginning of an entirely new class of people, a kind of rural proletariat called *pueri* or *pastores*, who were the victims of the economic revolution of the twelfth century. The group consisted primarily of younger sons of peasant families, who could not share in the paternal inheritance if it were not to be fractionalized, and who therefore could not marry. Thus they had to support themselves as day laborers, farm workers and cotters possessing no land and making ends meet by keeping herds of animals.... The fact that practically all sources call the participants in the Children's Crusade *pueri* and *pastores* suggests that they belonged to this social group (of the new poor)' (P. Raedts, a.c., 297–298).

58. Roscher, o.c., 278–280; '*Quia maior* aimed at capturing and harnessing mass popular support for the crusade' (Powell, o.c., 20). But there were limits to these recruiting practices. Thus cardinal Robert Courçon, the papal legate in France, was reproached because he 'detracted from the crusade through his indiscriminate signing. Brito [in his *Gesta Philippi Augusti Francorum regis*] alleges that when Robert recruited "the children, the old, women, and those who were lame, blind, deaf, and leprous" for the crusade, he served only to repel the wealthy upon whom the success of the campaign ultimately would depend. Because of these complaints, Robert incurred such

odium and came under such sustained attack from some of the French clergy that at the Fourth Lateran Council (November 1215) Innocent was com-
pelled to cancel his legation in France' (Cole, o.c., 128).

59. PL 216, 822; Riley-Smith, o.c., 131. Later correspondence with Bishop
    Conrad of Regensburg shows that for him four mounts were not sufficient
    because with such a small number he would not dare to venture as far as
    two miles outside his own city on account of the evils of the time (PL 216,
    906; Riley-Smith, o.c., 132). See also Powell, o.c., 22–27; Cole, o.c., 109.

60. Kedar, o.c., 57–74 passim.

61. For this and what follows, see Roscher, o.c., 286–287.

62. Kedar, o.c., 47.

63. Kedar, o.c., 68–69.

64. Kedar, o.c., 62–64. Albert mentions, among other things, that 'negotiations
    are scheduled to determine whether the inhabitants of Tarsus should
    remain pagan or convert to Christianity'; that 'Peter the Hermit offered
    Kerbogha, the ruler of Mosul, a chance to convert or join the battle with
    the crusaders' and that 'Tancred, the Norman prince of Galilee, in 1100 sent
    six knights to Duqaq of Damascus to demand that he surrender the city
    and become Christian. (The Turk executed five knights; the sixth preferred
    to become Muslim.)'

65. Kedar, o.c., 66–67, where other texts are also given.

66. See below, 36.

67. Kedar, o.c., 72: 'so that we may be able to convert the perfidious and worth-
    less people, so that they ought duly to believe with us in the Holy Trinity
    and in Your nativity and in Your passion and death and resurrection, so that
    Your name be invoked throughout the world and be blessed in all eternity.'

68. Cole, o.c., 141.

69. Roscher, o.c., 292–294; Donovan, o.c., 28, 33; H. Dilcher, 'Honorius III,' in:
    Theologische Realenzyklopädie XV, Berlin, 1986, 568–571.

70. 'Honorius's correspondence from January to April 1217, however, reveals
    that preparations for the crusade were in disarray and that the crusade was
    in danger of foundering. In many areas interest in the crusade was waning,
    and the clergy were proving difficult and uncooperative over the collection
    and the distribution of the twentieth' (Cole, o.c., 142).

71. COD 270.

72. *Regesta Honorii Papae III*, ed. P. Pressuti, Romae, 1888, I, 272.

73. See e.g., D. Flood, 'Peace in Assisi in the Early Thirteenth Century,' *FranzSt*
    64 (1982) 67–80. Reprinted in *FrancDig* I, 1 (May 1991) 1–20, abbreviated Peace
    in Assisi.

74. '...the relationship between the communes and the bishops varied consider-
    ably throughout this period. In some places, bishops played an important
    part in the formation of the earliest communal government.... Nevertheless,
    grounds for conflict were certainly more abundant than bases for coopera-

tion. Under the leadership of the reformed papacy, the episcopacy of northern Italy aggressively pursued efforts to maintain and enlarge the patrimonies of its churches.... A study of the documents [regarding Volterra] shows that all of those named as crusaders were supporters of the bishop. In every instance, they used their crusader status to pursue legal claims, largely against the commune, before ecclesiastical courts manned by judges delegate appointed by the legate' (Powell, o.c., 70).

75. C. Thouzellier, 'La légation en Lombardie du Cardinal Hugolin (1221): un épisode de la cinquième croisade,' *Revue d'histoire ecclésiastique* 45 (1950) 508–542, here 511–512.

76. D. Flood, 'Cardinal Hugolino on Legation,' *Haversack* 11, 2 (December 1987) 3–9.

77. See especially Powell, o.c., 69–74; also O. Guyotjeannin and G. Nori, 'Venezia e il trasporto dei crociati: a proposito di un patto del 1219,' *Studi Medievali* 30 (1989) 309–321.

78. For the opposition against the fraternity within the Roman curia, see J. Powell, 'The Papacy and the Early Franciscans,' *Franciscan Studies* 36 (1976) 248–262, here 258–259: 'Two documents are important in showing the nature and locus of this opposition. Writing in the spring of 1220, Jacques de Vitry, who had praised the Franciscans so unstintingly earlier, expressed serious concern about the order. "This religion seems very dangerous to us because not only the perfect, but also the young and imperfect, who ought to be disciplined and proved for some little time under conventual discipline, are divided two by two through the whole world." The strength of this objection becomes more apparent when we note that the Papal bull *Cum secundum consilium* (September 20, 1220) required a year in probation prior to profession in the order and forbade anyone to leave its obedience.... Furthermore, about this time, Cardinal Hugolino warned St. Francis about opposition to the order in the curia. This external danger may well have been of greater importance than any problems faced by Francis from within the order in persuading him to ask Honorius to appoint Hugolino as Cardinal Protector of the order, a step which might best be explained as a way of quieting the critics of the order. All of these separate pieces of evidence suggest a serious threat to the continued existence of the Franciscans. The main focus of this opposition lay in the Papal curia.... However, it is important to note here that conventual discipline rather than poverty was the issue that threatened the existence of the Franciscans in 1220.'

79. *LegPer*, 82.

80. This view is not shared by F. Cardini, 'Nella presenza del Soldan superba,' *Studi Francescani* 71 (1974) 199–250. He writes: 'Anyone who thinks about the crusade in its exclusive aspect of war in the East, forgets its corresponding aspect of peace in the West.... In the light of such considerations, one can no longer fail to notice the extraordinary accord between crusading propa-

ganda and Franciscan preaching, both from their respective beginnings equally concentrating on the need to put an end to the internal wars which stained Italy with blood, and to do penance. The Franciscan movement of peace among the cities, however new and renewing it might be, inserts itself in a tradition parallel to the crusading movement' (221–222). A somewhat similar opinion can be found in Powell's interpretation of Francis' visit to the sultan: 'What Francis was attempting was nothing less than an extension of the aims of the western peace movement to the struggle with Islam. This was entirely consistent with the objectives of the papacy' (o.c., 159).

81. In this connection, the observation which Manselli makes in his biography of St. Francis seems improbable. According to him, during their meeting in Florence, cardinal Hugolino, by his words and his activities, would have strengthened Francis in his plans to go to the Holy Land. R. Manselli, *St. Francis of Assisi*, Chicago, 1988, 217.

82. Roscher, o.c., 287; Powell, o.c., 195–200; Jeusset, o.c., 79–81.

83. James' date of birth is not known with certainty. T. F. Crane, *The Exempla of Jacques de Vitry*, New York, 1890, xxiv, thinks that he was born 'some time before 1180.' P. Funk, *Jacob von Vitry*, Leipzig, 1909, places James' date of birth in 1170. R. B. C. Huygens, *Lettres de Jacques de Vitry*, Leiden, 1960, mentions 1160/1170.

84. Crane, o.c., xxv–xxvii; see also Cramer, o.c., 211–212; Kedar, o.c., 117.

85. Cole, o.c., 113–114: 'Towards the end of the twelfth century it was becoming increasingly evident that there was a need for more popular preaching. Various reasons for this have been canvassed, but one important factor was the threat which heretical preachers were presenting to the church.' In order to make this preaching as effective as possible, Alan of Lille develops a series of 'model sermons *ad status*, to soldiers, advocates, princes, cloistered religious, priests, people about to be married, widows and virgins. Each sermon is tailored to address the moral and spiritual concerns which Alan thought appropriate to each of these social states.' Thus he gives 'a new socio-moral basis' to preaching which before was mainly practiced in the academic world of the schools where there was little or no room for lay people and both masters and students were clerics. James follows a similar method directed to various groups in his *sermones vulgares*. See note 86.

86. The sermon in question is sermon 48 of the *sermones vulgares*, a series of 74 sermons which James held for various groups like prelates and priests, scholars, judges and lawyers, theologians and preachers, monks, nuns, regular canons, hermits and recluses, Franciscans, lepers and other sick, the poor and afflicted, soldiers, merchants and money-changers, laborers, sailors, servants, married people, widows and virgins. In contrast to Alan of Lille, James' series also contains six crusade sermons: 37 and 38, to the brothers of the military order; 47 and 48, to crusaders and those about to become crusaders; 49 and 50, to pilgrims. For the complete list of these sermons, see

Crane, o.c., xlii–xlvi. Here I have used a summary made by Cole (o.c., 135). See also Kedar, o.c., 116–117.

87. '...the Fifth Crusade, of which James of Vitry was one of the principal preachers' (Riley-Smith, o.c., 133). 'Of all the preachers of the Fifth Crusade, however, the most remarkable was Jacques de Vitry.... It is a sign of the stature of Jacques de Vitry that so many of his writings have survived' (Cole, o.c., 132–133).

88. Crane, o.c., xxvii.

89. Huygens, o.c., 73–74. For his journey, see also R. Pernoud, *The Crusaders*, Edinburgh, n.d., 170.

90. Huygens, o.c., 75–76; *Omnibus*, 1608.

91. Huygens, o.c., 77–78; Pernoud, o.c., 177 and 171, where she also briefly describes the traveling conditions of ordinary crusaders. They were far less comfortable than James'.

92. Latin *Pullani*, French *Poulains*: descendants of crusaders who had settled in the Latin states of the East and married Christian women of Syrian or Armenian origin. Cf. *Grand Larousse* 8 (Paris 1963) 732.

93. Huygens. o.c., 83–87. James gives a brief, largely unfavorable description of each group and of their peculiarities of faith and morals. He was deeply shocked indeed by the situation which he found in Acre.

94. Huygens, o.c., 87–88.

95. Huygens, o.c., 88–89.

96. Huygens, o.c., 91ff: '*Milites vero Tyrenses armati conduxerunt me*', '*...milites civitatis michi obviam venirent*', '*...conduxerunt me cum manu armata.*' Cf. Kedar, o.c., 118.

97. Huygens, o.c., 91–92: '*...et ego fraudem Machometi et execrabilem eius doctrinam pro posse meo eis detexi.*'

98. Huygens, o.c., 94.

99. To what extent James' desire to preach to the Saracens has also been influenced by canon law is difficult to know with certainty. There existed a canon in the *Decretum Gratiani* which 'encouraged debates between Christians and infidels so that nonbelievers might be led to the true faith by the force of rational argument' (J. Muldoon, *Popes, Lawyers, and Infidels*, Liverpool, 1979, 4). This canon, however, was first meant for the non-Christian inhabitants of Europe. It is of course possible that James, knowing this canon, considered himself bound by it in his activities as bishop in the Holy Land. The text of the canon is as follows: '*Infideles non possumus Christo lucrari, si colloquium eorum vitamus et convivium. Unde et Dominus cum publicanis et peccatoribus manducavit et bibit*' (C.23 q.4 c.17, *Infideles, Corpus Iuris Canonici*, ed. E. Friedberg, I, 905). See also Kedar, o.c., 117–118, where the remark about James who carried the finger of Mary of Oignies with him, is documented.

100. Huygens, o.c., 96: '*...errorem eorum et legis nostre veritatem eis ostendebam.*'

101. Huygens, o.c., 96–97.
102. Huygens, o.c., 98.
103. Huygens, o.c., 108.
104. Huygens, o.c., 127–128; cf. Kedar, o.c., 118–119.
105. Huygens, o.c., 137: '...*eo, quod inter suos quicquid libebat licebat, diutius nobis-cum manere non sustinebant, sed ad consuetas inmundicias paganorum reverte-bantur a nobis occulte recedentes.*'
106. PL 207, 1061–1064.
107. PL 207, 1069–1070. This interpretation of Peter of Blois is mainly based on the fact that, as Siberry indicates in her *Criticism of Crusading 1095–1274*, Peter wrote his treatise as 'an impassioned appeal in support of the Third Crusade' (55). Peter therefore did not want anything better than that the kings and powerful would give up their reasons for delaying the crusade and instead get ready to travel with their armies to the Holy Land in a good spirit, i.e. in the spirit of poverty and humility. Hence, Raedts' conclusion that, according to Peter of Blois, 'only from the poor who possess noth-ing but their trust in God, can the liberation of Jerusalem still be hoped for' (a.c., 308), does not seem to be correct. As a result, it appears that there is no solid basis to see Peter of Blois as a forerunner of Francis, as Raedts does.
108. PL 207, 1068.
109. A. D. v. den Brincken, 'Islam und Oriens Christianus in den Schriften des Kölner Domscholasters Oliver (✠1227),' *MiscMed* 17, Berlin 1985, 86–102, here 96–97.
110. Huygens, o.c., 106; cf. Powell, o.c., 140–145.
111. Huygens, o.c., 123–124. I only quote the passage about Mohammed from the Latin text here: '*et ubi tociens invocatum est nomen maledictum perfidi Machometi, nomen abominabile, quod os demonis nominavit, invocetur amodo nomen benedictum Iesu Christi, nomen gloriosum quod os domini nominavit.*'
112. See also the above mentioned letter of Innocent III to King Alfonso VIII after the victory over the Moors at Las Navas de Tolosa in 1212 (PL 216, 703–704).
113. Here it concerns sermon 38 of the *sermones vulgares: ad fratres ordinis mili-taris*. As I have not been able to consult the Latin text of this sermon, I fol-low the English translation made by Riley-Smith, o.c., 68–69; a rather exten-sive summary can be found in Cramer, o.c., 244–247.
114. These texts are quoted in the *Decretum Gratiani*, C.23 q.1. See Siberry, o.c., 210.
115. This last story is taken up in the collections of *exempla* which later, on the basis of the *sermones vulgares*, were put together by preachers for their own use. See Crane, o.c., xlvi–liii.
116. This is the conclusion which Siberry reaches in her *Criticism of Crusading 1095–1274*. Her conclusion, that a radical opposition against the very idea of

the crusades is very rare, is shared by J. Brundage (*Speculum* 62 (1987) 722–723) and by M. Brols (*Studi Medievali* 28 (1987) 1045–1048).

117. See above, note 35.

118. See above, 22–3.

119. *Jordan*, 9; *Omnibus*, 1609.

120. See, for example, the passage in his first letter where he gives his vision on the Lesser Brothers and the Lesser Sisters: 'I believe that through these simple and poor men and women the Lord wants to save many souls before the end of the world, to the shame of the prelates who are like dumb dogs who do not have the strength to bark' (Huygens, o.c., 76; *Omnibus*, 1609). See above, note 90.

121. In this connection I basically disagree with Kedar who sees James and Francis as representatives of the same religious movement that keeps Europe under its spell: 'These two pioneer preachers to the Muslims pursued different careers and had a quite dissimilar impact on posterity, yet both were bent on a return to evangelical life, and participated in the current of intense religiosity that spread through Europe beginning in the eleventh century' (o.c., 119). I disagree also with the emphasis Kedar places on preaching as the aim of Francis' mission. Here the consequences of the fact that Kedar did not study *Regula non bullata* 14 and 16 in depth become evident.

122. See below, 55.

PART ONE: Chapter 2

1. 'The *Regula non bullata* is an important source for our knowledge of the history of the beginnings of the order founded by Francis. It is perhaps the most authentic source: did it not take shape, line by line, during the chapters of the first Franciscan generation?' (K. Esser in his foreword to D. Flood and T. Matura, *The Birth of a Movement: A Study of the First Rule of St. Francis*, Chicago, 1975, vii–viii). This view on the importance of the *Regula non bullata* is followed by almost all authors. Thus Stanislao da Campagnola writes in his introduction to the writings of Francis in *Fonti francescane*, Assisi, 1978, that the *Regula non bullata* 'does not present itself so much as a legislative text, than as a faithful mirror of the early Franciscan experience' (62).

2. D. Flood, *Die Regula non bullata der Minderbrüder*, Werl, 1967, 129.

3. 'At the Fourth Lateran Council (1215)... the Pope ordered the reconquest of Jerusalem, if need be by fire and sword. Francis was among those touched by the fever of the crusade; however, he did not simply go along with the others. His life had been deeply influenced by the gospel. Hence, he listened constantly to the instructions Jesus gave to his disciples in the gospels. A crusade with arms was for him out of the question. The humili-

ty of the cross is incompatible with the force of arms. Against this background Francis developed a different and alternative strategy, which he formulated in the mission statute of the Rule of 1221' (Lehmann, *Features*, 1–2). One year later, Lehmann appears less certain: 'the question remains whether the chapter has been influenced, directly or indirectly, by Innocent's idea of the crusade. If so, then we have to qualify it as a contrast program.' However, Lehmann suggests, such a qualification can lead us in the wrong direction. Hence, with several other authors, he interprets chapter 16 rather—and here he quotes Walter Bühlmann—'as an elaboration and an echo of his journey to Egypt' (L. Lehmann, 'Prinzipien franziskanischer Mission nach den frühen Quellen,' *Laur* 26 (1985) 322–323; abbreviated: Prinzipien).

4. G. Golubovich, 'San Francesco e i Francescani in Damiata,' *StFranc* 12 (1926) 307–330; L. Lemmens, 'De Sancto Francisco Christum praedicante coram Sultano Aegypti,' *AFH* 19 (1926) 559–578; F. Gabrieli, 'San Francesco e l'Oriente islamico,' in *Espansione*, 107–122.

5. Bühlmann, a.c., 88 and 96–97. Other authors who share the same opinion, are H. De Roeck, *De normis Regulae OFM circa missiones inter infideles ex vita primaeva franciscana profluentibus*, Roma, 1961, 106; Stanislao da Campagnola, *Fonti Francescane*, vol. I, Assisi, 1977, 60; F. De Beer, *We saw Brother Francis*, Chicago, 1983, 90.

6. Rotzetter, Missionary Dimension, 55–56.

7. In our commentary on this text, we will return to this in greater detail. It may be good, though, to observe here that traces of Francis' experiences among the Muslims can also be found in other writings of Francis, especially in his Letters to the Custodians and the Letter to the Rulers of the Peoples. See L. Lehmann, 'Der Brief des hl. Franziskus an die Lenker der Völker, Aufbau und missionarische Anliegen,' *Laur* 25 (1984) 287–324. English translation: 'The Letter of Saint Francis to the Rulers of the Peoples. Structure and Missionary Concerns,' *FrancDig* IV, 2 (December 1994) 25–62; abbreviated: Rulers. L. Lehmann, 'Die beiden Briefe des hl. Franziskus an die Kustoden, Ansätze für eine christlich-islamische Oekumene im Loben Gottes,' *FranzSt* 69 (1987) 3–33. English translation: 'The Two Letters of St Francis to the Custodians: Beginnings of a Christian-Muslim Ecumenism in Praising God,' *FrancDig* I, 1 (May 1991) 21–56; abbreviated: Custodians.

8. When speaking about the prohibition of engaging in arguments or disputes, Lehmann does not mention the use of apologetic methods by the brothers and the possible reason for this practice. He only paraphrases the text: 'The profession of faith must be preceded by a living witness of fraternal harmony and an attitude of reconciliation. The brothers are not to quarrel with people of other faiths, nor are they to insist that they are right

or show themselves superior. Such words must have sounded very strange and new in those times of bitter wars of religion among Christians and Muslims' (Features, 6). See also Prinzipien, 331–332. A similar approach can be found in Rotzetter, Missionary Dimension, 51.

9. *Jordan*, 7 and 9. See O. v. d. Vat, *Die Anfänge der Franziskanermissionen und ihre Weiterentwicklung im nahen Orient und in den mohammedanischen Ländern während des 13. Jahrhunderts*, Werl, 1934, 41–42.

10. For James of Vitry, see the previous chapter. To what extent the brothers may have been influenced here by the dominant ecclesiastical climate under Innocent III, who reconciled the Waldensian groups of Durand of Huesca and Bernard Prim with the church and entrusted them with the task of challenging and eliminating the heretics by means of *disputationes*, is difficult to determine. It is interesting to read, however, what the Propositum of Durand says with regard to their preaching activity: 'Since we are for the greater part clerics and almost all literate, we have decided to devote all our energy to lectures, exhortations, teachings and disputes against all heretic sects. The disputes, however, will be organized by the more learned brothers who are experts in the catholic faith and well instructed in the law of the Lord, so that the enemies of the catholic and apostolic faith will be confounded' (PL 215, 1513). See R. Zerfass, *Der Streit um die Laienpredigt*, Freiburg, 1974, 213–229.

11. *Historia Occidentalis*, ch. 32, 15; *Omnibus*, 1612–1613. 'It is not clear from this passage of the *Historia* whether the missionary activity mentioned there had started already before the arrival of St. Francis in the East, or whether the initiative had come from him. The first supposition seems to be the more probable one, even though it remains strange that James of Vitry does not speak at all about the Franciscans and their activity in the Holy Land in the five letters which he wrote from the East to his friends in Europe between Easter 1217 and summer 1220' (v. d. Vat, o.c., 57).

12. v. d. Vat, o.c., 4–5.

13. Cf. *LegPer* 67; 3 *Comp* 37.

14. Flood comes to the same conclusion: 'Francis spoke with the Sultan. We do not know what transpired between them, save that the encounter came off humanly, to the honor of them both. Francis had not fallen victim to the propaganda of the Christian West. That, too, came from leaving the world. He journeyed to the Saracens as their brother and servant. That became movement policy, with Chapter Sixteen in the Early Rule, in a sharp rejection of the Church's policy toward the Saracens. While among them Francis kept his eyes open and his wits lively' (*Francis of Assisi*, 135). See also his article, Assisi's Rules, where he writes: 'We can also conclude that it [i.e., the encounter between Francis and the sultan] resulted in the expansion of the Franciscan outlook. For Francis and his brothers added a chapter to their

basic document which sanctioned the extension of their Christian service to men and women beyond the spheres of Christian life' (91).

15. Th. Desbonnets, *De l'intuition à l'institution*, Paris, 1983, 49–58; H. Nolthenius, *Een man uit het dal van Spoleto*, Amsterdam, 1988, 141–146.

16. J. F. Godet, 'Le rôle de la prédication dans l'évolution de l'Ordre des Frères Mineurs d'après les écrits de saint François,' *FranzSt* 59 (1977) 53–64. English translation: 'The Role of Preaching in the Evolution of the Order of Friars Minor According to the Writings of Saint Francis,' *FrancDig* IV, 1 (June 1994) 17–33. See also Th. Desbonnets, o.c., 85–94; D. Flood, 'The Politics of "Quo Elongati,"' *Laur* 29 (1988) 370–385. Reprinted in *FrancDig* III, 1 (June 1993) 39–55; abbreviated: The Politics.

17. 'It is also very well possible that several ministers showed little understanding for a missionary activity in the way Francis thought about it, just as they also held a different opinion than Francis in many other questions. It was a matter of energetically defending the good right of this mission and of the missionary enthusiasts among the brothers against those tendencies and of resolutely keeping the way open for them to go to their mission country' (v. d. Vat, o.c., 15–16).

18. Lehmann, Features, 2–3; A. Rotzetter, *Die Funktion der Franziskanischen Bewegung in der Kirche: Eine pastoraltheologische Interpretation der grundlegenden franziskanischen Texte*, Schwyz, 1977, 160; abbreviated: *Die Funktion*. See also Jeusset, o.c., 60. Francis and his first brothers certainly used this verb to indicate the going from one place to another. And it was this going about in the world which was the central idea uniting these three chapters with each other. Hence we cannot agree with D. Dozzi, *Il Vangelo nella Regola non bollata di Francesco d'Assisi*, Roma, 1989, 207 and 211, who thinks that, in these chapters of the *Regula non bullata*, the going about in the world is probably not so much to be considered as a geographie-spatial, but rather as a socio-theological category. According to him, the going about in a geographic sense disappears into the background. It only indicates a circumstance (14:2) or a possibility (16:3), but is not considered essential for mission.

19. Flood, *Die Regula non bullata*, 124.

20. See also Rotzetter: 'When proclaiming the Kingdom of God, the Franciscans stand on the front line between the spirit of the sermon on the mount, i.e., the ethic of the Kingdom of God, and the 'wisdom of the world,' the so-called rational way of thinking that closes itself up within the sphere of what belongs to this world. Hence the danger arises that they limit themselves to a purely verbal proclamation and externally feign a religious life that is shaped by the Kingdom of God, while internally they are addicted to the *prudentia carnis*. The true heralds of the Kingdom of God, on the other hand, are guided by the Spirit of the Lord, who struggles against, and mortifies, the 'carnal' way of thinking insofar as it operates

within their own person. Moreover, the Spirit strives for humility, patience and the pure, simple, true and spiritual peace in the relationship with their neighbors' (*Die Funktion*, 163). It is a pity that Rotzetter places the struggle between the spirit of the flesh and the Spirit of the Lord almost exclusively within the individual person and does not concretize it in a material-historical way, on the socio-economic level, in the struggle between the economic system of Assisi and that of the brotherhood. At the end of his book Rotzetter does speak about the prophetic importance of the social criticism of the Franciscan movement in relation to the problems around work, Third World and the promotion of nonviolence (282–293). However, this could have been integrated much better into the whole of the book if the social criticism of Francis and his brothers would have been explained more clearly in the preceding chapters. Now it functions only as a kind of appendix. A similar individualizing interpretation can be found in O. v. Asseldonk, 'Verso un cuore puro con la pura, semplice e vera pace dello spirito (RegNB 17,15),' *Laur* 33 (1992) 488–489. He is right, however, in pointing out the great importance of the theme of the opposition between the spirit of the flesh and the Spirit of the Lord which occurs more than 15 times in the writings of Francis (486).

21. Flood, Assisi's Rules, 104. In my opinion, Flood's article is by far the best with regard to the connection between chapter 16 and chapters 14 and 17, which originally belonged together and between which chapter 16 has been inserted later on. Hence, chapter 16 must not only be read in connection with chapter 14, but also in connection with the present chapter 17. From a historical-literary point of view it seems to me incorrect to state, as Bühlmann does, that the so-called *'Wanderschaftsstatut'* (the statute about 'wandering,' chapters 14–17) 'is placed at the centre of the Rule,' and then to conclude that 'the apostolate of the evangelization must not be considered as a deviation and degeneration, but rather as the very core and climax of the Franciscan identity' (a.c., 98).

22. When the Lord revealed the greeting of peace to Francis is not clear. Probably this revelation has been made in a gradual process during the years of his conversion and the first years of the brotherhood. The experience which he had in Spoleto on his journey to Apulia, where he wanted to join the papal troops, or, according to Nolthenius, the army of the emperor, has certainly had a great influence. In both interpretations, this experience implied a rejection of power and violence, on which the system of Assisi was also based, as not in accordance with the will of the Lord who wants peace. That it still took some time before Francis recognized his mission to consist in the passing on of Jesus' greeting of peace in word and deed, is quite natural. For the stories about Francis' experience in Spoleto, see 1 *Cel* 4–5; 2 *Cel* 6; *AnPer* 5–6; 3 *Comp* 5–6. For the interpretation of Nolthenius, see her book, 211 and 323.

23. Nolthenius, o.c., 67–68. For this part, I rely very much on Flood, Peace in Assisi, 67–80. See also G. P. Freeman, 'Franciscus' vrede: een goed verhaal,' in *De Heer geve u vrede: Drie beschouwingen over Franciscus' vredespiritualiteit*, Franciscaanse Studies 6, Utrecht, 1990, 34–38. English translation: 'Francis' Peace: A Good Story,' *FrancDig* V, 2 (December 1995) 40–46. See also H. Von der Bey, *"Der Herr gebe dir den Frieden!"*, Werl, 1990.

24. Z. Zafarana, 'La predicazione francescana,' in *Francescanesimo*, 205.

25. D. Flood, 'Die wirtschaftliche Grundlage der franziskanischen Bewegung in ihrer Entstehungszeit,' *WissWeis* 44 (1981) 186–187. For what follows, see especially Flood, *Francis of Assisi*, 14–23.

26. Something similar happened in Milan with regard to the Humiliati. Basing himself on a study of Manselli, Flood writes: 'Manselli explained how officials in Milan entrusted the Humiliati with delicate tasks of communal importance.... They served as tax assessors and collectors, as weight controllers for corn and flour and bread and as city treasurers. They were entrusted with these tasks because they were honest and industrious and innocent of party politics. The people of Assisi had such an idea in mind when they offered the brothers work in finance and in records (*camerarius* and *cancellarius*). One role required civil honesty, the other professional competency.... In their offer to the brothers, the Assisians recognized their abilities. More important, the Assisians interpreted their Christian commitment. In their refusal, the brothers refused the Assisian interpretation of their "rule and life." They said in sum: "Do not use the story of the Humiliati to explain to yourself what we are doing and what it means." Historians do precisely that. They put Waldensians, Humiliati, and Franciscans together in one category. They explain them as the moral prophets of their age. Yet in this passage the brothers excluded as contrary to their life an economic function in Assisi similar to the one exercised by the Humiliati in Milan. In other words, they distinguished themselves economically from Assisi. They were not merely honest and modest; they were different in the way they related to things and to people. In the difference lies the story' (*Francis of Assisi*, 21–22).

27. '...life as a subject is from the very beginning one of the characteristics of the life of Francis and his brothers (Test 19). In this way they indicate their place in the society of their days,' not only in the world of work (RegNB 7:2), but also with regard to the Saracens and other nonbelievers (16:6). Francis expresses himself most radically in the Salutation of the Virtues, where he speaks about being subject 'even to all beasts and wild animals' (16–18). See Sevenhoven, a.c., 203–204. 'To be subject... was for Francis not a specific virtue which was to be realized separately and constituted an addition to his real resolve. Rather, it was a part, even the central part, the very heart, of the *Vita evangelii*... His concern is the imitation of the historical Christ of the gospels as the earthly-human, visible, tangible form of the

Son of God who appeared to us in humility' (K. V. Selge, 'Franz von Assisi und die Römische Kurie,' *Zeitschrift für Theologie und Kirche* 67 (1970) 129–161, here 149 and 151). Within the context of his article, Selge speaks only about being subject to the ecclesiastical authorities. He does not however research the origin of Francis' vision: that the Lord, and no one else, revealed this original form of evangelical life to Francis after he had left Assisi. It is precisely this origin which gives a totally different accent to Francis' wish to be subject. As will be shown in the following pages, Francis and his brothers saw their 'being-subject' first and foremost as an alternative way of life and as a protest against the use of power and violence in church and society. This original Franciscan interpretation, which Francis repeated in his Testament, should also be taken into account when interpreting the more legal, and not typically Franciscan use of the expression 'always to be subject and prostrate at the feet of the same holy church' at the end of chapter 12 of the *Regula bullata*. It will then appear that Francis and his brothers with their 'being-subject' to the Saracens for God's sake were not obeying the official church policy with regard to the crusades and the Saracens, sanctioned by pope and council, but were following the form of the gospel which the Lord had revealed to them. See also the commentary on verse 6 in the next chapter.

28. Flood, *Francis of Assisi*, 168–173.

29. We differ here from Lehmann: 'Wherever a brother may go, among Christians or non-Christians, all claims to power, all arrogance are excluded. The Franciscan does not rule over others, he allows himself to be ruled by others. He does not impose new structures, but starts by submitting himself to the existing ones, in order then, if need be, to dissolve the unjust structures from within' (Features, 6; Prinzipien, 332). As we have explained, Francis clearly decided not to be subject to the system and, if need be, to remove its unjust structures, but to radically break with it: 'I left the world' (Test 3), and to take care that this world would not return: 'it shall not be like this among the brothers' (RegNB 5:10). In their interpretation of Francis, many authors understand certain words very traditionally in accordance with the dominant form of religious spirituality. They pay too little attention to the fact that Francis' break with Assisi and its value system resulted, among other things, in that several keywords obtained a completely different meaning in the brotherhood. For this see D. Flood, 'A Brief Survey of Early Franciscan History,' *Haversack* 1, 5 (May–June 1978), 7–9.

30. The emphasis which Francis laid on submission and service may sound alien and alienating to people who in whatever way, individually or as group, are forced into submission. Indeed, we are dealing here with words that are historically and culturally loaded. However, Francis used them as a challenge and a protest against the power politics of the rich and the mighty which he had experienced as sinful. This sin can only be destroyed and true peace

established if the rich and mighty give up every sense of power, every feeling of superiority, for these exclude true sister- and brotherhood which are based on mutual service in a spirit of equality and respect for the other as other.

31. For the essential importance of this attitude of vulnerability for the dialogue with people of other religions and cultures, see J. van Gerwen, 'Christian Faith and (In)Tolerance,' *Louvain Studies* 16 (1991) 220–241, here especially 239: 'Real tolerance presupposes unconditional love, rather than calculation, because one has to be ready to accept the risk of being misunderstood, hurt, or even killed by the other, before a common basis of understanding will be reached. I need to risk myself (my identity) honestly and unconditionally, hoping (not being sure) that the other will do the same to me. It is necessary that I make the first move, not waiting for the other's opening.'

32. See Flood, *Assisi's Rules*, 95–100, where he develops the different knowledge which the brothers had obtained with regard to the asking of alms (And let them know... RegNB 9:7). Alms are for the brothers 'a heritage and a right due to the poor, which our Lord Jesus Christ acquired for us,' while for the rich alms are an act of charity. *Mutatis mutandis,* Francis' awareness that the knowledge of the brothers is different from that of Assisi, can also be applied to the understanding of 'being subject.' See also Flood, *Francis of Assisi*, 51–54.

33. 'This much is evident: the gospel texts of this chapter do not have the "decorative" role which one would have liked to attribute to them. For what would remain, if they would be eliminated? We are convinced, therefore, that the choice of these texts goes back to Francis, while the editing has been done by Caesar of Spires' (B. Vollot, 'Césaire de Spire et la Règle de 1221,' *Laur* 32 (1991) 3–28; 33 (1992) 175–220, here 175). In what follows Vollot shows clearly how the hand of an expert has joined and harmonized the texts of Lk 9:3 and 10:4 in RegNB 14:1: '... *nihil* (Lk 9) *portent* (Lk 10) *per viam neque* (Lk 9) *sacculum neque peram* (Lk 10) *neque panem neque pecuniam neque virgam* (Lk 9),' whereby '*neque virgam*' has been shifted from the beginning to the end of the list. That Caesar of Spires is this expert, indeed, is assumed on the basis of the witness of the Chronicle of Jordan of Giano: 'Since Francis saw that Caesar was well versed in sacred science, he commissioned him to embellish with the words of the gospel the Rule which he had conceived in simple words' (15). See also K. Esser, *Die Opuscula des hl. Franziskus von Assisi: Neue textkritische Edition*, Grottaferrata, 1989, 57–58; 403. Vollot advocates, however, another translation of the verb '*adornare*' than the usual French '*orner*,' or English 'embellish.' After a detailed lexigraphical examination, he concludes: 'All these considerations help us to understand better the role of Caesar of Spires: he has 'arranged' the gospel texts. In a first draft, Francis had in his own words

explained to him the gospel passages which he wanted to figure in the rule. Caesar has formed them in the original way of presentation which we know now. They have worked together in close collaboration' (a.c., 9).

34. 'The Franciscan movement and the communal system dealt with people and with things in two diametrically opposed fashions. The brothers declared their solidarity with lepers; they made the goods of life circulate among all. The rising communal class excluded the poor and the weak, claimed a lion's share of the social product, and polished up San Rufino to count God in on the commune's blessings. Given the social model of 1210 and the model of social action in Chapter XIV, there arose a sharp conflict between the movement and its milieu.., between Franciscan peace and communal peace' (Flood, Assisi's Rules, 94; see also Francis of Assisi, 70–76). A somewhat similar idea can be found in Rotzetter. When, according to him, Francis selects certain gospel texts from Lk 6 and Lk 10 to be the guiding principle for his brothers in RegNB 14, 'it should be clear that the Franciscan life is to be understood as a confrontation between the Kingdom of God and the world. By their going about through the world Franciscans want, at least as far as their intention is concerned, to realize the Kingdom of God as a reality that is coming near' (*Die Funktion*, 162).

35. *LegPer* 67. See C. Delcorno, 'Origini della predicazione francescana,' in *Francesco*, 125–160, here 132: 'In fact, to speak about peace in a society which is suffocated by the violence of weapons and laws seemed a provocative foolishness.'

36. Dozzi, o.c., 221–222.

37. Godet, a.c., 19: 'It is interesting to note in passing that the breeches are walking clothes. It is a matter of decency: one would tie up one's tunic to walk better. Wearing breeches permanently implies therefore that one travels frequently, a certain itinerancy.' See also Desbonnets, o.c., 28–30.

38. J. Le Goff, 'Franciscanisme et modèles culturels du XIIIe siècle,' in *Francescanesimo*, 83–128, here 90–91. It is striking that for the first Christians too the house is central. See J. H. Elliott, 'Household and Meals vs. Temple Purity, Replication Patterns in Luke-Acts,' *Biblical Theology Bulletin* 21 (1991) 102–108. It would go too far to presuppose here a dependence. It remains interesting, however, to see how both movements take the house as model for the new social relations of solidarity and inclusivity which they want to create as an expression of the values of the gospel, especially with regard to the marginalized.

39. Desbonnets, o.c., 30.

40. Godet, a.c., 20–21. See also Flood, The Politics, 371–375. A somewhat stray echo of this way of life of the first brothers can still be found in 1 *Cel* 39. Long after he has told us that Francis started preaching immediately after he had heard the gospel in the Portiuncula chapel (1 *Cel* 23), Celano informs us in that later passage about the first form of life of the brothers: 'During

the day, those who knew how labored with their hands, staying in the houses of lepers, or in other places where they could do a useful and decent job, serving all humbly and devotedly.'

41. 'We may conclude that in our section the oral preaching, fundamental in the gospel passages about mission, has been placed in the background.... In our context, the attention is directed rather to a witness of the gospel through one's life' (Dozzi, o.c., 211–212). Dozzi presupposes, and correctly in my view, that Francis made a selection and that the omission of the texts about preaching implies that he moved preaching into the background. Here Dozzi differs fundamentally from Rotzetter who writes with regard to RegNB 14:1–3: 'Since this quotation is composed from the missionary discourses of the Lord to the twelve (Lk 9) and to the seventy (Lk 10), the basic idea of the statute about wandering, which is identical with the primary function of the order, could be described as being sent to proclaim the kingdom of God. In accordance with the words of the Lord which are not directly quoted, but presupposed in the RegNB, this formula implies *the liberation of the world from the power of the demon, the healing of the sick and preaching on the basis of the power and authority of Christ, given to his disciples*' (*Die Funktion*, 161).

42. See among others Dozzi: 'The "lives of St Francis"... present different faces of Francis by projecting on to the past problems, answers and aspirations of the present' (o.c., 33). Also G. Miccoli, who writes: 'The different biographies and collections of materials on the life of Francis arise from various situations in the order—from various commitments in response to various needs' ('Francis of Assisi's Christian Proposal,' *Greyfriars Review* 3, 2 (August 1989) 130).

43. 'The community which Francis of Assisi wishes to establish, is much more a community of followers of Christ than of preachers' (R. Zerfass, *Der Streit um die Laienpredigt*, Freiburg, 1974, 236–237). But when they preach, then 'the proclamation of the word constitutes an integral part of the life according to the form of the gospel, and not an isolated apostolic or ecclesiastical function' (ibid., 239–240).

44. This happens rather soon. Thus Burchard of Ursperg (✠1231) in his *Chronicon* presents the Friars Minor and the Friars Preachers as the orthodox successors of the Humiliati and the Poor Men of Lyons. See *Omnibus*, 1604–1605. More recently, among others, K. Esser, *Anfänge und ursprüngliche Zielsetzungen des Ordens der Minderbrüder*, Leiden, 1966, 54–60. His opinion is followed by Lehmann: 'According to the early sources, the friars minor form a community of itinerant preachers' (Features, 3). In a later article, Lehmann qualifies this observation: 'Certainly, they are not in the first place concerned with preaching but, inspired by a strong Christocentrism, with the imitation of the wandering life of Jesus in poverty and in a renunciation of possessions, power and violence' (Prinzipien, 330). But why does

Lehmann all the same continue to use the model of the itinerant preachers? It can only create a false impression. Further, it is remarkable that Lehmann in his later qualification does not mention manual work, which is exactly what Francis is concerned with (Test 20). See also D. Berg, 'Kreuzzugsbewegung und Propagatio Fidei: Das Problem der Franziskanermission im 13. Jahrhundert und das Bild von der islamischen Welt in der zeitgenössischen Ordenshistoriographie,' *MiscMed* 17, Berlin, 1985, 60: 'The main activity of the merchant's son... consisted in the apostolic itinerant preaching (*Wanderpredigt*). At the same time the brothers were concerned to underline the content of their penitential sermons through an exemplary conduct.... The care for the salvation of their fellow humans, of prime importance in the communal areas which were pastorally inadequately taken care of, stood therefore at the center of the life of the Poverello and his first companions.' This interpretation is not only found in the German-speaking world, but also in Italy. Delcorno writes: 'To present Francis as an itinerant preacher may seem a reduction of his rich and many-sided personality; yet, all things considered, this is the most useful approach to understand the most authentic motivations of his work' (a.c., 129). *Mutatis mutandis*, the critical observation which G. P. Freeman makes with regard to Esser's opinion about the influence of the Cathari on the first admonition of Francis, holds good here too: 'A generation ago, it was a bright idea of Esser to oppose Francis and the Cathari of his time. The Poverello became thus more firmly inserted in his time or, more precisely, in the picture of his time that is current among church historians since Grundmann. According to that picture, Waldensians, Cathari and Friars Minor belong together as "religious movements." The problem is, however, that Francis never expressly criticizes the Cathari or mentions them by name...' ('Zur Interpretationsgeschichte der ersten Ermahnung des hl. Franziskus,' *WissWeis* 51 (1988) 123–143, here 136).

45. PL 216, 648. See Zerfass, o.c., 223.
46. Very enlightening here is Flood, Assisi's Rules, 93.
47. A completely different interpretation is given by Vazquez. After rejecting the views of Basetti-Sani and De Beer, expressed in articles in the review *Concilium* 149 (1981), he formulates his own hypothesis as follows: 'Francis had a strong desire to go to the sultan. He went there in fact to seek permission for himself, his brothers and perhaps all Christians to visit freely the holy places, especially the Holy Sepulchre... Since a number of years a law of the sultan was in force according to which every Christian wishing to visit the Holy Sepulchre would have to pay a considerable sum of money... Because of this Francis planned to clear this situation... It seems to me that this hypothesis becomes more probable when we consider it in the light of the memories of brother Illuminatus of Rieti, Francis' companion

during his visit of the sultan....' After the presentation and a short analysis of the story of brother Illuminatus, Vazquez concludes: 'No invitations to conversion, no polemics against the Koran, no insults against Mohammed and his followers. Francis asked only two precise things: a) respect for one's own religion—so that the name of Christ would not be cursed—; b) freedom to practice one's own faith and personal devotions without being hindered or alienated' (I. Vazquez, 'I Francescani e il Dialogo con gli Ebrei e i Saraceni nei secoli XIII–XV,' *Antonianum* 65 (1990) 538–540). For the story of brother Illuminatus, see *Omnibus* 1614–1615. See also below, note 58.

48. v. d. Vat, o.c., 4–5. If v. d. Vat is correct in his opinion that Francis did not have a direct example, it makes little sense to devote so much attention, as K. Elm does, to attempts made in the eleventh century to establish contact with Muslims in Spain or to the visit of Peter the Hermit to the king of Antioch during the first crusade (1098) or to the missionary activity of the Camaldulensians in Poland at the end of the tenth century. All these events are completely outside Francis' scope. At the same time, however, Elm totally forgets to take into account the direct, immediate context of the fifth crusade in his own interpretation of Francis' understanding of mission. Further, Elm himself acknowledges that in none of the religious movements at the time of Francis anything can be found that resembles a missionary activity outside the Christian world. K. Elm, 'Franz von Assisi: Busspredigt oder Heidenmission?,' *Espansione*, 71–103.

49. For this reason Freeman writes: 'I hesitate as to whether this journey [to Damietta] must be placed among Francis' attempts to establish peace. The motives which moved Francis to go unarmed to the sultan and preach to him the Christian faith, are disputed in the sources. Did he look for martyrdom? Did he want to convert the sultan in order to put an end to the crusades? Or did he mainly go to the crusaders to tell them that their undertaking would be disastrous? Whatever the case may be, his disarming behavior made a great impression among both Christians and Muslims' ('Schooiers om vrede: Over de vroeg franciscaanse beweging als vredesbeweging,' in *Geweld-tegen-geweld?* Hilversum, 1984, 11–32, here 21). Because of my interpretation of chapter 16 in the light of its context, I do not share his hesitation.

50. See his 'St. Francis and Islam,' *Concilium* 149 (1981) 11–20. Reprinted in 'Mission in the Franciscan Tradition,' *Spirit and Life: A Journal of Contemporary Franciscanism* 6 (1994) 161–175. In what follows I will refer to this last publication, abbreviated: Francis and Islam.

51. 1 *Cel* 55–57; *Bonaventura* IX 5 and 7.

52. *Omnibus*, 1609; the original text of Ernoul, a French knight who spent most of his life in the Middle East and continued there the chronicle of William of Tyre, can be found in G. Golubovich, *Biblioteca bio-bibliografica della Terra Santa e dell'Oriente francescano*, Quaracchi, 1906, I, 12–13; abbreviated: *BBT*.

53. *Omnibus*, 1612.

54. For the original text of Bernard, see *BBT*, 13–14.

55. After the disastrous defeat of the crusaders on August 29, 1219, sultan al-Malek al-Kamil made them a generous peace offer, in which he proposed to return Jerusalem to the Christians in exchange for the withdrawal of the crusaders' army from Egypt. During the negotiations which ultimately remained without success because, against the advice of John of Brienne, cardinal Pelagius rejected the sultan's offer, Francis made good use of the truce and went to visit the sultan, according to Lemmens (a.c., 560–561). Cf. Powell, o.c., 159–160; H. von der Bey, *"Der Herr gebe dir den Frieden!"* Werl, 1990, 99. In this case, Francis' visit had no influence on the peace offer of the sultan. Donovan thinks, however, that Francis' visit to the sultan could have contributed to a peace offer or at least the offer of a truce from the side of the sultan (o.c., 61–63). According to E. Grau, *Thomas von Celano, Leben und Wunder des hl. Franziskus von Assisi*, Franziskanische Quellenschriften 5, Werl, 1988, 122, Francis' visit to the sultan probably took place only after the truce which lasted till September 26. His argumentation is based on 1 *Cel* 57: 'In the thirteenth year of his conversion Francis set out for Syria, at a time when great and severe battles were raging daily between the Christians and the pagans; he took with him a companion, and he did not fear to present himself before the sultan of the Saracens.'

56. For the original text, see *BBT*, 14.

57. J. Powell, 'Francesco d'Assisi e la Quinta Crociata: Una Missione di Pace,' *Schede Medievali*, 4, Gennaio-Giugno, 1983, 68–77. Later, in my exegesis of chapter 16, I will return to this article.

58. *Omnibus*, 1614–1615. See also Nolthenius, o.c., 140 and 229. Without any further examination of the historical trustworthiness of the story of brother Illuminatus, Nolthenius concludes, incorrectly in my opinion: 'The words which Illuminatus has passed on to us ("It is written: if your eye hinders you, tear it out. Sultan, you are that eye") clearly indicate the extent of his [Francis'] tolerance... and moreover the limits of his pacifism. Peace must reign among the Christians themselves. A holy war is a category apart: terrible, but not to be condemned indiscriminately' (229). Elm comes to a similar conclusion. In his view, the opinion about the just character of the crusade, which the story of Illuminatus attributes to Francis personally, 'considerably restricts the thesis of the unconditional criticism of the crusade on the part of the Saint,' (a.c., note 96). Maier concludes his chapter on Francis and the fifth crusade: 'But if anything at all can be said about the visit to Damietta, the conclusion, on balance, must be that Francis did not come to Damietta to stop the Fifth Crusade. On the contrary, his overall objective was the same as that of the crusaders. Francis, like the crusaders, wanted to liberate the holy places in Palestine from Muslim rule. What was different was his strategy: Francis went beyond the idea of simply expelling

the Muslims from where they interfered with Christian life. He wanted their total submission to the Christian faith. Short of this total submission there would be no peace; short of this, for Francis too, was the necessity, if not the duty, to crusade against the enemies of faith' (o.c., 16–17).

59. On the basis of his examination of the texts of James of Vitry, Ernoul and others, De Beer concludes: 'This unarmed and disarming dimension has not escaped the notice of the sources and, above all, Jacques de Vitry, our privileged witness. Francis deliberately disengaged himself from the crusade. He risked being misunderstood by everyone' (*We Saw Brother Francis*, Chicago, 1983, 75–76; abbreviated: *Brother Francis*).

PART ONE: Chapter 3

1. In preparing my translation of chapter 16, I have consulted and made use of D. Flood, *The Birth of a Movement*, Chicago, 1975, 84–89; I. Brady, *The Writings of Saint Francis of Assisi*, Assisi, 1983, 76–77; R. Armstrong and I. Brady, *Francis and Clare: The Complete Works*, New York, 1982, 121–122.

2. D. Flood, 'Franciscans and Money,' *Haversack* 4, 2 (Dec. 1980), 12–21, here 13; see also his *Francis of Assisi*, 24–25.

3. v. d. Vat, o.c., 3–4, comes to the same conclusion. For him too Francis' going among the Saracens cannot be derived in a deductive manner from Jesus' missionary discourse. In this v. d. Vat clearly differs from B. v. Leeuwen who writes: 'He [Francis] has from the very beginning understood his call and that of his brothers as universal, after the image of the apostles, and hence also as a call to live and work among non-Christians as well as among Christians' ('Leven te midden van niet-christenen volgens de regel van 1221 en 1223,' *FL* 58 (1975) 217–230, here 220). Manselli holds a similar opinion, when he writes that Francis' going among the Saracens is a 're-elaboration of evangelical data,' and concerns 'an attitude that is born from meditating the gospel, from Francis' own evangelism' (*Espansione*, 21). See also De Roeck, o.c., 26 and 88–89; Esser, a.c., 19; Lehmann, Prinzipien, 122.

4. A good example is provided by the use of the text: 'If anyone wishes to come after me, let him deny himself and take up his cross and follow me' (Mt 16:24). Innocent III used this text as an appeal to a crusade against the Saracens in order to defend the interests of Western Christianity, whereas Francis, on the basis of his interpretation of the reality of Assisi, recognized in the text an invitation to live as a servant, not in power but in submission, among the people and even among the Saracens and to suffer patiently the eventual persecution that might be connected with this choice.

5. For a similar view, though somewhat differently argued, see v. d. Vat: 'No other word of the Savior could have expressed more clearly what the missionary activity meant to Francis in the first place: a risky undertaking, full of sacrifices, which demanded great prudence and strong courage from the

missionary. A missionary assignment, so authoritative as Christ's mission-ary command: "Go, therefore, and teach all nations" would not really have been in harmony with the peculiar character of Francis' view on mission,' (o.c., 12).

6. Dozzi, o.c., 210–214.

7. De Beer sees in the choice of this text an allusion 'to a tiny historical detail. After leaving the crusader camp Francis and his companion met two sheep just before being attacked by the Saracens' (Francis and Islam, 171). Cf. De Beer, *Brother Francis*, 90–91; De Roeck, o.c., 99. It is probably more correct to assume that this 'fact' which is mentioned by Bonaventure (IX, 8), finds its origin in the text of the rule.

8. Peter of Blois writes in 1188–1189: 'What foolishness is it, I ask, at the time of such great need, to allow the wolf to rage out on the flock, and only then to prepare for help when he has devoured all the sheep' (PL 207, 1064). Peter rebuked here the kings who continued to delay the crusade while in the meantime the 'wolf' devoured the sheep. It is clear that Peter wanted to motivate the kings to take up the fight against the 'wolf' and to drive him away, whereas Francis had something completely different in mind. Interesting too is a prayer that the soldiers of Genoa prayed when they attacked Damietta. We read therein: 'and like the sheep without their shep-herd tremble with fear in the midst of the wolves, so we will not be able to conquer the treacherous infidels without Your [i.e., God's] help.' Cf. A. Fortini, *Francis of Assisi*, New York, 1981, 403.

9. Thus Jordan tells us that Francis 'was received with honor (*gloriose*) and humanely (*humane*) treated because of his sickness' (10).

10. Sevenhoven, a.c., 204–208. According to Rotzetter, however, the image of the sheep between the wolves refers exclusively to the opposition and the perse-cution which the brothers may encounter and of which Francis is very well aware. See his Missionary Dimension, 48–49. The same opinion is also found in L. Lehmann, *Tiefe und Weite*, Werl, 1984, 239–240. Lehmann refers to the restoration of paradise (243), but this idea has no influence on his interpretation of what it means to go as sheep in the midst of wolves. See also Dozzi, o.c., 206.

11. See e.g., Adm 3, 8–9; 6, 2; 9, 1; Test 6; 25; RegB 10, 9–11. Further, we find numerous stories of this kind in the biographies, starting with the persecu-tion by his father: 1 *Cel* 10–15. Very interesting are the observations which are made in *AnonPer* 17b–c; 18b–c; 20a–24b. There we read, among other things: 'The brothers were treated well by this man, but he was an excep-tion' (23a).

12. As regards prudence, De Beer writes: 'The tact and the prudence that Francis requires of his missionary brothers coming to grips with another culture must be emphasized here' (*Brother Francis*, 92). As regards simplicity, Berg observes: 'Only in a later, second phase of communication could the

Friar Minor—always preserving peace—start with the proclamation of the word of God. This too should not take place in a polemical form, but with the specific Franciscan attitude of the *simplicitas*,' (a.c., 63). Jeusset relates simplicity to the life of the Friar Minor. By living as very ordinary people among the Saracens, they will be able to confess in all simplicity that they are Christians: 'confesser simplement,' 'la simple présence,' (o.c., 63–64).

13. The most detailed elaboration is given by De Beer, *Brother Francis*, 91–95. Instead of relating the gospel text to the twofold way of being 'spiritually' present among the Saracens (6–7), he considers the text as determining the structure of the whole chapter in three corresponding parts: the sheep— verses 1–4; the serpent—verses 5–9; the dove—verses 10–21. It is not at all clear, however, what the nonviolence of the sheep has to do with obtaining the permission of the minister, nor how the simplicity of the dove relates to the readiness to suffer martyrdom. Sevenhoven relates the gospel text to the twofold presence, though somewhat less systematically (a.c., 208). Dozzi rejects any relation between the gospel text and the structure of the chap- ter. 'Our text integrally reports Mt 10:16 in chapter 16:1–2, but the norms that follow (to go among the nonbelievers, to be subject to all, to confess that they are Christians, to proclaim the word of God) do not really appear to be typical examples of simplicity and especially of prudence' (213). 'It was certainly not "prudent" to go among the Saracens: it was tantamount to going to the slaughter, to martyrdom' (222). He does however link the image of the sheep with being subject and with possible persecution (206).

14. Lehmann, Prinzipien, 325–326, where he concludes: 'the negative under- standing of prudence explains perhaps why this word has no further effect on the description of the manner of working among the Saracens as well as on the writings in general.' It is indeed true that the gospel text is only quoted here, but this does not imply that the text does not have an effect on our passage. On the contrary, as Lehmann himself explicitly mentions in his commentary, with their emphasis on waiting with their preaching until they see that it pleases the Lord, Francis and his brothers clearly indicated their wish that those brothers who live among the Saracens proceed in a 'prudent' manner. 'The preacher must be able to get the feeling of the situa- tion and to discover God's will. The utmost attention toward God and humans is required' (a.c., 333).

15. For this and what follows, see Lehmann, Features, 4–5; Prinzipien, 323–324.

16. Also chapters 3 and 8 of the *Regula non bullata* and Admonitions 1, 2, 3 and 9 start in the same way. Cf. Lehmann, Prinzipien, 323.

17. At the Fourth Lateran Council more than 400 bishops from 80 ecclesiastical provinces were present, together with more than 800 abbots and priors. It was the most magnificent church assembly of the medieval West.

18. Powell, o.c., 90–93.

19. Together with Flood, Bühlmann, Lehmann, and Armstrong we keep to the

words *divina inspiratio*. Esser has omitted these words in his critical edition of the writings of Francis. Hence they are absent in most of the recent translations, with the exception of the English translations of Flood and of Armstrong-Brady. Esser's argumentation is based on the fact that these words are absent in Angelus Clarenus who would never have omitted them if they had been in the original. Next, Esser explains the presence of these words in the other manuscripts by assuming that the transcribers who knew the *Regula bullata* by heart, added these words as it were automatically from *Regula bullata* 12:1. Most authors think Esser's arguments to be rather weak. Thus Lehmann writes: 'This argumentation is extremely weak, because: 1) Angelus Clarenus is an unreliable witness, as Esser himself has shown in several places; 2) the expression would hardly have come into the *Regula bullata* if it had not already been in the *Regula non bullata*, for it was the intention to shorten the latter. In RegB 12:1 we have in fact a pitiful remainder of RegNB 16:3; 3) "divine inspiration" is closely linked with what two verses later is called "to live spiritually" (RegNB 16:5); 4) the expression is so typical for Francis that it must be considered original here as well for reason of internal coherence. Anyone who wishes to imitate Christ, does so under the inspiration of the Holy Spirit' (Prinzipien, 326–327). To this may be added, in my opinion, that Francis inserted the verses 3b–5a into chapter 16 in order to defend the conscientious choice of the individual brother against the policies of certain ministers. If so, it is very unlikely that Francis would not have used the words *divina inspiratio* to characterize the brother's choice to go among the Saracens.

20. My translation differs from the existing ones. While the French and Dutch translations do not specify whom or what the ministers should not oppose, the English translations of Flood and of Armstrong-Brady have 'and not oppose them,' i.e., the brothers who wish to go among the Saracens. So also the German translation. We prefer to relate the words *minister... non contradicat* to the opening words *Dicit Dominus*. The Lord says (*dicit*) and hence the minister should not contradict (*non contradicat*), but allow the brother to go, for it is the Lord who by his word sends him.

21. *Jordan* 16. According to *LegPer* 114 there would have been even more than five thousand brothers present. According to Freeman, 'Jordan deserves a greater credibility because he was personally present. However, medieval chronicles often show a tendency to exaggerate when great numbers are involved' (*Ze kwamen op blote voeten*, Haarlem, 1991, 31, note 23).

22. v. d. Vat, o.c., 13. It is not clear whether the ministers also referred eventually to canon law. The *Compilatio Secunda*, compiled after 1210 by John of Wales, contains a decision, taken from a letter of Clement III (1187–1191), in which permission was given to a bishop in the Baltic countries that religious who were fit to proclaim the gospel to the pagans might freely join him after they had asked and obtained the approval of their superior. Cf. II

Comp. 5, 4, 4=X 5. 6. 11, *Corpus Iuris Canonici*, ed. Friedberg, 2, 775. Did the ministers know this canon and did they insist that they too should give their approval? Most probably, as indicated in the text, the rule involves the ministers in the sending out of the brothers because of the fast expansion of the brotherhood.

23. See for this and what follows: L. Iriarte, *Geschiedenis van de franciskaanse beweging*, Utrecht, n.d., 51–52; J. Hoeberichts, 'Ministry to the Friars in the Writings of Francis and the Early Biographers,' *FIA Contact* 6, 4 (Nov. 1985) 2–9. In translating *rectitudo vitae nostrae* as 'the right direction of our life,' we differ from Flood's 'the determinations of our [way of] life' (o.c., 71), Brady's 'the pattern of our life' (o.c., 67), and Armstrong-Brady's 'the integrity of our life' (o.c., 113).

24. 'These words bespeak inner agitation, a certain repugnance. Evidently, Francis finds himself here in a defensive position against the ministers' (v. d. Vat, o.c., 15). See also above, 48–9.

25. See also the story about obedience in 2 *Cel* 152. 'Another time, speaking about the same subject (of true obedience) he said that according to him that obedience was the highest and was without anything of flesh and blood by which one goes by divine inspiration among the infidels either for the salvation of one's neighbors or out of a desire for martyrdom. To ask for this obedience he thought was highly acceptable to God.' However, the dialectic struggle in this story happens more on the individual, personal level between, on the one hand, 'flesh and blood,' in the sense of the 'natural' person who acts out of self-interest and, on the other, the supernatural, divine inspiration by which a person is invited to put aside his or her own interests and even to risk his or her own life by going among the unbelievers. The ecclesiastical and political aspects are not at all taken into consideration. Yet it seems to me that the latter stand in the foreground in Francis' Testament when he states emphatically: 'No one showed me what I should do, but the Most High himself revealed to me that I should live according to the form of the holy gospel' (14).

26. Such a dialectical interpretation is generally not followed in commentaries on chapter 16. Certainly, Lehmann does write in the introduction of one of his articles that 'Francis developed another alternative strategy' which has been 'formulated in the mission statute of the *Regula non bullata*,' but he does not further elaborate on this. When afterwards he speaks about the *divina inspiratio*, he does not contrast this with the thinking then prevailing in the church, but with an eventual acting on their own authority by the brothers without indicating what this concretely might consist in. In fact, Lehmann does not go beyond some general remarks which are not further contextualized: 'Francis and his companions consider themselves to be sent. They do not act on their own, but by order of the Lord: "by divine inspiration." The Lord is the origin of their mission and its content. The fact as

well as the form of their mission derive from the words of the Lord' (Features, 5). Because of the absence of any contextualization, these general remarks could also be applied to the crusaders. They too considered themselves to be sent; they too did not act on their own, but by order of the Lord. What is the difference then between Francis and the crusaders? The real difference becomes manifest only in the contrasting ideas, views and positions of Francis and his brothers, on the one hand, and of the church officials and crusaders, on the other, as brought to the fore by the dialectical interpretation.

27. 'Charissimi, obsecro vos tanquam advenas et peregrinos abstinere vos a carnalibus desideriis, quae militant adversus animam, conversationem vestram inter gentes habentes bonam.' Cf. S. J. P. van Dijk, The Ordinal of the Papal Court from Innocent III to Boniface VIII and Related Documents, completed by J. H. Walker, Fribourg, 1975, 307, where this reading is assigned for the Terce of the Second Sunday after the Octave of Easter. See also O. v. Asseldonk, 'Le lettere di S. Pietro negli scritti di S. Francesco,' Collectanea Franciscana 48 (1978) 67–76. He does not, however, refer to this text in his article.

28. AnPer 10–11. As regards this story A. Jansen writes: 'Especially remarkable is... the reaction of the three (Francis, Bernard and Peter): "This is what we desire." We have here the same reaction as Francis expressed after the reading of the missionary discourse in... 1 Cel 22. Is this not an indication that the story of 1 Cel has been separated from the original unit and has become an independent double story? Maybe Celano wanted to place the little church of Portiuncula more clearly into the limelight as the place where the Friars Minor had been founded. If Francis would have discovered the gospel there, this little church would even more clearly be the "foundation" of the order. A beautiful idea, but we doubt whether it is historically correct. Moreover, we know that Celano does not write history. For him the facts are meant to illustrate the ideas and, if need be, he is prepared to adapt the facts to the ideas' ('Franciscus ontdekt het evangelie,' FL 66 (1983) 2–12, here 10–11).

29. Bühlmann, a.c., 102; Jeusset, o.c., 59.

30. Rotzetter, Missionary Dimension, 53.

31. G. P. Freeman and H. Sevenhoven, De nalatenschap van een arme, Utrecht, 1989, 26; an English translation of this study has been published in installments in FrancDig III, 1 (June 1993) and following issues under the title: 'The Legacy of a Poor Man'; here FrancDig III, 1, 13–14.

32. Lehmann puts a different emphasis: 'On the other hand, one must not overlook here that the founder of the order is bound by the linguistic usage and the ideas of his time, when he counts the Muslims among the unbelievers (infideles). Evidently Francis considers all people who are not Christian, be they Jew or Muslim, as unbelievers who are to be converted' (Prinzipien, 328). In my opinion, the whole tenor of chapter 16 points in another direc-

tion, as I have tried to indicate in my commentary.

33. See James of Vitry, *Historia Occidentalis* 32, 14 in *Omnibus*, 1612.

34. Esser, followed by Bühlmann and Lehmann, speaks about a threefold way of being present among the Saracens: 'Francis distinguishes a threefold way to convince non-Christians of the truth of the gospel; a threefold way which breaks radically with the categories of this world' (a.c., 14). Cf. Bühlmann, a.c., 105; Lehmann, Prinzipien, 336. This third way is described in the verses 10–21. See further our commentary on these verses on 114.

35. The text of 1 Pe 2:12 can probably also be heard in the second letter of James of Vitry where he writes about his trip to Sarepta, '.. where I stayed for the night preaching to the Christians whom I found there, the word of God and showing them how they ought to live in a commendable way among the Saracens (*qualiter inter Sarracenos commendabiliter deberent conversari*)' (Huygens, o.c., 191–192). But whereas James was mostly concerned to remove the bad name of the Christians by a more commendable way of life and so to enhance their esteem in the eyes of the Saracens, Francis wished first of all that his brothers, faithful to their calling, live among the Saracens 'in the Spirit of the Lord.' Whether the Saracens were going to hold the brothers in higher esteem because of this or not, was of less importance to Francis and his brothers. Even if they would be tortured or persecuted because of their allegiance to the Lord, they would always remember that they 'have given themselves and have abandoned their bodies to the Lord Jesus Christ' (RegNB 16:10).

36. Esser places a different emphasis here. According to him, the brothers work 'spiritually' among the non-Christians when they perform their work in a way which 'corresponds to the Spirit of the Lord, and not in accordance with the norms that hold good among humans.' This presupposes that 'all egoism has been overcome and that, to speak in the words of Francis, the spirit of the ego has been replaced by the Spirit of the Lord.' It is evident here that Esser remains on the individualistic and moralistic level, and does not really place Francis in his historical context. Francis' going among the Saracens and his being subject to them is thus mainly seen as a personal victory over the egoism within himself, as an act of personal virtuousness, and not as taking a stand in 'the Spirit of the Lord' against the policies of the church which were dominated by the 'spirit of the flesh,' as an act of social and political involvement in what was happening in the society of his days. Cf. D. Flood, 'The Spirit's Action,' *Haversack* 9, 2 (Dec 1985) 19.

37. It is really remarkable how Francis and his brothers came to a totally different understanding of the expression: the inheritance of Christ. Notwithstanding all that they continually heard in sermons about the Holy Land as the inheritance of Christ, Francis and his brothers applied the expression to alms as the rightful share of the poor in the goods of the earth which Christ had won for them. Cf. RegNB 9:8.

38. See above, 46. Lehmann relates the expression 'not to engage in arguments and disputes' also to the behavior of the brothers among themselves: 'The expression regards at one and the same time the behavior of the brothers among themselves as well as toward people outside the brotherhood: they should not engage in arguments or disputes, but live as brothers among each other' (Prinzipien, 331; Features, 6). This interpretation has been inspired by the text: 'Nor should they argue among themselves or with others' (RegNB 11:3: cf. RegB 3:10). See also Rotzetter, Missionary Dimension, 51. In the context of the brothers who are going among the Saracens, the application to the behavior of the brothers among themselves appears improbable.

39. Cf. the saying of Peter the Venerable mentioned above: 'not with arms but with words; not with violence but with reason; not with hate but with love.' Rotzetter makes an immediate connection between Peter and Francis. 'Certainly Francis did not stand completely alone in his peaceful attitude. At least, in the middle of the 12th century, Peter the Venerable, abbot of Cluny, wrote in his *Adversos nefandam sectam Saracenorum* sentences like the following: not with arms but with words... Francis and his mission statute must be seen against the background of this work. While Peter expected the conversion of the Saracens from the use of science supported by the spirit of love, Francis wanted to concentrate on the fascination of a life full of love and devotion. In this way Francis came, even more clearly than Peter the Venerable, into conflict with the crusading mentality of most of his contemporaries, even of Innocent III' (*Die Funktion*, 165–166). See also his article 'Kreuzzugskritik und Ablehnung der Feudalordnung in der Gefolgschaft des Franziskus von Assisi,' *WissWeis* 35 (1972) 121–137, here 122; abbreviated: Kreuzzugskritik. We doubt whether there exists any connection at all between Peter the Venerable and Francis. Apart from the fact that Francis probably never heard of Peter and his work, Francis and Peter were very different personalities and their ideals varied greatly. In a letter to the grandmaster of the order of the Templars, Peter who was in favor of using reason rather than the sword, expressed nevertheless his great admiration for the continuous battle of the order against the Saracens. And in a letter to a king of Jerusalem whom he did not mention by name, Peter wrote that, since he could not join him with the sword in his hand in order to destroy the enemies of Christ, he would try to help him with his prayer. He also informed king Louis VII that he hoped the king would destroy the Saracens just as once Moses and Joshua did with the Amorites and Canaanites. Further, I have already referred to the very negative language which Peter maintained with regard to Mohammed and Islam. Hence it is very difficult to see in Peter a forerunner of Francis who tried precisely to break through the crusade ideology and did not use any negative language with regard to Mohammed and Islam in his writings. For Peter the

Venerable, see Kedar, o.c., 99–103; Torrell, a.c., 275–280; E. Siberry, 'Missionaries and Crusaders, 1095–1274: Opponents or Allies?' *Studies in Church History*, vol. 20, 1983, 104.

40. Rotzetter holds the opposite view while referring to Peter the Venerable who in his *Adversus nefandam sectam Saracenorum* is opposed to 'such vehement disputes (*talium litium animosas contentiones*), which do not take place because of a desire to find the truth, but because of a stubborn zeal to defend one's own opinion. Christian moderation clearly condemns the arrogant and furious confrontations (*superbas ac furiosas lites*).' According to Rotzetter, it follows from this that 'the virtue of moderation demands a sober, down-to-earth way of arguing. Hence, when Francis excluded arguments and disputes, he spoke about that particular way of arguing which moves away from a sober, down-to-earth attitude in the direction of lack of self-control, wild gestures, anger, rashness and passionate quarreling, but also that way of dialoguing which is more concerned about one's own preconceived opinion than about the truth and which therefore takes place on the level of right and self-assertion instead of on that of love which cares about the salvation of the other,' (*Die Funktion*, 166–167). I do not deny that the apologetic approach of Peter the Venerable may have influenced James of Vitry and, through him, the brothers who worked in Syria. It is however also possible that James during his time as a student in Paris had come in contact with Alan of Lille and his *De fide catholica contra hereticos* (PL 210, 305–430). In this work, divided in four books, Alan takes on four different heretical groups: the Cathari, the Waldensians, the Jews and finally the pagans or Muslims (*Liber quartus. Contra paganos seu Mahometanos*). Cf. A. G. Weiler, 'Tolerantie van christenen in de middeleeuwen ten opzichte van joden en moslims: apartheid, verbanning en verovering,' *Begrip* 114 (June–July 1993), 5–23, here 10. Or was James familiar with the apologetic method from his days as a crusade preacher against the Albigensians? For as is clear from the mission which Innocent III entrusted to the reconciled Waldensian groups of Durand and Bernard Prim, it was acknowledged papal policy to fight heretics in disputationes. Cf. Zerfass, o.c., 213–229; Cole, o.c., 102. However this may be, a reference to Peter the Venerable and his objections against certain forms of arguing and dialoguing seems incorrect here. For the brothers were definitely concerned, not about their own being right, but about the truth of Christ which they wanted to preach in order to offer the Saracens the possibility of salvation. Moreover, Francis forbade all arguments and disputes without distinction, whereas Peter was opposed only to those which were too vehement and were not directed toward finding the truth. In other words, whereas Francis forbade all aggressiveness, Peter took a critical posture only toward certain excessive forms of it. The famous saying of Peter opens very explicitly with the words: 'I attack (*aggredior*)... you not with arms but with words....' Add to

this that Peter trusted in words and in reason, while Francis wanted his brothers to preach by their deeds (RegNB 17:3). The opinion of Rotzetter is followed by Elm, a.c., 79. References to Peter the Venerable are also found in Berg, a.c., 64, Kedar, o.c., 102.

41. Huygens, o.c., 96–97. Cf. chapter I, 35.

42. 'Faithful to the demand of the *vita minorum* to be humble and *minores* everywhere, Francis limited himself first to gaining the confidence of the non-Christians through his behavior and his appearance' (Berg, a.c., 63).

43. The expression: *'tu es humilitas,'* which Francis uses in his Praises of God, does in this succinct form not occur at the time of the Fathers nor in the Middle Ages. See further J. B. Freyer, 'Humilitas und Patientia in den Ermahnungen des hl. Franziskus,' *WissWeis* 53 (1990) 19–31.

44. This idea has been taken from A. Jansen, 'Thuis op de hele wereld: De spanning tussen broederschap en identiteit,' *FL* 73 (1990) 172–181, here 178–179.

45. *Passio sanctorum martyrum fratrum Berardi...,* in *Analecta Franciscana* III, 593. See further: v. d. Vat, o.c., 47–49; De Roeck, o.c., 49–56.

46. *Jordan,* 7–8. Cf. L. Pelegrini: 'Let us not forget a certain insistence of the sources on the thirst for martyrdom on the part of Francis: an attitude which seems to be contradicted by the witness of Jordan of Giano. He presents us Francis who indignantly rejected the *legenda* of the Franciscan martyrs of Morocco... One gets the impression, if one must believe Jordan, that Francis had clearly warned the brothers of the drama or rather the tragedy they were to encounter, precisely because of their thirst for martyrdom which led them to risk their lives. Hence there follows that whole series of precautions which characterize the formulation of the mission, as given in chapter 16 of the *Regula non bullata*' ('Verbali delle sedute,' *Espansione,* 23). See also G. Basetti-Sani, *L'Islam e Francesco d'Assisi,* Firenze, 1975, 199–202. He comes to the following conclusion: 'Francis could certainly not approve the way of apostolate used by his brothers in Morocco. They went imprudently to insult their neighbor in his own house, which was truly not very evangelical. For this reason Francis ordered that the story of their martyrdom be destroyed' (201). Cf. De Beer, a.c., 169.

47. BBT 12–13. A similar story can also be found in Bernard the Treasurer (ibid., 13–14).

48. *Bonaventura* IX, 8. Cf. G. Basetti-Sani, 'Chi era il vecchio famoso che incontrò San Francesco a Damietta,' *Studi Francescani,* 82 (1985) 209–244. After mentioning several authors who deny the story about the ordeal by fire or are sceptical about it, Basetti-Sani concludes: 'St. Bonaventure has personally known brother Illuminatus of Rieti who was the only brother to accompany St. Francis to the sultan... and it is on the authority of Francis' companion Illuminatus that he reports the fact. Hence we have here to do with an event that is certainly historical' (214). However, his argumentation is not

very convincing. v. d. Vat has his doubts about the historical character of the story, especially since James of Vitry, Jordan of Giano and Celano do not mention the ordeal by fire at all. According to him, there exists no more than 'a certain probability' (o.c., 55). De Roeck thinks that the story is to be considered as a medieval literary embellishment rather than as a historical fact (o.c., 71). Cardini concludes that we are dealing here with a legend (a.c., 228).

49. *Omnibus*, 1614. In the above mentioned article, Basetti-Sani writes about this 'fable of the carpet full with crosses' that, according to the editors of the *Fonti Francescane*, 'the episodes of the carpet and of the justification of the crusades are not reported by Bonaventure, "although they speak in such an extensive and well-informed way about the mission to the sultan." The reason is that both episodes are "apocryphal." The anecdote of the crosses on the carpet can be found in the story of a Coptic patriarch in Egypt and a non-Christian (Muslim) king.... The friars later attributed this to St. Francis.... The same holds good for the justification of the crusade which was the theological argument of some Latin authors even before the Saint' (a.c., 211–212, n. 7).

50. Lehmann comes to a similar conclusion: 'The eyes of the hagiographers remained closed to the fact that the unarmed pilgrim [Francis]... succeeded in meeting the sultan on a totally different level than was customary, namely on the level of giving witness without condemning the other; of confession without any ulterior political or military motives; of preaching the faith without wanting to be right all the time; of tolerance without denying one's own point of view' (Custodians, 45).

51. I. Vazquez, 'I Francescani e il Dialogo con gli Ebrei e i Saraceni nei secoli XIII–XV,' *Antonianum* 65 (1990) 541.

52. Esser, a.c., 15.

53. Features, 6; Prinzipien, 332–333. In his commentary on the Salutation of the Virtues Lehmann sees in its recommendation of being subject to all people, and even to all beasts, 'a witness to Francis' idea of nonviolent mission...which replaces the crusade by the dynamic of the lived example and the sword by the readiness to lay down one's life' (*Tiefe und Weite*, 239).

54. Bühlmann, a.c., 103.

55. 'Le Lettere di S. Pietro negli Scritti di S. Francesco,' *Collectanea Franciscana* 48 (1978) 70–71.

56. Missionary Dimension, 51–52.

57. Ibid., 50.

58. The word *subditus* occurs twice in the *Regula bullata*, but in a context that is very different from both the *Regula non bullata* and the Testament. In RegB 10:1–2 the rule speaks about the distinction within the brotherhood between 'the brothers who are the ministers and servants of the other brothers,' and 'the brothers who are subject.' In this sense *subditus*, subject,

is a rather strange, monastic sounding expression in the Franciscan world where, properly speaking, there is no place for a relation *superior-subditus* as the text itself indicates by emphasizing that the leaders of the brotherhood are ministers and servants of all. In RegB 12:4 *subditus* refers to an attitude of submission towards the church: 'always submissive and prostrate at the feet of the same holy church.' As such being *subditus* presupposes a hierarchical relationship which differs from, and even can come into conflict with, Francis' understanding (see 222, note 27). Cf. Godet: 'Whereas the exhortation to be subject to the others returns in Admonitions 19 and 23 as well as in the Letter to the Faithful, it is absent from the *Regula bullata*, where moreover the word *minor* is used only in the opening sentence: "The rule and life of the Friars Minor..."' (a.c., 29).

59. I am not very happy with the view of Freeman who writes: 'To be subject is for Francis a means at the service of the proclamation of peace.... To be subject is a condition for the credibility of peace' (a.c., 18 and 21). To be subject is a way of life which the brothers choose because 'being-subject' is an evangelical (counter)value worth being realized for its own sake, and not because it is a means to be more credible to others in their preaching. To be subject is no strategy, but a fundamental choice of life which the brothers make independently from the fact whether they will become more credible in the eyes of the others or not. In fact, the 'being-subject' as the brothers practice it, does not lead to a greater credibility at all. On the contrary, the brothers are often ill-treated and even persecuted. See above, 64, and also my commentary on verses 11–21, 118ff.

60. D. Flood, 'Working and Preaching, 1,' *Haversack* 9, 3 (Feb. 1986) 22–23; D. Flood, *Francis of Assisi*, 21–23.

61. v. d. Vat writes: 'Francis did not consider the life of the brothers in mission countries to be much different from that in Christian countries. At least that is the impression which chapter 16 gives. Settling down at some abandoned place or at a place left to them, they should sanctify their life through prayer and work. Through their work they should also earn their livelihood. If the wages for their work were not sufficient or if wages were refused to them, then begging should take their place. The contact with the people that this would involve, should be used by the brothers for their apostolic work....' Unfortunately, this apostolic work is not defined in view of the peace mission of the brothers but, strangely enough, in terms of the contempt of this world. 'For it is precisely the Franciscan life when lived to the full, that would be the most important means to bring the non-Christians to the contempt of this world, to conversion and to reflection' (o.c., 22).

62. '*Subiecti igitur estote omni humanae creaturae propter Deum: sive regi quasi praecellenti: sive ducibus tanquam ab eo missis...quia sic est voluntas Dei.*'

63. Lehmann, Features, 6–7; Prinzipien, 333. I do not agree with v. d. Vat, who

looks for an explanation of Francis' emphasis on 'being-subject' in the fanaticism of the Saracens: 'Surely Francis explicitly emphasized the virtues of peacemaking, tolerance and submission in the mission chapter because they appeared to him especially necessary for the missionaries in their contact with the unbelievers, the enemies of Christ, and, above all, the fanatic Saracens' (o.c., 16).

64. *Omnibus*, 1612. For an extensive commentary on this text, see De Beer, *Brother Francis*, 73–76.

65. C. W. Troll, 'Mission und Dialog am Beispiel des Islam,' *CIBEDO* 4 (1990) 101.

66. Huygens, o.c., 119.

67. Huygens, o.c., 123.

68. Huygens, o.c., 130–131.

69. For the various sources, see J. P. Donovan, *Pelagius and the Fifth Crusade*, Philadelphia, 1950, 65.

70. Huygens, o.c., 126 and 134. For Oliver, see Cole, o.c., 144: 'Concerning the fate of the Muslim population, Oliver waxes euphorically over the thought of the 30,000 who had died.' See also: v. den Brincken, a.c., 86–102.

71. Huygens, o.c., 126–127. See also Powell, o.c., 162; Donovan, o.c., 65.

72. Huygens, o.c., 126.

73. Basetti-Sani, o.c., 138–142.

74. Huygens, o.c., 135. James also reports how in those dark days people under the false name of pilgrims (*peregrini falsi nominis*) enter into the camp and exercise a bad influence. Or, as he writes earlier in his sixth letter, there are 'many thieves and robbers and people who are pilgrims in name only' in the camp (Huygens, o.c., 127). See also Powell, o.c., 162–163; Donovan, o.c., 65–67.

75. BBT, 14.

76. While the main reason to omit the word *subditus* lies in the profound changes which had taken place in the brotherhood and against which Francis continued to protest until the very end of his life, as the Testament indicates, regarding chapter 12 the learned brothers may have found an official ally in the rules of canon law.

77. See *Quinque Compilationes Antiquae*, ed. A. Friedberg, Leipzig, 1882.

78. See *Corpus Iuris Canonici, Pars Secunda: Decretalium Collectiones*, ed. A. Friedberg, Leipzig, 1881. The *Decretales* of Gregory IX, also known as *Liber Extra*, will be abbreviated as X.

79. P. Herde, 'Christians and Saracens at the Time of the Crusades: Some Comments of Contemporary Medieval Canonists,' *Studia Gratiana*, 12 (1967) 360–376.

80. Muldoon, o.c., 4.

81. 'Praesenti concilio Deo auctore sancimus, ut nullum Christianum mancipium Iudaeo deinceps serviat...quia nefas est quem Christus Dominus redemit blasphemum Christi in servitutis vinculis detinere' (I Comp., 5.5.1=X 5.6.1).

82. '...*iustum non esset, ut Christi abluti baptismo, paganis gentibus deservirent...*' (I *Comp*. 5.5.2). This decree is not taken up in the *Decretales*.

83. '*Servi, subditi estote in omni timore dominis, non tantum bonis et modestis, sed etiam dyscolis. Haec est enim gratia, si propter Dei conscientiam sustinet quis tristitias, patiens iniuste.... In hoc enim vocati estis: quia et Christus passus est pro vobis, vobis relinquens exemplum ut sequamini vestigia eius: qui peccatum non fecit, nec inventus est dolus in ore eius: qui cum malediceretur, non maledicebat: cum pateretur, non comminabatur: tradebat autem iudicanti se iniuste*' (1 Pet 2:18–19; 21–23).

84. '*Testimonium quoque Christianorum adversus Iudaeos in omnibus causis...recipiendum esse censemus, et anathemate decernimus feriendos, quicumque Iudaeos Christianis voluerint in hac parte praeferre, cum eos subiacere Christianis oporteat...*' (I *Comp*. 5.5.5 (Conc. Lat. III, 26)=X 2.20.21).

85. '*Mancipia quoque Christiana nulla cum eis habitare permittas,...ne forte ex ipsorum conversatione ad Iudaismi perfidiam convertantur*' (I *Comp*. 5.5.7 = X 5.6.4).

86. '...*ne ipsi (Christiani) Iudaeorum servitio se assidue pro aliqua mercede exponant...quoniam Iudaeorum mores et nostri in nullo concordant, et ipsi de facili ob continuam conversationem et assiduam familiaritatem, instigante humani generis inimico, ad suam superstitionem et perfidiam simplicium animos inclinarent*' (II *Comp*. 5.4.2.=X 5.6.8).

87. '*Inhibemus ergo districte, ne de cetero nutrices vel servientes habeant Christianos, ne filii liberae filiis famulentur ancillae, sed tanquam servi a Domino reprobati, in cuius mortem nequiter coniurarunt, se...recognoscant servos illorum, quos Christi mors liberos, et illos servos effecit*' (III *Comp*. 5.3.c.un=X 5.6.13).

88. '*Quum sit nimis absurdum, ut blasphemus Christi in Christianos vim potestatis exerceat, quod super hoc Toletanum concilium provide statuit, nos propter transgressorum audaciam in hoc generali concilio innovamus, prohibentes, ne Iudaei publicis officiis praeferantur.... Hoc idem extendimus ad paganos*' (IV *Comp*. 5.4.2 (Conc. Lat. IV, 69) =X 5.6.16). With regard to this rule Jeusset remarks: '...it is clear that, in the spirit of the legislators, it was not allowed to serve the Saracens but, thanks to God, Francis hardly read the papal *bullaria*' (o.c., 62–63). Cf. De Beer, *Brother Francis*, 93.

89. Innocent III writes to his legates: 'The devout and holy plan to aid the Holy Land..which with God's inspiration we have conceived and are striving to lead to success' (PL 216, 822). Cf. Riley-Smith, o.c., 130. See also Introduction.

90. Esser, o.c., 15; Dozzi, o.c., 215; De Beer, *Brother Francis*, 92–93. Together with Esser, Dozzi and De Beer, I see the witness of life and the confession of being Christians as one and the same activity: it is by their way of life that they confess to be Christians. Lehmann, however, sees the brothers' confession of being Christians as a more or less separate activity which 'is preced-

ed by the living witness of fraternal harmony and an attitude of reconciliation' (Features, 6; Prinzipien, 333). It is difficult to understand how v. d. Vat
can write with regard to this confession of the brothers, 'Certainly, the mission chapter does not lack a certain aggressive element which comes to the
fore in the demand for a courageous profession of their faith' (o.c., 24).

91. Against this background, it is difficult to agree with the observation of
Cardini, 'One can think with certainty that Francis has effectively been a
crusader. He has thus taken the cross with a particular ceremony, made
special promises, obtained the indulgences, worn the sign of the cross during the time he was in the Holy Land...—a cross fastened or stitched on his
tunic—and hence has been able to call himself a crusader' ('La Crociata nel
pensiero e nella spiritualità di san Francesco e di santa Caterina,' in *Francesco
e Caterina*, Roma, 1991, 68). A similar observation is made by v. d. Vat with
regard to the mission of brother Elias in Syria, 'Hence we will hardly be
mistaken when we state that Elias and his companions were sent to Syria
with the sole purpose of promoting in their own way the crusading enterprise and to plant the order in the Christian crusading states' (o.c., 42). See
also De Roeck, o.c., 58.

92. In this context Jansen makes the following remark: 'It belongs to the fundamental structure of every communication that it is clear who is speaking,
who is being addressed, what the position is with regard to each other and
what the message is about.... [This implies] that the brothers must also clarify their own position when preaching. This they do..when they are sent to
the Saracens and other unbelievers. Among them the brothers may not
engage in arguments and disputes, but they must tell them who they are,
namely 'Christians.' If they do not do so, their way of behavior cannot be
understood and there will be no communication' ('De grote dankzegging en
aansporing,' *FL* 75 (1992) 216–217). The reverse is, of course, also true. By
saying who you are, it is also possible to block communication. Francis and
his brothers experienced this quite often. In elaborating chapter 16, they
take this possibility into account, as is evident from verses 10–21.

93. v. d. Vat, o.c., 25–26.
94. Bühlmann, a.c., 106–107.
95. v. d. Vat, o.c., 26–27.
96. LegPer, 72.
97. Bühlmann, a.c., 107.
98. Features, 5; Prinzipien, 124.
99. *Brother Francis*, 92.
100. Francis and Islam, 172. De Beer adds: 'And this (to be subject to every
human creature for God's sake) cannot leave Islam indifferent: the believer
is above all one who is "subject" to God in peace.' Here it is a matter, in my
opinion, of two different things: to be subject to God and to be subject to

every creature. The latter, which is emphasized by Francis in RegNB 16, is unknown in Islam.

101. Sevenhoven, a.c., 208. For this reason I cannot agree with v. d. Vat when he writes that Francis 'explicitly desires from the missionaries that they show themselves subject and peaceful to the unbelievers. Thus he opposed the pride and the fighting spirit of the Saracens with an apostolate of peace, humility and patience; and the religious fanaticism of the Muslims with a strong and unshakable faith which, when necessary, was prepared to sacrifice one's life for the truth' (o.c., 24).

102. In my opinion, it is here that we have to search for the origin of the typical expression of Francis, 'the holy names and words of God' (LetCler 1.3.6.12; 1 LetCust 2.5; Test 12). Other authors find an explanation for this expression in the writings of Denis the Pseudo-Areopagite (Cornet); in the New Testament and especially in the high-priestly prayer of the gospel of John from which Francis regularly quotes texts in which the word 'name' occurs (Asseldonk, Viviani); in Francis' daily prayer, which consists of both psalms and the Our Father (Lehmann). These authors mainly try to explain the presence of the word 'names.' Their explanations, however, do not enlighten us on the origin of the unique combination of the expression 'names and words,' because this cannot be found in the sources they quote. Yet, it is precisely this combination which is typical for Francis. For a short summary of the discussion, see L. Lehmann, 'Das schriftliche Mahnwort des hl. Franziskus an alle Kleriker,' *WissWeis* 52 (1989) 147–178, here 166–169. English translation: 'The Letter to All Clerics: A Written Exhortation of Saint Francis to all Clerics,' *FrancDig* V, 2 (December 1995) 1–36, here 22–24. We cannot at all agree with Armstrong-Brady in whose translation 'written words,' the typical combination of Francis simply disappears. In a footnote they give the rather far-fetched justification that 'their translation "written words" is based on the assumption that *nomen* means noun, *verbum* means verb. Since Saint Francis places such high value on the words of the Lord, it seems more appropriate to translate this phrase simply as "written words"' (o.c., 49–50, note 1).

103. A totally different, very negative appreciation of the Muslim call to prayer can be found about a century later at the council of Vienne (1311–1312). In canon 25 which betrays a gross ignorance on the part of Clement V and other ecclesiastical authorities with regard to Islam and the place of the prophet Mohammed, we read: 'It is an insult to the holy name and a disgrace to the Christian faith that in certain parts of the world subject to Christian princes where Saracens live, sometimes apart, sometimes intermingled with Christians, the Saracen priests, commonly called Zabazala, in their temples or mosques, in which the Saracens meet to adore the perfidious Mohammed, loudly invoke and extol his name each day at certain hours from a high place, in the hearing of both Christians and Saracens, and

there make public professions in his honor. There is a place, moreover, where once was buried a certain Saracen whom other Saracens venerate and worship as a saint. A great number of Saracens flock there quite openly from far and near. This brings no small disrepute on our faith and causes great scandal in the hearts of the faithful. These practices cannot be tolerated any further without displeasing the divine majesty. We therefore, with the sacred council's approval, strictly forbid such practices henceforth in Christian lands. We enjoin catholic princes, one and all, who hold sovereignty over the said Saracens and in whose territory these practices occur,...to remove this offense altogether from their territories and take care that their subjects remove it, by expressly forbidding the aforesaid public invocation or profession of the sacrilegious name of Mohammed. They shall also forbid anyone in their dominions to attempt in future the above mentioned pilgrimage or in any way to support it' (COD 380). Cf. N. Daniel, *Islam and the West: The Making of an Image*, Edinburgh, 1960, 116, and *The Arabs and Medieval Europe*, London, 1975, 258–259. He writes: 'There are truthful elements here, embedded in ignorance. The Pope pretends that the Prophet is adored in the mosque, but only says that he is extolled by the muezzin. On the pilgrimage he speaks with complete ignorance; it is almost as though he thinks the pilgrimage is itself within Christian territory.... We might almost suppose that he was speaking of the local cult of some Muslim saint, but the commentary makes it clear that the "certain Saracen" means Muhammad, and the "place," Mecca. However we judge the historical and geographical knowledge of the Curia, it comes out unambiguously that the affront to God lies in permitting the public practice of Islam.'

104. Lehmann, Rulers, 48–54; Custodians, 40–46.

105. *Bonaventura*, IX 8.

106. The recognition that all good comes from God and that we therefore are not allowed to appropriate it but have to render it back to God, is very concisely formulated at the original ending of the *Regula non bullata* in chapter 17:17–19. This text constitutes as it were a brief summary of Francis' vision of God and man, of his anthropology. Cf. Flood, Assisi's Rules, 91–104. See also Th. Zweerman, '"Danken" en "dragen". Twee dimensies van de vrijheid volgens Franciscus van Assisi,' in *Franciscus, wegwijzer naar de ware vrijheid*, Haarlem, 1983, 13–62.

107. R. Reijsbergen sees in this story an illustration of the fact that 'Francis was rooted in an oral culture and considered the written word as something sacred' (*Omkeer van een verdwaalde mens: Poging tot een maatschappijhistorische interpretatie van de Lofzang op de deugden van Franciscus van Assisi*, Doktoraalscriptie Erasmus Universiteit, Den Haag, 1989, 29). If this were true, it is all the more surprising that so little of this respect for the written word, and especially for the written words of the Lord, appeared among

Francis' contemporaries, although they too belonged to the same oral culture. The situation seemed so bad in Francis' eyes that, on several occasions, he found it necessary to enjoin not only his brothers but also the clergy, to collect the written words of the Lord which they found in unbecoming places and to keep them in a place that was becoming. Since in all this Francis acted quite differently from his contemporaries, it seems that we must not look for an explanation of this typical Franciscan injunction in the oral culture which he had in common with his contemporaries, but in some personal experience of Francis himself. I think that this experience occurred during his visit to the Saracens when he saw their reverence for their holy book. Moreover, respect for the written word within an oral culture does not per se include respect for the written word of the pagans. It is about the latter that the story of 1 *Cel* 82 speaks.

108. Schwinges, o.c., 46–50.
109. See also 1 *Cel* 57, where Celano describes the crusade as 'a war between Christians and pagans.' James of Vitry too called the Saracens 'pagans,' e.g., when he spoke about Saracens who, after their conversion to Christianity, returned to their old Muslim practices, *ad consuetas inmundicias paganorum revertebantu*; or when he referred to the camp of the Saracens as *castra paganorum* (Huygens, o.c., 137). Further, see note 40, where I mention that Alan of Lille directs the fourth book of his *De fide catholica contra hereticos* against the pagans or Muslims: *Contra paganos seu Mahometanos*.
110. Schwinges, o.c., 19–46 (life and works of William of Tyre); 116–117 (theological significance of Mohammed and Islam); 129–131 (appreciation of Nur ad-Din). With regard to the latter, William wrote: 'Nur ad-Din, a man prudent and discrete and God-fearing in accordance with the superstitious traditions of those people' (129). From this religious appreciation, Schwinges concludes that William admitted that Islam, within its own system, offers the possibility of a highly organized religiosity. Schwinges emphasizes here particularly the fact that William called Nur ad-Din a God-fearing person. 'After all, the fear of God is one of the most respected predicates for a religious person, and Nur ad-Din, a Muslim, shares it in William's view without any reservation with persons of the Old and New Testament, with Christian princes and men of the church' (130; see also 282). H. Möhring, however, does not consider Schwinges' opinion very plausible, precisely because of William's theological rejection of Islam. See his 'Salahadinus Tyrannus, 2: Die Haltung Wilhelms von Tyrus gegenüber Islam und Muslimen,' *Deutsches Archiv für die Erforschung des Mittelalters* 39 (1983) 439–466, here 451. Moreover, William added a clear qualification: Nur ad-Din is God-fearing in accordance with the superstitious traditions of his people. In other words, even though Nur ad-Din is God-fearing, his religious tradition is and remains superstitious and hence to be rejected. Möhring also has his doubts regarding the positive picture which William

gives of Nur ad-Din. According to him, William's judgement was so positive 'not because William judged the individual persons according to their
personal value, but according to the political advantage for the crusading
states' (ibid., 452).

111. Cf. above, 21–2.
112. v. den Brincken, a.c., 92.
113. 'These efforts always gained the upper hand with Oliver when it did not go
well with the crusaders during the fifth crusade: religious dialogues must
help to compensate for failing luck of war' (v. den Brincken, a.c., 98). These
religious dialogues, however, did not mean that Oliver gave up his crusading
ideal. See below.
114. For the text of the letter, see Lemmens, a.c., 564–565. See also v. den
Brincken, a.c., 98–102. Very clear is Riccoldus of Montecroce (1243–1320) who
spent many years in the Middle East: 'We are amazed how in a law of such
great perfidy works of such great perfection can be found. For who would
not be amazed if he would see how great among the Saracens is their solici-
tude for study, their devotion in prayer, their mercy toward the poor, their
reverence for the name of God and for the prophets and the holy places,
their seriousness of life, their affability toward strangers, their concord and
their love toward their own?' Quoted by F. Gabrieli, 'San Francesco e
l'Oriente Islamico,' in *Espansione* 119. Cf. O. Delcambre, 'Riccoldo da Monte
di Croce, pèlerin d'Orient,' *Peuples du Monde* 202 (April 1987) 32–33.
115. For these stories about the priest king Johannes, the Indian king David, and
a Christian king from Nubia, see v. den Brincken, a.c., 96–98.
116. Ibid., 102.
117. James of Vitry wrote in this connection: 'Also in many other churches
within the bounds of the city, after the ejection of the perfidious
Mohammed, the divine office is continually being recited both day and
night to the honor of God and of his saints' (Huygens, o.c., 127). See also
Donovan o.c., 85–88.
118. These ideas will be further developed in the second part of this study. See
also my article: 'Solidariteit en dienstbaarheid: Dialoog in franciskaans perspectief,' *FL* 73 (1990) 212–227.
119. Lehmann, Features, 7–9.
120. Bühlmann, a.c., 104.
121. Ibid.
122. See 35, where the text of James' letter is quoted.
123. E. Siberry, 'Missionaries and Crusaders, 1095–1274: Opponents or Allies?'
Studies in Church History, 20, 1983, 103–110, here 105.
124. Cf. what Francis said about the appropriation of the office of preacher: 'And
no minister or preacher should appropriate to himself the ministry of the
brothers or the office of preaching, but at whatever hour he is enjoined to
do so he should give up his office without any protest. Therefore, in the

love which is God, I beg all my brothers, preachers, speakers and workers, whether cleric or lay, to strive to humble themselves in all things, not to glory nor to rejoice in themselves nor to pride themselves inwardly about their good words and works, or indeed about any good which God sometimes does, says or works in them and through them' (RegNB 17:4–6).

125. Lehmann, Features, 7; Esser, a.c., 16–17.

126. See above, 23.

127. The text of this letter can be found in Basetti-Sani, o.c., 121–122.

128. It concerns here sermon 48 of the *Sermones vulgares*. For a summary of this sermon, see R. Röhricht, 'Die Kreuzpredigten gegen den Islam: Ein Beitrag zur Geschichte der christlichen Predigt im 12. und 13. Jahrhundert,' *Zeitschrift für Kirchengeschichte* 6 (1884) 550–572, here 569.

129. This discussion may also have been influenced by the peace offer which al-Malek al-Kamil made to the crusaders to lift their occupation of Egypt in exchange for the return of Jerusalem and of the Holy Cross, at least when this offer was made in June 1219, as Basetti-Sani supposes. King John of Brienne was prepared to accept the offer, but cardinal Pelagius, the papal legate, opposed it (o.c., 136). However, according to common opinion, based on Oliver of Cologne and James of Vitry, the peace offer was made only after the defeat of the crusaders on August 29, 1219. See Lemmens, a.c., 560; Powell, o.c., 159. In this last case, the peace offer of the sultan had no influence on Francis' discussion (sermon), because it was held before the defeat of the crusaders, as 2 *Cel* 30 tells us.

130. 2 *Cel* 30. Cf. R. Reijsbergen, *Inleiding bij de tweede druk van de nederlandse vertaling van de Eerste en Tweede levensbeschrijving van Franciscus van Assisi door Thomas van Celano*, Utrecht, 1990, 10.

131. Vazquez disagrees with this view: 'The fifth crusade, just like the other preceding ones, had been willed by the Holy See and was being conducted by an apostolic delegate. The supposed opposition of Francis to the crusade would therefore have been directed against the whole church as its target. Such an attitude, however, is not in the least manifest in any of his own writings or in other trustworthy contemporary sources. It is not even manifest in the *Vita prima* of Celano, although it deals with the stay of Francis at Damietta. The first notice about Francis' sermon against the battle of Damietta appears in the *Vita secunda* which was written to satisfy those brothers who wanted a Francis who would be less a conformist and more a reformer, not only in the church but also of the church' (a.c., 536).

132. J. M. Powell, 'Francesco d'Assisi e la Quinta Crociata: Una Missione di Pace,' *Schede Medievali* 4, January–June 1983, 68–77, here 74–77. According to Powell, Francis was not the only one to hold this view. Joachim of Fiore, too, rejected the idea of the *tempus acceptabile*. Because of this, Powell concludes that there is an affinity between the ideas of both. Thereby he does not want 'to infer that Francis was already a complete follower of Joachim,

like some Franciscans after him.' Rather, he wants 'to suggest the strict relation between Francis and the ideas of his time' (77), ideas with which Francis probably first came in contact during his stay in the camp of the crusaders. On the basis of 2 *Cel* 30, Cardini comes to the conclusion, totally improbable in my opinion, that his sermon before the crusaders shows us Francis 'involved as a military chaplain (*impegnato in una Militärseelsorge*). He grew up in a world which resonated with the heroic deeds of crusaders; his order had acquired an increasing importance thanks to the protection of two popes who were convinced supporters of the *iter ultramarinum*; the beginning of the presence of the Friars Minor in the Holy Land was probably linked with the departures of the crusaders in 1217: is it possible in this situation to believe that he who wanted to preach to the unbelievers and who in fact preached to the birds, the wolves and to the robbers, would have been prepared to forget precisely those brothers in Christ who in His name risked their life far away from their fatherland?' (a.c., 227).

133. It would lead us too far to insert here a biography of sultan al-Malek al-Kamil. While James of Vitry describes him as 'a cruel beast' who, on seeing Francis, becomes sweetness itself (*Omnibus*, 1612), Oliver of Cologne is much more positive in the letter which he writes to the sultan after the fall of Damietta. See above, 92–3. For more complete data, see H. L. Gottschalk, *Al-Malik al-Kamil von Egypten und seine Zeit*, Wiesbaden, 1958.

134. Huygens, o.c., 132–133; *Omnibus*, 1609.

135. De Beer, *Brother Francis*, 22.

136. *Omnibus*, 1612.

137. 'The mystical experiences of Francis took place because he had a special openness towards feelings which could lead him into ecstasy. These feelings resemble those of a child. They are overflowing with joy and enthusiasm and show a mysticism which is absorbed in the ineffable astonishment about the experiences he has gained' (H. Sevenhoven, 'Oorspronkelijk en ontroerend: Franciscus' omgang met de dieren,' *FL* 75 (1992) 193–201, here 199).

138. For this idea, see J. Slomp, 'Is Knitter's model in Nederland bruikbaar?' *Wereld en Zending* 15 (1986) 108–112, here 111.

139. For this idea, see the Document of the Secretariat for the non-Christian Religions on 'The Attitude of the Church Towards the Followers of Other Religions: Reflections and Orientations on Dialogue and Mission,' no. 44: 'We live therefore in the age of the patience of God for the church and every Christian community, for no one can oblige God to act more quickly than He has chosen to do' (*Bulletin* 56 (1984) 141). And in 'Dialogue and Proclamation: Reflection and Orientations on Interreligious Dialogue and the Proclamation of the Gospel of Jesus Christ,' the joint document of the Pontifical Council for Interreligious Dialogue and the Congregation for the Evangelization of Peoples, published May 19, 1991, we read: 'All, both

Christians and the followers of other religious traditions, are invited by God himself to enter into the mystery of his patience, as human beings seek his light and truth. Only God knows the times and stages of the fulfillment of this long human quest' (*Bulletin* 77 (1991) 210–250, here 248–249). About the significance of these texts in the present papal thinking about Islam, see below, 143–159.

140. Lehmann is of a different opinion: 'One cannot deny that this view (everyone who is not a Christian is an unbeliever who has to be converted) combined with the then already generally accepted principle "*extra ecclesiam nulla salus*" has been an essential motive for Francis' missionary engagement.' But Lehmann himself softens his opinion when he writes next: 'His [Francis'] other way of behavior: not to take any hostile or polemical action against the Saracens, but to live among them,...softened, and even frustrated, his opinion which he shared with his contemporaries' (Prinzipien, 328–329). If Francis' way of behavior frustrated certain theological opinions, it is difficult to accept that these opinions have been 'an essential motive' for his action. See also Bühlmann: 'Francis obviously agreed with the medieval idea that "outside the church there is no salvation," and that "everyone who is not baptized, will be condemned,"—an idea that was still being maintained until about thirty years ago' (a.c., 104).

141. F. van der Horst, *Das Schema über die Kirche auf dem I. Vatikanischen Konzil*, Paderborn, 1963, 223–228; F. A. Sullivan, *Salvation outside the Church? Tracing the History of the Catholic Response*, New York, 1992, 44–62.

142. '*Quae [heresis] quidem olim diaboli machinatione concepta, primo per Arrium seminata, deinde per istum Sathanam scilicet Mahumet provecta, per Antichristum vero ex toto secundum diabolicam intentionem complebitur*' (Petrus Venerabilis, *Summula totius haeresis sarracenorum*, in J. Kritzeck, *Peter the Venerable and Islam*, Princeton, 1964, 208–209). Cf. G. Rizzardi, 'Islam, errore o eresia? Aspetti e tendenze della teologia missionaria dei sec. XII–XIV,' *Renovatio* 22 (1987) 415–451; 489–532, especially the first chapter: 'I teologi del secolo XII si interrogano sull'Islam,' ibid., 418–451, here 432–433.

143. In another context D. Scheltens writes about this 'contradiction' between life and doctrine, experience and formulation, praxis and theory: 'Francis was no man of theory. He was not concerned to justify his attitude towards nature and its connection with God in theoretical insights. Whenever Francis spoke about God and world, he did so with the theological language of his time. He did not criticize or renew the dualism between God and world which characterizes to a certain extent the theological language of that tradition. His originality consisted in his life which was so intense and original that no theology could cause it any harm. For Francis life was stronger than doctrine' ('Ecologische spiritualiteit,' *FL* 72 (1989) 241–249, here 249). 'Tradition is the reflection of the Church's life, and it develops as that

life is lived in new contexts with new opportunities and difficulties. The highly trained theologian may possess the most accurate reflective state-ment of the Church's doctrine, and that is not a negligible accomplishment. But the believer who most deeply lives life in communion with his or her brothers and sisters has the fullest pre-reflective grasp of the meaning of the Church's doctrine. And that is the fruit of the Holy Spirit' (M. J. Himes, 'The Ecclesiological Significance of the Reception of Doctrine,' The Heythrop Journal 33 (1992) 146–160, here 153).

144. See below: 'Pope John Paul II and Islam,' 143–159.

145. *BullFranc* I, ed. J. H. Sbaraglia, Rome, 1759, 24.

146. v. d. Vat, o.c., 27–28.

147. v. d. Vat, o.c., 25. On the other hand, A. Camps writes: 'It is our thesis that Francis by his actions [i.e. his stay among the Saracens] and by his writing [RegNB 16] opened up a new era in missions' ('Franciscan Dialogue with Other Religions,' in L. Boff and W. Bühlmann, ed., *Build Up My Church: Franciscan Inspirations for and from the Third World*, Chicago, 1984, 131–148, here 137). The same opinion is followed by K. Esser, *Anfänge und ursprüngliche Zielsetzungen des Ordens der Minderbrüder*, Leiden, 1966, 237. Zerfass writes in this context about 'Francis, the Father of modern world mission' (o.c., 284), while Bühlmann calls Francis 'the pioneer of the new mission era' (a.c., 25).

148. We cannot therefore agree with Delcorno who writes: 'It would not be cor-rect to deny that the saint's journey to Egypt had any connection with the crusade, or rather with "the theology of the crusade as a new Exodus and at the same time a new crucifixion," which Innocent III had developed in his opening sermon of the Fourth Lateran Council. The preaching before al-Malek al-Kamil, planned as a search for martyrdom and hence as the crown of the imitation of Christ, represents the most radical realization of the cru-sading ideal' (a.c., 139).

149. Jeusset. o.c., 65.

150. *Omnibus*, 1612.

151. M. Roncaglia, *St. Francis of Assisi and the Middle East*, Cairo, 1957, 28.

152. Lehmann does not agree: 'The content of catechetics and proclamation is the distinctively Christian belief in the triune God. With a belief in the all-powerful God, also Muslims and Jews could agree, for they too adore the all-powerful God. However, in the Christian belief in a triune God they see a danger for their strict monotheism. Over against this the Christian preacher must explicitly speak about the Father, the Son and the Holy Spirit' (Features, 7).

153. 'The formulations of this chapter of the rule are very well chosen. They enable Christians and Muslims to establish a fruitful contact with each other because they pay explicit attention to what unites them: the faith in

the all-powerful God, the Creator of all things, who alone is good. Anyone who wishes to establish contact with Muslims, will have to pay attention to the belief in God's transcendence and put greater emphasis on the theocentric rather than on the christocentric aspects of the faith' (Sevenhoven, a.c., 208). See also De Beer, Francis and Islam, 173. An objection against this interpretation could be that in chapter 21 Francis gives an almost identical sermon model to the brothers for their proclamation, their *exhortatio* to the Christians. See below, 107.

154. For this and what follows, see the analysis of the texts in Nguyên-van-Khanh, *Le Christ dans la Pensée de saint François d'Assise d'après ses Écrits*, Paris, 1989, 107–118, here 108.

155. 'And we thank you because as you created us (*creasti*) through your Son, so also, by your holy love..., you willed to redeem us (*redimi voluisti*) by his cross and blood and death. And we thank you for your Son will come again (*venturus est*)...' (RegNB 23:3–4). 'Let us all love the Lord God..who created us and redeemed us, and will save us by his mercy alone (*qui nos creavit, redemit et sua sola misericordia salvabit*)' (RegNB 23:8). See Nguyên-van-Khanh, o.c., 110–111.

156. A somewhat similar view can be found in Lehmann. But whereas I develop the themes of Francis' preaching to the Saracens mostly in contrast to the preaching of James of Vitry and other contemporaries, Lehmann does not directly consider this context. Hence he remains much more general in his discussion of the preaching to the Saracens envisioned in chapter 16: 'Consequently, the image of God to be transmitted by the missionaries is not a static but a dynamic one. It is not a quiet God who is enthroned far beyond and above the happenings in this world and is not interested in humankind, but a God who is a most intimate relationship within himself (Father-Son-Holy Spirit), living, creative, reaching out towards humankind and the world in order to save them' (Features, 8).

157. Lehmann, Prinzipien, 333–334.

158. Rotzetter, Missionary Dimension, 53–54.

159. Jeusset, o.c., 67.

160. The word *exhortatio* had different meanings at the time of Innocent III, even in official documents. For a good survey, see Zerfass, o.c., 225–227.

161. Rotzetter, Missionary Dimension, 54.

162. COD, 239–240.

163. 'The bishops are obliged to appoint collaborators who in their place and in their diocese take care of the service of the word.... Since the sacrament of penance is also to be administered, only priests are suitable for this special pastoral care' (Zerfass, o.c., 247–248). See also Godet, a.c., 63–64.

164. For a good survey of the situation at the time of Innocent III, see Zerfass, o.c., 192–253.

165. COD 234–235. See F. Vocking, 'Franciscus en het IVe Lateraans Concilie,' *FL* 46 (1963) 12.

166. Jeusset, o.c., 63.

167. Here I follow Godet, a.c., 31. The similarity between chapter 16 and the opening verses of chapter 17 is also noticed by Rotzetter in one of his earlier publications. Cf. *Die Funktion*, 168. For Rotzetter's later interpretation, see above, 107.

168. This is also the opinion of Vocking, a.c., 16–17. His reconstruction, however, is somewhat different and places other accents. See also Godet, a.c., 31; L. Hardick and E. Grau, *Die Schriften des heiligen Franziskus von Assisi*, Werl, 1980, 315–316. They write with regard to chapter 16: 'There Francis advises next to proclamation by the preaching of the word..very explicitly also proclamation of faith through life itself (RegNB 16:6).'

169. The observation which Bühlmann makes with regard to this text seems rather far-fetched: 'It is worth noticing that Francis does not quote the hard words of Mark (16:16), but the much more nuanced, more dynamic, more spiritual words of John (3:5) which refer to the Holy Spirit and the kingdom of God. Once again this is in full accord with the "divine inspiration"... For Francis it is only the life according to the Spirit and according to one's conscience that counts' (a.c., 104).

170. Lehmann, Features, 9; Prinzipien, 334.

171. Of course, it is also possible to take the quoted gospel text as a starting point and to conclude that Francis, like all his other contemporaries, insisted on the necessity of baptism for salvation. In the light of this conclusion, one could then try to interpret the text about the two ways of presence among the Saracens. Such an attempt seems to me, however, to be doomed to failure because it cannot be reconciled with the missionary praxis which Francis and his brothers clearly formulated on the basis of their own personal experiences and which presupposes a new missionary theology, even though this appears not to have been thought through in all its consequences in what followed. Moreover, it is of the greatest importance not to limit oneself to the continuous repetition of traditional theological points of view, but to pay more attention to the experiences of people and to make the questions which they raise the starting point of theological reflection. For this offers the only possibility of developing a truly living theology of dialogue. As J. v. Lin and G. Speelman write, 'We have the impression that till this very moment the desire for meetings is too much influenced by predetermined theological positions. The time has come that we allow our theology of religions to be more clearly determined by the questions and the directions of the answers as they arise from the praxis of the meetings with people of other faiths' ('Moslims en christenen in Nederland: Uitnodiging tot oecumenische dialoog.' *Wereld en Zending* 15 (1986) 139–147, here 146–147).

172. Lehmann, Prinzipien, 335.

173. Esser follows a different interpretation: 'The brothers must only preach those things which please the Lord, that is, they must not act according to the rules of human rhetoric and respect; for they "must not be wise and prudent according to the flesh; rather [they] must be simple, humble and pure"' (a.c., 17).

174. See the commentary on verse 6 above, 73.

175. See B. Vollot, 'Césaire de Spire et la Règle de 1221,' *Laurentianum*, 33 (1992) 183.

176. Lehmann, Prinzipien, 335.

177. Vollot, a.c., 182–183.

178. Features, 10; Prinzipien, 335.

179. See above, note 34.

180. Prinzipien, 335.

181. Features, 10–11 and 16; Prinzipien, 335–336. The same idea can be found in Rotzetter, Kreuzzugskritik, 124.

182. LegPer, 82.

183. See my commentary on verse 1, 62–3. The opposite view can be found in Dozzi, o.c., 222–223.

184. 1 *Cel* 55–57. For a good analysis of this and similar stories written by friars, cf. De Beer, Francis and Islam, 164–167. Authors like Pellegrini, Cardini, and Vazquez attribute little value to Celano and Bonaventure on this point. Lehmann, on the other hand, writes, ' [Chapter 16 of the *Regula non bullata*] very clearly acknowledges the possibility of martyrdom. The desire for martyrdom which the Franciscan sources, especially Celano and Bonaventure, describe as the main motive for Francis' journey to the sultan, has thus a good basis in the writings of Francis as well. This all the more so since we must take into account that the readiness to suffer martyrdom is not only expected of those brothers "who go among the Saracens," but of "all the brothers wherever they are" (v. 10)' (Prinzipien, 339).

185. BBT, 12–13.

186. Elm, a.c., 83–85, 95, where he also makes the following very unlikely observation: 'In his *Regula non bullata*, he [Francis] bases the missionary task precisely on those texts from the New Testament in which persecution, fear, terror and death, in short: martyrdom, are described as certain and necessary for the way to salvation.'

187. 'Since he [Francis] was weak at the time, Elias spoke whatever he had to say to the chapter.... "There is a certain region called Germany, in which there live devout Christian people.... Since brothers sent to them have occasionally returned badly treated, our Brother [Francis] requires no one to go to them. However, he wants to give the same obedience, indeed a fuller obedience, to those who want to go, inspired with zeal for God and souls, than he would give to those going across the sea. If there are any who want to go,

they may rise and withdraw to that corner." Inflamed with this desire, about ninety brothers got up, offering themselves for death' (*Jordan*, 17).

188. Lehmann, Features, 11–12; Prinzipien, 336.

189. PL 216, 817; Riley-Smith, o.c., 120. The theme of the lord and his vassals occurs also in the first sermon to the crusaders (sermon 47 of the *Sermones vulgares*) of James of Vitry. Cf. Röhricht, a.c., 565. For an English translation, see Riley-Smith, o.c., 134.

190. For the importance of this image at that time, see Nguyên-Van-Khanh, o.c., 54–55. As Francis never mentions it, the observation which Pernoud makes regarding Francis' presence at Damietta seems rather improbable. She writes: 'Saint Francis embodied both the poor man and the knight—the two forces which had set out together in olden times along the road to the Holy Land and had retaken Jerusalem' (o.c., 222).

191. J. Hoeberichts, 'The Admonitions of Saint Francis: Words of Life and Salvation: The Fifth Admonition,' *FIA Contact*, 5, 4 (1984) 22–31. See also Nguyên-Van-Khanh, o.c., 98–104; P. van Leeuwen and S. Verheij, *Woorden van heil van een kleine mens: Commentaar op de Vermaningen van Franciscus van Assisi*, Utrecht, 1986, 43–49; R. Armstrong, 'Prophetic Implications of the Admonitions,' *Laurentianum* 26 (1986) 396–464, here 426–428; A. Jansen, 'De grote dankzegging en aansporing II, Geloofsbelijdenis en smeekgebed,' *FL* 75 (1992) 258–269, here 262–263.

192. *St. Francis and the Song of Brotherhood*, London, 1980, 60.

193. J. Hoeberichts, 'Een bevrijdingstheologisch perspectief op Franciscus en zijn keuze voor de armen,' *FL* 72 (1989) 219–233. English translation: 'Francis and His Option for the Poor from a Liberation-Theological Perspective,' *FrancDig* VI, 1 (April–June 1996) 27–43.

194. With regard to 'the holding captive' in Adm 10:3—a text which he quotes as related to our passage—Lehmann writes: 'Here the attention is turned to the enemy within the interior of man. To have oneself under control is a prerequisite for overcoming one's visible enemies.... Self-control is also required to overcome one's invisible enemies, their temptations and demonic promptings. The stories about Francis contain enough examples on this point' (Prinzipien, 338). 'Self-control,' however, is a word that does not seem to fit Francis very well, as is evident from the texts which we quoted from his writings. They stress not so much the 'self,' but rather the obedience to God, to the Spirit.

195. For this text, see the commentary on *subditus* in verse 6, on 75ff where I strongly emphasized the social meaning of being subject. See also R. Reijsbergen, 'Bevrijdende gehoorzaamheid: Het mysterie van de gehoorzaamheid bij Franciscus van Assisi,' *FL* 74 (1991) 60–71. Unfortunately, he does not relate the obedience to the Spirit by being subject to all people to the political choice of Francis and his brothers to leave Assisi and its socio-economic system. This aspect is also absent in his already quoted master's the-

sis on the Salutation of the Virtues, *Omkeer van een verdwaalde mens*, Den Haag, 1989. This does not come as a surprise because the publications of David Flood are not at all mentioned in his bibliography. The political character of Francis' choice is taken into account by A. Jansen, 'Lofzang op de deugden,' *FL* 75 (1992) 60–74; 167–182, especially 172–176.

196. Lehmann, Features, 12–14. See also O. van Asseldonk, 'San Giovanni evangelista negli scritti di S. Francesco,' *Laurentianum* 18 (1977) 225–255, here 245; A. Rotzetter, '"Aus Liebe zur Liebe". Zu einem Wort des hl. Franziskus,' *WissWeis* 44 (1981) 154–167.

197. A survey of the different interpretations of this controversial passage, which in the Dutch translation of Francis' writings as well as in the *Omnibus* has by far the longest footnote, can be found in O. Schmucki, 'La "Lettera a tutto l'Ordine" di San Francesco,' *L'Italia Francescana* 55 (1980) 245–286; translated into English under the title: 'St. Francis's Letter to the Entire Order,' *Greyfriars Review* 3, 1 (April 1989) 1–33. See also A. Rotzetter, *Franciscus van Assisi: De weg van het evangelie*, Haarlem, 1983, 122–123; Lehmann, Features, 13. Schmucki thinks that Francis advises against the celebration of several masses because of the stipends attached to them which could lead to the 'acquisition of earthly goods' (cf. LetOrder 14). Rotzetter, on the other hand, is of the opinion that, with the somewhat enigmatic motive: 'for love of love' (*per amorem caritatis*), Francis appeals to the brothers-priests to forego the celebration of private masses out of a spirit of brotherly love and a desire for unity: 'The eucharist may not become a place of dispersion; rather it should be the place where the brothers are gathered together.' I in turn try to do justice to the immediate context where the love of Jesus in the eucharist is described in terms of humility and total giving. Out of love for this love of Jesus, the brothers-priests should not hold on to the priestly ministry when this is not necessary for the community. If they do so, they contradict the love of Jesus as it has found expression in the eucharist.

198. Against the opinion of Esser who refers to Mt 25:46, we follow Vollot, a.c., 183.

199. Lehmann gives a somewhat different interpretation: 'Analysing this list, one notes that words expressing suffering and endurance are predominant. Especially at the beginning of the section a gloomy atmosphere prevails, even though it is interrupted by two beatitudes. The invitation to rejoice comes only in verse 16, but is then immediately mentioned twice: "rejoice and be glad!"' (Features, 15).

200. 'Le Diatesseron et la Première Règle de Saint François,' *FranzSt* 72 (1990) 341–364, here 344–345; 'Cèsaire de Spire et la Règle de 1221,' *Laurentianum* 33 (1992) 184–185. The 'slalom' goes as follows:

a)   Beati estis cum (Mt)

b) vos oderint homines (Lk)

a) et maledixerint vobis
   et persequentur vos (Mt)

b) et separaverint vos
   et exprobaverint
   et eiecerint nomen vestrum
   tamquam malum et cum (Lk)

a) dixerint omne malum
   adversum vos mentientes,
   propter me. (Mt)

b) Gaudete in illa die
   et exsultate, (Lk)

a) quoniam merces vestra (Mt)

b) multa est (Lk)

a) in coelis. (Mt)

On the basis of Vollot's analysis, I disagree with Lehmann where he characterizes verses 11–21 as 'a typical mixed text which we find frequently in Francis' writings when he tries to express his thoughts freely in the language of the bible' (Features, 11).

201. *BullFranc*, 26. See also v. d. Vat, o.c., 89; Vazquez, a.c., 543. Vazquez shows a very positive appreciation for the bull *Ex parte vestra*, precisely because it approves the attempts of the brothers to adapt themselves to the concrete situation in the interest of their pastoral ministry, even though this means setting aside certain prescriptions of the Rule. It will not come as a surprise that Vazquez in his article does not refer to Francis' Testament and its explicit prohibition not to ask for any letter of privilege from the Roman curia.

202. *BullFranc*, 24.

203. A somewhat different interpretation, which does not consider so much the danger that the pastoral policy of the church implies for Francis' original ideal, can be found in G. P. Freeman and H. Sevenhoven, *De nalatenschap van een arme*: 'In a story passed on by brother Leo (LegPer 115) some brothers complain that they sometimes have to wait for days before a bishop gives them permission to preach. Would it not be more practical if the brothers would ask the pope for a general permission to preach? Francis' answer can throw light on the question we are discussing here [about not asking privileges]. Francis says that they do not understand the will of God. It is important to convince prelates by humility and respect that they are dealing with pious men. This will lead to their conversion. The permission to preach will then follow automatically. When you show them an expensive bull, you outdo the local clergy with a means of power. This leads to self-exaltation and to envy among the clergy.... Credibility is more impor-

tant to Francis than beautiful words. To follow Christ's humility is more in accordance with the gospel than to try and impress people with papal bulls' (80. English translation: 'The Legacy of a Poor Man,' *FrDig* IV, 2 (December 1994) 70). We doubt however whether Francis was so much concerned about credibility in the eyes of others. His main concern, especially in his Testament, was the brothers' faithfulness to the original ideal which was threatened by the papal attempts to insert the brothers into the pastoral policies of the church at that time.

PART TWO: Introduction

1. F. Cardini, 'Gilberto di Tournai: un francescano predicatore della crociata,' *StFranc* 72 (1975) 31–48; 'Crociati, Pellegrini e Cavalieri nei "Sermones" di Gilberto di Tournai,' *StFranc* 73 (1976) 373–387. See also C. T. Maier, *Preaching the Crusades: Mendicant Friars and the Cross in the Thirteenth Century*, Cambridge, 1994; cf. Part I, Introduction, note 16.

2. G. Rizzardi, 'La controversia con l'Islam di Johannes Guallensis, O.F.M.,' *StFranc* 82 (1985) 245–269.

3. *Bonaventura* IV, 7.

4. For this and what follows, see A. Camps, 'De receptie van Franciscus' benadering van Saracenen en andere ongelovigen in de loop van de franciskaanse missiegeschiedenis tot op de dag van vandaag,' in *Franciscus en de islam*, Franciscaanse Studies 7, Utrecht, 1991, 36–49. Also v. d. Vat, o.c., 60–123.

5. J. Hoeberichts, 'Solidariteit en dienstbaarheid: dialoog in franciskaans perspectief,' *FL* 73 (1990) 212–227.

6. *Nostra Aetate*. Declaration on the Relationship of the Church to Non-Christian Religions, 2.

7. Both these documents can be found in *Franciscan Missionary Charism in Contemporary Franciscan and Church Documents*, Quezon City, 1987. It is surprising how little the brothers have been guided by RegNB 16 in their statements about mission and dialogue in the OFM documents of Medellin, 1971 and Madrid, 1973 and in the OFM Cap. document of Mattli, 1978. The latter contains an appendix about Franciscan missionary spirituality, in which RegNB 16 is dealt with more extensively, without however referring to the dialogue with other religions.

PART TWO: Chapter One

1. *Bulletin* No. 79 (1992) 9.

2. I refer to *Lumen Gentium* 16 here: 'The plan of salvation also includes those who acknowledge the Creator. In the first place among these there are the Muslims, who, professing to hold the faith of Abraham, along with us adore the one and merciful God, who on the last day will judge

humankind.'

3. *Nostra Aetate* 3.

4. Karl Rahner was a pioneer in this connection. See 'Christianity and the Non-Christian Religions,' *Theological Investigations* 5, 115–134. See also Sullivan, o.c., 171–174.

5. For a good survey, see P. Rossano, 'The Major Documents of the Catholic Church regarding the Muslims,' *Bulletin* No. 48 (1981) 204–215; T. Michel, 'Islamo-Christian Dialogue: Reflections on the Recent Teachings of the Church,' *Bulletin* No. 59 (1985) 172–193; T. Michel, 'Pope John Paul II's Teaching about Islam,' *Seminarium* 26 (1986) 73–82.

6. *Ecclesiam suam* 111; see Michel, 'Islamo-Christian Dialogue,' 175–176.

7. Michel, ibid.; Rossano, a.c., 210.

8. Rossano, ibid.

9. *Evangelii Nuntiandi* 53.

10. A. Camps, 'Een nieuwe uitgave van de handleiding voor de dialoog met moslims,' *Wereld en Zending* 13 (1984) 340–346.

11. *Redemptor Hominis* 6.

12. Ibid., 11.

13. Michel, 'Islamo-Christian Dialogue,' 177–178.

14. Cf. the Declaration *Dignitatis Humanae*, to which the pope explicitly refers in *Redemptor Hominis* 12.

15. See *Redemptoris Missio* 10 for the latest development in this matter.

16. *Nostra Aetate* 3: '...Abraham ad quem fides islamica libenter sese refert.'

17. *Lumen Gentium* 16: '...Musulmanos, qui fidem Abrahae se tenere profitentes.'

18. *Chiesa e Islam*, 12. See also note 21.

19. 'Islamo-Christian Dialogue,' 184.

20. *Redemptor Hominis* 7.

21. *Chiesa e Islam. Discorsi del Papa Giovanni Paolo II ai Musulmani nei primi tre anni del Suo Pontificato*, Vatican City, 1981.

22. Ibid., 14–15.

23. Ibid., 26.

24. Ibid., 33–34.

25. Ibid., 37.

26. Ibid., 40.

27. Ibid., 50; 52–53.

28. The pope's speeches to various groups of Muslims can be found in *Bulletin*, published by what was first called the Secretariat for non-Christians, and is at present known as the Pontifical Council for Interreligious Dialogue, Vatican City.

29. 'The Speech of the Holy Father John Paul II to Young Muslims during his Meeting with them at Casablanca (Morocco) August 19th, 1985,' *Seminarium* 26 (1986) 13–22.

30. *Bulletin* 60 (1985) 222–223.

31. M. Borrmans, 'Le discours de Jean-Paul II aux jeunes de Casablanca,' *Seminarium* 26 (1986) 44–71, here 57.

32. According to Borrmans, the pope seems to refer here to a verse in the Koran which places the final reason for religious pluralism in God: 'If Allah had so willed, he would have made you a single people, but he wanted to test you in what he has given you. So as in a race compete with each other in all virtues. Allah is your common goal. He will show you the truth of the matters about which you dispute' (5,48).

33. 'The Attitude of the Church Towards the Followers of Other Religions: Reflections and Orientations on Dialogue and Mission 44,' *Bulletin* 56 (1985) 141.

34. 'Dialogue and Proclamation: Reflection and Orientations on Interreligious Dialogue and the Proclamation of the Gospel of Jesus Christ 84,' *Bulletin* 77 (1991) 248–249.

35. J. Slomp, 'Is Knitter's model in Nederland bruikbaar?' *Wereld en Zending* 15 (1986) 108–112, here 111.

36. *Redemptoris Missio* 5.

37. All speeches of the pope with regard to the World Day of Prayer for Peace are published in *Bulletin* 64 (1987) 11–99; here 15. John Paul could have very well quoted here from Francis' Letter to the Custodians where he expresses his wish that the custodians 'may announce and preach [the Lord's] praise to all peoples in such a way that, at every hour and whenever the bells are rung, praise and thanks always be given to the all-powerful God by all the people throughout the whole world' (8). See L. Lehmann, 'The Two Letters of St. Francis to the Custodians: Beginnings of a Christian Muslim Ecumenism in Praising God,' *FrancDig* I, 1 (May 1991) 21–56. Cf. my commentary on RegNB 16, 6.

38. Ibid., 22.

39. Ibid., 30.

40. Ibid., 40.

41. Ibid., 40–41.

42. Ibid., 54.

43. For commentaries on *Redemptoris Missio*, see J. van Lin, 'Missio! Moet dat nog?' *Wereld en Zending* 20 (1991) 94–101; P. Holtrop, 'De schrale wind van de nieuwe lente,' ibid., 101–105; G. Evers, 'Interreligiöser Dialog und Mission nach der Enzyklika "Redemptoris Missio,"' *ZMR* 75 (1991) 191–209; T. Balasuriya, 'Note on Pope John Paul II's Encyclical: *Redemptoris Missio* (1990),' *The Japan Missionary Bulletin* 45 (1991) 217–224; J. Neuner, 'Mission in *Ad Gentes* and in *Redemptoris Missio*, *VJTR* 56 (1992) 228–241; A. Camps, 'Discussies gevoerd in de Encycliek 'Redemptoris Missio' en Aziatische reacties,' *Wereld en Zending* 22 (1993) 12–17; J. Neuner, 'Mission Theology after Vatican II, Magisterial Teaching and Missiological Approaches in India,' *VJTR* 58 (1994) 201–214.

44. *Bulletin* 77 (1991) 247. For a good commentary on this document, see I. Puthiadam, 'Dialogue and Proclamation: Problem? Challenge? Grace-filled Dialectic?' *VJTR* 56 (1992) 289–308. See further R. Fitzmaurice, 'The Roman Catholic Church and Interreligious Dialogue: Implications for Christian-Muslim Relations,' *Islam and Christian-Muslim Relations*, Vol. 3, No. 1 (June 1992) 83–107; J. Dupuis, 'Dialogue and Proclamation in Two Recent Documents,' *Bulletin* 80 (1992) 165–172.

45. 'Christmas address to the Roman Curia, 22 December 1986,' *Bulletin* 64 (1987) 61; *Redemptoris Missio* 29.

46. *Redemptoris Missio* 2.

47. Ibid., 5.

48. Ibid., 28.

49. Ibid., 55.

50. It will not come as a surprise that this has not yet happened in John Paul's book, *Crossing the Threshold of Hope*, New York, 1996, where among other things he states that the Holy Spirit works outside the visible structures of the church 'on the basis of the *semina Verbi* which are, as it were, a common saving root of all religions.' In other words, the working of the Holy Spirit in other religions is restricted to what they have in common with Christianity. Further, they have a saving effect insofar as they possess *semina Verbi*. There is as such no appreciation expressed for other religions in their otherness. On the contrary, where they differ from Christianity, they are considered defective.

PART TWO: Chapter 2

1. Surveys of the activities of the FABC can be found in A. Poulet-Mathis, 'Ecumenical and Interreligious Dialogue in Asia: Concerns and Initiatives of the Federation of Asian Bishops' Conferences,' *FABC Papers* No. 49 (1987) 10–29; A. Fernandes, 'Dialogue in the Context of Asian Realities,' *VJTR* 55 (1991) 545–560; J. Knight, 'Mission and Dialogue in Asia: Can We Plumb the Depths?' *VJTR* 56 (1992) 125–134; J. Dupuis, 'FABC Focus on the Church's Evangelising Mission in Asia Today,' *VJTR* 56 (1992) 449–468.

2. For the complete text of the final document, see *Message of the Asian Bishops' Meeting, Manila 29 November 1970*, in *For All the Peoples of Asia: Federation of Asian Bishops' Conferences Documents from 1970–1991*, ed. G. B. Rosales and C. G. Arévalo, Manila 1992, 3–7. This publication will be abbreviated FAPA.

3. Ibid., 17, FAPA, 5. Notwithstanding improvements that were made in the course of years, this complaint will often be repeated. Cf. BIRA I, 3, FAPA, 110. For the origin and purpose of the so-called BIRAs, see note 25.

4. Ibid., 19. This idea is further elaborated in 20–22, FAPA, 5–6.

5. Ibid., 24, FAPA 6.

6.   *Resolutions of the Asian Bishops' Meeting*, 12, FAPA, 9.
7.   Ibid., 1, FAPA, 8.
8.   *Evangelization in Modern Day Asia*, 9, FAPA, 14.
9.   Ibid., 12, FAPA, 14.
10. Ibid., 14–15, FAPA, 14.
11. . Ibid., 19, FAPA, 15.
12. Ibid., 16, FAPA, 14–15.
13. *Message*, 17, FAPA, 5.
14. 'It is our belief that only in and through Christ and His Gospel, and by the outpouring of the Holy Spirit, that these quests (for meaning) can come to realization. For Christ alone, we believe, is for every man "the Way, the Truth and the Life," (Jn 14:6) "who enlightens every man who comes into the world" (Jn 1:9). We believe that it is in Him and in His good news that our peoples will finally find the full meaning we all seek, the liberation we strive after, the brotherhood and peace which is the desire of all our hearts.' *Evangelization in Modern Day Asia*, 7, FAPA, 13. See also 26–27, FAPA, 16.
15. For the final document, *Prayer–The life of the Church of Asia*, see FAPA, 29–39.
16. Ibid., 5, FAPA, 30.
17. Ibid., 28, FAPA, 34.
18. Ibid.
19. Ibid., 30, FAPA, 34–35.
20. Ibid., 36, FAPA, 35.
21. Ibid., 35, FAPA 35.
22. Ibid., 36, FAPA, 35. About a year later, in October 1979, the bishops wrote during BIRA I: 'We enter as equal partners into the dialogue in a mutuality of sharing and enrichment contributing to mutual growth. It excludes any sense of competition. Rather, it centers on each other's values. All the partners in dialogue participate in their own culture, history and time. Hence, dialogue brings the partners more deeply into their own cultures and bears the characteristics of inculturation' (BIRA I, 12, FAPA, 111). For the origin and purpose of the BIRA's, see note 25.
23. *Prayer*, 42, FAPA, 36.
24. *Towards a New Age in Mission*, 19, FAPA, 131. See FABC I, 25–28, where the three forms of dialogue are mentioned, but are unclearly defined as three forms of the one dialogue which constitutes the essence of evangelization. For more background information on this view, see M. Amaladoss, 'Evangelization in India: A New Focus?' *VJTR* 51 (1987) 7–28; Amaladoss, 'Proclaiming the Gospel,' *VJTR* 57 (1993) 26–32.
25. The so-called *Institutes* are a kind of seminar, organized by the various departments of the FABC, to further develop and realize the policies and programs of the Federation. Next to the BISAs, there are BIMAs (Bishops' Institute for Missionary Apostolate) and BIRAs (Bishops' Institute for Interreligious Affairs). I will pay special attention to this last group. The

first three BIRAs dealt with the relation of the church to Buddhism (October 1979), Islam (November 1979) and Hinduism (November 1982). BIRA IV was held as a series of 12 seminars between October 1984 and February 1991. They discussed the important problems with which the theology of dialogue is confronted today.

26. For the background and the implications of this development, see F. Wilfred, 'Once Again... Church and Kingdom,' *VJTR* 57 (1993) 6–25. For the history of the integration of this idea within the FABC, see especially Dupuis, a.c., 455–461.

27. BISA III, 6 and 8, FAPA, 208–209.

28. BIRA I, 4, FAPA, 110.

29. BIRA II, 10, FAPA, 114. The formulation here and in the following paragraphs is clearly inspired by the Muslim view of faith.

30. Ibid., 10–13, FAPA, 114–115.

31. Ibid., 14, FAPA, 115.

32. *Consultation on Christian Presence among Muslims in Asia*, 8, FAPA, 166.

33. Ibid., 13, FAPA, 167.

34. Ibid., 14, FAPA, 167–168.

35. On the other hand, BIRA II does not speak about the problem of inculturation, while this is treated in *Consultation*, 31–32, and also in its *Pastoral Recommendations*, 6. See FAPA, 170–171 and 172–173. The changing composition of the group of participants, who all have their own experiences and interests, as well as the short duration of the seminars, have certainly contributed to this lack of continuity with regard to these essential aspects of the mission of the church in Asia.

36. Since BIRA IV was planned as a series of conferences on the most important problems of a theology of dialogue, the first meeting (BIRA IV/1, October 1984) was devoted to an inventory of these problems. One of the conclusions is that a profound study of the relationship between church and kingdom of God was needed (*Brief Report on the Assembly*, 9, FAPA, 248). This relationship then became the theme of BIRA IV/2. See Poulet-Mathis, a.c., 21; Dupuis, a.c., 456–457.

37. BIRA IV/2: 3; 6; 8, 1–3; 10; 12, 1–3; 15, FAPA, 251–255.

38. 'We [i.e., the Asian bishops] realize too that we must deepen in ourselves the spirit of servanthood taught to us by Him who lived in our midst "as one who serves" and who came "to give his life for the redemption of all"' (*Message*, 15, FAPA, 5).

39. BIRA IV/3: 5; 6; 12; 16; 17, FAPA, 258–261.

40. 'The local church constantly moves forward in mission, as it accompanies all humankind in its pilgrimage to the Kingdom of the Father' (*The Church—A Community of Faith in Asia*, 15, FAPA, 60).

41. BIRA IV/4: 2, FAPA, 300.

42. BIRA IV/6: 3; 6, FAPA, 304.

43. Ibid. 5, FAPA, 304.
44. For this idea, see G. Evers, 'Interreligiöser Dialog und Mission nach der Enzyklika "Redemptoris Missio,"' *ZMR* 75 (1991) 191–209, here 204–205.
45. BIRA IV/10: 8–9, FAPA, 314.
46. In a talk, given to the college of cardinals at its consistory (April 4–7, 1991), Tomko states, without giving any further evidence, 'The abandonment of missionary stations, of preaching the Gospel and of catechesis by missionaries, the clergy and women religious, and the flight to social work, as well as the great reductive talk about the "values of the kingdom" (justice, peace) is a widespread phenomenon in Asia and is propagated by some missionary centers on other continents, too.' The great culprits are, according to Tomko, some Indian theologians who 'have developed unacceptable and destructive doctrines, which can be reduced to three principal themes: Christ, the Spirit and the kingdom.' At the end of his talk, he warns against them: 'If India is the epicenter of these tendencies and Asia their main territory, similar ideas are already circulating in Oceania, in some countries of Africa and in Europe. The mission is then doubly deceived regarding the direct evangelization in the missionary territories and regarding the negative influence on missionary vocations in the churches of ancient Christianity. The question is thus posed in total seriousness: What should be done so that the word of God about the salvation given to us uniquely in Christ may be proclaimed in its purity, *"Ut verbum Dei currat et clarificetur?"'* (*Origins* 20 (1991) 753–754).
47. 'Christian Mission in Asia Today,' in 'The Emerging Challenges to the Church in Asia in the 1990s: A Call to Respond,' *FABC Papers* No. 59, 11 and 19. A good report can be found in F. Wilfred, 'Fifth Plenary Assembly of FABC: An Interpretation of its Theological Orientation,' *VJTR* 54 (1990) 583–592.
48. *Journeying Together*, 3.1.2 and 3.3.1, FAPA, 280–281.
49. Ibid., 4.1 and 4.3, FAPA, 281–282.
50. Ibid., 6. 3–6, FAPA, 283–284.
51. Tomko, a.c., 13; *Redemptoris Missio* 1; 4–11. See J. Neuner, 'Mission in *Ad Gentes* and in *Redemptoris Missio*,' *VJTR* 56 (1992) 228–241.
52. *Journeying Together*, 3.1.1. and 3.2.2, FAPA, 279–280.
53. Ibid., 4.6, FAPA, 282. The same idea also comes to the fore in the following texts, 'Our challenge is to proclaim the Good News of the Kingdom of God: to promote justice, peace, love, compassion, equality and brotherhood in these Asian realities. In short, it is to work to make the Kingdom of God a reality.... Our challenge is to cooperate with all people of goodwill in God's action in the world in the service of justice and peace' (ibid., 1.7, FAPA, 275). 'The challenge for the Church is to work for justice and peace along with the Christians of other Churches, together with our sisters and brothers of other faiths and with all people of goodwill, to make the Kingdom of

God more visibly present in Asia' (ibid., 2.3.9, FAPA, 279).

54. This approach will be criticized in *Redemptoris Missio* 17–18. See for a defense of the Asian approach, F. Wilfred, 'Once Again...Church and Kingdom,' *VJTR* 57 (1993) 6–25.

55. Neuner, a.c., 240–241.

56. See F. Wilfred, 'Images of Christ in the Asian Pastoral Context: An Interpretation of Documents from the Federation of Asian Bishops' Conferences,' *Concilium* 1993/2, 51–62.

57. *Journeying Together*, 9. 1.5.7, FAPA, 288–289.

58. BIRA IV/12: 7, FAPA, 326.

59. Ibid., 9, FAPA, 326–327.

60. Ibid., 12, FAPA, 328.

61. Ibid., 26, 29–30, FAPA, 330.

62. Ibid., 36–38, FAPA, 331.

63. See section VII, 'Dialogue is Entry into the Other's Language.' This section introduces a new element in the reflections of the BIRAs which, as the document says, 'is of vital importance in enabling us to undertake this new venture of pilgrimage together.... Language is the very soul of a culture. It can make or mar progress in interreligious communication' (ibid., 42, FAPA, 332). In all this we have to be well aware that 'religious terms like sin, forgiveness, heaven, have nuances inextricably linked with a Judeo-Christian world view which is different from that of other traditions. Genuine communication is possible only when the hidden content of these words is uncovered' (ibid., 43, FAPA, 332).

64. Ibid., 44, FAPA, 332.

65. Ibid., 40, FAPA, 331.

66. Ibid., 48–50, FAPA, 332–333.

67. Ibid., 51, FAPA, 333. The addition of 'proclamation' to the threefold dialogue with other religions, with other cultures and with the poor, does not really fit in 'the dialogical model' of the local church in Asia, which the Asian bishops have developed ever since FABC I in 1974. This addition is the result of the influence of cardinal Tomko, the prefect of the Congregation for the Evangelization of the Peoples. This is clear from the talk which he gave during the consistory of the college of cardinals on April 5, 1991, a few weeks after BIRA IV/12. As we have seen, in this talk he attacks Asian theologians, and especially their 'reductive talk about the values of the kingdom.' In this connection, he further states: 'Evangelization in the global sense, in which the "new focal point" is the construction of the kingdom or of a new humanity, would consist merely of dialogue, inculturation and liberation. Strangely and significantly, the message or proclamation is omitted' (*Origins* 20 (1991) 754). Cf. Dupuis, a.c., 454. For a defense of the Asian view, see M. Amaladoss, 'Proclaiming the Gospel,' *VJTR* 57 (1993) 26–32.

68. Ibid., 58, FAPA, 334; 55, FAPA, 333.

69. For this idea of entering into the language and culture of others, see especially F. Wilfred, 'Dialogue Gasping for Breath? Towards New Frontiers in Interreligious Dialogue,' *FABC Papers* No. 49 (1987) 32–52, here 46–48; Wilfred, 'World Religions and Christian Inculturation,' *Indian Theological Studies* 25 (1988) 5–26; 'Asia on the Threshold of the 1990s: Emerging Trends and Socio-Cultural Processes at the Turn of the Century: A Position Paper for the Fifth Plenary Assembly of the FABC,' *FABC Papers* No. 55 (1990) 1–43, here 25–27.

70. 'More than listening to lectures on theology, we shared the often moving experience of many who unselfishly take part in interreligious dialogue, as encouraged in the encyclical *Redemptoris Missio*' (BIRA IV/12: 57, FAPA, 334).

71. *Conclusions of the Theological Consultation*, 13 and 15, FAPA, 337–338. For the triple dialogue and the Roman reaction to it, see note 67.

72. Ibid., 20–21, FAPA, 339–340.

73. Ibid., 23–25, FAPA, 340.

74. Ibid., 53, FAPA, 347.

75. Ibid., 36–51, FAPA, 343–346.

76. Ibid., 52–53, FAPA, 346–347.

77. It is interesting to mention here that the Congregation for the Evangelization of Peoples, in its campaign against Asian theologians, ordered the FABC Papers to publish an English translation of an originally Italian article which speaks very negatively about a number of Asian theologians who are mentioned by name. This is directly contrary to the policies of the FABC Papers. For, as the colophon states, 'FABC Papers is a project of the FABC, designed to bring the thinking of Asian experts to a wider audience and to develop critical analysis of the problems facing the church in Asia from people on the scene.' The article in question is 'Asia, il Vangelo Dimezzato,' geschreven door Domenico Colombo PIME. In October 1991, it was published in English under the title: 'Another Gospel for Asia?' *FABC Papers* No. 62.

PART TWO: Chapter 3

1. For this difference in approach and its consequences, see F. Wilfred, 'A Matter of Theological Education: Some Critical Reflections on the Suitability of "Salvation History" as a Theological Model for India,' *VJTR* 48 (1984) 538–556; Wilfred, 'Dialogue Gasping for Breath? Towards New Frontiers in Interreligious Dialogue,' *FABC Papers* No. 49 (1987) 32–52, here 40–43; Wilfred, 'Dialogue and Mission in Context,' *CTC Bulletin* VIII, 3 (December 1989) 5–18, here 10–11.

2. 'Dialogue and Mission in Context,' 5–8; Wilfred, 'Asia on the Threshold of the 1990s: Emerging Trends and Socio-Cultural Processes at the Turn of the Century: A Position Paper for the Fifth Plenary Assembly,' *FABC Papers* No. 55 (1990) 1–43, here 2–10.

3. *Journeying Together Toward the Third Millennium*, 3.1.2; 4.1, FAPA, 280 and 282.

4. Ibid., 9.5, FAPA, 288.

5. BIRA IV/12: 38, FAPA, 331.

6. Whereas the Asian bishops prefer to speak about a spirituality of *kenosis*, a term taken from the hymn in Phil 2:5–11, Francis does not use the Latin translation of this term, *exinanitio*. The hymn, as such, was certainly known to Francis, as it was read on Palm Sunday and on the feastdays of the Invention of the Cross (May 3) and the Exaltation of the Cross (September 14). Yet, although there exist several similarities between the view on Christ expressed in this hymn and Francis' understanding, Francis does not quote the hymn as such. A resonance of the hymn we find, however, in Adm 1,16–18 and in LetOrder 27–29 where Francis speaks about Jesus, 'the Lord of the universe, God and the Son of God, who humbles himself.' Apparently it is not the rather difficult expression *'semetipsum exinanivit,'* which moreover occurs only once in the New Testament, which strikes Francis, but rather the more familiar *'humiliavit semetipsum.'* See Paul Zahner, 'Der Kenosisgedanke in der mittelalterlichen Auslegung des Philipperhymnus unter besonderer Berücksichtigung Francisci und Bonaventuras,' *WissWeis* 55 (1992) 94–110, here 104.

7. *Redemptoris Missio* 34.

8. *Journeying Together Toward the Third Millennium*, 4.3, FAPA, 282.

9. See M. Amaladoss, 'Encounter of Religions: Some Concerns as We Face the 1990's,' in *Making All Things New: Mission in Dialogue*, Anand, Gujarat, India, 1990, 131–144; Amaladoss, 'Rationales for Dialogue with World Religions,' *Origins* 19 (1990) 572–577; Amaladoss, 'Liberation: An Inter-religious Project,' *East Asian Pastoral Review* 28 (1991) 4–33; Amaladoss, 'Religious Conflict and Spirituality,' *Jeevadhara* XXIII, 133 (January 1993) 27–35; F. Wilfred, 'World Religions and Christian Inculturation,' *Indian Theological Studies* 25 (1988) 5–26; Wilfred, 'Dogma and Inculturation,' *VJTR* 53 (1989) 345–353; Wilfred, 'Towards an Anthropologically and Culturally Founded Ecclesiology: Reflections from an Asian Perspective,' *VJTR* 54 (1990) 501–511; Wilfred, 'Some Tentative Reflections on the Language of Christian Uniqueness: An Indian Perspective,' *VJTR* 57 (1993) 652–672.

Bibliography

I. FRANCIS OF ASSISI

R. Armstrong, 'Prophetic Implications of the Admonitions,' *Laurentianum* 26 (1986) 396–464.

O. v. Asseldonk, 'San Giovanni evangelista negli scritti di S. Francesco,' *Laurentianum* 18 (1977) 225–255.

_____. 'Le lettere di S. Pietro negli scritti di S. Francesco,' *Collectanea Franciscana* 48 (1978) 67–76.

_____. 'Verso un cuore puro con la pura, semplice e vera pace dello spirito' (RegNB 17,15), *Laurentianum* 33 (1992) 481–531.

G. Basetti-Sani, 'Franciscus van Assisi,' *Concilium* 4, 7 (1968) 11–26.

_____. *L'Islam e Francesco d'Assisi. La missione profetica per il dialogo*, Firenze, 1975.

_____. 'Chi era il vecchio famoso che incontrò San Francesco a Damietta,' *Studi Francescani* 82 (1985) 209–244.

D. Berg, 'Kreuzzugsbewegung und Propagatio Fidei: Das Problem der Franziskanermission im 13. Jahrhundert und das Bild von der islamischen Welt in der zeitgenössischen Ordenshistoriographie,' *Miscellanea Mediaevalia* 17, Berlin 1985, 58–76.

W. Bühlmann, 'Das Missionsverständnis bei Franziskus nach der Regula non bullata,' in A. Camps and G. Hunold, *Erschaffe mir ein neues Volk*, Mettingen, 1982, 13–29. English translation 'Francis and Mission According to the Rule of 1221,' *Spirit and Life: A Journal of Contemporary Franciscanism* 6 (1994) 87–107.

A. Camps, 'Franziskanischer Dialog mit anderen Religionen,' in L. Boff and W. Bühlmann, *Baue meine Kirche auf. Franziskanische Inspirationen aus der Dritten Welt*, Düsseldorf, 1983, 88–106. English translation 'Franciscan Dialogue with Other Religions,' in L. Boff and W. Bühlmann, *Build Up My Church: Franciscan Inspirations for and from the Third World*, Chicago, 1984, 131–148.

_____. 'De receptie van Franciscus' benadering van Saracenen en andere ongelovigen in de loop van de franciscaanse missiegeschiedenis tot op de dag van vandaag,' *Franciscaanse Studies* 7, Utrecht, 1991, 36–49.

F. Cardini, 'Nella presenza del Soldan superba,' *Studi Francescani* 71 (1974) 199–240.

———. 'La Crociata nel pensiero e nella spiritualità di san Francesco e di santa Caterina,' in *Francesco e Caterina*, Roma, 1991, 53–76.

E. H. Cousins, 'Francis of Assisi and Interreligious Dialogue,' *Dialogue and Alliance* 5, 2 (Summer 1991) 20–33.

E. R. Daniel, *The Franciscan Concept of Mission in the High Middle Ages*, Lexington, KY, 1975.

F. De Beer, 'Francis and Islam,' *Concilium* 149 (1981) 16–27. Reprinted in *Spirit and Life: A Journal of Contemporary Franciscanism* 6 (1994) 161–175.

———. *François, que disait on de toi?* Paris, 1977. English translation *We Saw Brother Francis*, Chicago, 1983.

C. Delcorno, 'Origini della predicazione francescana,' in *Francesco d'Assisi e Francescanesimo del 1216 al 1226*, Assisi, 1977, 125–160.

H. De Roeck, *De normis Regulae OFM circa missiones inter paganos ex vita primaeva franciscana profluentibus*, Roma, 1961.

S. J. P. v. Dijk, *The Ordinal of the Papal Court from Innocent III to Boniface VIII and Related Documents*, completed by J. H. Walker, Fribourg, 1975.

Th. Desbonnets, *De l'intuition à l'institution*, Paris, 1983. English translation *From Intuition to Institution: The Franciscans*. Chicago, 1988.

E. Doyle, *St. Francis and the Song of Brotherhood*, London, 1980.

D. Dozzi, 'Come Francesco cita e interpreta il Vangelo: note metodologiche ed esemplificazioni,' *Laurentianum* 29 (1988) 347–369.

———. *Il Vangelo nella Regola non bollata di Francesco d'Assisi*, Roma, 1989.

K. Elm, 'Franz von Assisi: Busspredigt oder Heidenmission?' in *Espansione del Francescanesimo tra Occidente e Oriente nel secolo XIII*, Assisi, 1979, 69–103.

K. Esser, *Anfänge und ursprüngliche Zielsetzungen des Ordens der Minderbrüder*, Leiden, 1966.

———. 'Das missionarische Anliegen des hl. Franziskus,' *WissWeis* 35 (1972) 12–18.

D. Flood, *Die Regula non bullata der Minderbrüder*, Werl 1967.

———. 'A Brief Survey of Early Franciscan History,' *Haversack* 1, 5 (May–June 1978) 2–14.

———. 'Franciscans and Money,' *Haversack* 4, 2 (December 1980) 12–21.

———. 'Die wirtschaftliche Grundlage der franziskanischen Bewegung in ihrer Entstehungszeit,' *WissWeis* 44 (1981) 184–204.

———. 'Peace in Assisi in the Early Thirteenth Century,' *FranzSt* 64 (1982) 67–89. Reprinted in *FrancDig* I, 1 (May 1991) 1–20.

———. 'Assisi's Rules and People's Needs: The Initial Determination of the Franciscan Mission,' *FranzSt* 66 (1984) 91–104. Reprinted in *FrancDig* II, 2 (June 1992) 69–89.

———. 'The Spirit's Action,' *Haversack* 9, 2 (December 1985) 18–22.

———. 'Working and Preaching 1,' *Haversack* 9, 3 (February 1986) 21–24.

____. 'Cardinal Hugolino on Legation,' *Haversack* 11, 2 (December 1987) 3–9.

____. 'The Politics of "Quo Elongati,"' *Laurentianum* 29 (1988) 370–385. Reprinted in *FrancDig* III, 1 (June 1993) 39–55.

____. *Francis of Assisi and the Franciscan Movement*, Quezon City, 1989.

D. Flood and T. Matura, *The Birth of a Movement: A Study of the First Rule of St. Francis*, Chicago, 1975.

A. Fortini, *Francis of Assisi*, New York, 1981.

G. P. Freeman, 'Schooiers om vrede. Over de vroege franciscaanse beweging als vredesbeweging,' *Geweld-tegen-geweld?* Hilversum, 1984.

____. 'Zur Interpretationsgeschichte der ersten Ermahnung des hl. Franziskus,' *WissWeis* 51 (1988) 123–143.

____. 'Franciscus' vrede: een goed verhaal,' in *De Heer geve u vrede: Drie beschouwingen over Franciscus' vredesspiritualiteit*, Franciscaanse Studies 6, Utrecht, 1990. English translation: 'Francis' Peace: A Good Story,' *FrancDig* V, 2 (December 1995) 37–73.

G. P. Freeman and H. Sevenhoven, *De nalatenschap van een arme*, Utrecht, 1989. English translation: 'The Legacy of a Poor Man,' *FrancDig* III, 1 (June 1993) 1–18; III, 2 (December 1993) 80–96; IV, 1 (June 1994) 34–63; IV, 2 (December 1994) 63–83.

J. B. Freyer, 'Humilitas und Patientia in den Ermahnungen des hl. Franziskus,' *WissWeis* 53 (1990) 19–31.

F. Gabrieli, 'San Francesco e l'Oriente islamico,' *Espansione del Francescanesimo tra Occidente e Oriente nel secolo XIII*, Assisi, 1979, 105–122.

J. F. Godet, 'Le rôle de la prédication dans l'évolution de l'Ordre des Frères Mineurs d'après les écrits de saint François,' *FranzSt* 59 (1977) 53–65. English translation: 'The Role of Preaching in the Evolution of the Order of Friar Minors According to the Writings of Saint Francis,' *FrancDig* IV, 1 (June 1994) 17–33.

G. Golubovich, 'San Francesco e i Francescani in Damiata,' *Studi Francescani* 12 (1926) 307–330.

L. Hardick and E. Grau, *Die Schriften des heiligen Franziskus von Assisi*, Werl, 1980.

J. Hoeberichts, 'The Admonitions of Saint Francis: Words of Life and Salvation: The Fifth Admonition,' *FIA Contact* 5, 4 (1984) 22–31.

____. 'Ministry to the Friars in the Writings of Francis and the Early Biographers,' *FIA Contact* 6, 4 (November 1985) 2–9.

____. 'Een bevrijdingstheologisch perspectief op Franciscus en zijn keuze voor de armen,' *FL* 72 (1989) 219–233.

____. 'Solidariteit en dienstbaarheid. Dialoog in franciskaans perspectief,' *FL* 73 (1990) 212–227.

____. 'Franciscus en de Islam,' *Franciscaanse Studies* 7, Utrecht, 1991, 1–35.

____. 'Francis and Mission,' *FrancDig* II, 1 (January 1992) 43–59.

L. Iriarte, *Geschiedenis van de franciskaanse beweging*, Utrecht, n.d.

A. Jansen, 'Franciscus ontdekt het evangelie,' *FL* 66 (1983) 2–12.

_____. 'Thuis op de hele wereld: De spanning tussen broederschap en identiteit,' *FL* 73 (1990) 172–181.

_____. 'Lofzang op de deugden,' *FL* 75 (1992) 60–74; 167–182.

_____. 'De grote dankzegging en aansporing,' *FL* 75 (1992) 213–217; 258–269; 76 (1993) 18–21, 85–97.

J. G. Jeusset, *Dieu est courtoisie: François d'Assise, son Ordre et l'Islam*, Nantes, 1985.

J. LeGoff, 'Franciscanisme et modéles culturelles du XIII siécle,' *Francescanesimo e vita religiosa dei laici nel 200*, Assisi, 1981, 83–128.

B. v. Leeuwen, 'Leven te midden van niet-christenen volgens de regel van 1221 en 1223,' *FL* 58 (1975) 217–230.

P. v. Leeuwen and S. Verheij, *Woorden van heil van een kleine mens: Commentaar op de Vermaningen van Franciscus van Assisi*, Utrecht, 1986.

L. Lehmann, *Tiefe und Weite: Der universale Grundzug in den Gebeten des Franziskus von Assisi*, Werl, 1984.

_____. 'Grundzüge franziskanischen Missionsverständnisses nach Regula non bullata 16,' *FranzSt* 66 (1984) 68–81. English translation: 'Main Features of the Franciscan Understanding of Mission according to the Rule of 1221,' *FrancDig* II, 1 (January 1992) 1–20.

_____. 'Der Brief des hl. Franziskus an die Lenker der Völker: Aufbau und missionarisches Anliegen,' *Laurentianum* 25 (1984) 287–324. English translation: 'The Letter of Saint Francis to the Rulers of the Peoples: Structure and Missionary Concerns,' *FrancDig* IV, 2 (December 1994) 25–62.

_____. 'Prinzipien franziskanischer Mission nach den frühen Quellen,' *Laurentianum* 26 (1985) 311–360.

_____. 'Die beiden Briefe des hl. Franziskus an die Kustoden: Ansätze für eine christlich-islamische Oekumene im Loben Gottes,' *FranzSt* 69 (1987) 3–33. English translation: 'The Two Letters of St. Francis to the Custodians: Beginnings of a Christian-Muslim Ecumenism in Praising God,' *FrancDig* I, 1 (May 1991) 21–56.

_____. 'Das schriftliche Mahnwort des hl. Franziskus an alle Kleriker,' *WissWeis* 52 (1989) 147–178. English translation: 'The Letter to All Clerics: A Written Exhortation of Saint Francis to All Clerics,' *FrancDig* V, 2 (December 1995) 1–36.

L. Lemmens, 'De Sancto Francisco Christum praedicante coram Sultano Aegypti,' *Archivum Franciscanum Historicum* 19 (1926) 559–578.

C. T. Maier, *Preaching the Crusades: Mendicant Friars and the Cross in the Thirteenth Century*, Cambridge, 1994.

G. Miccoli, 'La proposta cristiana di Francesco d'Assisi,' *Studi Medievali* 24 (1983) 17–76. English translation: 'Francis of Assisi's Christian Proposal,' *Greyfriars Review* 3, 2 (August 1989) 127–172.

N. Nguyên-Van-Khanh, *Le Christ dans la pensée de Saint François d'Assise d'après ses écrits*, Paris, 1989.

H. Nolthenius, *Een man uit het dal van Spoleto: Franciscus tussen zijn tijdgenoten*, Amsterdam, 1988.

J. M. Powell, 'The Papacy and the Early Franciscans,' *Franciscan Studies* 36 (1976) 248–262.

____. 'Francesco d'Assisi e la Quinta Crociata: Una Missione di Pace,' *Schede Medievali* 4 (1983) 68–77.

R. Reijsbergen, *Omkeer van een verdwaalde mens: Poging tot een maatschappijhistorische interpretatie van de Lofzang op de deugden van Franciscus van Assisi*, Doktoraalscriptie Erasmus Universiteit, Den Haag, 1989.

____. 'Bevrijdende gehoorzaamheid: Het mysterie van de gehoorzaamheid bij Franciscus van Assisi,' *FL* 74 (1991) 60–71.

M. Roncaglia, *St. Francis of Assisi and the Middle East*, Cairo, 1957.

A. Rotzetter, 'Kreuzzugskritik und Ablehnung der Feudal ordnung in der Gefolgschaft des Franziskus von Assisi,' *WissWeis* 35 (1972) 121–137.

____. *Die Funktion der franziskanischen Bewegung in der Kirche: Eine pastoraltheologische Interpretation der grundlegenden franziskanischen Texte*, Schwyz, 1977.

____. '"Aus Liebe zur Liebe"? Zu einem Wort des hl. Franziskus,' *WissWeis* 44 (1981) 154–167.

____. *Franciscus van Assisi: De weg van het evangelie*, Haarlem, 1983.

____. 'Die missionarische Dimension des franziskanischen Charismas,' *FranzSt* 66 (1984) 82–90. English translation: 'The Missionary Dimension of the Franciscan Charism,' *Spirit and Life: A Journal of Contemporary Franciscanism* 6 (1994) 47–57.

O. Schmucki, 'La "Lettera a tutto l'Ordine" di San Francesco,' *L'Italia Francescana* 55 (1980) 245–286. English translation: 'St. Francis's Letter to the Entire Order,' *Greyfriars Review* 3, 1 (April 1989) 1–33.

K. V. Selge, 'Franz von Assisi und die römische Kurie,' *Zeitschrift für Theologie und Kirche* 67 (1970) 129–161.

H. Sevenhoven, 'Leven te midden van de Saracenen,' *FL* 73 (1990) 201–211.

O. v. d. Vat, *Die Anfänge der Franziskanermissionen und ihre Weiterentwicklung im nahen Orient und in den mohammedanischen Ländern während des 13. Jahrhunderts*, Werl, 1934.

I. Vazquez Janeiro, 'I Francescani e il Dialogo con gli Ebrei e i Saraceni nei secoli XIII–XV,' *Antonianum* 65 (1990) 533–549.

S. Verhey, *Der Mensch unter der Herrschaft Gottes*, Düsseldorf, 1960.

F. Vocking, 'Franciscus en het IVe Lateraans Concilie,' *FL* 45 (1962) 47–59; 78–94; 132–152; 46 (1963) 6–20; 40–50; 67–81; 109–123; 131–143.

B. Vollot, 'Le Diatesseron et la Première Règle de Saint François,' *FranzSt* 72 (1990) 341–364.

____. 'Césaire de Spire et la Première Règle de Saint François,' *FranzSt* 73 (1991) 310–323.

____. 'Césaire de Spire et la Règle de 1221,' *Laurentianum* 32 (1991) 3–28; 33 (1992) 175–220.

H. Von der Bey, *'Der Herr gebe dir den Frieden'*, Werl, 1990.

Z. Zafarana, 'La predicazione francescana,' *Francescanesimo e vita religiosa dei laici nel 200*, Assisi, 1981, 203–250.

P. Zahner, 'Der Kenosisgedanke in der mittelalterlichen Auslegung des Philipperhymnus unter besonderen Berücksichtigung Francisci und Bonaventuras,' *WissWeis* 55 (1992) 94–110.

R. Zerfass, *Der Streit um die Laienpredigt: Eine pastoral-geschichtliche Untersuchung zum Verständnis des Predigtamtes und zu seiner Entwicklung im 12. und 13. Jahrhundert*, Freiburg, 1974.

Th. Zweerman, '"Danken" en "dragen". Twee dimensies van de vrijheid volgens Franciscus van Assisi,' *Franciscus, wegwijzer naar de ware vrijheid*, Haarlem, 1983, 13–62.

II. THE CRUSADES

A. Bredero, *Christenheid en Christendom in de Middeleeuwen*, Kampen, 1986.

A. D. v. den Brincken, 'Islam und Oriens Christianus in den Schriften des Kölner Domscholasters Oliver (✠1227),' *Miscellanea Mediaevalia* 17, Berlin, 1987, 86–102.

R. I. Burns, 'Christian-Islamic Confrontation in the West: The Thirteenth-Century Dream of Conversion,' *The American Historical Review* 76 (1971) 1386–1434.

F. Cardini, 'I musulmani nel giudizio dei crociati all'inizio del Duecento,' *Archivio Storico Italiano* 146 (1988) 371–388.

P. J. Cole, *The Preaching of the Crusades to the Holy Land, 1095–1270*, Cambridge, Massachusets, 1991.

V. Cramer, *Die Kreuzzugspredigt zur Befreiung des Heiligen Landes, 1095–1270, Studien zur Geschichte und Charakteristik der Kreuzzugspropaganda*, Köln, 1939.

T. F. Crane, *The Exempla of Jacques de Vitry*, New York, 1890.

E. R. Daniel, 'Apocalyptic Conversion: The Joachite Alternative to the Crusades,' *Traditio* 25 (1969) 127–146.

N. Daniel, *Islam and the West: The Making of an Image*, Edinburgh, 1960.

⎯⎯⎯. *The Arabs and Mediaeval Europe*, London, 1975.

O. Delcambre, 'Riccoldo da Monte di Croce, pèlerin d'Orient,' *Peuples du Monde* 202 (April 1987) 32–33.

J. P. Donovan, *Pelagius and the Fifth Crusade*, Philadelphia, 1950.

H. Gilles, 'Législation et doctrine canoniques sur les Sarracins,' *Islam et chrétiens du Midi (XIIe–XIVe s.)*, Toulouse, 1983.

O. Guyotjeannin and G. Nori, 'Venezia e il trasporto dei crociati: A proposito di un patto del 1219,' *Studi Medievali* 30 (1989) 309–321.

P. Herde, 'Christians and Saracens at the Time of the Crusades: Some Comments of Contemporary Medieval Canonists,' *Studia Gratiana* 12 (1967) 360–376.

R. B. C. Huygens, *Lettres de Jacques de Vitry (1160/1170–1240)*, Leiden, 1960.

B. Z. Kedar, *Crusade and Mission, European Approaches toward the Muslims*, Princeton, 1984.

J. Kritzeck, *Peter the Venerable and Islam*, Princeton, 1964.

J. Leclercq, 'Gratien, Pierre de Troyes et la seconde croisade,' *Studia Gratiana* 2 (1954) 585–593.

H. Möhring, 'Heiliger Krieg und politische Pragmatik: Salahadinus Tyrannus. 2. Die Haltung Wilhelms von Tyrus gegenüber Islam und Muslimen,' *Deutsches Archiv für die Erforschung des Mittelalters* 39 (1983) 439–466.

J. Muldoon, *Popes, Lawyers, and Infidels*, Liverpool, 1979.

R. Pernoud, *The Crusaders*, Edinburgh, n.d.

J. M. Powell, *Anatomy of a Crusade, 1213–1221*, Philadelphia, 1986.

P. Raedts, 'The Children's Crusade of 1212,' *Journal of Medieval History* 3 (1977) 280–323.

J. Riley-Smith, *What were the Crusades?* London, 1977.

____. 'Kreuzzüge,' *Theologische Realenzyklopädie*, Vol. XX, Berlin, 1990, 1–10.

L. and J. Riley-Smith, *The Crusades: Idea and Reality, 1095–1274*, London, 1981.

G. Rizzardi, 'Islam, errore o eresia? Aspetti e tendenze della teologia missionaria dei sec. XII–XIV,' *Renovatio* 22 (1987) 415–451; 489–532.

R. Röhricht, 'Die Kreuzpredigten gegen den Islam: Ein Beitrag zur Geschichte der christlichen Predigt im 12. und 13. Jahrhundert,' *Zeitschrift für Kirchengeschichte* 6 (1884) 550–572.

H. Roscher, *Papst Innocenz III und die Kreuzzüge*, Göttingen, 1969.

S. Runciman, *A History of the Crusades, Vol. III: The Kingdom of Acre and the later Crusades*, Cambridge, 1954.

G. Schwaiger, 'Innocenz III,' *Theologische Realenzyklopädie*, Vol. XVI, 175–182.

R. Schwinges, *Kreuzzugsideologie und Toleranz: Studien zu Wilhelm von Tyrus*, Stuttgart, 1977.

E. Siberry, 'Missionaries and Crusaders, 1095–1274: Opponents or Allies?' *Studies in Church History* 20 (1983) 103–110.

____. *Criticism of Crusading 1095–1274*, Oxford, 1985.

H. Tillmann, *Pope Innocent III*, Amsterdam, 1980.

C. Thouzellier, 'La légation en Lombardie du Cardinal Hugolin (1221): Un épisode de la cinquième croisade,' *Revue d'histoire ecclésiastique* 45 (1950) 508–542.

J. P. Torrell, 'La notion de prophétie et la méthode apologétique dans le Contra Saracenos de Pierre le Vénérable,' *Studia Monastica* 17 (1975) 257–280.

Th. C. Van Cleve, 'The Fifth Crusade,' *A History of the Crusades, Vol. II: The Later Crusades 1189–1311*, ed. K. M. Setton, Philadelphia, n.d., 377–428.

A. G. Weiler, 'Tolerantie van christenen in de middeleeuwen ten opzichte van joden en moslims: apartheid, verbanning en verovering,' *Begrip* 114 (June–July 1993) 5–22.

III. INTERRELIGIOUS DIALOGUE

For a more complete bibliography, see 'Bibliography on Interreligious Dialogue,' *Theology in Context, Supplements* 7, Aachen, 1992. This list is limited to articles which I consulted.

M. Amaladoss, 'Evangelisation in India: A New Focus?' *VJTR* 51 (1987) 7–28.

_____. 'Encounter of Religions: Some Concerns as We Face the 1990's,' *Making All Things New: Mission in Dialogue*, Anand, Gujarat, India, 1990, 131–144.

_____. 'Rationales for Dialogue with World Religions,' *Origins* 19 (1990) 572–577.

_____. 'Liberation: An Inter-religious Project,' *East Asian Pastoral Review* 28 (1991) 4–33.

_____. 'Religious Conflict and Spirituality,' *Jeevadhara* XXIII, 133 (January 1993) 27–35.

_____. 'Proclaiming the Gospel,' *VJTR* 57 (1993) 26–32.

T. Balasuriya, 'Note on Pope John Paul II's Encyclical: *Redemptoris Missio* (1990),' *The Japan Missionary Bulletin* 45 (1991) 217–224.

M. Borrmans, 'Le discours de Jean-Paul II aux jeunes de Casablanca,' *Seminarium* 26 (1986) 44–71.

A. Camps, 'Een nieuwe uitgave van de handleiding voor de dialoog met moslims,' *Wereld en Zending* 13 (1984) 340–346.

_____. 'Discussies gevoerd in de Encycliek "Redemptoris Missio" en Aziatische reacties,' *Wereld en Zending* 22 (1993) 12–17.

J. Dupuis, 'Dialogue and Proclamation in Two Recent Documents,' *Bulletin* 80 (1992) 165–172.

_____. 'FABC Focus on the Church's Evangelising Mission in Asia Today,' *VJTR* 56 (1992) 449–468.

G. Evers, 'Interreligiöser Dialog und Mission nach der Enzyklika "Redemptoris Missio,"' *ZMR* 75 (1991) 191–209.

A. Fernandes, 'Dialogue in the Context of Asian Realities,' *VJTR* 55 (1991) 545–560.

R. Fitzmaurice, 'The Roman Catholic Church and Interreligious Dialogue: Implications for Christian-Muslim Relations,' *Islam and Christian-Muslim Relations* 3, 1 (June 1992) 83–107.

P. Holtrop, 'De schrale wind van de nieuwe lente,' *Wereld en Zending* 20 (1991) 101–105.

J. Knight, 'Mission and Dialogue in Asia: Can We Plumb the Depths,' *VJTR* 56 (1992) 125–134.

J. v. Lin, 'Missio! Moet dat nog?' *Wereld en Zending* 20 (1991) 94–101.

T. Michel, 'Islamo-Christian Dialogue: Reflections on the Recent Teachings of the Church,' *Bulletin* 59 (1985) 172–193.

_____. 'Pope John Paul II's Teaching About Islam,' *Seminarium* 26 (1986) 73–82.

J. Neuner, 'Mission in *Ad Gentes* and in *Redemptoris Missio*,' *VJTR* 56 (1992) 228–241.

_____. 'Mission Theology After Vatican II: Magisterial Teaching and Missiological Approaches in India,' *VJTR* 58 (1994) 201–214.

A. Poulet-Mathis, 'Ecumenical and Interreligious Dialogue in Asia: Concerns and Initiatives of the Federation of Asian Bishops' Conferences,' *FABC Papers* No. 49, 10–29.

I. Puthiadam, 'Dialogue and Proclamation: Problem? Challenge? Grace-filled Dialectic?' *VJTR* 56 (1992) 289–308.

P. Rossano, 'The Major Documents of the Catholic Church Regarding the Muslims,' *Bulletin* 48 (1981) 204–215.

J. Slomp, 'Is Knitter's model in Nederland bruikbaar?' *Wereld en Zending* 15 (1986) 108–112.

F. Wilfred, 'A Matter of Theological Education: Some Critical Reflections on the Suitability of 'Salvation History' as a Theological Model for India,' *VJTR* 48 (1984) 538–556.

_____. 'Dialogue Gasping for Breath? Towards New Frontiers in Interreligious Dialogue,' *FABC Papers* No. 49 (1987) 32–52.

_____. 'Some Heuristic Propositions on the Relationship of Christianity to Non-Christian Religions and Cultures,' *Indian Theological Studies* 24 (1987) 220–229.

_____. 'World Religions and Christian Inculturation,' *Indian Theological Studies* 25 (1988) 5–26.

_____. 'Dogma and Inculturation,' *VJTR* 53 (1989) 345–353.

_____. 'Dialogue and Mission in Context,' *CTC Bulletin* VIII, 3 (December 1989) 5–18.

_____. 'Asia on the Threshhold of the 1990s: Emerging Trends and Socio-Cultural Processes at the Turn of the Century: A Position Paper for the Fifth Plenary Assembly of the FABC,' *FABC Papers* No. 55 (1990) 1–43.

_____. 'Towards an Anthropologically and Culturally Founded Ecclesiology: Reflections from An Asian Perspective,' *VJTR* 54 (1990) 501–511.

_____. 'Fifth Plenary Assembly of FABC: An Interpretation of its Theological Orientation,' *VJTR* 54 (1990) 583–592.

_____. 'The Politics of Culture: Critical Reflections on Culture and Human Development from a Third World Perspective,' *Jeevadhara* 127 (1992) 59–80.

_____. 'Once Again... Church andz Kingdom,' *VJTR* 57 (1993) 6–25.

_____. 'Images of Jesus Christ in the Asian Pastoral Context: An Interpretation of Documents from the Federation of Asian Bishops' Conferences,' *Concilium* 1993/2, 51–62.

_____. 'Some Tentative Reflections on the Language of Christian Uniqueness: An Indian Perspective,' *VJTR* 57 (1993) 652–672.

_____. 'Ecumenism as a Movement of Justice: Focus on Asia,' *VJTR* 58 (1994) 573–583.